Claims
for
Poetry

Claims for Poetry

Donald Hall, Editor

Ann Arbor   **The University of Michigan Press**

Copyright © by the University of Michigan 1982
All rights reserved
Published in the United States of America by
The University of Michigan Press
Manufactured in the United States of America
♾ Printed on acid-free paper

2000   1999   1998   1997   14   13   12   11

Library of Congress Cataloging in Publication Data
Main entry under title:

Claims for poetry.

   1. Poetry—Addresses, essays, lectures.   I. Hall,
Donald, 1928–
PN1064.C59   1982   801'.951   82-2580
ISBN 0-472-06308-1   AACR2

Acknowledgments

A. R. AMMONS, "A Poem Is a Walk" reprinted by permission of Mr. Ammons.

MARVIN BELL, "The Impure Every Time" reprinted by permission of Mr. Bell.

WENDELL BERRY, "Damage" reprinted by permission of Mr. Berry.

ROBERT BLY, "A Wrong Turning in American Poetry" and "What the Image Can Do" reprinted by permission of Mr. Bly.

HAYDEN CARRUTH, "The Question of Poetic Form" reprinted by permission of Mr. Carruth.

ROBERT CREELEY, "On the Road: Notes on Artists and Poets 1950–65," "To Define," "A Note," "A Note on the Local," "'Statement' for Paterson Society," and "Poems Are a Complex," from *A Quick Graph* and *Was That a Real Poem,* copyright 1970 // 1979 by Robert Creeley. Reprinted by permission of Four Seasons Foundation.

ROBERT DUNCAN, "Ideas of Meaning of Form" reprinted by permission of Mr. Duncan.

RUSSELL EDSON, "Portrait of the Writer as a Fat Man: Some Subjective Ideas or Notions on the Care and Feeding of Prose Poems" reprinted by permission of Mr. Edson.

TESS GALLAGHER, "The Poem as Time Machine" reprinted by permission of Ms. Gallagher.

SANDRA M. GILBERT, "My Name is Darkness: The Poetry of Self-Definition" reprinted by permission of Ms. Gilbert. The essay first appeared in *Contemporary Literature* 18, no. 4 (Autumn, 1977).

JOHN HAINES, "The Hole in the Bucket" reprinted by permission of Mr. Haines.

DONALD HALL, "Goatfoot, Milktongue, Twinbird: The Psychic Origins of Poetic Form" reprinted by permission of Mr. Hall.

For Joyce Peseroff

Editor's Note

It is commonly supposed that contemporary poets are uncritical, reacting against the New Criticism of the fathers and grandfathers. Surely they place less emphasis on their criticism, but in order to write poetry it seems necessary to think about it, and poets do their thinking in print. Over the past several years, numbers have collected their critical prose into books: Denise Levertov, Adrienne Rich, Robert Creeley, Gary Snyder, Richard Hugo, W. D. Snodgrass.... And the University of Michigan Press's *Poets on Poetry* series has collected volumes by Stafford, Kinnell, Kumin, Wakoski, Piercy, Ignatow, Francis, Levine, Simpson, Bly, Kostelanetz, Haines, Logan, Bell, and Ostriker.

Volumes like these each assemble one poet's notions of poetry, often demonstrating growth or change over decades. Perhaps a book like this one may perform another function—a volume not dedicated to the promulgation of any school, eclectic to the point of disorder, but containing various essays which set forth different claims for poetry—conflicting, overlapping, contentious; avant-garde, reactionary; immemorial, neoteric; light, heavy, angry, funny, political, aesthetic, academic, psychological, innovative, practical, high-minded, abstract, frivolous, pedagogic.

The alphabet supplies the order of authors, a grid which proclaims the arbitrary. I take delight in the accidents of juxtaposition, as one might take pleasure in inviting enemies to sit next to each other at table. When I began to collect these notions, I thought I would find affinities within groups; of course there is some affinity, but in the end I found less coherence than I had expected, or less expected coherence; I found friends opposing each other and enemies in agreement.

If there is no consensus, even among associates, is there any point to putting this collage of contentions into the same frame? I think so. Although some writers are perfectly literary, although some argue a poetics inseparable from politics, although some make historical surveys, diversity does not preclude conversation. Mind you, some forms of speech inhibit dialogue, as credo fits ill with history, and manifesto with enigma: sometimes these confrontations attempt dialogue between speakers of Old Norse and Bengali, but in the Babel of this mixed assemblage, the attentive listener who admits diversity of aim and purpose may assemble from various clauses his own symposium. Without dialogue we are speechless; without conflict we go to sleep.

Criticism marches, it has been claimed, insofar as it emerges from the atelier. These essays are by-products of palette and canvas, produced by the makers themselves. If a poet's criticism appears obscure, it often becomes clearer when we measure it against the same poet's poems. Each product of the same pen clarifies other products, and the criticism in this volume does not exist as its own end.

Usually it exists to advance one sort of poetry—the sort written by the critic-poet in question. This purpose may be as inadvertent as it is ineluctable. When Eliot wrote his essay on Hamlet, he meant to bring light to Hamlet; if he shed darkness on Shakespeare's play, he brought illumination to our reading of "The Waste Land" and "The Journey of the Magi"—the result not of narcissism but of obsession, accomplished through the lucky delusion which characterizes the superior artist.

Yet the personal may need to believe that it is general before it will be spoken. In collecting these essays, I have mostly avoided prose in which poets wrote directly about their own work; although I found them fascinating in the particular, I usually found them lacking in generality. For the same reason I have avoided book reviews, accurate to another writer's particular qualities; I wanted instead to collect prose containing, however fragmentarily, implications of a poetics. Some good poets have written no such prose, and will not be found here. On a few occasions I have reprinted early formulations of a poet's ideas, like an essay-review by Robert Bly and some notes by young Robert Creeley; most are more recent summations of concern. Varied as they are in manner and purpose, I hope that each may serve some purpose.

D. H.
Wilmot, N.H.
26 June 1981

Contents

A. R. Ammons

A Poem Is a Walk
1967

*Nothing that can be said
in words is worth saying.*

Laotse

I don't know whether I can sustain myself for thirty minutes of saying I know nothing—or that I need to try, since I might prove no more than you already suspect, or, even worse, persuade you of the fact. Nothingness contains no images to focus and brighten the mind, no contrarieties to build up muscular tension: it has no place for argumentation and persuasion, comparison and contrast, classification, analysis. As nothingness is more perfectly realized, there is increasingly less (if that isn't contradictory) to realize, less to say, less need to say. Only silence perfects silence. Only nothingness contributes to nothingness. The only perfect paper I could give you would be by standing silent before you for thirty minutes. But I am going to try this imperfect, wordy means to suggest why silence is finally the only perfect statement.

I have gone in for the large scope with no intention but to make it larger; so I have had to leave a lot of space "unworked," have had to leave out points the definition of any one of which could occupy a paper longer than this. For though we often need to be restored to the small, concrete, limited, and certain, we as often need to be reminded of the large, vague, unlimited, unknown.

I can't tell you where a poem comes from, what it is, or what it is for: nor can any other man. The reason I can't tell you is that the purpose of a poem is to go past telling, to be recognized by burning.

I don't, though, disparage efforts to say what poetry is and is for. I am grateful for—though I can't keep up with—the flood of articles, theses, and textbooks that mean to share insight concerning the nature of poetry. Probably all the attention to poetry results in some value, though the attention is more often directed to lesser than to greater values.

Once every five hundred years or so, a summary statement about poetry comes along that we can't imagine ourselves living without. The greatest statement in our language is Coleridge's in the *Biographia*. It serves my purpose to quote only a fragment from the central statement: that the imagination—and, I think, poetry—"reveals itself in the balance or reconciliation of opposite or discordant qualities." This suggests to me that description, logic, and hypothesis, reaching toward higher and higher levels of generality, come finally to an antithesis logic can't bridge. But poetry, the imagination, can create a vehicle, at once concrete and universal, one and many, similar and diverse, that is capable of bridging the duality and of bringing us the experience of a "real" world that is also a reconciled, a unified, real world. And this vehicle is the only expression of language, of words, that I know of that contradicts my quotation from Laotse, because a poem becomes, like reality, an existence about which nothing that can be said in words is worth saying.

Statement can also achieve unity, though without the internal suspension of variety. For example, All is One, seems to encompass or erase all contradiction. A statement, however, differs from a work of art. The statement, All is One, provides us no experience of manyness, of the concrete world from which the statement derived. But a work of art creates a world of both one and many, a world of definition and indefinition. Why should we be surprised that the work of art, which over-reaches and reconciles logical paradox, is inaccessible to the methods of logical exposition? A world comes into being about which any statement, however revelatory, is a lessening.

Knowledge of poetry, which is gained, as in science or other areas, by induction and deduction, is likely to remain provisional by falling short in one of two ways: either it is too specific, too narrow and definite, to be widely applicable—that is, the principles suggested by a single poem are not likely to apply in the same number or kind in another poem: or, the knowledge is too general, too abstract and speculative, to fit precisely the potentialities of any given poem. Each poem in becoming generates the laws by which it is generated: extensions of the laws to other poems never completely take. But a poem generated by its own laws may be unrealized and bad in terms of so-called objective principles of taste, judgment, deduction. We are obliged both to begin internally with a given poem and work toward generalization *and* to approach the poem externally to test it with a set—and never quite the same set—of *a priori* generalizations. Whatever we gain in terms of the existence of an individual poem, we lose in terms of a consistent generality, a tradition: and vice versa. It is Scylla and Charybdis again. It is the logically insoluble problem of one and many.

To avoid the uncertainty generated by this logical impasse—and to feel assured of something definite to teach—we are likely to prefer one side or the other—either the individual poem or the set of generalizations—and then to raise mere preference to eternal verity. But finally, nothing is to be gained by dividing the problem. A teacher once told me that every line of verse ought to begin with a capital letter. That is definite, teachable, mistaken knowledge. Only by accepting the uncertainty of the whole can we free ourselves to the reconciliation that is the poem, both at the subconscious level of feeling and the conscious level of art.

One step further before we get to the main business of the paper. Questions structure and, so, to some extent predetermine answers. If we ask a vague question, such as, What is poetry?, we expect a vague answer, such as, Poetry is the music of words, or Poetry is the linguistic correction of disorder. If we ask a narrower question, such as, What is a conceit?, we are likely to get a host of answers, but narrower answers. Proteus is a good figure for this. You remember that Proteus was a minor sea god, a god of *knowledge,* an attendant on Poseidon. Poseidon is the ocean, the total view, every structure in the ocean as well as the unstructured ocean itself. Proteus, the god of knowledge, though, is a minor god. Definite knowledge, knowledge specific and clear enough to be recognizable as knowledge, is, as we have seen, already limited into a minor view. Burke said that a clear idea is another name for a little idea. It was presumed that Proteus knew the answers—and more important The Answer—but he resisted questions by transforming himself from one creature or substance into another. The more specific, the more binding the question, the more vigorously he wrestled to be free of it. Specific questions about poetry merely turn into other specific questions about poetry. But the vague question is answered by the ocean which provides distinction and non-distinction, something intellect can grasp, compare, and structure, and something it can neither grasp, compare, nor structure.

My predisposition, which I hope shortly to justify, is to prefer confusion to over-simplified clarity, meaninglessness to neat, precise meaning, uselessness to over-directed usefulness. I do not believe that rationality can exhaust the poem, that any scheme of explanation can adequately reflect the poem, that any invented structure of symbology can exceed and thereby replace the poem.

I must stress here the point that I appreciate clarity, order, meaning, structure, rationality: they are necessary to whatever provisional stability we have, and they can be the agents of gradual and successful change. And the rational, critical mind is essential to making poems: it protects the real poem (which is non-rational) from blunders, misconceptions, incompetences; it weeds out the second rate. Definition, rationality, and structure are ways of seeing, but they become prisons when they blank out other ways of seeing. If we remain open-minded we will soon find for any easy clarity an equal and opposite, so that the sum of our clarities should return us where we belong, to confusion and, hopefully, to more complicated and better assessments.

Unlike the logical structure, the poem is an existence which can incorporate contradictions, inconsistencies, explanations and counter-explanations and still remain whole, unexhausted and inexhaustible; an existence that comes about by means other than those of description and exposition and, therefore, to be met by means other than, or in addition to, those of description and exposition.

With the hope of focusing some of these problems, I want now to establish a reasonably secure identity between a poem and a walk and to ask how a walk occurs, what it is, and what it is for. I say I want a reasonably secure identity because I expect to have space to explore only four resemblances between poems and walks and no space at all for the differences, taking it for granted that walks and poems are different things. I'm not, of course, interested in walks as such but in clarification or intensification by distraction, seeing one thing better by looking at something else. We want to see the poem.

What justification is there for comparing a poem with a

walk rather than with something else? I take the walk to be the externalization of an interior seeking, so that the analogy is first of all between the external and the internal. Poets not only do a lot of walking but talk about it in their poems: "I wandered lonely as a cloud," "Now I out walking," and "Out walking in the frozen swamp one grey day." There are countless examples, and many of them suggest that both the real and the fictive walk are externalizations of an inward seeking. The walk magnified is the journey, and probably no figure has been used more often than the journey for both the structure and concern of an interior seeking.

How does a poem resemble a walk? First, each makes use of the whole body, involvement is total, both mind and body. You can't take a walk without feet and legs, without a circulatory system, a guidance and co-ordinating system, without eyes, ears, desire, will, need: the total person. This observation is important not only for what it includes but for what it rules out: as with a walk, a poem is not simply a mental activity; it has body, rhythm, feeling, sound, and mind, conscious and subconscious. The pace at which a poet walks (and thinks), his natural breath-length, the line he pursues, whether forthright and straight or weaving and meditative, his whole "air," whether of aimlessness or purpose—all these things and many more figure into the "physiology" of the poem he writes.

A second resemblance is that every walk is unreproducible, as is every poem. Even if you walk exactly the same route each time—as with a sonnet—the events along the route cannot be imagined to be the same from day to day, as the poet's health, sight, his anticipations, moods, fears, thoughts cannot be the same. There are no two identical sonnets or villanelles. If there were, we would not know how to keep the extra one: it would have no separate existence. If a poem is each time new, then it is necessarily an act of discovery, a chance taken, a chance that may lead to fulfillment or disaster. The poet exposes himself to the risk. All that has been said about poetry, all that he has learned about poetry, is only a partial assurance.

The third resemblance between a poem and a walk is that each turns, one or more times, and eventually *re*turns. It's conceivable that a poem could take out and go through incident after incident without ever returning, merely ending in the poet's return to dust. But most poems and most walks return. I have already quoted the first line from Frost's "The Wood-Pile." Now, here are the first three lines:

> Out walking in the frozen swamp one grey day,
> I paused and said, "I will turn back from here.
> No, I will go on farther—and we shall see."

The poet is moving outward seeking the point from which he will turn back. In "The Wood-Pile" there is no return: return is implied. The poet goes farther and farther into the swamp until he finds by accident the point of illumination with which he closes the poem.

But the turns and returns or implied returns give shape to the walk and to the poem. With the first step, the number of shapes the walk might take is infinite, but then the walk begins to "define" itself as it goes along, though freedom remains total with each step: any tempting side-road can be turned into on impulse, or any wild patch of woods can be explored. The pattern of the walk is to come true, is to be recognized, discovered. The pattern, when discovered, may be found to apply to the whole walk, or only a segment of the walk may prove to have contour and therefore suggestion and shape. From previous knowledge of the terrain, inner and outer, the poet may have before the walk an inkling of a possible contour. Taking the walk would then be searching out or confirming, giving actuality to, a previous intuition.

The fourth resemblance has to do with the motion common to poems and walks. The motion may be lumbering, clipped, wavering, tripping, mechanical, dance-like, awkward, staggering, slow, etc. But the motion occurs only in the body of the walker or in the body of the words. It can't be extracted and contemplated. It is non-reproducible and nonlogical. It can't be translated into another body. There is only one way to know it and that is to enter into it.

To summarize, a walk involves the whole person; it is not reproducible; its shape occurs, unfolds; it has a motion characteristic of the walker.

If you were brought into a classroom and asked to teach walks, what would you teach? If you have any idea, I hope the following suggestions will deprive you of it.

The first thought that would occur to you is, What have other people said about walks? You could collect all historical references to walks and all descriptions of walks, find out the average length of walks, through what kind of terrain they have most often proceeded, what kind of people have enjoyed walks and why, and how walks have reflected the societies in which they occurred. In short, you could write a history of walks.

Or you could call in specialists. You might find a description of a particularly disturbing or interesting walk and then you might call in a botanist to retrace that walk with you and identify all the leaves and berries for you: or you might take along a sociologist to point out to you that the olive trees mentioned were at the root—forgive me—of feudal society: or you might take along a surveyor to give you a close reading in inches and degrees: or you might take a psychoanalyst along to ask good questions about what is the matter with people who take walks: or you might take a physiologist to provide you with astonishment that people can walk at all. Each specialist would no doubt come up with important facts and insights, but your attention, focused on the cell structure of the olive leaf, would miss the main event, the walk itself.

You could ask what walks are good for. Here you would find plenty: to settle the nerves, to improve the circulation, to break in a new pair of shoes, to exercise the muscles, to aid digestion, to prevent heart attacks, to focus the mind, to distract the mind, to get a loaf of bread, to watch birds, to kick stones, to spy on a neighbor's wife, to dream. My point is clear. You could go on indefinitely. Out of desperation and exasperation brought on by the failure to define the central use or to exhaust the list of uses of walks, you would surrender, only to recover into victory by saying, Walks are useless. So are poems.

Or you could find out what walks mean: do they mean a lot of men have unbearable wives, or that we must by outward and inward motions rehearse the expansion and contraction of the universe; do walks mean that we need structure—or, at an obsessive level, ritual in our lives? The answer is that a walk doesn't mean anything, which is a way of saying that to some extent it means anything you can make it mean—and always more than you can make it mean. Walks are meaningless. So are poems.

There is no ideal walk, then, though I haven't taken the time to prove it out completely, except the useless, meaningless walk. Only uselessness is empty enough for the presence of so many uses, and only through uselessness can the ideal walk come into the sum total of its uses. Only uselessness can allow the walk to be totally itself.

I hope you are now, if you were not before, ready to agree with me that the greatest wrong that can be done a poem is to substitute a known part for an unknown whole and that the choice to be made is the freedom of nothingness: that our experience of poetry is least injured when we accept it as useless, meaningless, and non-rational.

Besides the actual reading in class of many poems, I would suggest you do two things: first, while teaching everything you can and keeping free of it, teach that poetry is a mode of discourse that differs from logical exposition. It is the mode I spoke of earlier that can reconcile opposites into a "real" world both concrete and universal. Teach that. Teach the distinction.

Second, I would suggest you teach that poetry leads us to the unstructured sources of our beings, to the unknown, and returns us to our rational, structured selves refreshed. Having once experienced the mystery, plenitude, contradiction, and composure of a work of art, we afterwards have a built-in resistance to the slogans and propaganda of over-simplification that have often contributed to the destruction of human life. Poetry is a verbal means to a non-verbal source. It is a motion to no-motion, to the still point of contemplation and deep realization. Its knowledges are all negative and, therefore, more positive than any knowledge. Nothing that can be said about it in words is worth saying.

Marvin Bell

The Impure Every Time
1980

American poetry has changed utterly in the past twenty-five years. It changed partly because America changed. On the one hand, there was a proliferation of individual styles by the poets of the generation born late in the twenties. This happened mainly in the late fifties and early sixties. On the other, poetry changed because in the seventies we began to speak about it differently. Some women wanted to speak of it differently. Some Blacks wanted to speak of it differently. Chicanos and Oriental-Americans wanted to. Native American Indians wanted to. All kinds of outsiders wanted to. And poets who were increasingly translated into English and published in America spoke about it differently.

I can remember having to defend my practice of "free verse" in workshops. Someone might raise an eyebrow and say, "This appears to be written in free verse." "Oh no," I'd reply, "it's written in sprung accentuals with variant lines." I can remember when a prose-poem had to prove it was poetry, and when it seemed to matter. Now James Wright's wonderful book, *To a Blossoming Pear Tree,* can include a piece of prose (prose? prose-poetry?) about a scoutmaster in Martins Ferry, Ohio, and no one doubts that it is poetry. And I can remember when particular attitudes, even styles, were permitted Oriental poets, Russian poets, or poets of Eastern Europe, say, but were forbidden to American poets.

It's changed because we have gone back to thinking of poetry as something more than a bundle of techniques. Which is to say that we have gone back to emphasizing that there is something more to poetry than accomplishment.

Poetry has content, public as well as private. It has content not available elsewhere. That is why no good poets are dumb. If your uneducated relatives can spot the quality that is poetry, why can't you? Because you've been educated and acculturated away from your instincts, away from your heartbeat and pulse, away from the physical.

While good poetry has to be well-written, no one quite knows what it means to write well. Everyone knows that writing well, even in lines, even in meters and rhymes, doesn't necessarily make poetry. It makes verse. Poetry is better than verse.

J. V. Cunningham wouldn't agree. Years ago he published an essay in which he argued that verse was rational, could be judged, and had a civic role, while poetry was irrational, could not be judged, and therefore had no assured civic role. He chose verse, the surer accomplishment.

I choose poetry. I choose the ugly as well as the beautiful, knowing it will all be beautiful soon enough. I choose the unknown (for now), the mystery rather than the accepted solution, the cracked bowl over the flawless one, the voice that has a little spit and phlegm in it, the used shoes, imagination over analysis, Williams over Stevens, the impure every time.

As a reader I don't have to choose between Stevens and Williams. They are equally great. I used to think I didn't have to choose as a writer, either, but I was wrong. They don't represent merely different styles. They represent opposite attitudes, opposing principles, about what the subject of poetry is.

I like to see visible indications of mentality in poems: the poem proceeding intelligently as well as *sensefully*. But I prefer that the subject matter not *be* the intelligence—as it is, I think, for Stevens. Without a greater engagement with the world than one finds in Stevens, language is an accomplished liar. I think Williams is, in the end, a more intelligent poet than Stevens. To write as Williams did, one has to have made sophisticated decisions about the nature of language. Moreover, while Stevens's work is singular, an achievement almost baroque, Williams's experiments and stylistic advances are far more daring and inventive as well as more influential.

We know now that poetry is a quality of imagination and language inextricably bound up with the recognizable world. We know that it's a kind of flying, that it gets up and goes.

The literary career is sometimes a hideous notion. It brings out the worst in critics and reviewers. It develops cliques and antagonistic loyalties when what a poet most needs is to learn from that which most opposes him or her, most disturbs, most confronts. Instead of support, the poet gets knee-jerk hostility from other "camps," and equally reflexive self-imaging praise from friends.

I remember walking across a lawn with Allen Ginsberg in the sixties. A young man called out to him, "What do you think of Creeley's new book?" His tone was clear: he himself didn't think so much of it. Maybe Ginsberg didn't either. But he turned and said, "Whatever Bob's doing, I'm *for* him." A little more of that would go a long way toward a great American poetry.

One of the reasons why America often seems to have no place for great poets of the people is that the critics will always choose Stevens over Williams while Williams is alive. They will always choose poetry which labors to be "poetic," whether by remembered forms or by a nostalgic, privately-pained tilt of the head and vocal cords. Ah yes, they say, that's poetry, just as we studied it. The obscure will sometimes get a hearing, for the empty journals are always waiting for material. Hugh Kenner dismissed James Wright's gorgeous book of poems, *To a Blossoming Pear Tree,* essentially because it didn't suggest to him anything to say about it. That attitude makes poetry just an occasion for critical conversation. The use of excerpts from poems in reviews and books promotes the (false) notion that poems are just pieces put together.

Good poems transcend these problems, and we find them. More to the point, the act of writing transcends everything for those of us who need to write. They can take away from you everything but this: the poems you have written, the poems you are writing.

There is a valuable elitism which encourages quality, but there is an evil elitism which attempts to forbid participation. We see it now in the decrying of the proliferation of poets in America. Some blame the NEA, some blame universities, some probably blame IBM and Xerox, but none think to place the "blame" where it belongs: in the guts and brains of the people who want to write. Millions of people who have played baseball but not well know something about it because they tried and now they go to watch. Is it wrong for people who can't write well to write as well as they can? In the great scalepan of human vices, a bad poem doesn't weigh very much. We could use a little modesty about publishing, we could usefully bind and gag a few poets who blanket the country with annual requests for paid readings, but then these are not such great vices either. Alas, the coin of the realm in the world of poetry is reputation, and there will always be those who will attempt to steal some for themselves.

I started out to say that poetry is an accomplishment beyond technique. Of course we always knew. Meanwhile, the Academy spoke of technique in one or two ways, the Black Mountaineers spoke of technique in another way, the Deep Imagists in their way, the minimalists briefly, etc. Do you know why more and better articles about books of poetry don't appear? Because now that poetry is no longer written between the lines, the critics don't know what to say.

The critics have gone off into structuralism, post-structuralism, cartographies of misinterpretation, talk about semiotics and hermeneutics—which is to say they have left the scene.

For American poetry this is a time of rapid growth not separate from profound cultural/political/psychological changes. It was probably necessary to get the critics out of town for a while, to have a period when one was seldom being told what it was one had done and could not do. With all the damn talk about the particulars of writing nowadays, it's sometimes hard to imagine anyone doing anything new, but of course there will always be some who don't know any better.

Wendell Berry

Damage
1975

I

I have a steep wooded hillside that I wanted to be able to pasture occasionally, but it had no permanent water supply.

About halfway to the top of the slope there is a narrow bench, on which I thought I could make a small pond. I hired a man with a bulldozer to dig one. He cleared away the trees, and then formed the pond, cutting into the hill on the upper side, piling the loosened dirt in a curving earthwork on the lower.

The pond appeared to be a success. Before the bulldozer quit work, water had already begun to seep in. Soon there was enough to support a few head of stock. To heal the exposed ground, I fertilized it and sowed it with grass and clover.

We had an extremely wet fall and winter, with the usual freezing and thawing. The ground grew heavy with water, and soft. The earthwork slumped; a large slice of the woods floor on the upper side slipped down into the pond.

The trouble was the familiar one: too much power, too little knowledge. The fault is mine.

I *was* careful to get expert advice. But this only exemplifies what I already knew. No expert knows everything about every place, not even everything about any place. If one's knowledge of one's whereabouts is insufficient, if one's judgment is unsound, then expert advice is of little use.

II

In general, I have used my farm carefully. It could be said, I think, that I have improved it far more than I have damaged it.

My aim has been to go against its history and to repair the damage of other men. But now a part of its damage is my own.

The pond was a modest piece of work, and so the damage is not extensive. In the course of time and nature it will heal.

And yet there *is* damage—to my place, and to me. I have carried out, before my own eyes and against my intention, a part of the modern tragedy: I have made a lasting flaw in the face of the earth, for no lasting good.

Until that wound in the hillside, my place, is healed, there will be something impaired in my mind. My peace is damaged. I will not be able to forget it.

III

It used to be that I could think of art as a refuge from such troubles. From the imperfections of life, one could take refuge in the perfections of art. One could read a good poem—or, better, write a good one.

Art was what was truly permanent, therefore what truly mattered. The rest was "but a spume that plays / Upon a ghostly paradigm of things."

I am no longer able to think that way. That is because I now live in my subject. My subject is my place in the world, and I live in my place.

There is a sense in which I no longer "go to work." If I live in my place, which is my subject, then I am "at" my work even when I am not working. It is "my" work because I cannot escape it.

If I live in my subject, then writing about it cannot "free" me of it or "get it out of my system." When I am finished writing, I can only return to what I have been writing about.

While I have been writing about it, time will have changed it. Over longer stretches of time, *I* will change it. Ultimately, it will be changed by what I write, inasmuch as I, who change my subject, am changed by what I write about it.

If I have damaged my subject, then I have damaged my art. What aspired to be whole has met damage face to face, and has come away wounded. And so it loses interest both in the anesthetic and in the purely esthetic.

It accepts the clarification of pain, and concerns itself with healing. It cultivates the scar that is the course of time and nature over damage: the landmark and mindmark that is the notation of a limit.

To lose the scar of knowledge is to renew the wound.

An art that heals and protects its subject is a geography of scars.

IV

"You never know what is enough unless you know what is more than enough."

I used to think of Blake's sentence as a justification of youthful excess. By now I know that it describes the peculiar condemnation of our species. When the road of excess has reached the palace of wisdom it is a healed wound, a long scar.

Culture preserves the map and the records of past journeys, so that no generation will permanently destroy the route.

The more local and settled the culture, the better it stays put, the less the damage. It is the foreigner whose road of excess leads to a desert.

Blake gives the just proportion or control in another proverb: "No bird soars too high, if he soars with his own wings." Only when our acts are empowered with more than bodily strength do we need to think of limits.

It was no thought or word that called culture into being, but a tool or a weapon. After the stone axe we needed song and story to remember innocence, to record effect—and so to describe the limits, to say what can be done without damage.

The use only of our bodies for work or love or pleasure, or even for combat, sets us free again in the wilderness, and we exult.

But a man with a machine and no culture—such as I was when I made my pond—is a pestilence. He shakes more than he can hold.

Robert Bly

A Wrong Turning in American Poetry
1963

I

American poetry resembles a group of huge spiral arms whirling about in space. Eliot and Pound are moving away at tremendous speeds. Moore and Jeffers are driving into space also. This island universe is rushing away from its own center. Let me contrast this picture with another. Spanish poetry of this century is moving inward, concentrating. Antonio Machado stands at the center of Spanish poetry, standing at the center of himself as well. His poems are strange without being neurotic. His thought is abundant and clear, near the center of life. The younger Spanish poets can judge where they are from where he is. They can look in, and see him standing there.

In American poetry on the other hand a young poet cannot take Pound, Eliot, or Moore for a master without severe distortion of his own personality. They whirl about so far out that anyone who follows them will freeze to death. If American poetry had a center it would seem to be William Carlos Williams. His poetry however shows a fundamental absence of spiritual life. He is in fact as much caught up in destructive expansion as the others.

II

Eliot, Pound, Moore, and Williams, all born within five years of each other, form a poetic generation we might call the generation of 1917. They support certain ideas with great assurance. Eliot's support of the idea of the "objective correlative" is an example. His phrasing of the idea is as follows: "The only way of expressing emotion in the form of art is by finding an 'objective correlative', in other words, a set of objects, a situation, a chain of events which shall be the formula of that particular emotion." The tone is final, but the statement is not true. With "objective" here, we stumble onto a word we will find over and over again in the work of the 1917 generation. These men have more trust in the objective, outer world than in the inner world. As poets, they want to concern themselves with objects. The word "formula" above suggests the desire to be scientific, to study things. Eliot says in essence that *objects* are essential in a poem. He wants to arrange them in a formula, as a scientist would, so that the controlled experiment can be repeated any number of times.

As a program, the search for the objective correlative merely obstructs poetry. What does the search for this formula result in? The impulse for the poem does not flow forward into the language. Instead the impulse is stopped: the poet searches about for the proper formula in the public world. This means working up the poem as an idea—for example, in terms of the lower classes ("Sweeney Erect") or in terms of Greek myth ("Sweeney Agonistes"). Greek myths and the lower classes are thought to be very objective. However the impulse to the poem is broken. True freshness and surprise are impossible. The poet's eyes are not on the impulse but are constantly looking over the public world for reliable sets of objects. Finally the poet's own mind becomes objective: he becomes the public.

Modern Spanish poetry—to continue our contrast—denies Eliot's thesis of the relevance of the objectivizing process. Ricardo Gullon, for example, has said that the purpose of poetry "is to transfer an intuition." How is an intuition to be transferred? Guillaume de Torre, the greatest contemporary Spanish critic, holds up the personal, even the intimate poem. Intuition is embodied in experiences private to the poet (which the reader can nonetheless share) "and not in common experiences from the public domain masquerading as unique and vital. T. S. Eliot's 'objective correlative' and other vulgarities dressed up in cryptic terms are nothing but so many frauds."

Lorca has a poem describing his emotions while walking on the streets of New York, feeling that he is aging, being rapidly killed by the sky. He does not talk of Circe, or the clothes of bums sleeping on the sidewalk. He says:

Among the forms which are moving toward the serpent,
And the forms which are searching for the crystal,
I'll grow long hair.

With the tree of amputated limbs which does not sing,
And the boy child with the white face of the egg,

With all the tiny animals who have gone insane,
And the ragged water which walks on its dry feet.

Lorca conveys his emotion not by any "formula" but by means which do not occur to Eliot—by passion. The phrase "objective correlative" is astoundingly passionless. For Lorca there is no time to think of a cunning set of circumstances that would carry the emotion in a dehydrated form to which the reader need only add water.

Pound said in 1911: "I believe that the proper and perfect symbol is the natural object." Pound considers poetry to be fundamentally a repository of wisdom. He wishes to put into the *Cantos* as many important thoughts and conversations as he can, the most important fragments of all classic books, so that should a man be able to own only one book he could own the *Cantos* and thereby possess all truth on economics, culture, and government. The poem is thus defined with no reference to the unconscious. Instead of the unconscious there is economics. Relations between parts of the outer world take the place of inner relations and of the inner world. The book takes what it needs by force. As a poem, the *Cantos* annexes other people's ideas, facts, other languages. The poem is like an infinitely expanding metropolis, eating up more and more of the outer world, with less and less life at the center. The personality of the poet is driven out of the poem. The expanding poem, like the expanding city, has no personality. The idea of the poem as infinite concentration of the personality—Yeats believed this is what a poem was—is entirely lost. How can the personality be present if the unconscious is pushed out?

Marianne Moore's poetry also represents a treasure house—a feminine one. The objects in the poem are fragments, annexed, and the poem is a parlor full of knickknacks carefully arranged. Melville leaves such a room and goes to sea: there he sees whales moving about in the sea their whole lives, winds thrashing freely, primitive forces that act out their own inward strength. Returning to land he becomes a revolutionary because in society he sees such elementary forces curtailed; he asks why they must be checked and lamed. The purpose of Marianne Moore's art is exactly opposite: it is to reconcile us to living with hampered forces. She brings in animals and fish, but only fragments of them—beaks of birds, single wings of dragonflies, the dorsal fin of a whale, the teeth of snakes, the forepaw of an otter—all adapted to domestic life. Everything is reduced in size, reduced to human dimensions, as in old New England parlors, where there was "a shark's backbone made into a walking stick." The poem becomes a temporary excursion into the dangerous world of nature, with an immediate and safe return already envisioned— a kind of picnic. The fragments of animals that appear are separated from their inner force, their wildness, and turned from living things into objects. A poem is conceived as an exercise in propriety.

William Carlos Williams's work shows a similar attachment to objects. "No ideas but in things!" he said. His poems show great emotional life mingled with the drive of the intelligence to deal with outward things—but no inward life, if by inward life we mean an interest in spiritual development. Williams was a noble man, of all the poets in his generation the warmest and most human. Still, his ideas contained something destructive: there is in them a drive toward the extinction of personality. Williams's "No ideas but in things!" is a crippling program. Besides the ideas in things there are ideas in images and in feelings. True, bits of broken glass are preferable for poetry to fuzzy generalities such as virtue or patriotism. But images like Lorca's "black horses and dark people are riding over the deep roads of the guitar" also contain ideas and give birth to ideas. Williams asked poetry to confine itself to wheelbarrows, bottlecaps, weeds—with the artist "limited to the range of his contact with the objective world." Keeping close to the surface becomes an obsession. The effect of Williams's thought, therefore, was to narrow the language of poetry—to narrow it to general remarks mixed with bits of glass and paper bags, with what Pound called "natural objects." Williams says, "The good poetry is where the vividness comes up true like in prose but better. That's poetry."

Between Walls

The back wings
of the

hospital where
nothing

will grow lie
cinders

in which shine
the broken

pieces of a green
bottle

In that Williams poem the personality and the imagination
are merely two among many guests. The imagination has to
exist as best it can in a poem crowded with objects. In the bare
poems of some of Williams's followers the personality of the
poet is diffused among lampposts and matchfolders, and van-
ishes. The poet appears in the poem only as a disembodied
anger or an immovable eye.

The point in contrasting Lorca's language with Williams's
is not that Lorca's poems are richer but that Lorca approaches
his poetry with entirely different artistic principles—among
them the absolute essentiality of the image. These ideas bear
fruit in the poems. Lorca's poems have many things in them,
sharply observed ("black doves puttering in the putrid
waters"), but they also have images, also passion, wild leaps,
huge arsenic lobsters falling out of the sky.

Charles Olson, about fifty, is generally considered the main
transmitter of the ideas of Williams and Pound to the present
generation. In Olson's prose their outward direction is set
down even more programmatically, as in "Projective Verse"—
an essay which echoes T. E. Hulme—in which Olson says:

> Objectism is the getting rid of the lyrical interference of the
> individual as ego, of the "subject" and his soul, that peculiar
> presumption by which western man has interposed himself
> between what he is as creature of nature (with certain instruc-
> tions to carry out) and those other creations of nature which
> we may, with no derogation, call objects.

In demanding that the poet get rid of himself as a subjective person Olson is simply restating Eliot's belief in the desirability of "extinguishing the personality." To Olson the poet's inwardness is "lyrical interference." Some Zen teachers use language like this, but their meaning is exactly the opposite. The aim of Zen, as of a poet like Rilke, is to make men more and more inward until they stop admiring objects, at which point they will be able to see them clearly, if they wish to.

The ideas of the 1917 generation are quite consistent. Eliot and Pound conceive maturity as a growth of outwardness. Eliot's later plays are naturally more outward than his earlier plays, the *Cantos* more outward than *Lustra*. The opposite is true of Yeats and Rilke. Rilke was more inward at thirty than at twenty; more inward at fifty than at thirty.

In this country we have a great reluctance to admit that ideas can be incompatible. We want to follow both the Pound-Olson direction and the Rilke direction. Yet in *Letters to a Young Poet* Rilke writes: "Give up all that. You are looking outward, and that above all you should not do now. There is only one single way. Go into yourself." And he tells Kappus that poetry will come "from this turning inward, from this sinking into your private world." Rilke believes the poet actually experiences the soul, does not share the mass's preoccupation with objects.

If we are to develop clear principles in our poetry we must honestly say that we cannot reconcile the ideas of Rilke with the ideas of the Williams-Pound-Olson movement. This is why Pound talks of Rilke so little. A man cannot turn his face at the same moment toward the inward world and the outer world: he cannot face both south and north.

III

I have tried to point out that the 1917 generation had a rather unified set of ideas centered on objectivism—shared by all the major poets of that generation despite their other differences. All later poetry has been written, necessarily, under the influence of these ideas. Now how can we describe our poetry since the twenties in a way that will include Winters as well as Lowell, Eberhart as well as Ciardi?

It is first of all a poetry without spiritual life.

For the sake of contrast, consider a brief Spanish poem by Juan Ramon Jiminez.

Oceans

I have a feeling that my boat
Has struck, down there in the depths,
Against a great thing.
    And nothing
Happens! Nothing... Silence... Waves...
—Nothing happens? Or has everything happened
And are we standing now, quietly, in the new life?

Can we imagine finding a kin of that by one of us in the *Kenyon Review* or the *Evergreen Review?*

The beginning of spiritual life is a horror of emptiness which our people feel every day, but it is Rilke who has described such a state, not one of us.

Already the ripening barberries are red
And in their bed, the aged asters hardly breathe.
Whoever now is not rich inside, at the end of summer,
Will wait and wait, and never be himself.

Whoever now is unable to close his eyes
Absolutely certain that a crowd of faces
Is only waiting till the night comes
In order to stand up around him in the darkness—
That man is worn out, like an old man.

Nothing more will happen to him, no day will arrive,
And everything that does happen will cheat him.
Even you, my God. And you are like a stone
Which draws him daily deeper into the depths.

Our recent poetry is also a poetry in which the poem is considered to be a construction independent of the poet. It is imagined that when the poet says "I" in a poem he does not mean himself, but rather some other person—"the poet"—a dramatic hero. The poem is conceived as a clock which one sets going. This idea encourages the poet to construct automated and flawless machines. Such poems have thousands of intricately moving parts, dozens of iambic belts and pulleys, precision trippers that rhyme at the right moment, lights flashing alternately red and green, steam valves that whistle like birds. This is the admired poem. Richard Wilbur, for all his ability, fell a victim to this narrow conception of the poem. His early "Water Walker," written before this oppressive concept of the poem penetrated him, remains his most personal and freshest poem. Robert Lowell in *Lord Weary's Castle* constructed machines of such magnitude that he found it impossible to stop them. Like the automated, chainreacting tool of the sorcerer's apprentice, the poems will not obey. The references to Mary or Jesus that end several of them are last-minute expedients, artistically dishonest and resembling a pile of cloths thrown into a machine to stop it.

The great poets of this century have written their poems in exactly the opposite way. In the poems of Neruda, Vallejo, Jiminez, Machado, Rilke, the poem is an extension of the substance of the man, no different from his skin or his hands. The substance of the man who wrote the poem reaches far out into the darkness and the poem is his whole body, seeing with his ears and his fingers and his hair.

Here is a poem of Machado's, written before the death of his wife; here the "I" *is* the poet.

> From the doorsill of a dream they called my name . . .
> It was the good voice, the voice I loved so much.
>
> —Listen. Will you go with me to visit the soul?
> A soft stroke reached up to my heart.
>
> —With you always . . . And in my dream I walked
> Down a long and solitary corridor,
> Aware of the touching of the pure robe,
> And the soft beating of blood in the hand that loved me.

Next, the poetry we have had in this country is a poetry without even a trace of revolutionary feeling—in either language or politics.

It is startling to realize that in the last twenty years there have been almost no poems touching on political subjects, although such concerns have been present daily. The *Kenyon Review*, under Ransom, and the *Southern Review*, under Tate, have been effective forces here. The guiding impulse in both Ransom's and Tate's minds is fear of revolution. As southerners they act to exaggerate the fear felt by even northerners.

This kind of southerner thinks of himself as a disinherited aristocrat. Their holding position in poetry has more resemblance to the attitude of Governor Ross Barnett of Mississippi than most people would be willing to admit. LaForgue says, "The only remedy is to break everything." Ransom says, in effect, that the only remedy is to keep everything. This is why there is so much talk of Donne and New Criticism in the *Kenyon Review*—such concerns tend to damp down any tendencies toward revolution. Ransom wanted poems that knew how to behave in a drawing room. Dylan Thomas was not welcome, and certainly not Neruda or Brecht.

If revolution in thought is put down, revolution in language also dies. The absence of any interest in fresh language in literary magazines shows up in the thirties and forties. Compared with that of Hart Crane or Cummings the language of Nemerov or Ciardi is inexpressibly dull. And Jarrell, for example, opens a poem:

> One looks from the train
> Almost as one looked as a child. In the sunlight
> What I see still seems to me plain.

There is almost no contrast inside the line. A poet who has higher standards in language can put together inside a line words that have different natures—like strange animals together in a wood. Mallarmé uses this kind of contrast as a foundation for his poems. Awareness of the different kinds of fur that words have is instantly apparent in Lorca's poems:

> One day
> The horses will live in the saloons
> And the enraged ants
> Will throw themselves on the yellow skies that
> have taken refuge in the eyes of cows.

Compare this with a typical stanza of ours:

> Youth comes to jingle nickels and crack wise;
> The baseball scores are his, the magazines
> Devoted to lust, the jazz, the Coca Cola,
> The lending library of love's latest.
>
> Karl Shapiro, "The Drug Store"

In Shapiro's stanza all the words have the same spirit: gray.

The poetry of the thirties and forties moves backward. Art Buchwald once described the scene he imagined could take place as a Fly Now—Pay Later plan collides with a failure to make a payment on time. A man from the travel agency comes to your house with a curious electric machine. You sit down in it, the current is turned on, and the machine removes all your memories of Europe. In the poetry of the thirties and forties we are supposed to forget that there were even any ideas of a different language for poetry—forget that the German Expressionist poets ever lived, forget the experiments in language represented by French poets and later by Alberti and Lorca. Poetry is forgotten, if by poetry we mean exploration into the unknown, and not entertainment; an intellectual adventure of the greatest importance, not an attempt to teach manners; an attempt to face the deep inwardness of the twentieth century, not attempts to preserve the virtues of moderation. The forties generation succeeds in forgetting both the revolution in language and any revolutionary feeling toward society.

Our postwar poets defend the status quo. Nemerov, Ransom, and Ciardi, for instance, by their examples, urge poets not to make too much trouble in the universities. Ransom urges us to have a "civilized attitude." Most of these men are merely accepting the ideas of T. S. Eliot, who supports the Establishment. Hölderlin wrote a short poem on this subject which has great common sense.

> Deep down I despise the herd of leaders and ministers,
> But I despise even more the genius who takes their side.

The poetry we have had here is a poetry without the image.

The only movement in American poetry which concentrated on the image was Imagism, in 1911–13. But "Imagism" was largely "Picturism." An image and a picture differ in that the image, being the natural speech of the imagination, cannot be drawn from or inserted back into the real world. It is an animal native to the imagination. Like Bonnefoy's "interior sea lighted by turning eagles," it cannot be seen in real life. A picture, on the other hand, is drawn from the objective "real" world. "Petals on a wet black bough" can actually be seen.

We have merely to glance at a typical American stanza of

the last years to see that the image is destroyed before birth by pressure of the direct statement or the picture.

> Now mist takes the hemlocks and nothing
> stirs. This is a gray-green and a
> glassy thing and nothing stirs. A plane
> to or from Newark burrs down idling on
> its flaps or grinds full-rich up its
> airy grade, and I hear it.
>
> John Ciardi

But if there is no image how is the unconscious going to make its way into the poem? Let us consider the typical "formal poem." Suppose there is no image: then such a statement in a poem as "I must perfect my will" is composed by the conscious mind, rhymes searched for and found by the conscious mind. The efficient workaday conscious mind creates the entire poem. The important thing about an image, on the other hand, is that it is made by both the conscious and the unconscious mind. This is true of Yeats's image of the beast of the "Second Coming" and of Lorca's "the glasses of the dawn are broken."

Finally, then, our poetry has been a poetry essentially without the unconscious.

This is not surprising. Two of our strongest traditions have been puritanism (our so-called religious tradition) and business (our secular tradition). The mind of the puritan shows a fear of the unconscious—a belief that only ugly and horrible images and ideas come from it. All animal life and sexual life are met with fear and disdain. These are the impulses behind the poetry of Eliot and Pound, and that of the neoclassical school as well. The impulses do not describe the poetry of Hart Crane and Theodore Roethke, exceptions to almost all the points I have been making.

Max Weber showed that the apparent asceticism of the puritan had a secret purpose: to adapt the man to an efficient life in business. Working in business "ascetically" fifteen hours a day is the mark of a man who has resisted Satan; success in outward things becomes a proof of religious virtue. The drive toward outward things in the 1917 generation and in recent poets is essentially obedience to business traditions.

These two strains—puritan fear of the unconscious and the business drive toward dealing in outer things—meet in our poetry to push out the unconscious. The 1917 poets tried to adapt poetry to business and science. They looked for "formulas." They tried to deal efficiently with natural objects. They studied to develop "technical skill"—like engineers.

Then with their brandishing technical skill the poets of the thirties and forties evict the unconscious. And poetry sinks—plunges, sometimes—into the outer world. Titles of books indicate this in an interesting way. Richard Wilbur's third book is called *Things of this World*. Shapiro entitled his first book *Person, Place, and Thing*, and his new one *The Bourgeois Poet*.

IV

Ortega y Gasset in *Man and Crisis* suggests that the intellectual history of a nation hinges on the differences between generations. Members of the younger generation when they get to be about thirty years old find that the ideas of the older men do not seem to describe the world accurately. As the young man "meditates on the world in force" (the world of the men who in his time are mature) he finds "his problems, his doubts, are very different from those which these mature men felt in their own youth." The ideas of mature men seem false or at least no longer adequate. The men of the younger generation therefore advance their own ideas and attack the ideas of the older generation. In this debate—in which all can take part—the old ideas are examined, ideas themselves are made real, new ideas hammered out. A nation's intellectual life depends upon this struggle between generations.

I have discussed briefly the generation of 1917. (Frost and Stevens, considerably older men, belong to an earlier group.) After the 1917 generation a group of this country's poets appeared who might be called the Metaphysical Generation. Not only were these poets of the twenties and thirties profoundly influenced by the English metaphysical poets, but their basic attitude was detached, doctrinaire, "philosophical." Eberhart's poetry is destroyed, in most poems, by philosophical terms used with fanaticism. Poetry becomes abstract. The poet takes a step back, and brings doctrines between himself and his experience. The presence of doctrines, metaphysical or political, marks both the puritan metaphysicals and the left-wing radicals—Eberhart and Tate as well as the *New Masses* poets. The interest in doctrine is all taken from the 1917 poets. Tate for example is a disciple of Eliot, a man nearly a decade older.

The next clearly defined generation is that of 1947—the war generation, including Karl Shapiro, Robert Lowell, John Berryman, Delmore Schwartz, Randall Jarrell, Howard Nemerov. Their convictions about poetry are so impersonal and changeable that it would be truer to say they have no convictions at all. Ortega remarks, "Imagine a person who, when in the country, completely loses his sense of direction. He will take a few steps in one direction, then a few more in another, perhaps the exact opposite." We are reminded of Shapiro, who in his first book has a vicious attack on D. H. Lawrence; this is followed by wholehearted praise of Lawrence; his worship of New Criticism is followed by pointed disgust for it; he pursues the academic style in his own poetry, and then discards it for the Ginsberg style. Both styles are for him equally bankrupt.

The generation of 1947 might very well be called the Hysterical Generation. Its response to the question of literary style or content is hysterical. In fact, hysteria itself is often a subject matter of these men's poetry, as in Berryman's *Homage to Mistress Bradstreet*. The history of Lowell's style shows the same pattern as Shapiro's. Accepting Tate's ideas, Lowell adopts a fanatically formal verse only to abandon it abruptly for the prose style of *Life Studies*. The sad fact is that he is not really fitted for either of these styles, and his own style remains undiscovered.

The progress of the generations since 1917 might then be described as the progress from the objectivist generation to the metaphysical generation to the hysterical—three clearly marked psychic steps. They are not steps toward irrationality but toward dullness and lack of conviction. They are states that succeed one another in a process of disintegration of personality. After the initial step away from inwardness, and toward the world of things, this country's poets increasingly lose touch with their own inward reality and become less and less sure of themselves. They no longer stand firmly inside their own convictions.

The outstanding characteristic of the generation of 1947 is its reluctance to criticize ideas handed to them. That new generation did not create an idea of its own. Randall Jarrell's criticism is occupied with praise of Marianne Moore and others, without any serious discussions of ideas. If Richard Wilbur has any criticism of the ideas or poetry of men older than himself, he doesn't mention it. Robert Lowell recently reviewed Yvor Winters's collected poems for *Poetry* and reported that the reason Winters had been left out of so many anthologies was that he is "so original and radical," an "immortal poet." In the *Hudson Review* Lowell later gave a similar blanket endorsement of William Carlos Williams. There is something intellectually shameful about his accepting the standards of both of these men, since their standards are not only different but contradictory. Such acceptance of the ideas of older men by younger men is unnatural as well as unhealthy.

What is the result of this strange lack of intellectual struggle between the generations? Ortega remarks, "Entire generations falsify themselves to themselves; that is to say, they wrap themselves up in artistic styles, in doctrines, in political movements which are insincere and which fill the lack of genuine convictions. When they get to be about forty years old, these generations become null and void, because at that age one can no longer live in fictions."

V

I have been putting forward general ideas about poetry. Let us see if these ideas hold up when poems are in front of us.

Here is an entire poem by Juan Ramon Jiminez which has an inner intensity.

> Music—
> Naked woman
> Running mad through the pure night!

And here are lines in which the intensity is all on the surface:

> Would you perhaps consent to be
> The very rack and crucifix of winter, winter's wild
> Knife-edged, continuing and unreleasing,
> Intent and stripping, ice-caressing wind?
> > Delmore Schwartz, "Will You Perhaps"

This is the opening of a poem by Rafael Alberti, translated by Anthony Kerrigan:

> By the side of the sea and a river in my early days
> I wanted to be a horse.
> The reed shores were made of wind and mares.
> I wanted to be a horse.

And here are lines from a recent U.S. anthology:

> The old man accepts a Lucky Strike.
> He was a friend of my grandfather.
> We talk of the decline of the population
> And of codfish and herring
> While he waits for a herring boat to come in.
>
> Elizabeth Bishop, "At the Fishhouses"

In the Bishop poem we can feel the outer world driving in, invading the poem. The facts of the outer world push out the imagination and occupy the poem themselves. The lines become inflexible. The poem becomes heavy and stolid, like a toad which has eaten ball bearings.

Here are lines from *Life Studies:*

> Father and Mother moved to Beverly Farms
> to be a two-minute walk from the station,
> half an hour by train from the Boston doctors.
>
> Robert Lowell, "Terminal Days at
> Beverly Farms"

And from Jarrell:

> "In a minute the doctor will find out what is wrong
> and cure me," the patients think as they wait.
> They are patient as their name, and look childishly
> And religiously at the circumstances of their hope,
> The nurse, the diplomas, the old magazines.
>
> Randall Jarrell, "A Utopian Journey"

In this country's poems the facts are put in because they happened, regardless of how much they lame the poem. *Life Studies* is a very important book on the development of the outward poem, since it shows that the outward poem moves inevitably toward sociology. Here is a poem by Juan Ramon Jiminez, translated by Carlos de Francisco Zea, which makes an interesting contrast with the American sociological poem.

> I am not I.
>   I am this one
> Who goes by my side unseen by me;
> Whom I, at times, go visit,
> And whom I, at times, forget.
> He who keeps silent, serene, when I speak,
> He who forgives, sweet, when I hate,
> He who takes a walk where I am not,
> He who will remain standing when I die.

And one of ours:

> whenever he left a job,
> he bought a smarter car.
> Father's last employer
> was Scudder, Stevens, and Clark, Investment Advisors,
> himself his only client.
> While Mother dragged to bed alone,
> read Menninger....
>
>   "Commander Lowell'

This is seriously reviewed as poetry, since United States critics demand very little from our poets. And the poets demand very little from themselves.

Apollinaire insisted on the presence of poetry, even in four lines. His poem "Flies":

> Our flies know all the tunes
> Which they learned from the flies in Norway—
> Those giant flies that are
> The divinities of the snow.

The poem devoid of any revolutionary feeling, in politics or language, has no choice but to become descriptive prose, sociological prose—or worse, light verse. Often in recent United States poetry the poet adopts a genial, joshing tone, indicating that what he is saying doesn't seem to be of any importance, even to him. To point up the difference between real poetry and what passes among us for poetry, let me quote a stanza by the Peruvian poet Vallejo, followed by a stanza in the joshing tone.

> The anger that breaks a man down into small boys,
> That breaks the small boy down into equal birds,
> And the birds, then, into tiny eggs;
> The anger of the poor
> Owns one smooth oil against two vinegars.

And this is the opening of a poem by Howard Nemerov in *Fifteen Modern American Poets:*

> Her laughter was infectious; so, some found,
> Her love. Several young men reasonably
> Regret inciting her to gratitude
> And learning of her ardent facility.

Poetry without inwardness or revolutionary feeling has no choice but to end in a kind of fabricated grossness. Poetry on this level of imagination must become more and more coarse in order to achieve sensation. Poets like Karl Shapiro are convinced that if they can only make a poem gross or outrageous enough it will be a great poem. A poem, then, becomes defined as something more prosy than prose.

> New York, killer of poets, do you remember the day
> you passed me through your lower intestine? The troop
> train paused under Grand Central. That line of women
> in mink coats handed us doughnuts through the smutty
> windows. They were all crying. For that I forgave New
> York. (We smuggled a postcard off at New Haven.)
> *Partisan Review,* Summer, 1962

In this Shapiro passage the senses are completely dead. In fact, there has been a steady deadening of the senses in our poetry since 1918. There were fewer odors and colors in new poems in 1958 than there were in 1918. The absence of the senses in our poems at times is astonishing.

Here is a medieval Arabic poem called "Storm" followed by one of ours:

> Each flower in the dark air opens its mouth
> Feeling about for the breasts of the abundant rain.

Meanwhile armies of the black-skinned clouds, loaded
with water, march by
Majestically, bristling with the golden swords of lightning.

. . . .

The compass of the ego is designed
To circumscribe intact a lesser mind
With definition. . . .

Stanley Kunitz, from "Lovers Relentlessly"

Abstraction is merely another form of the flight from inwardness; the objectivist takes flight into the outward world, and the rationalist into the efficient intellect. Rationalists try to convince us that the atrophying of the senses is a good thing, and they describe it as the development of abstract language in poetry.

In this country intellectual statement about passion is thought to be superior to passion—or at least equal to it. Yvor Winters urges us to be sure our rational mind is present when we write a poem:

A poem is good in so far as it makes a defensible rational statement about a given human experience (the experience need not be real but must in some sense be possible) and at the same time communicates the emotion which ought to be motivated by that rational understanding of the experience.

"In Defense of Reason"

Passion cannot be trusted unless taken apart and put together again by the reason. The mind will tell us what we *ought* to feel.

Rilke has an entirely different vision of poetry:

O Lord, give each person his own personal death.
A dying that moves out of the same life he lived,
In which he had love, and intelligence, and trouble.

Here are Winters's lines:

This passion is the scholar's heritage,
The imposition of a busy age,
The passion to condense from book to book
Unbroken wisdom in a single look.

We return again and again to the idea of the 1917 generation that poetry involves the "extinction of the personality." If all senses die, all images die, all association with the unconscious dies, all revolutionary feeling dies, then, it is believed, we are near poetry. Let me quote as a final contrast a medieval Arabic poem—a true poem—followed by some lines of Louise Bogan.

> Never have I seen or heard of anything like this:
> A pearl that changes out of modesty into a red jewel.
>
> Her face is so white that when you look at its beauty,
> You see your own face under its clear water.

and Bogan:

> I burned my life that I might find
> A passion wholly of the mind,
> Thought divorced from eye and bone,
> Ecstasy come to breath alone.

Under the influence of objectivism and abstraction, not only does our poetry become mediocre but our criticism also. When the senses die, the sense within us that delights in poetry dies also. And it is this sense of delight that tells us whether a given group of words contains genuine poetry or not. A great poet and a great critic are like the mule who can smell fresh water ten miles away. There is a sense which tells us where the water of poetry is, abroad or at home, west or east, even under the earth.

When this sense is dead, critics have to decide whether certain books are poetry by the presence of forms, or of "important statements," or of wit, or even of length. The longer a poem is the more poetry it is thought to contain. The American lines I have quoted are often very bad and I chose them partially with that in mind. Yet in each case they show the direction of the quoted poet's work as a whole. Moreover, the very fact that the poet wrote them, printed them in a book, and allowed them to stand is evidence of the atrophying of the sense of poetry. It is possible that the American lines I have quoted are bad poetry, but another possibility is that they aren't poetry at all.

A human body, just dead, is very like a living body except

that it no longer contains something which was invisible anyway. In a poem, as in a human body, what is invisible makes all the difference. The presence of poetry in words is extremely mysterious. As we know from the Japanese experience of the haiku, as well as from the experience of many brief poems in the western tradition, poetry can be present in fifteen words, or in ten words. Length or meter or rhyme have nothing to do with it. Ungaretti has a poem of four words ("m'illumino/d'immenso") which is unquestionably a poem.

> Everyone is alone on the core of the earth
> pierced by a ray of sunlight;
> and suddenly it's evening.

This poem of Quasimodo's manages to slip suddenly inward.

A poem is something that penetrates for an instant into the unconscious. If it can penetrate in this way, freshly, several times, then it is a poem of several lines. But if it does not do this it is not a poem at all—no matter how long it is.

The outward poem is like a pine tree made half of tin and half of wood. The poem of things conceives itself to be describing the world correctly because there are pieces of the world in it. This poetry cannot sustain the poet or itself because the imagination has no privacy in which to grow. In the last thirty years in America the intelligence of the poet runs back and forth hurriedly between the world inside his head and the world outside. The imagination meanwhile is thinking in its chamber. The intelligence knocks at the door, demanding some imagination to put between a flat statement and a piece of glass, and rushes out with the gift. Then it hurries back to get a little more imagination to prevent two subway cars from rubbing together. The imagination is continually disturbed, torn away bit by bit, consumed like a bin of corn eaten gradually by mice.

The imagination does not want to hear these constant knockings on the door. It prefers to remain in its chamber, undisturbed, until it can create the poem all of one substance—itself. The imagination out of its own resources creates a poem as strong as the world which it faces. Rilke speaks of "die Befreiung der dichterischen Figur," which may be translated as "the liberation of the poetic image," "the releasing of the image from jail." The poet is thinking of a poem in which the image is released from imprisonment among objects. The domination of the imagination is established over the entire poem. When this happens the poem enters the unconscious naturally.

Our poetry took a wrong turning years ago. Some centuries have a profound spiritual movement; poetry, when vigorous, always is a part of it. We know ours is a century of technical obsession, of business mentality, of human effort dissipated among objects, of expansion, of a destructive motion outward. Yet there is also a movement in the opposite direction which is even more powerful. The best thought in this century moves inward. This movement has been sustained by Freud, by great poetry of Europe and South America, by painting, by the most intelligent men. This is the important movement. The weakness of our poetry is that it does not share in this movement.

Most of our poetry so far has nothing to give us because, like its audience, it drifts aimlessly in the outer world. A country's poetry can drift outward, like the lives of most of its people, or it can plunge inward, trying for great intensity. Inward poetry deepens all life around it. Other poets have given their countries this gift. If we fail in this, of what use is our life? As Lorca says, life is not a dream.

What the Image Can Do
1981

Before I talk about the image's function, I'd like to set down some thoughts about its place among the other powers that make up a good poem. I have asked myself what the powers are that make a poem forceful, and I have settled on six of these powers, elements, or energy sources. Sometimes they change in my mind, but I'll set down the six I see now.

As the first power, I'd name the image. An example is: "The blind man on the bridge is as gray as some abandoned Empire's boundary stone." The human intelligence in the image joins itself to something not entirely human. The image always holds to one of the senses at least, to smell or taste or touch or hearing, the seeing of color or motion. If one says, "The good of one is the good of all," one abandons the senses almost successfully. The image, by contrast, keeps a way open to the old marshes, and the naked hunter. The image moistens the poem, and darkens it, with certain energies that do not flow from a source in our personal life. Without that moistness the poem becomes dry or stuck in one world. Rilke composed the image above, and he seems to me the greatest contemporary master of the image.

As the second power I would name spoken language, that is, language with what Frost calls "sentence sound," embodying a lively music of pitches. The phrase "spoken language" implies two strengths: the first is diction free from archaisms. Words swiftly age, drop out of usage. We learn to leave archaic words behind, leave them, as Antonio Machado says, to the poets in whose age the words were not archaic. Walt Whitman, Robert Frost, and William Carlos Williams especially made American poets alert to which words are archaic and which are not, so that one does not use an archaic word without intending it. The second strength we see only on the wing, or hear only in flight—I mean the variety of pitches one hears in true poetry. The music of pitches enlivens spoken language, and its mastery in poetry is a secret not much discussed these last years. Much recent poetry achieves spoken language in the first sense, but not in the second. Perhaps our difficulty is connected with the overly simplified syntax we have been using. In variety of pitch, Yeats and Frost are both great masters.

As the third power I would name psychic weight. This power is less palpable than the other two, and has not lately had a critical champion. Poetry about important subjects can still lack psychic weight, and in fact, this power is most often noticed by its absence. Time after time in my twenties, after typing up a group of poems hopefully, I would notice an absence. The poems seemed well written, and yet a psychic weight was missing, something imponderable, that I seemed not in control of. I think this weight, which comes later than image or pitch, comes from opening the body to grief, turning your face to your own life, absorbing the failures your parents and your country have suffered, handling what alchemy calls "lead." Edwin Arlington Robinson's poems have psychic weight, *Lord Weary's Castle,* James Wright's best poems, Anna Akhmatova's work, Cesar Vallejo, Baudelaire.

I have set down some sketches of, or hints toward, three powers or energy sources in a poem: the image, that carries both the dark and light worlds, the music of pitches that makes its effect on the musical lobe, and an adult grief that makes the poem feel heavy, as if it were living on the earth. It takes a young poet ten years or so, I think, to develop the image well, perhaps five more to grasp the idea of spoken language and embody it, perhaps five or ten more to make the changes that will lead to weight. I don't think the order of the labors is important. Some poets may be given one power as a gift, and have to work on the others, or may work on all three simultaneously, or begin with some power not mentioned. The whole process seems to take an American poet twenty or twenty-five years; some European poets go through it more quickly.

I was forty-five or so before I felt in *This Body Is Made of Camphor and Gopherwood* all three energy sources present. The music of pitches is the most difficult for me, and ten years' work with the prose poem, whose intimacy allows one to hear pitches well, led up to that book. I was somewhat surprised then, on reading *Camphor and Gopherwood,* to realize that I was about halfway to my goal. I was surprised how little emphasis I had put on sound. Didn't ancient poetry put a lot of emphasis on sound?

As the fourth power, then, I'll name sound. We know the Druid poetry schools required the memorization of several thousand lines of Celtic poetry before instruction was given; and I think sound is slighted now because so few poets memorize their own poems or the great poems of the past. During their friendship Joseph Conrad and Ford Madox Ford once found that they could recite between them the entire text of *Madame Bovary* in French. Different sounds affect different parts of the body; a study of this was essential to Sanskrit poets. The poet needs to separate sound from meter, rhythm, or cadence, and study sound for itself; Gerard Manley Hopkins understood that. Some poets learn to make a sound-structure, with internal resonances, sounds calling to other sounds. In Wallace Stevens we can hear sounds calling to sounds:

> Supple and turbulent, a ring of men
> Shall chant in orgy on a summer morn

In Yeats:

> I will arise, and go now, and go to Innisfree,
> And a small cabin build there, of clay and wattles made

The sounds make a structure of beams, and even if all the words were taken away the beams would still stand. This internal structure of sounds holds up Pasternak's and Akhmatova's poems. Such an internal structure makes a poem a joy to memorize. We feel sound calling to sound in Hart Crane, and Richard Wilbur and Robert Francis; and we often feel a sound-structure in certain poems that Robert Creeley, Donald Hall, and William Everson have written; John Logan's poems have an immense amount of sound work. Recent critics tend to be deaf to this power, and tend not to comment on its presence or its absence.

As the fifth power I'll name the drumbeat. The power of the drumbeat I see as having two sources: first, the meaning that certain sequences of beats have, for example a unit of two beats, or three beats, or four beats, and secondly the meaning of the occasionally stronger beat. Robert Hass has written about the first source, the rhythmical units, in his article "Listening and Making," published in *Antaeus*, Winter-Spring, 1981. It is the best article on rhythm for twenty years. He wants to make sure we understand that he is not talking about meter. "I have already remarked that meter is not the basis of rhythmic form." Donald Hall has also written brilliantly about drumbeat power in his collection of essays called *Goatfoot Milktongue Twinbird*. The strong drumbeat he calls Goatfoot. If there is no drumbeat in the line, the goat's foot has not come down; perhaps a human foot has come down, but not a goat's foot. Yeats says:

> I asked if I should pray,
> But the Brahmin said:

The goat's foot comes down on "pray" and again on "But." Blake said:

> The little boy lost in the lonely fen,
> Led by the wand'ring light.

The goat's foot comes down on "lost," on "fen," and again on "Led."

As I understand it, the Whitman line takes no account of the goat's foot, because the drumbeat does not lend itself to the expansive; it belongs to the concentrative by nature; and, moreover, the goat's foot seems to require a different syntax than that prevalent in Whitman.

The prose poem, which is a further development of the Whitman line, tends to make do without the goatfoot. Conservative critics to the contrary, iambic meter does not insure its presence; no meter insures it. Contemporary iambic poets write in meter, but the goatfoot is missing there as much as in the prose poem. In other words, the drumbeat is hard to find in poetry by living Americans. I find very little of it in my own poems.

As the sixth power, I'll name the narrative, the story, the fiction, the tale, the imagined entertainment, the "Once upon a time." The poet, in order to enter this power, has to imagine personalities, not exactly "personas" either. Chaucer loves this power, so do Blake and the Parzival authors. Edgar Lee Masters did too, and loved it so much that in *Spoon River Anthology* he leaps to this stage, without having done much work on the other elements. Among living American poets Ed Dorn carries this power, so do Russell Edson, Louis Simpson, and, often, William Stafford; but the master in autobiographical narrative is Thomas McGrath in his *Letter to an Imaginary Friend.* No one, including our most active critics, pays any attention to it because we simply don't respect the power of the story, even though Homer, *Beowulf*, Aeschylus, Rumi, Dante, and Goethe make clear how important this energy is in the overall power of the poem.

With this said, we can return to a concentration on the image, but I wanted, by setting these thoughts down, to make clear that no matter how much I respect the image, I don't consider it to be the only important element in a poem, nor the most important. It is one of six or seven. American poets of the last twenty years have probably placed too much emphasis on the image, too much in relation to the other powers. The image in itself brings so much moistness to the poem that it cannot be overpraised.

1

The image belongs with the simile, the metaphor, and the analogy as an aspect of metaphorical language. Shelley said: "Metaphorical language marks the before unapprehended relations of things." Owen Barfield remarks in his marvelous book called *Poetic Diction* (which is about many other things as well) that he would like to alter only one detail in Shelley's sentence. He would change "before unapprehended relations" to "forgotten relations." Ancient man stood in the center of a wheel of relations coming to the human being from objects. The Middle Ages were aware of a relationship between a woman's body and a tree, and Jung reproduces in one of his books an old plate showing a woman taking a baby from a tree trunk. That would be an example of a forgotten relationship recently retrieved; and Greek myths, when studied, turn up others. Many relationships then have been forgotten—by us. They can be recovered. "For though they were never yet apprehended they were at one time seen," Barfield says. "And imagination can see them again." Whenever a poet through imagination discovers a true analogy, he or she is bringing up into consciousness a relationship that has been forgotten for centuries; the object is then not only more seen, but the poet receives a permanent addition to his knowledge.

The power of the image is the power of seeing resemblances, a discipline important to the growth of intelligence, and essential to a poet's intelligence. Emerson said of true analogies:

> It is easily seen that there is nothing lucky or capricious in these analogies, but that they are constant, and pervade nature. These are not the dreams of a few poets, here and there, but man is an analogist, and studies relations in all objects. He is placed in the center of beings, and a ray of relation passes from every other being to him.

Remembering forgotten relationships is then one of the great joys that comes from making up poetry. Of course not every image the mind makes up is a true one, and we have the right to ask of every image in a poem: Does this image help us to remember a forgotten relationship, or is it merely a silly juxtaposition, which is amusing and no more?

2

Barfield makes us see this distinction by emphasizing analogy, which contains the word "logic" in it. He maintains that every true image—every image that moves us or moves our memory—contains a concealed analogical sequence. The imagination calls on intuitive logic to help it create the true image. He gives this passage as an example of an analogical sequence.

> My soul is an enchanted boat,
> Which, like a sleeping swan, doth float
> Upon the silver waves of thy sweet singing.

I'll put down some suggestions. The analogy could be:

> My soul is to your singing
> as a boat is to water.

That may be adequate, but it's a bit bare.

> My soul is to your sounds
> as a sleeping swan is to water.

I prefer that sequence, because it includes the idea of enchantment, which has a secret resonance with "sleeping swan."

The true, or resonant, image then involves the logical intelligence; one has to be intelligent to create an image, and intelligent to understand it. It does not involve two "things" or "energies," but four.

> My soul is to your sounds
> as a sleeping swan is to water.

As a further example, Barfield quotes two lines of Shakespeare, more mysterious than the lines from Shelley.

> What is your substance, whereof are you made,
> That millions of strange shadows on you tend?

Enormous energy enters the poem with the word "*millions.*" Shakespeare gave that thought-energy to the creation of the image. Owen Barfield remarks that "sometimes in retracing the path back to the hidden analogy, a great deal of abstraction is necessary before we can arrive at the ratio." The *ratio* is his word for the sequence of analogies that we unravel slowly and laboriously, but which the imagination leaped to in an instant while it wrote the lines. What are the four points then that underlie Shakespeare's image? We could try this group:

> Your inner personality is to ordinary personality
> as a great magnet is to a stone.

That's solid, but it doesn't feel quite resonant enough. Let's try this:

> Your substance is to the mysterious interior being
> as a great medium is to ghosts longing to speak.

I like that better. But it's not what Barfield has. He suggests these four energies:

> My experience of you is to the rest of my experience
> as the sun is to the earth.

I like this delving. Delving like this makes clear that the true image has thought in it; complicated analogical, even logical, perceptions are called in, and imagination fuses them to make a strong image.

This statement is true in eternity, and to praise the meaning of image is important now, in order to balance the disparagement of image that one finds in much recent criticism. Ira Sadoff in *American Poetry Review* (November-December, 1980) says:

> While the deep image poem acted as an important corrective to the time-honored Anglo-Saxon tradition on the ascendancy of the head over the body, too often it also refused what can only be called intelligence, the possibility of reflection upon experience, the ability to make sense of our histories, our limits as well as our possibilities.

After this observation he sets down an image poem he made up in a minute, as if writing images were easy, as if any high school student could write as well as Trakl.

Ira Sadoff here is clearly warning the beginning poet that the fun of creating images can become a game, and a silly one, and I agree with him on that; but nowhere in his sentence, or his essay, does he distinguish between the true image and the silly juxtaposition. His essay suggests that he has a grudge against the image; and it sets forth the doctrine that the word *intelligence* is to be reserved for the discursive poem. But the discursive poem can also be silly.

I like intelligence when it debates, expansively, both sides of a question in the meditative or discursive poem, and I also like intelligence when it appears, concentratedly, in the image.

3

It seems to me there are two sorts of images, and I'll try in this section to distinguish them. One sort of image resembles a jar in the way it contains, or a house. The image is a house with a room for the light world and the dark world, for the conscious and the unconscious, for the world of the dead and the world of the living. It makes a house with a room for each. Trakl wrote:

The oaks turn green
in such a ghostly way over the forgotten footsteps of the dead.

It has a room for what we know, and for what we don't know.
These two lines are from a poem of mine:

> So much lies just beyond the reach of our eyes . . .
> what slips in under the door at night, and lies
> exhausted on the floor in the morning.

Neruda, in "Solo la Muerte" made a house with a room for
what is invisible in death:

> Death arrives among all that sound
> like a shoe with no foot in it, like a suit with no man in it,
> comes and knocks, using a ring with no stone in it, with no
> finger in it . . .
> Nevertheless its steps can be heard
> and its clothing makes a hushed sound, like a tree.

Bert Meyers, in his poem about his days as a frame maker and
wood polisher, said:

> At dusk I drive home
> the proud cattle of my hands.

These are not real cattle, but he is proud of his hands the way
the dairy farmer is proud of his superb Holsteins. So the
unconscious which doesn't care about large and small mo-
mentarily turned his small hands into immensely large
cows.

The first sort of image, which I've compared to a jar or a
house, unites within human consciousness various worlds,
dark and light. It joins what is present with what is not pres-
ent. The moistness comes from the world we don't know: the
underworld of the dead, the energies the ego has almost suc-
cessfully repressed, the absent foot, the interior sun in
another human being, the imaginary cattle.

I'd like to distinguish that from another sort of image,
which is less like a jar and more like an arm. It reaches out
beyond human consciousness to touch something else. The
Beowulf poet, speaking of Grendel's pond, says:

> At night that lake
> Burns like a torch. No one knows its bottom,
> No wisdom reaches such depths. A deer,
> Hunted through the woods by packs of hounds,
> A stag with great horns, though driven through the forest
> From faraway places, prefers to die
> On those shores, refuses to save its life
> In that water.
>
> Burton Raffel's translation

> Tiger, tiger, burning bright
> In the forests of the night

We sometimes hear the tale of Johnny Appleseed described as a myth, but it has no arm image. The true myth is the carrier for an arm image, and each myth depends, for its power, on at least one of these arm images. Chinua Achebe mentions that in his culture a myth says the whole world was created from a drop of milk. Around 1800, Goethe, Novalis, and Hölderlin open their poems to the arm image that reaches out beyond human consciousness, and open their poems in a way few English poets of the time were doing. A great strength in Yeats's work is that he opens the poem to the arm image:

> The terror of all terrors that I bore
> The Heavens in my womb.

Here we feel the nonhuman universe has entered the human through some sort of channel given by the image. There is terror in it. The imagination has placed the Milky Way inside the womb. We don't feel the image as an analogy. Such an image once found persists for centuries, and people never exhaust its possibilities.

In the myth of Persephone's descent into Hades, the narrative says that after her disappearance from the meadow, her mother did find the hole into the earth, but her footprints were gone, obliterated under the tracks of pigs. A herd of pigs had gone down with her. There is great power in that herd, and we catch an echo of it later in the pigs Christ drove over the cliff.

Images of the "arm" sort carry us into the area in which matter responds to the human unconscious. No one knows much about that; we hear it touched on in events that happen "synchronistically": after longing for a book for days you walk into a stranger's house and see it lying open on the table. It appears also in the sobering insights the subatomic physicists have had in the "Copenhagen experience," in which the particles apparently responded to the human presence, to the observer's unconscious.

4

I discussed in *News of the Universe* the idea, which human beings have been fond of through recent centuries, that the gap between us and nature is unbridgeable . . . in other words, that there is no arm. There is something in us that enjoys feeling that we are isolate, with our human reason, alone in the universe, unchangeably remote from the natural world. If we find this idea comforting and necessary, we avoid writing images, lest we come upon an arm image.

But the difference between a literature that includes the image, and a literature that excludes the image (such as the newspaper or the scientific Newtonian essay) is that the first helps us to bridge the gap between ourselves and nature, and the second encourages us to remain isolated, living despairingly in the gap. Many philosophers and critics urge us to remain in the gap, and let the world of nature and the world of men fall further and further apart. We can do that; or a human being can reach out with his right hand to the natural world, and with his left hand to the world of human intelligence, and touch both at the same moment. Apparently no one but human beings can do this. What is the power that enables us to do that reaching? Barfield says it is imagination. I recently came across an arm image the ancient Norwegians created for Thor: lightning over a ripe barley field. The barley field lies within the human world, but lightning belongs to some other world, and the arm image of Thor joins them. There it is again: the ancient Gothic imagination was unwilling to accept the severe categorizations of outer and inner, divine and human, intelligence and matter, that Aristotle and later Descartes acquiesced in.

Wallace Stevens, with his alive Gothic imagination, believes in this oneness of worlds, and states in "Sunday Morning" his belief that human beings will once more understand it:

And in their chant shall enter, voice by voice,
The windy lake wherein their lord delights,
The trees, like serafin, and echoing hills,
That choir among themselves long afterward.

The arm image continues to resonate, far beyond the personal, and is inexhaustible, endlessly abundant. This true union, this oneness of worlds, is what Wallace Stevens means by the word *Harmonium*. And it is the final purpose of the image and of all six powers of the poem to join in creating that resonance, the music of the octaves, the Harmonium.

Hayden Carruth

The Question of Poetic Form
1975

. . . 151. Sometimes when manufacturers go into business for the first time they give their products high model numbers, as if to suggest that they are old companies with long experience in similar antecedent productions. Well, in somewhat the same spirit, though I hope for reasons less specious, I begin here with paragraph no. 151. God knows I'm an old company, and perhaps only He knows the number of my antecedent productions. But, more specifically, what I want to suggest by my high model number is the time that has gone into the preparation of this particular product; my years of random "scholarship," my amassed notes, fragments, citations, experimental pages, scattered bibliographies, and so on, with which I sit surrounded now—more than enough, I assure you, to fill up 150 introductory paragraphs. Then rejoice with me, for they are all jettisoned. No footnotes, no quotations, and as few proper names as I can get by with: that is how I have decided to proceed. Let the thing be abstract, subjective, principled. Academic critics and philosophers have their reasons, I know, but their reasons are not mine; nor are they the reader's, at least not if my readers are the people I hope to address, my fellow poets and lovers of poetry.

152. Yet aside from the fact that I would find it personally too disheartening not even to mention my labors, a further point arises from these missing 150 paragraphs. For a long time I shuffled my papers, sorted them, fumbled them, trying to make my notes fall into some pattern that would be useful to me, until at last I saw the truth: there is no pattern. And the reason is clear; I knew it all along, but was intimidated from applying it by the manners of the very scholars whose works I was reading. Virtually every important theory of poetry has been invented by a poet. That is the nub of it. And each theory has sprung from the poet's own emotional and esthetic needs in his particular time and place—or hers, for many

important statements have come, especially recently, from women, though I must submit to grammar by masculinizing the métier hereafter—and moreover each theory has been derived from what the poet has observed of his own psychology and method in his own workshop. In short, the theories are subjective. Each theorist begins by returning, not to "first principles," since in art they do not exist, but to experience. The scholarship is irrelevant. And no wonder the theories are inconsistent and often in conflict; no wonder there is no pattern and the categories break down, so that the scholars end, as one of them has, by calling Pope a neoclassical romanticist or by using every term in their catalogues, ineffectually, for Ezra Pound. Yet the statements of Pope and Pound and other poets remain crucial, the indispensable documents of our poetic understanding. In them I find both urgency of feeling and the irrefragibility of knowledge, the real knowledge of what happens when a poem is written. Both qualities are what keep art and the artist alive.

153. There is no pattern then; quite the contrary. And consequently what I am doing here above all is asking for . . . but I don't know what to call it. It is neither reconciliation nor toleration. Among genuinely conflicting views reconciliation is impossible, while toleration implies indifference or a kind of petrified Quakerish absolutism of restraint. These are not what I mean at all. Yet it is true that I abhor sectarianism in the arts, or dogmatism of any kind. What I am asking for, I think, is the state of mind that can see and accept and believe ideas in conflict, without ambivalence or a sense of self-divisiveness. Call it eclecticism if you will. I have been accused of it often enough, the word flung out like a curse. But just as I, a radical, distrust other radicals who are not in part conservatives—i.e., who are ideologues—so I distrust poets who cannot perceive the multiplexity of their art, perceive it and relish it. Poetry is where you find it. I am convinced of this; convinced as a matter of temperament, as a matter of thirty years' intensive critical reading, and as a matter of my perception of human reality—the equivalence of lives and hence of values. So if you find poetry in Blake but not in Pope, or the other way around, that's OK, you are better off than people who find it in neither. But if you find it in both, then you are my kind of reader, my kind of human being.

154. Moreover poetry is a mystery. I don't mean the poem on the page, though that is difficult enough. I mean what went before: poetry as process, poetry as a function of what we call, lumping many things together, the imagination. Think how long science has worked, thus far in vain, to explain the origin of life, which appears to be a simple problem, comparatively speaking, involving few and simple factors. Then think of trying to explain the imagination; first the imagination in general, then a particular imagination; the factors are incalculable. I believe it will never be done. Hence what anyone says about poetry, provided it be grounded in knowledge, is as true as what anyone else may say, though the two sayings utterly conflict. Yet they can be held in the mind together, they can be believed together. And still the element of mystery will remain.

155. What about Aristotle? He was no poet; far from it. It shows unquestionably in his theory of poetry. He wrote about art from the point of view not of the artist but of the spectator, the playgoer. He described the psychology of aesthetic experience; pity and woe, the notion of catharsis. This is interesting and useful, and from it certain ideas may be extrapolated about the work itself, the play. But about playwriting, about art as process? No. And Aristotle's attempt to do it—the feeble theory of imitation—as well as the attempts of a great many others after him, have produced confusion and irrelevance for nearly twenty-five hundred years. To my mind this is the giveaway. A real theory of art begins with process and accepts the inevitability of mystery; it rests content with its own incompleteness. A spurious theory of art begins somewhere else and tries to explain everything.

156. The word that seems to incorporate most fully the essential idea of imaginative process is the word *form*. But at once the element of mystery makes itself known, for the word has been used in so many different ways, with so much looseness and imprecision, that clearly people do not know what it really means; or perhaps the word itself really means more, implicitly or innately, than the people mean, or can mean, when they use it. Hence the imprecision can never be eliminated; the craftiest philosopher will never produce anything but a partial definition. Yet this is no reason for not trying. A few years ago I was attacked by an eminent poet, publicly and bitterly, because in a short piece on another topic I had said

that the staggered tercets used by Williams in his later poems are a "form." Granted, I was using the word imprecisely, which is what one must do with these large, complex, mysterious terms, especially in short pieces, if one is to avoid a breakdown of communication. I am sure my readers knew what I meant. But the eminence was not satisfied; apparently he was infuriated. No, he said, the staggered tercets are merely a style; the form is something deeper, the whole incalculable *ensemble* of feelings, tones, connotations, images, and so on that bodies forth the poem; and I purposely, if somewhat quaintly, say "bodies forth" rather than "embodies" because I think this exactly conveys my attacker's meaning, and the distinction is worth attending to. Of course he was right. I agree with him; I agreed with him then and before then. But at the same time he was only partly right, and he was being dogmatic in just the sense I have referred to, i.e., by insisting arbitrarily that part of the truth is the whole of the truth, and by pinning everything upon an understanding of terms. This is what dogma is. Yet often enough in the past the meanings of our terms have been exactly reversed. *Form* has meant the poem's outer, observable, imitable, and more or less static materiality; *style* has meant its inner quality, essentially hidden and unanalyzable, the properties that bind and move and individuate. Indeed this was the common usage of the two words in literary theory from Lessing and Goethe to T. S. Eliot. And all that is proven by this is that poets are always talking about the same things, but with different names, different tones, different emphases, and different perceptual orientations. How could they otherwise, when each returns to his own experience for the knowledge from which he writes?

157. The danger is, as we have seen, that experience which leads to knowledge will lead further to dogmatism. It happens all the time, by no means more frequently among poets than among others. Yet it isn't necessary. Neither in human nor in categorical terms is this progression inevitable, and it can be interrupted anywhere by reasonableness and humility. What do we mean by the word *form* in ordinary speech? What is the form of an apple? Certainly it is not only the external appearance, its roundness, redness, firmness, etc. Nor is it only the inner atomic structure. Nor is it the mysterious genetic force that creates appleness in the apple. It is all these things and more, the whole apple. The form *is* the apple. We cannot

separate them. In philosophical terms it is the entire essence of the apple plus its existence, the fact of its being. I think that when we use the word *form* in reference to a poem we should use it in just this way. It means the whole poem, nothing less. We may speak of outer and inner form, and in fact I think we must, provided we remember that these are relative terms, relative to each other and to the objectives of any particular inquiry. An image, for example, may be an element of outer form at one time or of inner form at another; it depends on how you look at it. But the form *is* the poem.

158. As for style, to my mind it is not something different from form but something contained within form, a component of form. True, it is unlike other components. But they themselves are more or less unlike one another, so why should this cause difficulty? The best definition I can make is this: style is the property of a poem that expresses the poet's personality. Either his real personality or his invented personality; or, most likely, a combination of the two. It is manifested in the concrete elements of form: syntax, diction, rhythm, characteristic patterns of sound or imagery, and so on; and if one has sufficient patience these elements can be identified, classified, tabulated, they can be put through the whole sequence of analytic techniques; yet style will remain in the end, like the personality behind it (though not on the same scale), practically indemonstrable. Style consists of factors so minutely constituted and so obscurely combined that they simply are not separable and not measurable, except in the grossest ways. Yet we know a style when we see it, we recognize it and are attracted or repelled by it. One reason for this is the fact that style is a continuing element in a poet's work, it remains consistently itself from one poem to another, even though the poems in other respects are notably dissimilar. We speak of the "growth" and "maturity" of a poet's style in the same way that we speak of the growth and maturity of a person. This is an interesting fact; it may even sometimes be a crucial fact, as when we are attempting to explain the incidence of poetic genius. But it can also be a dangerous fact, for it leads to the state of mind in which style seems to be abstract from the poem, abstract from form itself. This is a delusion, I think, and moreover a delusion that brings us near the heart of the question of poetic form.

159. Some people will say that my assertion regarding

outer and inner form is sloppy. I don't see why. I am comfortable in my radical relativism, and am frankly unable to explain why other people shouldn't be comfortable in it too. Yet I know what they have in mind. Some kinds of outer form, they will say, are repeatable—sonnets, villanelles, that sort of thing; and of course it is quite true that the structures of meter and rhyme in some such poems may be indicated roughly but schematically by stress marks and letterings, and then may be imitated in new substances of words, images, feelings, experiences, and so on. My critics will say that this repeatability of certain elements of form makes them absolutely distinct from other elements that cannot be repeated. Again I don't see why. To me the poem in its wholeness is what is important, and I do not care for classifications. Besides, absolute classifications are a myth. Simply because we can state that two poems written a hundred years apart are both Petrarchan sonnets, does that make them the same? Obviously not. Moreover the statement itself seems to me to have only the most superficial classificative meaning; it is virtually useless. Oh, I know what immense complexes of cultural value may adhere to the Petrarchan sonnet or to other conventional classes of poetic structure, and how in certain contexts, outside the discussion of form, these values may be most decidedly *not* useless. OK. But here I *am* discussing form, and the point I want to make is that in reality no element of form is perfectly repeatable and no element is perfectly unique. Outer and inner form may approach these absolutes at either end, but they cannot reach them. They cannot reach them because the absolutes lie outside the poem. A rhyme scheme is not a poem; it is a complete abstraction which has only the absoluteness—if that is the right term—of a Euclidean triangle existing nowhere in nature. Similarly the combination of vital energies and individual referents at the heart of a poem, its inner form, may be almost unique, almost unanalyzable or indiscerptible, but it cannot be absolutely so, for then the poem would cease to be a product of human invention and would assume a status equivalent to that of the creaturely inventor himself, a part of *natura naturata;* and that, I believe—I fervently hope—is impossible. (Though I know many poets who claim just this for their own inventions and their own inventive powers). In short, it is not a question of repeatability but of imitation. And it is not a question of facsimile but of approximation. All we can say about the abstractability of form, including style, is that some elements of form, chiefly the outer, are more or less amenable to imitation, and that other elements, chiefly the inner, are more or less resistant to it. Yet this is saying a good deal. The form *is* the poem, and all its elements lie *within* the poem. Repeatability is a delusion. Finally, even style, though I have noted its continuance from poem to poem, does not continue by means of repetition but by means of self-imitation, that is to say, imperfectly, hence changeably and developmentally; an unchanging style would be a dead style, or no style at all and certainly not a part of poetry.

160. I don't know if what I have written in this last paragraph is clear. Let me reduce it to an analogy. By examining a number of apples one can draw up a generalized schematic definition of an apple, and by using modern methods of investigation one can make this definition account not only for the apple's external appearance but for its invisible internal structure and its animate energy, the forces that determine both its specificity and its individuality. Conceivably this definition might be useful, since by referring to it one could recognize another apple when one saw it. Beyond that, if one were inclined to make classifications, the definition would help in distinguishing the apple from other classes of fruit. But no one, not even the most ardent lovers of definitions, would say that the definition *is* the apple. Obviously the definition is only a definition. And yet some people say that the definition is the *form* of the apple. Can this be? I don't see how. Can a form exist apart from the thing it forms, or rather apart from the thing that makes it a form, that informs it? Can we have such a thing as an unformed form? No, a definition is only a definition, a generalization, an abstraction; and a form, by virtue of being a form, is concrete. No part of the apple's form can exist outside the apple.

161. When I put the matter in these terms the source of difficulty becomes clear right away, and of course it is the Platonic ideal. Well, it seems to me that Plato made a very shrewd observation of human psychology when he conceived his ideals—if he was the one who actually conceived them (I am ignorant of pre-Socratic philosophy). Unquestionably our imaginations do contain an abstracting faculty, with which we derive and separate ideas from things, and often these ideas

become ideals in both the Platonic and modern senses. They are universals, though that is not saying as much as people often mean when they use this word. They are what enable us to be perfectionists, knowing the ideal is unattainable yet striving always toward it; which is what accounts for human excellence, in poetry and in everything else. Every poet has in his head the "idea" of the perfect poem, though it has never been written and never will be. But to infer from this useful but passive quality that ideals—definitions, "forms"—are active or instrumental in the realm of practice, in poetry or in nature, seems to me mere fancy.

162. I should think poets ought to see this more easily than most people. A form is an effect, not a cause. Of course I don't say that in a chain of cultural actions and reactions a form, or rather the abstract definition of a form, may not play a causal role; without doubt it may, and obviously the element of convention in literature is large and important. But considered in conceptual purity, a form is not a cause. Do we work from the form toward the poem? That is the mode of the set piece, the classroom exercise—and we know what kind of "poems" come from that. No, we work from the thing always, from the perception or experience of the thing, and we move thence into feelings and ideas and other cultural associations, and finally into language, where by trial and error we seek what will be expressive of the thing. If we are lucky we find it, and only then do we arrive, almost by accident or as an afterthought, at form. In one sense form is a by-product of poetry, though this is not to deny its essentiality. Naturally I do not mean either that the actual complicated processes of poetic imagination can be reduced to any such simple progression as the one I have indicated. The whole transaction may occur in a flash, literally simultaneously. Formal intuitions may appear at the very beginning. I am convinced that no method of analysis will ever be contrived which is refined enough to isolate all the energies and materials combined in the poetic act. Yet at the same time I do suggest that form in itself is never the cause, and certainly never the instrument (the efficient cause) of real poetry, and I believe this is something all real poets can verify from their own experience.

163. Until now my strategy has been to avoid using the two words that in fact have been the crucial terms in all my speculations about poetic form for several years, the words *organic*

and *fixed*. Yet they are my reason for these paragraphs, as well as my incitement. The notions I have set down here must have been set down thousands of times before, I'm sure, frequently by writers more skillful and gifted than I. Hence what impels me is my awareness that each age attacks the perennial topics from the standpoint of its particular need, with its peculiar angle of vision and edge of feeling. And our age, speaking in terms of poetry, seems to revolve predominantly around these two terms. "Organic form" *vs.* "fixed form": that indicates how we look at the question of poetic form, and it pretty well suggests the quality of our feeling about it. Certainly we are earnest and combative, we are very acutely caught up. Have poets in earlier times worried themselves quite as much as we do about form in poetry? Even the word itself—*form*—has about it now a flavor of ultimacy, almost a numen, that I don't think it possessed in ages past. Of course there are good reasons for this, at least in terms of literary evolution. Anyone who has lived through the past thirty or forty years of poetry in America knows exactly how the conflict between "fixed form" and "organic form" came about, and why. But I am not interested here in the history or sociology of poetry; I am interested in the thing itself, and I hope what I have written so far indicates that I think both terms, *organic* and *fixed*, as they appear in common usage among poets today, are misapplied. Clearly this is the case with fixed form. If form cannot be abstracted it cannot be fixed; at best it can only be turned into a definition, a scheme. The case with organic form seems less clear, because in some sense the concept of organic form is close to what I have been saying about form as the effect or outcome of poetry. But frequently the advocates of organic form go further; they say that the forms of their poems are taken, if not from the ideal forms of Plato's heaven, then from forms in nature, in experience, in the phenomenal world. But forms in the phenomenal world are no more abstractions than any other forms, and transference is impossible. At best poetic form is an analogy to nonaesthetic form, but a very, very remote analogy; so remote indeed that I think it serves no purpose, and the citing of it only beclouds the issue. If what I have argued here is true, i.e., that form is the poem, then form is autonomous—it can be nothing else, which is only what poets have said in other ways for centuries. (Though this does not mean, I would insist, that the poem in its totality of feeling, meaning, and value is separable from morality or ordinary human relevance.) Well, if form is autonomous then let us treat it as such.

164. But if form is autonomous it is also indigenous. A particular poetic form is solely *in* a particular poem; it *is* the poem. Hence it inheres solely in the materials of that poem (which by extension or implication may include the poem's origins). From this I conceive that if an analogy exists between a poetic form and a form in nature, this analogy is solely and necessarily a coincidence, and it is meaningless. After all, what true or functional analogy can exist between the forms of generically differing materials? To say that a poetic form is analogous to a form in nature is the same as saying that a horse is like a pool table, or a dragonfly like a seraph.

165. Going back to *outer* and *inner,* these are the terms I prefer, applied with strict relativism. I think they are more exact than *fixed* and *organic.* Moreover I like them better because they imply no conflict, no war, but rather a consonance. To my mind warring poets, because they are dealing with the very substance of truth, i.e., our vision of reality, are almost as dangerous and a good deal sillier than warring generals.

166. Of course I do not mean to deny what is as plain as the nose on anyone's face, e.g., that Alexander Pope wrote virtually all his poetry is closed pentameter couplets. But I would say three things. First, the misnamed "heroic couplet," which seems to us the height of artifice, was just the opposite in the minds of those who used it. Dryden chose the couplet because he thought it the plainest mode available, the verse "nearest prose," and he chose it in conscious reaction against the artificial stanzaic modes that had dominated English poetry during most of the sixteenth and seventeenth centuries. In short, he and his followers thought they were liberating poetry, just as Coleridge and Wordsworth liberated it a hundred years later, or Pound and Williams a hundred years after that. The history of poetry is a continual fixing and freeing of conventions. It follows that these poets, Dryden and Pope, really were engaged in a liberation; and it follows too that we ought always to pay at least some attention to history and fashion, the worldly determinants, in our consideration of any poetry. Secondly, I do not think the couplet was a fixed form. I do not think it for the same reason that I do not think any form can be fixed. Granted, it was a pattern that was

imitated by many verse writers. But among the best poets it
was a form like any other poetic form: the natural, spontane-
ous (which does not mean instantaneous) effect of the causal
topics, feelings, and attitudes from which their poems de-
rived. It is evident in the best of Pope. He himself said: "I
have followed . . . the significance of the numbers, and the
adapting them to the sense, much more even than Dryden,
and much oftener than anyone minds it. . . . The great rule of
verse is to be musical." Today we do not like "numbers" and
"rules"; but I get from this the distinct feeling that when Pope
spoke of "adapting," he was thinking about poetic form in a
way close to my own. And I know for certain that what he
meant by "musical" had little to do with rhyming and every-
thing to do with the total harmony of language and substance.
Think of the material of Pope's poems. Could it have engen-
dered any other poetic form? I believe the closed pentameter
couplet was natural to Pope, "organic" if you like, and if his
poems are not as well unified *poetically* as any others of a
similar kind and scope, if the best of them are not *poems* in
exactly the same sense we mean today, then I don't know how
to read poetry. (But I do.) Thirdly, in another sense of the
word, different from the sense I have been using, every poetic
form is fixed. It cannot be otherwise. Unless a poem is de-
stroyed as soon as it is written, its form exists as a thing in the
world, to be observed by anyone who wishes to observe it,
particularly by the poet who created it. Thus every poetic
form exists in its permanent concreteness—relatively speak-
ing, of course—and thus it gives rise to influence. It produces
a convention, and this convention may reenter the poet's sen-
sibility and become part of the apparatus of imagination. It
happens with all poets. After all Whitman continued to follow
the conventions of his poems quite as narrowly as Pope fol-
lowed the conventions of his; and in this sense the "organic"
poets of today are writing in forms as fixed as any, as fixed,
say, as the heroic couplet. I grant it would be difficult in
practice to discriminate between what I am here calling a
convention and what I earlier called a style; yet in theory it
must be possible, because a style is what is expressive of a
poet's personality, whereas a convention is a generalized "feel-
ing" about language and structure, often with broadly cul-
tural associations, which can enter anyone's sensibility, not
just its creator's. It would be silly to deny a connection among

James Wright, Galway Kinnell, and W. S. Merwin, for instance, or among Denise Levertov, Robert Creeley, and Robert Duncan. And I suspect that in part these connections consist of the poets' common and mostly unconscious awareness of conventions that have arisen from the multiplicity and multiplexity of their own created, "fixed" poetic forms.

167. Poetry is where you find it. Its form is always its own. The elements of outer form, such as language, tone, or texture, may move sometimes from and sometimes toward the elements of inner form, such as structures of imagery and feeling, symbols, or scarcely revealed nodes of imaginative energy. But if the poem is a real poem its whole form will be integrated. No element of outer form, considered apart from the rest, can signify whether or not a poem, an old poem or a new poem, is real; nor can any element of inner form, so considered. Hence the classification of poems, old or new, is a hurtful, false endeavor. Let the warring cease.

Robert Creeley

On the Road
Notes on Artists and Poets, 1950–65
1974

Coming of age in the forties, in the chaos of the Second World War, one felt the kinds of coherence that might have been fact of other time and place were no longer possible. There seemed no logic, so to speak, that could bring together all the violent disparities of that experience. The arts especially were shaken and the *picture of the world* that might previously have served them had to be reformed. Of course, the underlying information of this circumstance had begun long before the time with which I am involved. Once the containment of a Newtonian imagination of the universe had been forced to yield to one proposing life as continuous, atomistic, and without relief, then discretions possible in the first situation were not only inappropriate but increasingly grotesque. There was no *place*, finally, from which to propose an objectively ordered reality, a world that could be spoken of as *there* in the convenience of expectation or habit.

The cities, insofar as they are intensively conglomerate densities of people, no doubt were forced to recognize and change previous to other kinds of place. The *neighborhood* had been changing endlessly, ever since the onslaught of the Industrial Revolution, and *change*, like it or not, had become so familiar a condition that there was even a dependence on the energy thus occurring. Nothing seemingly held firm and so one was either brought to a depressed and ironically stated pessimism concerning human possibilities, or one worked to gain location in the insistent flux, recognizing the nature of its shifting energies as intimate with one's own.

Put another way, this situation increasingly demanded that the arts, *all* of them—since no matter how disparate their preoccupations may sometimes appear, their roots are always fact of a commonly shared intuition or impulse—that these articulations and perceptions of the nature of human event *yield* the assumption of discrete reality, of objects to be hung on walls merely to be looked at, or words rehearsing agreed-to patterns of valuation and order, or sounds maintaining rationally derived systems of coherence; that the human event itself be permitted to enter, again, the most significant of its own self-realizations.

Hindsight makes all such statement far more tidy than it ever in fact was or could be. As a young man trying to get a purchase on what most concerned me—the issue of my own life and its statement in writing—I knew little if anything of what might be *happening*. I had gone through a usual education in the East, had witnessed in shock the terrifying conclusion of humans killing one another, had wobbled back to college, married (mistakenly) in the hope of securing myself emotionally, had wandered into the woods just that I had no competence to keep things together in the city, even left the country itself, with my tolerant wife, hoping that some other culture might have news for me I could at last make use of and peace with. But the world, happily or unhappily, offers only one means of leaving, and I was returned without relief again and again to the initial need: a *means* of making articulate the world in which I and all like me did truly live.

Most stable in these preoccupations was the sense that any *form*, any ordering of reality so implied, had somehow to come from the very condition of the experience demanding it. That is to say, I could not easily use a previous mode of writing that wasn't consequence of my own literal experience. I couldn't write like Eliot, for example, I couldn't even depend upon Stevens, whose work then much attracted me. So it was that I became increasingly drawn to the proposals of Ezra Pound ("We must understand what is happening . . .") and to the work of William Carlos Williams:

> From disorder (a chaos)
> order grows
> —grows fruitful.
> The chaos feeds it. Chaos
> feeds the tree.
>
> "Descent"

Then, in 1950, a chance contact with Charles Olson gained through a mutual friend, Vincent Ferrini, changed my mind entirely and gave me access at last to a way of thinking of the process of writing that made both the thing said and the way of saying it an integral event. More, Olson's relation to Black Mountain College (which led to my own) found me that company I had almost despaired of ever having. So put, my emphasis here seems almost selfishly preoccupied with *me*—but I was, after all, one of many, all of whom had many of these same feelings and dilemmas. I expect that one of the first tests of the artist is his or her ability to maintain attention and activity in an environment having apparently very little concern or interest in what seems so crucial to oneself. *Company,* then, is a particularly dear and productive possibility for anyone so committed. Mine was answer to every wish I had ever had.

Living in Europe, in France and then in Mallorca, I had come to know some painters, like they say. Ezra Pound had generously put me in touch with René Laubiès, the first to translate selections from the *Cantos* into French, and I found him a warm and intelligent friend. However, I felt rather gauche and heavy around his work, which was in some respects an extension of usual School of Paris preoccupations— that is, he did work to realize a thing in mind, a *sign* or *symbol* that had value for him apart from its occasion in the work itself. His dealer was Paul Fachetti, happily, and it was at this gallery I first saw Jackson Pollock's work, a show of small canvasses giving some sense of the *mode* but without the *scale* that finally seems crucial for him. In any case, these paintings stuck in my head very firmly so that even now I can recall them without difficulty. Lawrence Calcagno and Sam Francis were also showing at Fachetti's, but neither made much impression on me at the time, despite I was delighted they were Americans.

Possibly I hadn't as yet realized that a number of American painters had made the shift I was myself so anxious to accomplish, that they had, in fact, already begun to move away from the insistently *pictorial*, whether figurative or nonfigurative, to a manifest directly of the *energy* inherent in the materials, literally, and their physical manipulation in the act of painting itself. *Process,* in the sense that Olson had found it in Whitehead, was clearly much on their minds.

Coming to Black Mountain the spring of 1954 was equally gain of that *viability* in writing without which it, of necessity, atrophies and becomes a literature merely. Robert Duncan, in recent conversation, recalled his own intention then, "to transform American literature into a viable *language*—that's what we were trying to do." Speaking of Frank O'Hara, he noted that extraordinary poet's attempt

> to keep the *demand* on the language as *operative*, so that something was at issue all the time, and, at the same time, to make it almost like chatter on the telephone that nobody was going to pay attention to before . . . that the language gain what was assumed before to be its *trivial* uses. I'm sort of fascinated that *trivial* means the same thing as *three* (Hecate). Trivial's the *crisis*, where it always blows. So I think that one can build a picture, that in all the arts, especially in America, they are *operative*. We think of art as doing something, taking hold of it as a *process*.

At Black Mountain these preoccupations were insistent. For the painters, the information centered in the work of the Abstract Expressionists, many of whom had been either visitors or teachers there—although their large public approval was yet to come. What fascinated me was that they were entirely centered upon the requalification of the *occasion* of painting or sculpture, the sense of what it was given to *do*. Again, a *literature,* in this case art history and criticism, had grown over the viable condition of the possibility. So, as John Chamberlain put it, "a sculpture is something that if it falls on your foot it will break it," both foot and sculpture. It weighs a lot. It sits on a so-called pediment. In contrast, he wanted a new vocabulary to speak of what a sculpture might be, terms like "fluff" or "glare." When asked why he had used discarded automobile parts for much of his early work, his answer was that Michelangelo had had, apparently, a lot of marble sitting in his backyard, but junked automobiles were what Chamberlain found in his own. *Material* was crucial again, regaining the tensions, the instant-to-instant recognition of the nature of what *was* in hand as mind took hold of it. In contrast, John Altoon saw the School of Paris as so much "polishing of stones," what R. B. Kitaj calls a "patinazation," a concern with decorative texture which prevented perception of the possibilities of the *act* of painting itself.

In like sense, *all* assumptions of what a painting was were being intensively requalified. Hence the lovely definition of that time: *a painting is a two-dimensional surface more or less covered with paint.* Williams's definition of a poem is parallel: *a large or small machine made of words.* In each case there is the marked attempt to be rid of the overlay of a speciously "historical" "appreciation," a "tradition" which is finally nothing more than congealed "taste" or "style"—which, Duncan notes, is distinctly different from art. "No man needs an art unless he himself has to put things together—to find an equilibration. . . ." Style is predicated on the habit of discrimination previous to experience of the objects thus defined, whether these be so-called art objects or simply the clutter of a dump or city street. Duncan's point is that "the objects are not arriving [in perception or consciousness] that way, nor are the objects of thought arriving that way. . . ." The collage or assemblage art of Wallace Berman, George Herms, and Larry Jordan—all working in San Francisco in the fifties—makes use of a *conglomerate,* coming out of what people discard, out of *any* time.

Possibly the attraction the artist had for people like myself—think of O'Hara, Ashbery, Koch, Duncan, McClure, Ginsberg; or Kerouac's wistful claim that he could probably paint better than Kline—was that lovely, uncluttered directness of perception and act we found in so many of them. I sat for hours on end listening to Franz Kline in the Cedar Bar, fascinated by, literally, all that he had to say. I can remember the endless variations he and Earl Kerkham spun on the "It only hurts when I smile" saga, and if that wasn't instance of initial story telling (an *art*), I don't think I'll ever know what is or can be. Kline could locate the most articulate senses of human reality in seemingly casual conversation—as I remember he once did, painfully, moving, by means of the *flowers* in a flower shop a friend had just opened to the *roses* Kline had once brought to the pier to welcome his bride from England—to find that she had had a breakdown in passage. Those "flowers" gave us both something to hold on to.

It may also have been the *energy* these people generated which so attracted us, and we may have been there simply to rip it off in a manner Wyndham Lewis warned against long ago. Writers have the true complication of using words as initial material and then depending on them as well for a more reflective agency. It would be absurd to qualify artists as nonverbal if, by that term, one meant they lacked a generative vocabulary wherewith to articulate their so-called feelings and perceptions. The subtlety with which they qualified the possibility of *gesture* was dazzling. So Michael McClure speaks of having "totally bought Abstract Expressionism as spiritual autobiography" and of Pollock as "so integral [to his own life and thought] that his work began immersing my way of thinking in such a subtle way so early I can't tell you when. . . ."

The insistent preoccupation among writers of the company I shared was, as Olson puts it in his key essay, "Projective Verse" (1950):

> what is the process by which a poet gets in, at all points energy at least the equivalent of the energy which propelled him in the first place, yet an energy which is peculiar to verse alone and which will be, obviously, also different from the energy which the reader, because he is a third term, will take away?

Duncan recalls that painters of his interest were already "trying to have something *happen* in painting" and that painting was "moving away from the inertness of its being on walls and being looked *at*. . . ." *Action* painting was the term that fascinated him, and questions such as "to what degree was Still an Action painter?" He recognized "that you see the energy back of the brush as much as you see color, it's as evident and that's what you experience when you're looking." He notes the parallel with his work of this time, "The Venice Poem," which is "shaped by its own energies" rather than by a dependence on the pictorial or descriptive. Most emphatically, it is "not shaped to carry something outside of itself."

In his *Autobiography,* published in 1951, Williams reprints the opening section of "Projective Verse," feeling it "an advance of estimable proportions" insofar as Olson was "looking at the poems as a field rather than an assembly of more or less ankylosed lines." Earlier, seeing the text in manuscript, he had responded enthusiastically, noting that "Everything leans on the verb." *Energy* and *field* are insistently in mind in his attempt to desentimentalize accumulated senses of poetry by asserting its *thingness.* He uses his friend, the painter Charles Sheeler, as context:

> The poem (in Charles's case the painting) is the construction in understandable limits of his life. That is Sheeler; that, lucky for him, partial or possible, is also music. It is called also a

marriage. All these terms have to be redefined, a marriage has to be seen as a thing. The poem is made of things—on a field.

This necessity—to regain a focus not overlaid with habits of *taste* and the *conveniences* of the past—is found in all the arts at this time. At a retrospective show of his early work (in company with Claes Oldenburg and George Segal) Jim Dine said it constituted his own battle with "art history," his specific attempt to test and find alternatives for its assumptions. In like sense I once heard John Cage, speaking to a group of hostile and "classically" oriented music majors at a New York university, point out that the music with which they were engaged had to do with *concept* and its understanding, whereas the music to which he was committed had to do with *perception* and its arousal. He also made the point that their music occupied only one fourth of the spectrum from a theoretic silence to white noise. Being an American, as he said, he felt that wasteful, and was also particularly interested in the possibilities of what's called *noise* itself. Just as Williams had to fight all his life the curious stigma which labeled him "antipoetic" (a term unintentionally provided by Wallace Stevens in an introduction to his work, which Stevens wanted to separate from saccharine notions of poetry), so we had to fight to gain a specific diction common to lives then being lived. No doubt the implicit *energy* of such language was itself attractive, but the arguments against it, coming primarily from the then powerful New Critics, made its use an exhausting battle. Allen Ginsberg remembers coming offstage after his early readings of *Howl* often so nervously worn out and shocked by the public antagonism, that he'd go to the nearest toilet to vomit. In contrast—and in grotesque parallel indeed to what was the literal condition of the "world"—we both remembered the authoritative critical works of the time we were in college, books with titles like *The Rage for Order* and *The Well Wrought Urn*. Whatever was meant by *The Armed Vision*, the guns were seemingly pointed at us.

There was also the idea, call it, that poets as Ginsberg or myself were incapable of the formal clarities that poetry, in one way or another, has obviously to do with. Even now, at public readings in which I've read a sequence of poems whose structure has persistently to do with the parallel *sounds* of words having marked recurrence, someone inevitably (and too often one of my colleagues in teaching) will ask me if I've ever considered using rhyme? It blows my mind! I can't for the life of me figure out *where* they are in so-called time and space. As Pound pointed out, we don't all of us occupy the same *experience* of those situations, no matter we may be alive together in the same moment and place.

When my first wife and I decided at last to separate in 1955, we met in New York to discuss the sad responsibilities of that fact. At one point, locked in our argument, I remember we were walking along Eighth Street not far from the Cedar Bar, and suddenly there was Philip Guston, across the street, waving to us. My wife had not met him, and I had but recently, thanks to Kline—and had found him a deeply generous and articulate man. Most flattering was the fact he knew my work, although at that time it would have been hard to find it in any easily public condition. (It's worth noting that De Kooning, Kline, and Guston—the three I knew best—were all of them "well read," to put it mildly, and seemingly kept up with the new work of that time as actively as the writers themselves. Guston especially had a great range of "literary interest." A poem in *For Love* called "After Mallarmé" is actually a translation of a poem of Jouvet's which Guston quoted to me, having brought me up to his loft, with characteristic kindness, to show me the few paintings still there just previous to his first show with Sidney Janis. My "translation" is what I could make of the French he quoted, in my scattered recollection of it.) In any case, my wife had become increasingly suspicious of what she felt were the true incompetences of my various heroes, i.e., Kline painted the way he did because he couldn't draw, and Williams wrote in his fashion, because he couldn't rhyme. So here was one she could physically confront, and she didn't waste any time about it. Guston had brought us to a restaurant which had just opened, and so there were free *hors d'oeuvres*—to his and my delight. Once we were seated, she let him have it: *how do you know when a painting is finished* (painting the way you do). He answered very openly and clearly. Given the field of the painting, so to speak, given what might energize it as mass, line, color, *et al.*—when he came to that point where any further act would be experienced as a diminishment of that tension (when there was nothing more to *do*, in short), that was when he felt the painting was finished. She let the matter rest, but I knew she felt almost complacently dissatisfied. "He doesn't know what he is doing—he's just fooling around." She, like so many others than and now, did feel that there must be an intention factually outside the work itself, something to be symbolized there, some content elsewise in mind there expressed, as they say. But that a *process*—again to emphasize it—might be felt and acted upon as crucial in itself she had not considered. So a statement such as Olson's "We do what we know before we know what we do" would be only a meaningless conundrum at best. I guess she thought we were all dumb.

Far from it, for whatever use it proved. There was, first of all, a dearly held to sense of one's *professionalism,* as Duncan reminded me, and all of us *practiced* the art which involved us as best we could. He spoke of the "upsurge in the comprehension of the language" in each art, and "not only writing, or painting, was going on, but *reading,*" a veritable checking out of all the possibilities inherent in the physical situation and associative values pertaining. So painters are working "from a very solid comprehension of the visual language they come from, including anyone who may be looking." They know, as do the poets related, the *state* of the language—in a sense parallel to the scientist's saying something is in a volatile or inert *state*—so that "we do convey what we mean" and there is attention to what is happening in *every* part of the work, to keep "a tension throughout."

The diversity of possibilities gained by such an intensive inquiry is still the dominant condition. At times it may seem almost too large an invitation to accept, and in any situation where it is used either for convenience or habit, an expectable bag of tricks, then whatever it may have generated is at an end. This is to say, more vaguely, what Ezra Pound emphasized: "You cannot have literature without *curiosity*. . . ." Or what Olson's qualification of *attention* makes clear: "the exaction must be so complete, that the assurance of the ear is purchased at the highest—forty-hour-a-day—price. . . ." There is also the dilemma demonstrated by the story Chamberlain tells of his first wife: "She said she wanted to be a singer, but what she really wanted to be was famous." Good luck.

Possibly the complex of circumstances which made the years 1950 to 1965 so decisive in the arts will not easily recur. No one can make it up, so to speak. But there were clearly years before, equally decisive, and there will no doubt be those now after. This clothesline is at best an invention of pseudohistory, and the arts do not intend to be history in this way, however much they use the traditions intimate to their practice. When Duncan saw Olson for the last time, in hospital a few days before his death, he said to him, "important as history was to you, there are no followers—and as a matter of fact that isn't what happened in poetry." Olson grinned, and Duncan added, "It *was* an adventure. . . ."

It's always an *adventure*, thank god. When Rauschenberg arrived at the Art Students League in New York, one of his teachers, Morris Kantor, felt that his wife, who'd come with him, really had the more practical competence as a painter. But what Rauschenberg had as curiosity was fascinating, e.g., he'd put a large piece of butcher paper just in front of the door by which students came and went, would leave it there for a day or so, and then would examine it intently, to see the nature of pattern and imprint which had accumulated. Characteristically it is Rauschenberg who questions that an "art object" should live forever necessarily, or that it should be less valued than a car which manages to stay in pristine state for a very few years indeed.

What seems most to have been in mind was not the making of *models*, nor some hope of saving a world. As Duncan said of Olson's sense of a city, "You have to confront it and get with it," not "straighten it out. Optimism and pessimism have nothing to do with being alive." The question more aptly is, "How much aliveness is found in living in a city," as much to the point now as when Whitman made his own extraordinary catalog. Moral as the arts are in their literal practice, I do think they abjure such program in other respects. At least they do not serve easily such confined attention, however humanly good. I am sure Allen Ginsberg, despite the persistent concern he has shown for the moral state of this country, would nonetheless yield all for that moment of consciousness which might transform him.

But none of this, finally, has anything to do with any such argument at all. As Wittgenstein charmingly says, "A point in space is a place for an argument." You'll have to tell mother we're still on the road.

Placitas, N.M.
August 28, 1974

To Define
1953

The process of definition is the intent of the poem, or is to that sense—"Peace comes of communication." Poetry stands in no need of any sympathy, or even goodwill. One acts from bottom, the root is the purpose quite beyond any kindness.

A poetry can act on this: "A poem is energy transferred from where the poet got it (he will have some several causations), by way of the poem itself to, all the way over to, the reader." One breaks the line of aesthetics, or that outcrop of a general division of knowledge. A sense of the KINETIC impells recognition of force. Force is, and therefore stays.

The means of poetry are, perhaps, related to Pound's sense of the *increment of association;* usage coheres value. Tradition is an aspect of what anyone is now thinking—not what someone once thought. We make with what we have, and in this way anything is worth looking at. A tradition becomes inept when it blocks the necessary conclusion; it says we have felt nothing, it implies others have felt more.

A poetry denies its end in any *descriptive* act, I mean any act which leaves the attention outside the poem. Our anger cannot exist usefully without its objects, but a description of them is also a perpetuation. There is that confusion—one wants the thing to act on, and yet hates it. *Description* does nothing, it includes the object—it neither hates nor loves.

If one can junk these things, of the content which relates only to denial, the negative, the impact of dissolution—act otherwise, on other things. There is no country. Speech is an assertion of one man, by one man. "Therefore each speech having its own character the poetry it engenders will be peculiar to that speech also in its own intrinsic form."

A Note
1960

I believe in a poetry determined by the language of which it is made. (Williams: "Therefore each speech having its own character the poetry it engenders will be peculiar to that speech also in its own intrinsic form.") I look to words, and nothing else, for my own redemption either as man or poet. Pound, early in the century, teaches the tradition of "man-standing-by-his-word," the problem of *sincerity*, which is never as simple as it may be made to seem. The poet, of all men, has least cause and least excuse to pervert his language, since what he markets is so little in demand. He must find his living elsewhere. His aim must never be deflected by anterior commitment, even to those whom he loves. Words cannot serve responsibly as an apology for those who may wish to make them one.

I mean then *words*—as opposed to content. I care what the poem says, only as a poem—I am no longer interested in the exterior attitude to which the poem may well point, as signboard. That concern I have found it best to settle elsewhere. I will not be misled by the "niceness" of any sentiment, or its converse, malevolence. I do not think a poet is necessarily a nice man. I think the poem's morality is contained as a term of its structure, and is there to be determined and nowhere else. (Pound: "Prosody is the total articulation of the sound in a poem.") Only craft determines the morality of a poem.

Louis Zukofsky offers *A Test of Poetry* as "the range of pleasure it offers as sight, sound, and intellection." I am pleased by that poem which makes use of myself and my intelligence, as a partner to its declaration. It does not matter what I am told—it matters, very much, how I am there used. Our world has been so delivered to the perversion of language (the word *qua* trick or persuader) that my own soul, such as I know it, comes to life in whatever clarities are offered to it. Poems allow me to go on living, and I am grateful for my life.

A Note on the Local
1961

The local is not a place but a place in a given man—what part of it he has been compelled or else brought by love to give witness to in his own mind. And that is the form, that is, the whole thing, as whole as it can get.

I think we will be fools to be embarrassed by it. We know the other neatness possible, the way of the neat pattern, and the dodging which it must call for. Grace has no part in that. At some point reached by us, sooner or later, there is no longer much else but ourselves, in the place given us. To make that present, and actual for other men, is not an embarrassment, but love.

"Statement" for Paterson Society
1961

A poem is a peculiar instance of language's uses, and goes well beyond the man writing—finally to the anonymity of any song. In this sense it may be that a poet works toward a final obliteration of himself, making that all the song—at last free of his own time and place. It is curious that this can be most true of that most personal, wherein the man leaves the environment of years and faces, to make his own the poem. But he can only do this, it seems to me, by the most scrupulous localism—because only the particular instance proves free in this way.

Again and again I find myself saved, in words—helped, allowed, returned to possibility and hope. In the dilemma of some literal context a way is found in the words which may speak of it.

Poems Are a Complex
1965

Poems are a complex, and exist by virtue of many things. First, they are a structure of sounds and rhythms which cohere to inform the reader (whether he listen aloud or in silence) with a recognition of their order. In this respect, I much agree with Louis Zukofsky's note of his own poetics, which, as he says, comprise a function having as lower limit speech, and upper limit music. Pound's note, that "Prosody is the articulation of the total sound of a poem," has equal relevance.

Since words are the material, and words have meanings in other senses, that fact also has pertinence. But I do not feel that *thing* in the language we call a poem has to do with a literal issue of semantic meaning. Yet that aspect of meaning is a material also, and clearly enters into the issue of image, or statement—or all such effects of something said.

I think for myself the primary term is that words can move in the measure of song, although I do not wish to confuse poetry with music. But in a poem I tend to hear whatever can be called its melody long before I have reached an understanding of all that it might mean.

Finally, I use several measures though never with much literal consciousness. Two further statements of Pound's long ago attracted me: "Only emotion endures . . ." and "Nothing counts save the quality of the emotion. . . ." I have used that sense with respect to all instances of writing, but I would feel, as he, that poetry is that one most fully charged with meaning. To that I would now add a recent emphasis of Olson's: "That which exists through itself is what is called meaning."

In other words, poems are not referential, or at least not importantly so. They have "meaning" in that they do "exist through themselves." I have no very clear sense of where they may come from, but I have felt them most evident when least assumed. Lorca's "Theory and Function of the *Duende*" is interesting to me, although I would not so simply discredit either the Angel or the Muse to gain the "dark sounds" only. But I do feel poems to involve an occasion to which a man pays obedience, and which intentions alone never yield.

There are many ways indeed to say any of this, and I can't feel any one to be sufficient. I think I first felt a poem to be what might exist in words as primarily the fact of its own activity. Later, of course, I did see that poems might comment on many things, and reveal many attitudes and qualifications. Still, it was never what they said *about* things that interested me. I wanted the poem itself to exist and that could never be possible as long as some subject significantly elsewhere was involved. There had to be an independence derived from the very fact that words are *things* too. Poems gave me access to this fact more than any other possibility in language.

Robert Duncan

Ideas of the Meaning of Form
1961

Phases of meaning in the soul may be like phases of the moon, and, though rationalists may contend against the imagination, all men may be one, for they have their source out of the same earth, mothered in one ocean and fathered in the light and heat of one sun that is not tranquil but rages between its energy that is a disorder seeking higher intensities and its fate or dream of perfection that is an order where all light, heat, being, movement, meaning, and form are consumed toward the cold. The which men have imagined in the laws of thermodynamics.

But if our life is mixed, as the suspicion comes from the Gnostics and from Blake, and rays of many stars that are suns of all kinds. Aie! if we are so many fathered, or if, as theosophists have feared, we were many mothered in the various chemistries of the planets, still let the war be done and the adultery rage on, for my soul is sick with fear and contention whenever I remember the claim of mind against mind and some ass praises me because a line rimes who would despise me if he knew the meanings, and I am aroused myself toward thoughts of vengeance and triumph. Thus, I say, "Let the light rays mix," and, against the Gnostics, who would free the sparks of spirit from what is the matter, and against the positivists and semanticists who would free the matter from its inspirational chaos, I am glad that there is night and day, Heaven and Hell, love and wrath, sanity and ecstasie, together in a little place. Having taken thought upon death, I would be infected by what is.

> she said, Sir, it is a most beautiful fragrance,
> as of all flowering things together;

Thus, H.D., fifteen years ago, in *The Flowering of the Rod:* "But Kasper knew the seal of the jar was unbroken." And William Carlos Williams in the close of "Asphodel":

    Asphodel
            has no odor
                    save to the imagination
    but it too
            celebrates the light.
                    It is late
    But an odor
            as from our wedding
                    has revived for me
    and begun again to penetrate
            into all crevices
                    of my world.

The end of masterpieces . . . the beginning of testimony. Having their mastery obedient to the play of forms that makes a path between what is in the language and what is in their lives. In this light that has something to do with all flowering things together, a free association of living things then—for my longing moves beyond governments to a co-operation; that may have seeds of being in free verse or free thought, or in that other free association where Freud led men to re-member their lives, admitting into the light of the acknowledged and then of meaning what had been sins and guilts, heresies, shames, and wounds;

that may have to do with following the sentence along a line of feeling until the law becomes a melody, and the imagination, going where it will—to the stars! may return to penetrate, a most beautiful fragrance, into all the crevices of our world:

in this light I attempt to describe what I most abhor, what most seems to exclude or mistake the exuberance of my soul.

Convention, Conformities, and Regulated Meters

Form to the mind obsessed by convention, is significant in so far as it shows control. What has nor rime nor reason is a bogie that must be dismissed from the horizons of the mind. It is a matter of rules and conformities, taste, rationalization, and sense. Beyond, as beyond in the newly crowded Paris or London of the Age of Reason, lies the stink of shit and pestilence. Wherever the feeling of control is lost, the feeling of form is lost. The reality of the world and men's habits must be constricted to a realm—a court or a salon or a rationale—

excluding whatever is feared. It is a magic that still survives in Christian Science and the New Criticism, a magic that removes the reasonable thing from its swarming background of unreason—unmentionable areas where all the facts that reason cannot regulate are excluded and appear as error, savage tribes, superstitions and anarchical mobs, passions, madnesses, enthusiasms and bad manners. Metaphor must be fumigated or avoided (thought of as displaying the author's fancy or wit) to rid the mind of the poetic, where metaphor had led dangerously toward Paracelsus' universe of psychic correspondences, toward a life where men and things were beginning to mix and cross boundaries of knowledge. Poets, who once had dreams and epiphanies, now admit only to devices and ornaments. Love, that had been a passion, had best be a sentiment or a sensible affection. Rational piety and respect for God stood strong against divine inspiration and demonic possession. The struggle was to have ideas and not to let ideas have one. Taste, reason, rationality rule, and rule must be absolute and enlightened, because beyond lies the chiaroscuro in which forces co-operate and sympathies and aversions mingle. The glamor of this magic haunts all reasonable men today, surrounding them with, and then protecting them from, the shadows cast by the enlightenment, the darkness of possibilities that control cannot manage, the world of thought and feeling in which we may participate but not dominate, where we are used by things even as we use them.

This frame of mind still holds a dominant place today. In literary circles—(literary societies were an expression of this prophylactic genius against experience)—there are so many mentors of wit and taste, of what ought to be, "hoping with glory to trip up the Laureate's feet," whose meters must perform according to rules of iamb and spondee, these phantasms of the convention triumphing over the possible disorder or music that threatens in the contamination of actual stresses in the language.

So, one Miss Drew (selected by me at random from a library recommended-currents shelf to represent up-to-date academic opinion about form in poetry) defining the art of the poet: "A metrical scheme is itself simply a mechanical framework, a convention, within which and against which, the poet orders his individual poetic movement," reacts throughout against any thought that there might be, as Carlyle was not afraid to think, a music in the heart of things that the poet sought. What Carlyle saw was that the key to that music lay in the melody (which we must take it Miss Drew has never heard) of the language itself, where "all speech, even the commonest speech, has something of song in it: not a parish in the world but has its parish-accent;—the rhythm or *tune* to which the people there *sing* what they have to say." But Carlyle in those lectures in 1840 was concerned with the return of the heroic spirit. Miss Drew is a latter-day believer in men cut down to the proper size, a mistress of that critical demon that Pound in his *Cantos* calls Pusillanimity.

Contrast the voice and spirit of Carlyle, where imagination appears as an intuition of the real:

> All deep things are Song. It seems somehow the very central essence of us, Song; as if all the rest were but wrappages and hulls! The primal element of us; of us, and of all things. The Greek fabled Sphere-Harmonies: it was the feeling they had of the inner structure of Nature; that the soul of all her voices and utterances was perfect music. Poetry, therefore, we call *musical Thought*. The Poet is he who *thinks* in that manner. At bottom, it turns still on power of intellect; it is a man's sincerity and depth of vision that makes him a Poet. See deep enough, and you see musically; the heart of Nature *being* everywhere music, if you can only reach it.

Against which the voice and spirit of Miss Drew:

> The convention sets up a pattern of recurrent sound effects which is pleasant to the ear. It is an element in a larger movement, his rhythm. Rhythm means flow, and flow is determined by meaning more than meter, by feeling more than feet. It represents the freedom the poet can use within his own self-imposed necessity. It is the personal voice speaking through the formal convention.

What we see in the contrast is, in scope of imagination, style, intellect, unfair perhaps. Carlyle is so obviously a mind troubled by genius; Miss Drew is so obviously a mind troubled only by, as she calls it, "a self-imposed necessity." But the genius of convention, that was brilliant in the 17th and 18th centuries, in our own is liable to come out small or trivial. Carlyle's thought opens a vista toward what our own inspired science of linguistics has made part of our responsibility, if we are concerned with the nature of things. Carlyle's thought going toward the inner structure of Nature had intuitions of the inner structure of language. The science of Sapir and Whorf has its origins in the thought of *The Hero as Poet.* Just as, exemplified in Miss Drew, one of the stands of the conventional, of all reasonable men, is against the heroic.

"Pound's cult of *Imagism,*" Miss Drew goes on, "demanded no rhythmical stress at all, only a clear visual image in lines alleged to be in the pattern of the musical phrase. When read aloud, these patterns couldn't possibly be distinguished from prose. The result was a flood of poems such as William Carlos Williams's "Red Wheelbarrow," which proves perhaps only that words can't take the place of paint."

It is of the essence of the rationalist persuasion that we be protected, by the magic of what reasonable men agree is right, against unreasonable or upsetting information. Here, in order to follow Miss Drew's intelligence, we must be ignorant of (aggressively oppose the facts) or innocent of (passively evade the facts) history (what Imagism actually was), poetics (what Pound actually did say about tone and duration, stress and phrase), gestalt (what a pattern actually is in time, and how poetry and music have common characteristics by reason of that extension), linguistics (what the actual patterns of vowel and consonant, stress and pitch, are in the language); and, finally, we must be determined to read "The Red Wheelbarrow" to fit Miss Drew's determination that "these patterns couldn't possibly be distinguished from prose."

The base evil of Miss Drew's mind is that it must depend upon our taking its authority. Her evocation throughout of "mechanical framework," "orders his movement," "determined," "imposed," "alleged" and then "ought" and "ought not," "couldn't possibly," "can't" is the verbal effluvia of a mind holding its own ("self-imposed necessity") against experience. For were we to question her authority in light of the poem, we would find that there is some difference in movement between the poem she seems to have read that went as follows: "So much depends upon a red wheel barrow glazed with rain water beside the white chickens" and the actual poem. But it is part of her conviction that the appearance on the page of a line is a matter of convention, must indicate either following or disobeying what men have agreed on. Any other meaning, that the line might be a notation of how it is to be read, is intolerable.

So she must overlook or deny the lines as meaningful notation, where syllabic measures of variable number alternate with lines of two syllables to form a dance immediate to the eye as a rhythmic pattern:

> four syllables (two one-syllable words + one two-syllable word)
> one two-syllable word
> three syllables (three one-syllable words)
> one two-syllable word
> three syllables (three one-syllable words)
> one two-syllable word
> four syllables (one two-syllable word + two one-syllable words)
> one two-syllable word.

She must overlook, fail to hear, or deny the existence of riming vowels in "glazed" and "rain," "beside" and "white" that give a balanced emphasis to the measure in the close; much less an ear for the complex or subtle relations that syncopate the opening lines between "so much" and "barrow," "depends" and "red wheel," "a" and "upon."

At every level her mind was excited to resist against Williams's *so much depends.* Her goal in criticism was not to explore the meaning and form of the poem but to stand against it; to remain independent of red wheelbarrow, vowels and consonants, count of syllables and interchange of stresses, juncture, phrase.

"Whether this kind of thing pleases," she decides firmly, "must be a matter of personal taste, but it should not be called *verse,* since that word means that the rhythm *turns* and repeats itself; just as *prose* means that it runs straight on."

But criticism like this is a monster of poor sort. Though I am unread in contemporary verse of the conventional persuasion outside of the work of Marianne Moore, T. S. Eliot, and Robert Lowell, I realize that beyond these there is marshaled an imposing company of arbiters and camp followers, lady commandos of quatrains right! and myrmidons of the metaphysical stanza, holding the line against any occurrence of, much less the doctrines of, poetic genius or romantic imagination, handing out prizes (booby and otherwise) to balance the accounts and bolster standards. Schoolmarms and professors of literature affronted by the bardic presumptions of Dame Edith Sitwell.

Were our songs of the universe and our visions of that great Love who once appeared to Dante holding his smoking heart in his hand, were our feelings and thoughts that had flowed out of whatever originality they might have had into their origins in phrases of a melody, were our dreams and our architectures to come home at last, members of no more than a classroom education?

Convention, anyway, in these circles of literary critics and school masters, is a proper mode, and seldom rises to any height above the general conventionality, having its roots (like the unconventionality of "beats") in what other men think. But in the vitality of poets, of Marianne Moore or of Robert Lowell, some personal necessity rather than social opportunity gives substance and meaning to their conventional verse. The rigorously counted syllables, the certainty of end rimes, the conformation of stanzas arise along lines, not of a self-imposed necessity but of a psychic need.

Stanza must conform to stanza in the work of Marianne Moore wherever the charge of emotion is carried, because awareness at all depends upon a character structure that proves itself in awareness. "Tell me the truth, / especially when it is / unpleasant," she says in *Light Is Speech;* and there is the sense of facing the facts, of "Test me, I will resist." Power over things, which is the keynote of the aesthetic of the Man of Reason, is at least related to the power to survive things that inspires Marianne Moore's art. It is not subtlety of movement and interrelation but the challenge of obstacles and particulars that informs her dance. "No more fanatical adjuster," she remarks in lines that keep their own "constant of the plumbline, of the tilted hat / than Escudero." Her metaphor is never a device but a meaningful disclosure. She is not conventional then by social class or by prejudice, but by nature. But to be conventional by nature leaves her personal and vulnerable, erecting around herself an armored modesty, that can show also an irritable sense of possible violation. In her strength and in her weakness she shows her likeness to this constellation I have been drawing of the genius of defensive Reason.

Robert Lowell, too, is not merely conventional as a matter of what men approve but holds his line and establishes his rime at the edge of disaster. His precisions arise not from a love of the melos, the particles that contribute to the melody, but from a mistrust throughout of free movements. When in *Life Studies* his line grows irregular, it conforms to the movement straining for balance that a drunk knows. Betrayal is immanent:

> In the ebb-
> light of morning, we stuck
> the duck
> -'s web-
> foot, like a candle, in a quart of gin we'd killed.

The notation of these lines is as accurate as in William Carlos Williams, and the art as admirable. But the concept of the verse is not free, but fearful. Where in the later poetry of Williams the end juncture makes possible a hovering uncertainty in which more may be gathered into the fulfillment of the form, in the *Life Studies* of Lowell the juncture appears as a void in measure that is some counterpart of the void in content. How / we feel / can this / foot / get across to / that / line. There.

In *O to Be a Dragon* Marianne Moore sees in *Combat Cultural* terms which relate directly to the rise in the 17th and 18th centuries of the Reasonable Convention confronted by intolerable threat:

> I recall a documentary
> of Cossacks: a visual fugue, a mist
> of swords that seemed to sever
> heads from bodies—feet stepping through
> harp-strings in a scherzo.

As, perhaps another conventional soul, Charles Bell, writing in *Diogenes* 19, speaks of "the transformations of Renaissance and Baroque" that filled architecture of churches "with voluptuous riot," bringing religion into a vertigo, "the dramatic contrasts of assertive ego of later religious music, of Gabrielli and Bach." And we recall that the rationalist aesthetic was an heroic effort to find balance against this admission of vertigo, against the swirl of a vastly increased vision of what man might be.

"However," Marianne Moore pauses, and begins her next stanza:

> the quadrille of Old Russia for me:
> with aimlessly drooping handkerchief
> snapped like the crack of a whip;

The tension, the reality of the verse, depends upon its being sufficiently haunted by the thought of its energy as a violence and the thought of its form as repose for the poet to take her stance. But the "aimlessly drooping handkerchief / snapped like the crack of a whip" is an image of the unnecessary conventionality of Marianne Moore's later work where recognition and admiration have disarmed her of the struggle that gave reality to her vigorous lines. Challenged, she may be aroused to display her backbone, to bristle her armatures. But window shopping among the ads of the *New Yorker*, it is not to the aepyornis or rock challenged by time that the figure refers but to the qivies with winning ways.

In her career Marianne Moore began, in certain poems like "An Octopus" or "In the Days of Prismatic Color," with some promise of a free verse, where movement of language had the vigor of a feeling and thought that was not self-conscious. Here the number of lines in the stanza can vary with the immediate sense of movement, and the actual kept feeling of the tempo gives measure rather than the systematic repeated count of syllables or the emphasis of rimes at the end of lines. It is the uneasy definition of what is "sophistication" and what are "the initial great truths" that is one proposition of the poem; it is "the days of Adam and Eve," of "complexity . . . committed to darkness," of smoke, modified color, even murkiness, on the one hand; and "when Adam was alone," where color keeps its place in "the blue-red-yellow band / of incandescence" on the other. These poems imagine terms of a nature where things may mingle still, though the soul is troubled and the mind already resolved to outlast unsureness.

But in the work in which she found what was typical or original, the metaphor is that of animal or hero who survives by resistance of his spine (backbone) and his spiney armature (protective character structure). Conventionality breeds personality. She conforms to her own society. Individuality, yes, but dependent thruout upon rules and orders even as it insists upon its individuality. Her splendid achievement is to excite our admiration of her performance, her risky equilibriums, and her resistance to deeper thought and feeling where personality is lost. Her skill and her craft are unexcelled. But they depend upon increased self-consciousness, and they divert then the attention of the poet and our attention in reading from the question they beg of the avoidance of emotions too common to be personalized.

In the resolution of "In the Days of Prismatic Color" we note the conditions were already potential where truth is identified with what resists but not with the experience that is resisted: "The wave may go over it if it likes," she says, where "it" is Truth and the wave is experience. "Know that it will be there when it says, 'I shall be there when the wave has gone by.'" She evokes in her most famous poetry, with its images of rigorists and armored animals, a heroism of the isolated remnant, a constantly reiterated picture of her own personality as determined in a "little-winged, magnificently speedy running-bird" poetry, increasingly specialized. These poems were practices meant to insure habitual virtues. Vision and flight of the imagination were sacrificed to survival in terms of personal signature.

In pieces like "Hometown Piece for Messrs. Alston and Reese, Enough," and "In the Public Garden," she sacrifices character to the possibilities of what America loves in public personality. What had been a display of bony determination and admirable protective structure becomes now a projection of loveable peculiarity, a profession of charming helplessness. In her career she has performed a range that once in history had its hopeful beginnings in Dryden, then its heroic dimensions in the rage of Pope and Swift, and at last, its social occasions in our own day when "a British poet," as Auden writes in the Introduction to his 1956 *Book of Modern American Verse*, "can take writings more for granted and so write with a lack of strain and over-seriousness." We remember, for it applies here too, the "aimlessly drooping handkerchief" of *Combat Cultural* in this professional lack of over-seriousness, which is the secret superior possibility for Auden.

The vital phase of Rational Genius came as it met straight on the threat of an overwhelming expansion in consciousness that followed the breakthrough in the Renaissance on all levels. The inspiration of Reason was to close off consciousness in an area that was civilized, European, superior in race, practical and Christian (or at least rational in religion). The neo-Platonism and Hermeticism that had begun with Gemisthus Pletho, Ficino, and Pico della Mirandola and appeared in the Rosicrucianism of the early 17th century carried men's religious thought across barriers of right belief, church and civilization, into realms of imaginative synthesis. The agreement of reasonable men was to quarantine the fever of thought. Rationalism erected a taboo of social shame that still lasts against the story of the soul, against the dream and inner life of men the world over, that might be read were the prejudices of what's right and what's civilized lost. Only in the fairy-tales and lore of the common people or in the ritual and lore of cults whose members incurred the cost in their thought of their being outcast and shamed did the great imagination survive. Church-goer or atheist, the rational man was immune to revelation.

Ideas of race, of nation and progress, held and still in many circles hold against the recognition that mankind is involved in one life. Respectable critics and versifiers have been as shocked by the "Buddhism" of Allen Ginsberg or Kerouac as they are by the "sex." When the wall broke, and where it broke, orthodoxy or atheism was swept aside, and men began again to read inner meaning and experience in the arts of all places and times, the message of the soul in African masks, in Aeschylus or in Lady Murasaki, even as they read it in the lore of Catholic saints and Protestant mystics, letting the light from Asia come into their souls to wed and mingle with the light from Rome. It was against this flood of information that threatened once men began to explore the world that the genius of Reason was evoked. Against the imagination then.

The plagues and panics that swept men in their physical existence after 1492 had their counterparts in the plaguing contacts with fellow civilizations in America, Africa and Asia, and the panic that swept Christendom as time before Christendom and space beyond Christendom began to be real and men found their psychic resistances invaded. Up swirled minds and emotions, sciences and art, in a convulsive imagination. There were fearful architectures, gestures, efforts to hold what was not understood and might not be tolerable—in one swirling rhythm. So, in Milton's thundering syntax the heaped-up effort at architecture, majesty and vastness takes over the drama from even Satan, and leaves Adam and Eve impoverished in their identity and as overwhelmed as they are disobedient. How Eve is dwindled in conception from the vital conception of Lady Macbeth or Cleopatra.

There is then a lovely release in the Restoration. The beauty of what the Age of Enlightenment meant we can hear still in the "Ode on the Death of Henry Purcell," where Dryden and John Blow build their musical monument to the genius of art over chaos. Angels sing where demons had lurked in chaos. Had it held, had the lights and shadows played as they do in Watteau's pastoral charades, had all of humanity come in under the charm of the rational imagination, masked and playing in a masque, Eskimos and Congo warriors in costumes of the Commedia del'Arte, might it have been like that? a lovely surety gathering its strength in chaos and uncertainty, to banish care? But the art was based on care. Convention, as long as it was heroic, something greater and finer than what we mean today by conventional verse and conventional manners, held its own and needed care, could take nothing for granted. Those shepherds and milkmaids were what could stand against any thought of those who actually herded the sheep or milked. In a painting by Longhi, Venetian revelers give dimension that is real to a rhinoceros, an animal nature momentarily held in its place.

The crisis of the Enlightenment was the crisis that Keats saw recapitulated in Coleridge's collapse from the inspiration of "The Ancient Mariner" and "Cristobel" to the psychic despair, the rationalist obsession, of later years. "The Ancient Mariner" had evoked the revelation of the soul in terms of world exploration; "Cristobel" had evoked the revelation of the soul in the terms of psychic threat that came from sexual lore condemned by Christendom.

"*Negative Capability*," Keats wrote in a letter, December 21st, 1817:

> that is, when a man is capable of being in uncertainties, mysteries, doubts, without any irritable reaching after fact and reason—Coleridge, for instance, would let go-by a fine isolated verisimilitude caught from the Penetralium of mystery, from being incapable of remaining content with half-knowledge.

Science, too, in Newton, sought fact and reason, some order that did not verge upon uncertainty. Whitehead in *Ad-*

ventures in Ideas notes that "Literature preserves the wisdom of the human race; but in this way it enfeebles the emphasis of first-hand intuition." It is against some first-hand intuition that men strove to render wisdom sensible and the immediate experience passing, haunted by some premonition of the uncertainty principle in physical measurements that our own science must face, of the uncertainty of self-knowledge in terms of our psychology and physiology, of the uncertainty of our role in life raised by information of evolution. A psyche that is not all to be lightened! a universe that is not all to be ours!

Fact and reason are creations of man's genius to secure a point of view protected against a vision of life where information and intelligence invade us, where what we know shapes us and we become creatures, not rulers, of what is. Where, more, we are part of the creative process, not its goal. It was against such intolerable realizations that these men took thought. The rationalist gardener's art is his control over nature, and beauty is conceived as the imposed order visible in the pruned hedge-row and the ultimate tree compelled into geometric globe of pyramid that gives certainty of effect.

The poet's art was one of control over the common speech, forcing natural metaphor from all hint of meaningful experience or intuition of the universe and maintaining it as a form of speech, and disciplining syntax and line away from the energies of the language itself into balanced phrases, regular meters and heroic couplets. —As too, in military arts, manoeuvres and disciplines occupy the conscious mind. Men are drilled in order that there be an authority, removing them from immediate concern in the acts of killing and destruction involved. A Frederick the Great may be on the edge of knowing that his wars are devastations, not drills. But to such modern triumphs of the conventional mind as Roosevelt or Eisenhower decisions are matters of reason and plan. Disease, death, terror and the ruin of cities are not experienced but dealt with, where rational theory wages its war. The question of the use of disease as a weapon has already been decided by reasonable men who developed the diseases to use and who appointed the military power to use them. Wrathful inspiration (divine or demonic) will not move our rulers to war, nor will some romantic drive to power or suicidal imagination: it is convention, what reasonable men agree upon, that will decide all. War, too, becomes rational.

The game of tennis and the minuet both subject the Yahoo of the animal man to the manners and rules of a court and give authority to that trained horse (and house-broken, too, I hope) of the rational faculty that is a Houyhnhnm. But this Yahoo and this Houyhnhnm is one man divided against himself, phantasy of the Enlightenment in his formal wig performing his ritual dance towards the riddance of Yahoos who know nothing of tennis or minuet. I think of those wigs that marked men of fashion and wit from the uneducated and impoverished mob, the conventional wig and the unconventional cap alike perched on the universally lousy scalp.

But my point here is that the minuet, the game of tennis, the heroic couplet, the concept of form as the imposing of rules and establishing of regularities, the theories of civilization, race, and progress, the performances in sciences and arts to rationalize the universe, to secure balance and class—all these are a tribal magic against a real threat of up-set and things not keeping their place.

The tonal scale of Mozart, where, even among the given notes on the piano, scales are established, so that certain notes are heard as discordant in relation to other notes, threatening to harmony, is a scale imagined to hold its own against threat. A change in mode, in what was permitted, once threatened demonic disorder. Now, unconventional usages threatened loss of reason or insurrection. It is an architecture built up of symmetries, for the mind feels even visual departures from the norm will bring vertigo and collapse. There must be regular sequences and a repetition of stanzas, because thought must not wander, possibility must contain the reassurance of an end to possibilities.

Even in that beginning that I pictured as a kind of health realized by this creation of "Reason" after the whirling orders of the early seventeenth century, there is an uneasy strain. Dryden in his Preface to *All for Love* needs the reassurance of "a subject which has been treated by the greatest wits of our nation" and "their example has given me the confidence to try myself." Then there must be—why?—"the middle course," "motive," "the excellency of moral," "all reasonable men have long since concluded"—these are the terms of the conventional art at its youthful beginning. The tenor throughout is prophylactic. "*Since our passions are, or ought to be, within our power,*" Dryden proposes. In all fields, in poetry as in government or religion, the goal is system or reason, motive or morality, some set of rules and standards that will bring the troubling plenitude of experience "within our power." As long as the battle is for real, where so much depends upon control of self or of environment, there is pathos and even terror in the reasonable man, for there is so much in man's nature and experiences that would never be within his authority.

Frost is right in his sense that the meters and rimes of regulation verse have a counterpart in the rules, marked areas of the court (establishing bounds and out-of bounds), and net of the tennis game. ("I would as soon write free verse as play tennis with the net down.") But, for those who see life as something other than a tennis game, without bounds, and who seek in their sciences and arts to come into that life, into an imagination of that life, the thought comes that the counterpart of free verse may be free thought and free movement. The explorer displays the meaning of physical excellence in a way different from that displayed by the tennis player.

Linnaeus, who, as Ernst Cassirer describes him in *The Philosophy of the Enlightenment*, "selected arbitrarily certain qualities and features according to which he tries to group the plant world," removing his specimens from the field in which they had their living significance, has a counterpart in anthologists of our day who strive to rise above schools and movements, to remove poetry from any reference to its environment and living associations, and to present what suits their taste—orders that display their acumen and avoid any reference to what is. The stamp or flower collection, the tasteful anthology, the values, weights, standards—all these are justly subject, if we are concerned not with what "all reasonable men have long since concluded" is good, but with what is actually happening, to the criticism science had to make in time of Linnaeus. As given by Cassirer:

> He thinks he can give us a picture of the sequence, organization, and structure of this world on the basis of this procedure of mere arrangement, of analytical classification. Such a picture is possible only by a reversal of his procedure. We must apply the principle of connection rather than that of analytical differentiation; instead of assigning living creatures to sharply distinguished species, we must study them in relation to their

kinship, their transition from one type to another, their evolution and transformations. For these are the things which constitute life as we find it in nature.

So, a Cecil Hemley wishes that a Donald Allen's anthology had shown better taste, and would group the "best" of Allen's anthology with poets who never in their lives or thoughts were connected with Olson or Creeley or myself or Denise Levertov. Cecil Hemley reflects that he does not have a "taste" for the work of Robert Creeley. Since he has no other conceivable route to knowledge of that work, taste must suffice. But I can have no recourse to taste. The work of Denise Levertov or Robert Creeley or Larry Eigner belongs not to my appreciations but to my immediate concerns in living. That I might "like" or "dislike" a poem of Zukofsky's or Charles Olson's means nothing where I turn to their work as evidence of the real. Movement and association here are not arbitrary, but arise as an inner need. I can no more rest with my impressions of *Maximus* than I can indulge my impressions at any vital point: I must study thru, deepen my experience, search out the challenge and salvation of the work.

What form is to the conventional mind is just what can be imposed, the rest is thought of as lacking in form. Taste can be imposed, but love and knowledge are conditions that life imposes upon us if we would come into her melodies. It is taste that holds out against feeling, originality that tries to hold out against origins. For taste is all original, all individual arbitration. Dryden's "reasonable men" who "have long since concluded" are a bogie of his own invention (though they may be devoutly believed in at Oxford or Harvard today) and lead at last to the howling dismay and scorn of Pope, Swift, and Gibbon who must hold out everywhere against rampant Stupidity, Madness, and Superstition in the universe of man's psychic life. In the "Ode on the Death of Henry Purcell" the illusion is fresh, and the conflicts of conscience and intellect have not yet appeared, or, perhaps, are subsumed in the honest fact that the work is a tomb or memorial to its own genius.

How strangely Shakespeare's voice in Prospero's contrasts with Dryden's in that period when charm (a device, yes, but a reality of the psyche, no) is replaced by wit:

> Now my Charmes are all ore-throwne,
> And what strength I have's mine owne.

contrasted with Dryden's "their example has given me the confidence to try myself." Shakespeare, who imagined something of that Negative Capability that Keats defines, must rest not upon example but upon prayer, having his art by a grace that was not the grace Dryden knew of men's manners, but a mystery.

> Now I want
> Spirits to enforce; Art to inchant,
> And my ending is despaire

The Enlightenment was to correct even the spelling in its effort to postpone the knowledge.

Russell Edson

Portrait of the Writer as a Fat Man
Some Subjective Ideas or Notions on the Care and Feeding of Prose Poems
1975

... At first the fat man, who has seen himself only as the expanded borders of one larger than most, yet containing a consciousness of average size, perhaps smaller by the squeeze of his flesh, seeks now an episodic prose work, the novel; that harmony of diverse materials, his life. His novel is to be about a writer writing a novel about a writer writing a novel about a writer writing a novel, and so forth; a novel within a novel within a novel; an image reflected between two mirrors back and forth in ever receding smaller mirrors. . . .

He is a very fat person, more, simply than the bulk of flesh, he vaguely sees this, though classed with others of such heft; his soul is also fatted with the lack of ability.

Yes, he is a very fat person because there are thin people. It is relative. He supposes that there are fatter people than he. Of course there are; and probably fatter people than those who are fatter than he.

This is silly, I am simply a fat man whose eyes are of average size, from where I look out from my flesh like anyone else.

And so it is that he wants to write about a fat man such as himself, who now commits himself to composition, growing itchy in his bed, not only from his constant eating, much of which takes place in his bed for lack of love, but because of ideas, excellent fictives, which give rise to an increased heartbeat, and an optimism not fully justified by talent or metabolic levels. But of course this is no longer of moment. Talent is, as he would say, a dilettante measure in my new frame of mind. He casts it out as a silly ornament.

All is will and power, both growing from the other like a single club, with which I shall force a fiction—as though I scrubbed floors to send my son through college that he might get a high-paying job and buy me a castle to live in, where I spend my remaining days simpering and whimpering about how I went down on my knees with a scrub-pail to send my son through college. . . .

2

The fat man sat down to his typewriter almost as though he were sitting down to a dinner, his face set with that same seriousness that must attend all his sittings down to dinner, like a huge transport vessel taking on fuel; a gluttony that has grown far beyond simple self-indulgence.

3

The fat man sat before his typewriter and wrote, the fat man sat before his typewriter and wrote, the fat man sat before his typewriter and wrote: It was better to find a single defensible place, a philosophy, if not a material barrier, that by its very nature offered no challenge to anyone.

To live in the refuse of others is to live in the negative of their desire. Assuming all the while that existence itself is the highest premium. Therefore, that I go unchallenged is the platform upon which I build my durance.

The fat man wrote: Many species have outlived their tormentors simply by offering no challenge, but living where their tormentors would not, by eating what their tormentors felt not fit for those in the position of seemingly perfect choice.

The fat man wrote: The tormentor grows into dilettantism. The tormentor finds existence more an art than a practical concern. Nature becomes a drawing room where the fine music of bees is heard among the flowers, and the lisp of cool drink flows from glaciered mountains; and life with all its easy fruit becomes a boudoir of death. For nature is not constant, and turns like a restless sleeper in her bed; the earthquake, the flood. The clock of expectation cracks. The air is all in smoke, the hardy are run to gas, and the stink is everywhere. A stratum of complacency lays down its bones in the earth like a shredded lace.

The fat man wrote: There was a microbe that lived in the droppings of the great. The microbe had a much different set of values than the great, those who indulged themselves down the avenues of dependency, where only the rarest of flowers, mingled with the hissing of champagne, and a touch of indirect lighting in the warm summer evenings, gave moment to the endless ease....

The fat man wrote: The young microbe worked the fields of refuse....

The fat man wrote: Yet, the fat man may be the very one floundering in the easy avenue....

4

Is the typewriter not like the console of some giant musical instrument designed to ruin one's head? wrote the fat man writing about a fat man.

... A sudden rush of dream figures pulls the head's womb inside out.... Belly of soft plumbing, unhappy fat man....

The typewriter is the keyboard of an organ; the pipes run up through the world, contrived through trees and telephone poles...

5

... It was as if to buy a farm you bought a cabbage. The fat man smiled and fell out of his head. The moon had risen....
What of that?... The pulse of days, moon-thud, sun-thud, regularity, even if one's own has gone. One becomes used to living in areas of time. Islands of memory surrounded by nothing.

The twentieth century, a country someplace in the universe; my species suffocating itself to death with its groin. Piling its redundancy beyond love or renewal; stool and child dropped with equal concern... We were our own excrement.

Our young meant no more to us than mosquitoes. We burnt them, we starved them. We let the universe know that we meant nothing to ourselves. We hated God for igniting us with neuronic tissue. We created God as he had us. Why not, he didn't stop us? If we were made in his image, so was he also imprisoned in ours....

6

The human intelligence sees itself as the only thing different from all things else in the universe; an isolated witness to a seemingly endless cosmological process, ever burgeoning as galaxies and morning glories. Human intelligence recognizing its frail root and utter dependency on the physical universe.... That out of the vast mindlessness was it born.... Must look upon its situation as absurd. Intelligence is in the care of mindlessness....

7

The fat man comes to this: That the artifice of the novel is impossible for him; he has not enough faith to build a cathedral. He must work toward bits and pieces formed from memory... And yet, experience remains hidden and less important than the inscape it has formed. To find a prose free of the self-consciousness of poetry; a prose more compact than the storyteller's; a prose removed from the formalities of *literature*....

8

... A prose that is a cast-iron aeroplane that can actually fly, mainly because its pilot doesn't seem to care if it does or not. Nevertheless, this heavier-than-air prose monstrosity, this cast-iron toy will be seen to be floating over the trees.

It's all done from the cockpit. The joy stick is made of flesh. The pilot sits on an old kitchen chair before a table covered with oilcloth. The coffee cups and spoons seem to be the controls.

But the pilot is asleep. You are right, this aeroplane seems to fly because its pilot dreams....

We are not interested in the usual literary definitions, for we have neither the scholarship nor the ear. We want to write free of debt or obligation to literary form or idea; free even from ourselves, free from our own expectations.... There is more truth in the act of writing than in what is written....

9

... Growing your own writing without going to the Iowa Writers Workshop, and without sending your work to known poets—your own garden, your own meditation—isolation!— Painful, necessary! ... Finally the golden bubble of delight, one is saved by one's own imagination.

One comes to the writing table with one's own hidden life, the secret of the fat man; not dragging Pound's *Cantos*....

The trouble with most who would write poetry is that they are unwilling to throw their lives away.... They are unwilling....

How I hate little constipated lines that are afraid to be anything but correct, without an ounce of humor, that gaiety that death teaches!

What we want is a poetry of miracles—minus the "I" of ecstasy! A poem that as many people who read it each reads a different poem. A poetry freed from its time. A poetry that engages the Creation, which we believe is still in process, and that it is entirely an imaginative construction, which our creative acts partake of, and are necessary to. We are all helping to imagine the Universe.

Which means a poetry not caught and strangled on particular personalities. A poetry that can see itself beyond its obvious means.

And we wish above all to be thought of as "beneath contempt" by the pompous, those who have stood their shadows over the more talented.

How I despise the celebrity poet!

10

... The self-serious poet with his terrible sense of mission, whose poems are gradually decaying into sermons of righteous anger; no longer able to tell the difference between the external abstraction and the inner desperation; the inner life is no longer lived or explored, but converted into public anger.

Beware of serious people, for their reality is flat; and they have come to think of themselves as merely flat paste-ons. Their rage at the flatness of their lives knows no end; and they keep all their little imitators scared to death....

And they are meddlers, they try to create others in their own image because theirs is failing....

11

Poems of celebration in praise of the given reality are written by prayer writers and decorators. They, of course, have heaven in mind. In their bones they think they are securing a place next to God.

This kind of poet neglects content for form; always seeking the *way* to write; thus, in extremity, form becomes content. The ersatz sensibility that crushes vitality; the how-to poets with their endless discussion of breath and line; the polishing of the jewel until it turns to dust.

Of course this kind of poem must try to express itself as celebration and ecstasy, which is the empty mirror of soliloquy, the "I" poem, where the poet can't get past himself.

This is boring because it is not creative, it is middle-class mercantile morality. It is for those who in the name of craft, their hope of heaven, refuse to write poetry. Because at the heart of the "I" poem is little imagination and a total lack of humor; only the sensitive, self-serious soliloquist, who seems so dated and tiny in the box of mirrors he has built up around himself.

12

Being a fat man one must depend on external structures for support, walls, doorways, furniture; but this does not necessarily mean that one needs external support for one's vision. A fat man may have to make his mind do what his body cannot, more perhaps than others with more physical function. In the limitation is found both the bridge and the barrier, which is as necessary as friction to walking. I don't wish here to create a perfect box. But I do wish to suggest that beyond the sense that all is lost is yet the real hope, the excitement of knowing that there is always a little more; and that *little more* is the joyous place from where one writes.

This is the sense of nothingness, that life is always poised on the edge of decay, that seemingly solid structures long to become dust, that time adores the future more than the present, and only man holds the past with any tenderness. The sense that all is passing away, even as I write this, that in a way the *new* means death; this sense creates the Angel of Joy, which is for me the true Muse. The fat man who has nothing to lose is allowed to be silly, the Angel of Joy prescribes it. . . .

13

. . . A poetry freed from the definition of poetry, and a prose free of the necessities of fiction; a personal form disciplined not by other literature but by unhappiness; thus a way to be happy. Writing is the joy when all other joys have failed. Else, but for the unsavory careerists, why write? It is good fun to ruin the surface of a piece of paper; to, as it were, run amuck. One hurts no one, and paper is cheap enough.

The idle man finds symbolic work. And more, the fat man is only capable of symbolic work. You do agree, I hope? Men are happy when they are working. Even idle men are made happy by thinking of work, even if only thinking of others at work. It is always a pleasure to see the naughty little hands of man engaged in something other than scratching.

Thus the work is found. The writer comes to blank paper. The difficulty is *what to write about?* Believe it or not, subject matter is the first concern of the beginning writer, and will remain the concern of the *real* writer.

Subject matter? Well, of course it's the psychic material that longs to be substance. It is not simply a hook on which to hang form.

In other words, speaking of writing, the way a thing is written is far less important than what the thing is about. This may sound very unliterary, but, after all, the object of creative writing is not literature; at least it shouldn't be, for that is a worldly measure that has so little to do with the work at hand.

We say the *how* comes into being by virtue of the *what*. Surely, if the subject matter is fully imagined, its physicalness fully grasped, then the subject matter will predict its form. Nothing can exist without a shape. But form does not exist without substance. The *how* is merely, or should be, the shape of the *what*. If it is not, the writing is boring. BORING!

If a writer cannot collect his psyche into a physical reality, he ought to think seriously of trying something other than writing.

14

... Then the prose poem: Superficially a prose poem should look somewhat like a page from a child's primer, indented paragraph beginnings, justified margins. In other words, the prose poem should not announce that it is a special prose; if it is, the reader will know it. The idea is to get away from obvious ornament, and the obligations implied therein. Let those who play tennis play their tennis.

A good prose poem is a statement that seeks sanity whilst its author teeters on the edge of the abyss. The language will be simple, the images so direct, that oftentimes the reader will be torn with recognitions inside himself long before he is conscious of what is happening to him.

Regular poetry, even when it is quite empty of content, the deep psychic material, can manage with its ornaments of song and shape to be dimensional; which is to say, the ability to define space, which is very necessary to all the arts. Such a regular poem may seem the near "perfect object," albeit a beautiful box with nothing in it. Which is good enough; anything brought out of the abyss is to be honored. But *is* it good enough?! Isn't static predictability just rather boring?

As to the dimensional quality necessary to art, we mean depth, volume, in a word, shape; substance with a texture of parts that define space and durance. In the prose poem this sense of dimension is given by humor. The prose poem that does not have some sense of the funny is flat and uninformed, and has no more life than a shopping list. I don't mean the banal, high-schoolish snickering that one sees so often in so-called prose poems, but the humor of the deep, uncomfortable metaphor.

15

To come back to the prose poem. What makes us so fond of it is its clumsiness, its lack of expectation or ambition. Any way of writing that isolates its writer from worldly acceptance offers the greatest creative efficiency. Isolation from other writers, and isolation from easy publishing. This gives one that terrible privacy, so hard to bear, but necessary to get past the idea one has of oneself in relation to the world. I'm not talking about breaking oneself as a monk or a nun might, causing all desire and creativity to become the thick inky darkness that freezes function, but that the writer ought to look to himself, to his own means, that he may get past those means.

It is the paradox, that it is through ourselves we get to that place that is not ourselves; that is, in fact, all of us.

The fear of being alone is sometimes expressed in the elitist nonsense that the poet is some kind of special person owing something to the "inarticulate masses" (who in heaven ever coined that?), which is the same old messianic crap, that same old paranoia wrapped in the same old sentimental rags!

Oh where has the ideal of the ivory tower gone?

16

The prose poem is an approach, but certainly not a form; it is art, but more general than most of the other arts. This may sound odd because we know prose poems as things written on paper. But it is only incidental that they are written out; the spirit or approach which is represented in the prose poem is not specifically literary. My personal convenience is best served by writing only because writing is the fastest way. This kind of creation needs to be done as rapidly as possible. Any hesitation causes it to lose its believability, its special reality; because the writing of a prose poem is more of an experience than a labor toward a product. If the finished prose poem is considered a piece of literature, this is quite incidental to the writing. This kind of creating should have as much ambition as a dream, which I assume most of us look upon, meaning our nightly dreams, as throwaway creations, not things to be collected in a book of poems.

Abundance is also important. The re-working of something that might be saved is no good; better to go on and make something else, and then something else. Prose poems cannot be perfected, they are not literary constructions, unless anything written is to be so considered; prose poems have no place to go. Abundance and spontaneity; spontaneous abundance in imitation of the joy and energy of general creation and substance.

Tess Gallagher

The Poem as Time Machine
1979

Once, at an auction in upstate New York, I watched two men carry a mahogany box with a crank handle onto the lawn. One of the men turned the lever until he was satisfied and then put a large black disk into the box and opened the front of the box so the little doors, spread wide, made the whole contraption seem as though it might fly away. But instead, a chorus of voices, recorded many years before, scratched and muted by all that intervening time and space, drifted out over the crowd.

Before anyone in our group knew what I was doing, I had signaled my way to ownership and the two men were approaching us carrying the Victrola, its record still turning above their heads.

In hearing the phonograph I had not forgotten life in the jet age; in fact, the simultaneity of jets and hand-wound phonographs had only amplified my amazement with both inventions. A few months before, I had been in Iowa; then in hours I was in New York. The morning of the auction I had spoken by telephone with my parents on the West Coast. That night I would watch a TV news reporter in Egypt, another in Israel. Still, all these inventions for transcending time and distance had not kept me from the original magic of the phonograph music. I did not exclaim: "See how they used to do it," but rather: "Voices out of a flat disk, human voices singing out of a mahogany box!" I was like an astronaut dropped suddenly into my own moment.

I remember the day my father came home from the neighbors' in 1949 and said they had a radio with talking pictures. It was his way of explaining television to us in terms of what he knew: radio. Several years later I would sit on the rug with half a dozen neighborhood kids at the house down the block, watching Flash Gordon and advertisements for Buster Brown shoes.

Such early space-travel films may have marked my first encounter with the idea of time machines, those phone booths with the capacity to transpose one into encounters with Napoleon or to propel one ahead into dilemmas on distant planets. I was six or seven years old and already leading a double life as an imagined horse disguised as a young girl. I had long brown hair and a young friend named Koene Rasanen who suffered from the same delusions, which were, oddly, tolerated by our parents. There were several ridges behind my house which our horse-selves delighted in. Some of my freest moments still exist in those images of myself standing silhouetted on the highest knoll, pawing with one foot, tossing my thick pony mane and neighing for my friend with such authority that a real horse pastured down the block began to answer me.

To be called to the house to run errands or peel potatoes for dinner was to suffer a temporary malfunction of the time machine. Adults were those creatures who had suffered permanent malfunctions. If you neighed at them, they put it down to a sexual phase, or took it as a practical cue to shop for a horse.

When I got my first horse, at age ten, it was strangely unsatisfying. Already that exchange of the real object for the imagined embodiment had begun to disinherit me. I hadn't wanted a horse to ride, I had wanted to *be* a horse, and had, in the nearest human proximity, managed it.

Flash Gordon never became a horse by stepping into a time machine, but he could choose any one of countless masquerades at crucial moments in history or in the futures he hoped to outsmart. The whole idea of past or future being accessible at the push of a button seemed so natural to me as a child that I have been waiting for science to catch up to the idea ever since.

In the meantime, there have been a few wonderful gimmicks—Polaroid cameras and, lately, Polaroid movie cameras: instruments built to surprise the moment by reproducing it as close to its occurence as possible, thereby extending the past as present, a spectator's present at that. So we have Mother tying the bow in Polly's hair. And if we like, we can run the film backward and untie Polly's hair. We have then an ongoing past as a spectator's present.

With the country in a state of constant mobility, we depend

more than ever on telephones to keep friends who have been left behind at the last outpost. We can be in immediate touch. Two disparate people living in the "now" may hook up across the miles, talking their pasts into the present up to that point where the pie is burning in the oven or where someone has knocked at the door. We may hurtle the body through space into exotic places on jets. It costs a lot not to be where you're expected to be . . . that trip you took to get away from the familiar faces, those phone calls you charged to make up for having forgotten those people who are truly living too far away to be held constantly in mind. Already we are shaking ghosts like shaking hands, meeting ourselves as has-beens where we stand.

I can still see Mark Strand shuffling the poems on his knees in a classroom in Seattle, Washington, in 1970 and saying in that ironic, ghost-ship voice of his: "Time, that's the *only* problem."

Octavio Paz defined the poet's time as "living for each day; and living it, simultaneously, in two contradictory ways: as if it were endless and as if it would end right now." Stanley Kunitz has written a poem entitled "Change," which gives this dual sense of impermanence and the desire to be eternal. He also includes memory as it comments upon the present moment, often painfully.

> Dissolving in the chemic vat
> Of time, man (gristle and fat),
> Corrupting on a rock in space
> That crumbles, lifts his impermanent face
> To watch the stars, his brain locked tight
> Against the tall revolving night.
> Yet is he neither here nor there
> Because the mind moves everywhere;
> And he is neither now nor then
> Because tomorrow comes again
> Foreshadowed, and the ragged wing
> Of yesterday's remembering
> Cuts sharply the immediate moon;
> Nor is he always: late and soon
> Becoming, never being, till
> Becoming is a being still.

Here, Now, and Always, man would be
Inviolate eternally:
This is his spirit's trinity.

Always, as a maker of poems, I have been witness to the
images, have been led by the poem as it speaks into and with
itself and opens out of its contradictions to engage the reader.
But the reader is also the maker of the poem as it lives again
in his consciousness, his needs, his reception, and even his
denials. The poem is in a state of perpetual formation and
disintegration. It is not at the mercy of pure subjectivity, but,
as Ortega y Gasset would say, it is "the intersection of the
different points of view." This, then, brings about a succes-
sion of interpretations of which no single one, even that of the
poet, is the definitive one. In this way the poem enters and
becomes time. It becomes, as Paz phrases it, "the space that is
energy itself, not a container but an engenderer, a catalytic
arena open on all sides to the past, on all sides to the future."

This conception of time as an atmosphere, as the "now" of
the poem, which Paz calls "the Historical Now" or "the Ar-
chetypal Now," is what I would like to call "the point of all
possibilities." By this I mean the point at which anything that
has happened to me, or any past that I can encourage to
enrich my own vision, is allowed to intersect with a present
moment, as in a creation, as in a poem. And its regrets or
expectations or promises or failures or any supposition I can
bring to it may give significance to this moment that is the
language moving in and out of my life and my life as it meets
and enters the lives of others.

"Poems," says Paz, "search for the you." In America we
begin to ask who will colonize the "I," that island of cannibals,
of separations, of endings and be-alls, of my turn, of better-
than-you, of privilege and sweat-of-the-brow rectitude, of I
own this and you own that, homeland of the civilized
heartbreak where, if you leave, I shall get along anyway, I
shall do perfectly well without you. There are others and
others and you will not be one of them, where if your coat
were drowning, I would not save it. No, the "I" without its
search for the "you"—either by implication as the "I" in each
of us or in a direct reaching toward the other—this "I," whose
reaching *in* is not at the same time a reaching *out*, is like a

character in a novel who is running on empty. We cannot long be interested in its roadside reveries, its monologues with the vast interiors. Even if you are speaking to a "you" that will not listen, it is better than no "you" at all. This includes the "you" that is the self, of course, but as "other." We remember Yeats speaking endlessly to Maud Gonne; Emily Dickinson talking to Death as if to a suitor; Hamlet confiding in a skull; Colette, who, when her mother died, saw no reason to stop writing letters to her.

The time of the "I" is expanded when it considers the "you," and perhaps it is in the time that the poem makes that we can find courage enough for the risks yet to be taken in our "walking-around" lives. The poem not only makes time, it *is* time; it is made of time as is the bee who dances out the directions that are and are not the map of a place, the remembering of a way back to the flower feast that belongs to others, to the hive, and to the very moment that way is given.

I have, in a poem, called a man back from the dead if he has not answered me fully in life. Yeats, in "He Wishes His Beloved Were Dead," even rushes ahead of the fact to gain the right urgency in which he might be granted forgiveness.

> Were you but lying cold and dead,
> And lights were paling out of the West,
> You would come hither, and bend your head,
> And I would lay my head on your breast;
> And you would murmur tender words,
> Forgiving me, because you were dead:
> Nor would you rise and hasten away,
> Though you have the will of the wild birds,
> But know your hair was bound and wound
> About the stars and moon and sun.

The time of the poem is not linear, is not the time of "this happened, then this, then this," though I may speak in that way until I am followed and the language leads me out of its use into its possibilities. No one is buried so deeply in the past that he may not enter the moment of the poem, the point of all possibilities where the words give breath, in a re-imagining, so we know what was as what it is now and what it can become. If the language of commerce is a parade, then the language of the poem is that of a hive where one may be stung into recognition by words that have the power to create images strong enough to change our own lives as we imagine and live them.

The poet between poems is like a child called into the house to peel potatoes for supper. The time of the house is enigma to him. He cannot wait to be out the door again. *Time Is a River Without Banks* is the title of Chagall's painting of the winged fish flying through the air above the river. The fish is playing a fiddle above a clock which flies with it. In order to indicate the river there are houses and lovers and the reflections of houses. The lovers are not looking up. They are in love and at the point of all possibilities. They have transcended time, which is all around them like the unheard music of the fiddle.

It is the poet who refuses to believe in time as a container, who rushes into the closed room of time, who plunges through the bay window and slashes a hand across the harp, even if what results is not music so much as a passionate desecration of a moment, which, like the photograph in its effort to fix us, excludes us from our own past. The poet is always the enemy of the photograph. If she talks about her own appearance in the group smiling on the porch, she will inch her thumb into the lens to indicate that she has escaped. She will assault the image with words, changing the bride's dress into a cascade of petals. She will make sure the train pulls away from the platform.

The poem as time machine works in an opposite way from the time machine as used in H. G. Wells. In the latter, one is sent out like a lonely projectile into time past or future, casting the present into a future or a past. The poem, on the other hand, is like a magnet which draws into it events and beings from all possible past, present, and future contexts of the speaker. It is a vortex of associative phenomena. "A baby is crying / In the swaddling-pages / a baby," says Bill Knott. "'Don't cry. No Solomon's-sword can / divide you from the sky / You are one. Fly.'" We move from baby to swaddling pages to the threat of Solomon's sword dividing the baby not from itself but from the sky, then to the baby metamorphosed into the sky itself and told to fly. We remain in the present moment of the crying baby, but we are in touch with babies past; the baby Jesus in swaddling clothes, the baby who is being fought over by two women, each claiming to be its mother. And beyond this, we are given the possibility of flight, of a nature that is as indivisible as sky.

In poem-time, the present *accompanies* memory and eventuality; it is not left behind, since the very activity of the words generates the poem's own present no matter what tense the poet uses. The poem's activity in the consciousness of the reader is a present-time event which may, nevertheless, draw on his past, his expectations and hopes.

> All lives that has lived;
> So much is certain;

When Yeats says this in his "Quarrel in Old Age," it is more than salutary. It is an acknowledgment that the past is not a burial ground but a living fiber that informs and questions what is and will be.

I sit in a Montana café having a meal with my mother, who is visiting from Washington State. Suddenly she remembers a time when she was beautiful, when she had the power of beauty. I realize I never knew her in that time, though often she still acts from it, as from some secret legacy. I see that I have failed to make her know her present beauty, so she must return endlessly to that past—a reservoir. Even as I see her, I see myself, my own aging. I walk with her into "the one color / of the snow—before us, the close houses, / the brave and wondering lights of the houses." It has been snowing during our meal, and the houses have been transformed by a covering of snow, as though time in the form of snow has softened all contours, has fallen down about us deep enough, white enough, to put everything on the same plane spatially and temporally. The girlhood beauty of my mother accompanies us as we leave, gives the houses their brave and wondering lights, causes them to drift in a white sea under the covering of night.

Perhaps it is our very forgetting that allows these past images significance. If we remembered constantly, the time-fabric of our lives would remain whole and we would have no need of the poem to reinvolve us in what was a part of what is and may be.

"Forget! Forget it to know it," Robert Penn Warren says in his poem "Memory Forgotten."

How long
Has your mother been dead? Or did you, much older,

Lie in the tall grass and, motionless, watch
The single white fleck of cloud forever crossing the
blue—. . . .

How much do we forget that is ourselves—

Nothing too small to make a difference,
And in the forgetting to make it all more true?

That liquid note from the thicket afar—oh, hear!
What is it you cannot remember that is so true?

So Warren connects forgetting with what we feel to be true,
the smell or the sound from afar that, if we knew its signifi-
cance, would give us back some essential part of ourselves. He
makes forgetting a positive accident, like the money found in
a coat you hadn't worn for months, an accidental payload.
The truth that we are is bound up, it would seem, with our
partiality, our inability to hold everything of ourselves in
memory as we go. Every time we remember some forgotten
moment in a way that illuminates the present or causes the
present to mediate some past, then the boundaries we
thought were there between past, present, and future dis-
solve, if only for the time that is the poem.

It is believed that in the infant's first consciousness of the
events and objects passing before him, he does not separate
himself from them, but experiences his own identity simply as
an endless stream of stimuli. Even his response to events is not
so much toward as *in* them. The infant is immersed in objects,
and their time in space continues with him, is infinite.

The Hindus have a name for this continuing or fourth di-
mension of "being across time." It is called the *Linga-Sharira*,
that which remains the same in us though our cells change
completely every seven years and we are not in fact the same
in body that we were. Part of what the poem does is to restore
us to consciousness of the *Linga-Sharira* which continues
through change and which is immeasurable.

The poem, because it takes place at the point of all pos-
sibilities, in that it can intersect with all past, present, and
future expectations, is able to accommodate this fourth

dimension, the "something else" of the *Linga-Sharira,* which allows us to change yet to remain the same through time. "The same," in this instance, means the overview that can look at the total life at the same instant that it looks at any one point of the life and say, This is she as she is, was, and will be.

Proust reminds us that "perhaps the immobility of things that surround us is forced upon them by our conviction that they are themselves, and not anything else, and by the immobility of our conception of them." The past and future are linked to our apartness, our identity as beings cut off from this original immersion in a time without succession. In that time, the time of the infant, there were no landmarks apart from us to signal our departure or arrival, our movement toward or away; no forgetting or remembering was then possible.

Even the stopped moment of a photograph paradoxically releases its figures by holding them because the actual change, the movement away from the stilled moment, has already taken place without us, outside the frame of the photograph, and the moment we see ourselves so stilled, we know we have also moved on. This is the sadness of the photograph: knowing, even as you look, it is not like this, though it was. You stand in the "was" of the present moment and you die a little with the photograph.

Octavio Paz speaks of the poetic experience as one which allows us to deny succession, the death factor. "Succession," he says, "becomes pure present. . . . The poem is mediation: thanks to it, original time, father of the times, becomes incarnate in an instant." The poem then represents an overflowing of time, the instant in which we see time stopped without its "ceasing to flow." It overflows itself, and we have the sensation of having gone beyond ourselves.

"Poetry," says Paz, "is nothing but time, rhythm perpetually creative." In the time of the poem we are held, not as the photograph holds, but as in a simultaneity of recognitions which wake us up in the middle of our lives. The poem causes an expansion of the "now." Archibald MacLeish's "Epistle to be Left in the Earth" is a poem which expands the "now" by including the speaker's and the reader's deaths as encountered by those who live after.

... It is colder now
there are many stars
we are drifting
North by the Great Bear
the leaves are falling
The water is stone in the scooped rocks
to southward
Red sun grey air
the crows are
Slow on their crooked wings
the jays have left us
Long since we passed the flares of Orion
Each man believes in his heart he will die
Many have written last thoughts and last letters
None know if our deaths are now or forever
None know if this wandering earth will be found

We lie down and the snow covers our garments
I pray you
you (if any open this writing)
Make in your mouths the words that were our names.

Part of the recent popularity of the writing of poems in prisons, grade schools, poetry workshops in universities, and the wards of mental clinics has developed from the sense that we are traveling too fast through a time which has fewer and fewer of the future-maintaining structures with which we grew up. I mean the structures of marriage, of the family, of the job as a fulfillment of one's selfhood. These allowed one to look ahead into the near and far future of one's life with some expectation of continuity, which is a part of one's future-sense. We now have serial marriages, separations between parent and child, as well as jobs that come and go as the technology fluctuates even more crazily to accommodate a product-oriented society.

It may be that the poem is an anachronism of being-oriented impulses. It is an anachronism because it reminds us ironically that we stand at the point of all possibilities yet feel helpless before the collapse of the future-sustaining emblems of our lives. This has reduced us to life in an instantaneous "now." The time of the poem answers this more and more by allowing an expansion of the "now." It allows consequence to disparate and contradictory elements in a life. The "I," reduced to insignificance in most spheres of contemporary society, is again able to inhabit a small arena of its own making. It returns us, from the captivities of what we do and make, to what we are.

When the "now" expands, it includes before and after. The poem reminds us that the past is not only that which happened but also that which could have happened but did not. The future, says Ouspensky, in a similar way, holds not only that which will be, but everything that *may* be. He reminds us that if eternity exists at all, every moment is eternal. Eternal time is perpendicular at each instant to successionary time, which is time as we *misperceive* it. An example of an unrealized future enacted in a poem is Gene Derwood's "Elegy," where we read that the boy "lamentably drowned in his eighteenth year" will not fulfill the expectations of adulthood:

> Never will you take bride to happy bed,
> Who lay awash in water yet no laving
> Needed, so pure so young for sudden leaving.

All time is during. That is why it is so hard to exist in the present. Already we are speeding ahead so fast that we can only look back to see where we have been. I once said to a group of students that the poet is like a tuba player in a house on fire. Crucial events surround him, threatening to devour, while he makes inappropriate music with an instrument that cannot help causing its serious manipulator to look ridiculous.

This speeding up of the time-sense in contemporary life, through the technology of mobility and through the disintegrative nature of human relationships, has affected the language of the poem as a time-enacting mechanism. The poem has begun to move in simple sentences, in actions and images more than in ideas, to speak intensely about the relationship of one person to another, to attempt to locate its subject matter or its speaker, if only during the time of the poem, very specifically at 142nd Street on July 23, 1971. Many contemporary poems have opted for the present tense and a great suspicion has fallen over the past and future tenses. If they are used at all, they are converted into a present happening in order to insure immediacy. The sentences are simple perhaps because this slows the time-sense down and makes the language more manageable. Though some wonderful poems are being written with this pacing, I am often nostalgic for a more extended motion. It is no secret that the contemporary reader has begun to balk at the periodic sentence. The atrophy of even short-term recall in America has caused the mind to resist holding much information, or even verbal structures of the slightest complexity. When my Irish musician friend tells me of singers who can sing hundreds of songs that have been passed on to them, I see how far we have come from this kind of memory.

The poem as time machine has inherited a heavy responsibility from these strains on the language and on the human figure's diminishing stature among its self-perpetuating creations. The poem is expected to tell us, not that we're immortal, but simply that we exist as anything at all except contingencies. It has the old obligations to carry experience memorably in the language with few of the formal structures to maintain it. Its voices have become a chorus of one, the personal "I" venturing as far as the patio or the boathouse. But as regards man's relation to time, the poem has shown itself valiant. I am no longer envious of Flash Gordon and his time machine. The poem is the place where the past and future can be seen at once without forsaking the present.

In a poem I consecrate all that forgotten life which allows the incidence of memory, cast like a light on my life and the lives of others. The poet is the Lazarus of the poem, rising up with it. In the time of the poem it is still possible to find courage for the present moment. The life imagined in the poem has been known to affect the speaker, the reader, their sense of what can be salvaged or abandoned in a life. However, if we are like the blind man whose reality in the instant of "now" ends at the tip of his stick as he walks along the cliff, we must still believe in falling. The poem, for all its bounty, is a construct, and though the words in it may give the fiercest light, we cannot live there. Poems are excursions into belief and doubt, often simultaneously.

Mostly we are with the child peeling potatoes at the kitchen sink. We are too short for the view out the window except when we stand on the kitchen chair, which we are not supposed to do, but which we do. The time in the poem can be as useful as a kitchen chair, helping us to be the right size in a world that is always built for others. If I did not grow up to be a horse, I will not hold it against my life. I could not think fast enough to keep my two-leggedness from setting in. Still, I know there is a young girl in me who remembers the language of horses. She is with me in the time of the poem.

With all the modern time-savers, we have no better machine for the reinvention of time than the poem. I would not trade my least-loved poem for a Polaroid snapshot. The real time-savers are those that accommodate the mind, the heart, and the spirit at once.

Sandra M. Gilbert

"My Name Is Darkness"
The Poetry of Self-Definition
1977

"Something hangs in back of me," wrote Denise Levertov in "The Wings," a poem published in the middle sixties. "I can't see it, can't move it. // I know it's black, / a hump on my back. . . . black // inimical power."* A few years later, in 1972, Anne Sexton published a poem called "The Ambition Bird" that made a similar point:

> I would like a simple life
> yet all night I am laying
> poems away in a long box. . .
>
> All night dark wings
> flopping in my heart.
> Each an ambition bird.

Both poets, whether consciously or not, seem to have been echoing the terrified and yet triumphantly self-defining metaphors of Sylvia Plath's "Stings":

> I stand in a column
>
> Of winged, unmiraculous women, . . .
>
>   . . . but I
> Have a self to recover, a queen.
> Is she dead, is she sleeping?
> Where has she been,
> With her lion-red body, her wings of glass?
>
> Now she is flying
> More terrible than she ever was. . . .

---

*The double slash (//) indicates the break between stanzas.

117

And all three women—Plath, Levertov, Sexton—are writing in a vein of self-definition that has also been worked by other recent women poets as diverse as Adrienne Rich, Diane Wakoski, Muriel Rukeyser, Ruth Stone, Gwendolyn Brooks, Erica Jong, and Margaret Atwood. In fact, I'd like to speculate here that the self-defining confessional genre, with its persistent assertions of identity and its emphasis on a central mythology of the self, may be (at least for our own time) a distinctively female poetic mode.

"Confessional" poetry has, of course, been generally associated with a number of contemporary male poets, most notably Berryman, Lowell, and Snodgrass. A tradition of such writing, moreover, can easily be traced back through such male mythologists of the self as Whitman and Yeats to Wordsworth and Byron, those romantic patriarchs whose self-examinations and self-dramatizations probably fathered not only the poetry of what Keats called the egotistical sublime but also the more recent ironic mode we might call the egotistical ridiculous. Most male poets, however, have been able to move beyond the self-deprecations and self-assertions of confessional writing to larger, more objectively formulated appraisals of God, humanity, society. Writers like Bly and Snyder, though they, too, are descendants of Whitman and Wordsworth, cannot by any stretch of the vocabulary be called confessional. Such obviously confessional male poets as Lowell and Berryman write verse in which (as M. L. Rosenthal's definition of confessional poetry puts it) "the private life of the poet himself... often becomes a major theme." Yet they manage to be "at once private and public, lyrical and rhetorical" (as Rosenthal also notes) because the personal crisis of the male poet "is felt at the same time as a symbolic embodiment of national and cultural crisis." Thus, just as the growth of Wordsworth's mind stands for the growth of all self-fulfilling human minds, so "the 'myth' that Lowell creates is that of an America... whose history and present predicament are embodied in those of his own family and epitomized in his own psychological experience."

The male confessional poet, in other words, even while romantically exploring his own psyche, observes himself as a representative specimen with a sort of scientific exactitude. Alienated, he's nevertheless an ironic sociologist of his own alienation because he considers his analytic perspective on himself a civilized, normative point of view. Lowell, describing his own mental illness with desperate intensity, is still able to note with detachment the "hackneyed speech" and "homicidal eye" of "the kingdom of the mad," and, recalling an impassioned past, to describe his younger self with surgical precision as "boiled and shy / and poker-faced." Like other modern male *poètes maudits*, in short, he has a cool faith in his own ability to classify his own exemplary sufferings, a curious, calm confidence that even in madness he is in some sense at the intellectual center of things. Can it be (at least in part) that because he's a man, he can readily picture himself as Everyman?

Certainly, by contrast, the female confessional poet seems to feel no such paradoxical ease with her own anxieties. Even when she observes herself with amused irony, as Plath does in "Lady Lazarus" ("What a trash / To annihilate each decade. . . . It's the theatrical // Comeback in broad day. . . . That knocks me out"), she enacts as well as dissects her suffering, her rage, her anxiety:

> Herr God, Herr Lucifer
> Beware
> Beware.
>
> Out of the ash
> I rise with my red hair
> And I eat men like air.

The detached irony of a Lowell or a Berryman—the irony possible for a self-assured, normative sensibility—is largely unavailable to her, unavailable because even at her most objective she feels eccentric, not representative; peripheral, not central. More, she struggles with her suffering, grapples with it in bewilderment, writing what Plath (who is again paradigmatic here) called "sweating, heaving poems," because she cannot easily classify either herself or her problem. To define her suffering would be to define her identity, and such self-definition is her goal, rather than her starting point.

The male confessional poet—Lowell, Berryman, Yeats— writes in the certainty that he is the inheritor of major traditions, the grandson of history, whose very anxieties, as Harold Bloom has noted, are defined by the ambiguities of the past that has shaped him as it shaped his fathers. The female poet, however, even when she is not consciously confessional like Plath or Sexton, writes in the hope of discovering or defining a self, a certainty, a tradition. Striving for self-knowledge, she experiments with different propositions about her own nature, never cool or comfortable enough to be (like her male counterparts) an ironic sociologist; always, instead, a desperate Galileo, a passionate empiricist who sees herself founding a new science rather than extending the techniques and discoveries of an old one. It is for this reason, I believe, that otherwise radically different poets like Plath, Sexton, Rich, Wakoski, and Levertov all write verse characterized by such recurrent self-defining statements—hypotheses, really—as the following:

"I am your opus, / I am your valuable."
"I am a nun now. . . ."
"I am not a nurse. . . . I am not a smile."
"I am dark-suited and still, a member of the party."
"I am the arrow, / The dew that flies / Suicidal. . . ."
"I am a miner."
"I am a letter in this slot. . . ."
"I / Am a pure acetylene / Virgin."
"I think I may well be a Jew."
"I am not a Caesar."
"I am the magician's girl."
"I am no source of honey."
"I am no drudge. . . ."
"O God, I am not like you. . . ."

Sylvia Plath, *Ariel*

"I am a tree gypsy: you can't shake me out of your branches."
"Here I am. . . . a strange combination of images."
"I am like the guerrilla fighter / who must sleep with one eye / open for attack."
"I am blue, / I am blue as a blues singer, / I am blue in the face. . . ."
"My body dries out / and becomes a bone sceptre. . . ."
"I am the sword with / the starry hilt. . . ."
"I am ringless, ringless. . . ."
"I am a blackbird."

"I am / also a ruler of the sun, I am / the woman / whose hair
lights up a dark room, whose words are matches. . . ."
"I am solitary, / like the owls I never see. . . ."

Diane Wakoski, Inside the Blood Factor and
Dancing on the Grave of a Son of a Bitch

"I'm . . . a naked man fleeing / across the roofs. . . ."
"I am a galactic cloud . . . / I am an instrument in the shape of a
woman. . . ."
"I am a woman in the prime of life, with certain powers. . . ."
"I am the androgyne / I am the living mind you fail to de-
scribe. . . ."
"I am she: I am he / Whose drowned face sleeps with open
eyes. . . ."
"I am an American woman, / my body a hollow ship. . . . / I am
not the wheatfield / nor the virgin forest."

Adrienne Rich, Poems: Selected and New, 1950–1974

"Everyone in me is a bird, / I am beating all my wings."
"I am no different from Emily Goering."
"I am a watercolor. / I wash off."
"I'm Ethan Frome's wife. I'll move when I'm able."
"I am no longer the suicide / with her raft and paddle."
"I am not an idler, / am I?"
"Yes! I am still the criminal. . . ."
"I have become a tree, / I have become a vase. . . ."
"I am an ocean-going vessel. . . ."
"I am a small handful. . . ."
"I am not immortal. Faustus and I are the also-ran."

Anne Sexton, Love Poems, The Book of Folly, and
The Death Notebook

"The moon is a sow / . . . . and I a pig and a poet."
"Am I a pier, / half-in, half-out of the water?"
"I am faithful to / ebb and flow . . . / I hold steady / in the black
sky. . . . / There is no savor / more sweet, more salt / than to
be glad to be / what, woman, / and who, myself / I am, a
shadow / that grows longer as the sun / moves, drawn out /
on a thread of wonder."

Denise Levertov, O Taste and See and The Sorrow Dance

Though they were taken out of context, you probably recognized many of these lines. They might all have been by one, anxiously experimental, modern Everywoman, so strikingly similar are they in structure and intention. Considering and discarding different metaphors, different propositions of identity, each of these five writers seems to be straining to formulate an ontology of selfhood, some irreducible and essential truth about her own nature. While the male poet, even at his most wretched and alienated, can at least solace himself with his open or secret creativity, his mythmaking power, the female poet must come to terms with the fact that as a female she is that which is mythologized, the incarnation of otherness (to use de Beauvoir's terminology) and hence the object of anthologies full of male metaphors. Many of her hypotheses about herself are therefore in one way or another replies to prevalent definitions of her femininity, replies expressing either her distress at the disparity between male myths about her and her own sense of herself, or else her triumphant repudiation of those myths. Men tell her that she is a muse. Yet she knows that she is not a muse, she *has* a muse (and what is its sex?). Men tell her she is the "angel in the house," yet she doesn't *feel* angelic, and wonders, therefore, if she is a devil, a witch, an animal, a criminal. Men tell her that she is Molly Bloom, Mother Earth, Ishtar, a fertility goddess, a *thing* whose periodicity expresses the divine order (or is it the *disorder?*) of seasons, skies, stars. They tell her, echoing Archibald MacLeish's definition of a poem, that she should not mean but be. Yet meanings delight her, along with seemings, games, plays, costumes, and ideas of order, as they delight male poets. But perhaps, she speculates, her rage for order is mistaken, presumptuous?

"Alas!" complained Anne Finch, Countess of Winchilsea, in the late seventeenth century,

> a woman that attempts the pen,
> Such an intruder on the rights of men,
> Such a presumptuous Creature, is esteem'd,
> The fault, can by no vertue be redeem'd,
> They tell us we mistake our sex and way;
> Good breeding, fassion, dancing, dressing, play
> Are the accomplishments we shou'd desire;
> To write, or read, or think, or to enquire

Wou'd cloud our beauty, and exaust our time,
And interrupt the Conquests of our prime;
Whilst the dull mannage, of a servile house
Is held by some, our outmost art, and use.

"The Introduction"

Given these disadvantages, she admonished herself to "Be
caution'd then . . . and still retir'd . . . / Conscious of wants, still
with contracted wing, / To some few freinds [*sic*], and to thy
sorrows sing. . . ." Nevertheless, this modest poetess of "Spleen"
and sorrow, contending against a sense of her own con-
tracted wing, pioneered a poetic mode for other women, a
mode of reticence conquered by assertion and self-examination,
a mode of self-definition *within* and *against* the context of
prevailing male definitions of women.

Today, doubting her likeness to crops and fields, the
woman poet asks herself, with Adrienne Rich, "Has Nature
shown / her household books to you, daughter-in-law, / that
her sons never saw?" ("Snapshots of a Daughter-in-Law"),
and, refusing to be "a woman in the shape of a monster," she
defines herself instead as "an instrument in the shape / of a
woman trying to translate pulsations / into images for the
relief of the body / and the reconstruction of the mind"
("Planetarium"). With Esther Greenwood in *The Bell Jar* she
denies that she is the passive "place an arrow shoots off from"
and proposes, rather, to "shoot off in all directions" herself, to
be as active and full of intentions as "the colored arrows from
a Fourth of July rocket." Yet all the while, limited and defined
by others, enclosed in cells of history, she perceives that she is
supposed to be living quietly in her kitchen, adhering, as
Plath wrathfully wrote, "to rules, to rules, to rules" ("A Birth-
day Present"). And so she wonders if she is, after all, a mon-
ster like Spenser's Duessa. "A thinking woman sleeps with
monsters," notes Adrienne Rich. "The beak that grips her,
she becomes" ("Snapshots"). And Plath asks, "What am I /
That these late mouths"—the dissenting mouths of her
mind—"cry open . . . ?" ("Poppies in October").

What am I? Who am I? What shall I call myself? Another
aspect of the woman poet's struggle toward self-definition is
her search for a name. Significantly, the problems and pos-
sibilities of naming recur throughout the poetry of such
writers as Plath, Rich, Sexton, Levertov, and Wakoski.

Perhaps even more significantly, however, where the male confessional poet uses the real names of real people to authenticate his ironic sociology, the self-defining female poet uses names as symbolic motifs, as mythic ideas. Robert Lowell, for instance, entitles one of his books *For Lizzie and Harriet,* and confesses that "hand on glass / and heart in mouth [I] / outdrank the Rahvs in the heat / of Greenwich Village . . . ," while Dewitt Snodgrass sardonically insists that "Snodgrass is walking through the universe." But Levertov gives herself a generic name, reconciling herself with deep serenity to "what, woman, / and who, myself, / I am." And Plath, trapped in the identity crisis Levertov appears to have transcended, relinquishes her name, symbolic of a mistaken identity, with intense relief: "I am nobody; I have nothing to do with explosions. / I have given my name and my day-clothes up to the nurses . . ." ("Tulips").

Even Sexton, who seems at first to be playing with her name as Snodgrass toys with his, invents an imaginary Christopher to go with the reality of Anne and sets the two names in the context of a series of psalms outlining a private myth of origins: "For Anne and Christopher were born in my head as I howled at the grave of the roses. . . ." Adrienne Rich goes further still, defining herself as a participant in a mysterious universal reality—"The Stranger," "the androgyne"—and noting, therefore, that "the letters of my name are written under the lids / of the newborn child." Finally, Diane Wakoski, perhaps the most obsessed with names of all these poets, mythologizes one aspect of herself by emphasizing the various implications of her name: "If you know my name, / you know Diane comes across diamond in the word book," she writes in "The Diamond Merchant," "crossing my life . . . leaving me incomplete. . . ." Elsewhere she adds: "There is / an ancient priestess / whose tears make the spider-lilies grow. / She knows my name is darkness" ("The Mirror of a Day Chiming Marigold"). And she reveals a crucial tension between her name and her real identity: "Feeling the loneliness / of my cold name, / I live in a secret place, / behind a carved door. / My house is a diamond and my life / is unspoken" ("In the Secret Room, East of the Sun, West of the Moon").

This tension between the woman's name and the reality that it may not after all represent suggests, however, a central problem that shadows all the attempts at self-definition made by the female poets discussed here. For as she struggles to define herself, to reconcile male myths about her with her own sense of herself, to find some connection between the name the world has given her and the secret name she has given herself, the woman poet inevitably postulates that perhaps she has not one but two (or more) selves, making her task of self-definition bewilderingly complex. The first of these selves is usually public and social, defined by circumstance and by the names the world calls her—daughter, wife, mother, Miss, Mrs., Mademoiselle—a self that seems, in the context of the poet's cultural conditioning, to be her natural personality (in the sense of being both physiologically inevitable and morally proper or appropriate). The female poet's second self, however, is associated with her secret name, her rebellious longings, her rage against imposed definitions, her creative passions, her anxiety, and—yes—her art. And it is this *Doppelgänger* of a second self which, generating the woman's uneasiness with male myths of femininity, gives energy as well as complexity to her struggle toward self-definition.

For if the first self is public, rational, social, and therefore seems somehow "natural," this dark, other, second self is private, irrational, antisocial, and therefore—in the best romantic tradition—associated with the supernatural. Denise Levertov's poem "In Mind" outlines the dichotomy between the two selves better than any prose analysis could. Noting that the poet's mind contains two radically opposite (but implicitly complementary) selves, Levertov describes the first of these as "a woman / of innocence," a woman who is "unadorned" but sweet-smelling and "fair-featured." She wears

> a utopian smock or shift, her hair
> is light brown and smooth, and she
>
> is kind and very clean without
> ostentation—
>   but she has
> no imagination.

Shadowing this kindly public woman, however, the poet imagines a

> turbulent moon-ridden girl

or old woman, or both,
dressed in opals and rags, feathers

and torn taffeta,
who knows strange songs—

but she is not kind.

Innumerable male writers have also, of course, spoken in ways similar to this of doubles and otherness, imagining second supernatural selves ranging from good wizards like Superman to bad alter egos like Mr. Hyde. But the exploration of inner alterity is only one of many modes of self-analysis available to the modern male confessional poet, whereas all the women whose poetry has been discussed here seem to share a real obsession with the second, supernatural self. "The Other" and "Again and Again and Again" are just two of many poems by Sexton that deal with this phenomenon of otherness. In the first, interestingly, she describes her supernatural self—her "other"—as masculine, an early avatar, I suppose, of Christopher, the imaginary twin she associates (in *The Death Notebooks*) with the mad eighteenth-century poet Christopher Smart:

> Under my bowels, yellow with smoke,
> it waits.
> Under my eyes, those milk bunnies,
> it waits.
> It is waiting.
> It is waiting.
> Mr. Doppelgänger. My brother. My spouse.
> Mr. Doppelgänger. My enemy. My lover.

Like Levertov's second self, Sexton's is unkind and therefore unfeminine, aggressive, masculine. My "other," she writes, "swallows Lysol."

> When the child is soothed and resting on the breast...

> My other beats in a tin drum in my heart....

> It cries and cries and cries
> until I put on a painted mask
> and leer at Jesus in His passion.

Then it giggles.
It is a thumbscrew.
Its hatred makes it clairvoyant.
I can only sign over everything,
the house, the dog, the ladders, the jewels,
the soul, the family tree, the mailbox.

Then I can sleep.

Maybe.

Inhabited by such rage, it is no wonder that the woman poet often struggles, with a kind of feverish panic, to define herself, frantically clearing away the debris of alternative selves like "old whore petticoats"—to quote Sylvia Plath—in the hope of reattaining the blazing chastity, the unviolated singleness, of a "pure acetylene / Virgin" ("Fever 103°"). For, inhabiting her, the second self is a cry that keeps her awake—to go on quoting Plath—flapping out nightly and "looking, with its hooks, for something to love." Yet she can define it no more precisely, can define instead only her own pain, her fear of its otherness. "I am terrified by this dark thing / That sleeps in me . . . ," Plath continues in "Elm." "All day I feel its soft, feathery turnings, its malignity." In "Again and Again and Again" Sexton notes: "I have a black look I do not / like. It is a mask I try on. / . . . its frog / sits on my lips and defecates." Even Adrienne Rich, usually affirmative in her definition of a second, supernatural self, acknowledges the awful anxiety associated with such experiences of interior otherness: "A pair of eyes imprisoned for years inside my skull / is burning its way outward, the headaches are terrible" ("Ghazals: Homage to Ghalib"). Diane Wakoski, who writes of wanting "to smash through the fortified walls of myself / with a sledge," describes, in heavily sexual terms, "the anger of my own hair, / which is long / and wants to tie knots, / strangle, avenge this face of mine . . ." ("This King: The Tombed Egyptian One," and "Water Shapes"). Inhabited by this cry of fury, these self-assertive, witch-dark wings that flap inside so many women poets, she feels a sort of supernatural electricity "dripping" from her "like cream" and perceives the whole world as transformed, seething with magical dangerous blue phenomena: "blue trains rush by in my sleep. / Blue herons fly overhead. . . . / Blue liquid pours down my poisoned throat and blue veins / rip open my breast. Blue daggers tip / and are juggled in my palms. / Blue death lives in my fingernails" ("Blue Monday"). "The Eye altering alters all," as Blake observed so long ago, and the woman poet who defines herself as possessor of (or possessed by) a deadly second self inevitably begins to imagine that she's lost in a universe of death.

Where is the way out of such a universe? What kind of self-definition is possible to someone who feels herself imprisoned there, her back humped with black inimical power, black wings flapping in her heart?—to go back to the poems with which I began these speculations. One answer, the one Sylvia Plath most often chooses, is for the woman poet to completely reject the "natural" self—the public, outer self of roles and names—and instead to identify entirely with her supernatural self. "Mrs. Hughes," for instance, is clearly one of Plath's old whore petticoats, as are "Otto Plath's daughter" and "the Guest Managing Editor of *Mademoiselle.*" Her real self, she insists, is "no drudge" but a queen, unleashed and flying, more terrible than she ever was. Yet here the terror is not a cause of anxiety but a sign of life and triumph. Become celestial like Rich's woman-as-galactic-cloud, healing the wounds of self-division, Plath's supernatural self appears at last as a "red / Scar in the sky, red comet," flying "Over the engine that killed her— / The mausoleum, the wax house" of the dying "natural" self ("Stings").

Denise Levertov, on the other hand, opts in "The Wings" for a very different solution to the problem of her black inimical power, speculating that she may have *two* wings, two second selves, both equally supernatural but "one / feathered in soot, the other // . . . pale / flare-pinions." "Well—" she asks, repudiating the rage of Plath's terrible flying scar, "Could I go / on one wing, // the white one?" Perhaps, she implies, the second self is not witch, devil, animal, but in the best, Blakean sense, goddess, angel, spirit.

But, of course, to go on only one wing is a compromise, an admission of defeat and fragmentation akin to Anne Finch's sorrowful presentation of her "contracted wing." And Adrienne Rich, determined "to save the skein" of "this trailing knitted thing, this cloth of darkness, / this woman's garment" of enigmatic selfhood, refuses to compromise ("When We Dead Awaken"). Like both Plath and Levertov, however, she identifies primarily with a supernatural self, a self flying "lonely and level" as "a plane . . . / on its radio beam, aiming / across the Rockies" ("Song"). But unlike Plath in "Stings" or Levertov in "The Wings," she's untroubled by questions about the morality of this second self. Neither black nor white, neither terrible nor blessed, it exists, Rich suggests, because it has to, for the sake of the survival of all women. Thus, the second pair of eyes, which gave the poet headaches in the 1968 "Ghazals," reappears later in "From the Prison House" as a single, healthy, visionary, third eye that is impervious to pain, pure, objective, an instrument of accurate perception:

> Underneath my lids another eye has opened
> it looks nakedly
> at the light
>
> that soaks in from the world of pain
> even when I sleep . . .
>
> This eye
> is not for weeping
> its vision must be unblurred
> though tears are on my face
>
> its intent is clarity
> it must forget
> nothing.

Despite this affirmation of the justice and inevitability of her visionary anger, it's plain that Rich, too, sees herself as fragmented. Displacing her poetic vision onto a supernatural third eye and leaving the eyes of her outer, natural self merely for weeping, she implicitly concedes—at least in this poem—the difficulty of achieving a wholeness, a single, entirely adequate self-definition. And to be honest, very few women poets, from Anne Finch to the present, have in fact managed a definitive statement of self-assertion, a complete self-definition. Yet I hope that these preliminary speculations have at least partly recorded what I think women poets themselves have fully recorded: a difficult process of self-discovery that is in full progress, moving all women continually forward toward what D. H. Lawrence (for whom the problem was considerably simpler) called "self-accomplishment."

Like Lawrence, W. B. Yeats was an heir of the romantic movement's egotistical sublime, so it was natural for him to imagine a woman singing, "'I am I, am I; / The greater grows my light / The further that I fly,'" and to note, "All creation shivers / With that sweet cry." But soon, perhaps, such self-assertive imaginings will be equally natural for women poets. Already Muriel Rukeyser, in one of her most famous passages, has envisioned a radiant union of inner and outer selves, a first jubilant joining of the fragments into a true creative whole: "No more masks! No more mythologies! / Now, for the first time, the god lifts his hand, / the fragments join in me with their own music." And Denise Levertov, transcending her divided self of black and white wings, has proclaimed: "There is no savor / more sweet, more salt / than to be glad to be / what, woman, / and who, myself, / I am. . . ." As for the hump of black inimical power on her back, the burden of her wings, that other self can be assimilated, she suggests in "Stepping Westward," into a force that nourishes her wholeness:

> If I bear burdens
> they begin to be remembered
> as gifts, goods, a basket
>
> of bread that hurts
> my shoulders but closes me
>
> in fragrance. I can
> eat as I go.

John Haines

The Hole in the Bucket
1975

> . . . so poetry is arrested in its development if it remains an unmeaning play of fancy without relevance to the ideals and purposes of life. In that relevance lies its highest power.
>
> Santayana

American poetry lacks ideas. Like all large statements, this one covers a lot of ground and leaves plenty of room for error. I make it if for no other reason than to see what response I can provoke. But there are other reasons at hand, chiefly my dissatisfaction with the thinness, sameness, and dullness of so many contemporary poems. Our poems are characteristically occasional, and I do not mean by this that they are all written for or about occasions. Williams, after all, wrote many of his poems out of everyday encounters with things and persons; so did Stevens. Most poets do this. But I mean that the poems are generated by a sporadic and shallow response to things, and not within the context of a unified outlook on life.

This may be a way of saying that we have no major poets at this time. I myself would not be so foolish as to assert that. It has, however, been said not only that this is the case, but that we shouldn't expect things to be different. The statement may be true, but I feel dissatisfied with it. The notion that this is a time for the small and plentiful poet and not for the major talent seems to limit beforehand the possibilities. It is as if some of us wished to shrink the world to our own size since we cannot grow enough to equal it.

When hundreds of poems in magazine after magazine and in book after book reveal the same casual, happenstance character, the same self-limited frame of reference, the art of poetry itself may be called into question. What use is such an art beyond mere self-entertainment for the few? And without inclusive, authentic ideas it can't be otherwise.

By "idea" I mean, among other things, some kind of conviction about the world and the place of poetry in it. It is an insight, let's say, that makes of experience and perception a particular way of seeing: what we sometimes call the poet's "vision." The insight may come as a sudden revelation, but it is more likely to be achieved slowly as a result of simply living and responding to things in the world, of reading and thinking, and of the daily work of writing poems and thinking about writing poems. After a while, if one is lucky, some pattern emerges; the substance of one's efforts begins to be clear. The process is all one piece, one way of being. And the value of the idea, once it is formed, is that it furnishes the means by which, in a world lacking unity, all that the poet sees and feels has meaning. Things fall into place. Every writer of poems seeks to accomplish something like this in single poems, or it seems to me that we would not write them at all. The task is to go beyond the single lucky poem, or even the single gift of a volume, and by a vigorous kind of self-exploration and a "prodigious search of appearances" (Wallace Stevens) develop and extend the meaning of the insight. We no longer have at hand the unifying outlook on life common to all which society may once have provided its artists and citizens; but every poet who aspires to more than occasional composition must sooner or later create the idea for himself, the personal myth, much as Stevens attempted to do with his theory of the imagination. The idea itself can be criticized, but the effort needs to be made.

All the work we value most from the past sixty or seventy years was nourished by ideas. Ideas are present and abundant in Yeats and Eliot, in Pound, in Stevens, in Jeffers, and in Lawrence, to name but a few. And those poets of the same period who now seem to us to be "minor" are precisely those in whose work ideas are either weak or commonplace, or do not exist at all. Mark Van Doren's poems, for example, show that it is possible to write graceful and often interesting poems without strong ideas. This doesn't mean that the work of such poets has no permanent value: only that we must look elsewhere for the most authentic voice of the period.

Even a casual reading of modern poetry in Spanish would lead one to a similar conclusion. In Unamuno, in Machado, in Jimenez, and in Paz, the fire of the idea, the passion of it, lights up the best poems. The same is true of much contemporary European poetry in our time. Here and there in contemporary American poetry the conviction rises, where it does not freeze into dogmatism or mere gesture, only to sink again. The merest appearance of it, and the excitement it generates, seems to me to provide sufficient evidence for what I am saying.

Possession of an idea, of a conviction about human history, rescues a poet like Edwin Muir from mediocrity. In Muir's case the idea was formed in early childhood out of a series of clear glimpses into the original order of things. His memory of these, and his slowly maturing belief in the symbolic truth of dreams, and in what he called the "fable" of human life—the Fall and journey out of Eden toward some eventual reconciliation—allowed him to write late in life a poem like "The Horses" in which his vision is complete. Actually, Muir is remarkable for his fidelity to his vision and for the steady growth in his power of utterance.

Williams is another poet in whom an important idea began to form relatively early. We speak a new language on this continent, one no longer English, and some means of measuring this language as verse must be invented if we are to have the poetry we need. The slow clarification of this idea can be traced in Williams's work. Whatever the ultimate value of the idea, it allowed, in fact made necessary, his continued growth as a poet.

Even though an idea may appear to have negative qualities, as is sometimes the case in the work of Robinson Jeffers, behind the apparent negation can be seen the positive figure of life-enhancement. Most genuine poets have understood that one great quality of art, and it may be its most important quality, is that it enhances life for us. In more common terms, it gives us something to look up to. Things are changed, made visible in another, or ideal light; they are removed from the ordinary and become part of some very old, interior story in which we recognize something of ourselves. Poetry can hardly do this successfully when the emotion and thought generated in the words halts at the boundaries of the poem. The task, then, is to make connections, to invest the "I" of the poem with significance beyond the ordinary, to make of one's own predicament a universal case. Or to state it another way, it is to allow something besides the self to occupy the poem, to matter as much as the self. And this requires, beyond insight, honesty and imagination, two qualities not always in good supply.

Having valid ideas about poetry implies having a keen regard for poetry itself. For this a certain shifting of attention may be necessary, away from personality and career, or an abandonment of ambition in the narrow sense of it. But it also requires a sure awareness that poetry has been written for thousands of years by men and women in all sorts of places and circumstances. It is still an art; and the individual brings to this art what gifts and insights he or she possesses.

All our competence with words and with verses, with images and metaphors, asks for substance and purpose if poetry is not to be a slightly superior form of amusement. It must become more serious and more profoundly involved with the life of its time. And should anyone think I am being merely cranky, I would like to quote one of my favorite remarks by Wallace Stevens, written in a letter in 1946 and still valid:

> If people are to become dependent on poetry for any of the fundamental satisfactions, poetry must have an increasingly intellectual scope and power. This is a time for the highest poetry. We never understood the world less than we do now nor, as we understand it, liked it less. We never wanted to understand it more or needed to like it more.

It may not be true that poetry requires criticism in order to be written. The poems will appear when it is time for them and not otherwise. Nevertheless, lack of serious ideas about poetry implies an absence of criticism. There are two kinds of criticism. One of them is the sort that defines and places works of the past. It tells, as well as it can, something of where we have been, what we have been, and what we have done. At its most abundant (and dull), this is the sort that endlessly sifts and classifies the past; it is essentially an academic activity, one that keeps literary scholars eternally occupied. The second and much rarer sort attempts to define the conditions for the art of the present—what we want poetry to be for us now and tomorrow. This is the kind written by Pound and by Williams, sometimes by Lawrence, and by a few others. It often conveys a sense of urgency, of necessity. The best criticism accomplishes a double task: it both defines the past and attempts to describe the present and future possibility. Of this kind we have had very little for a generation or more. The literary journals are filled with commentators, but the commentaries in most cases amount to little more than book reviewing and trivial shoptalk—the eternal and boring "nuts and bolts" of most "craft" essays. I will except from this description Robert Bly, whose erratic but often daring pieces scattered in many journals over the past dozen years or more have done as much as anything to fill a considerable void. Donald Hall should also be mentioned for the intelligence of his numerous contributions on contemporary poets and poetry.

The main value of criticism is that it provides a space in which creation can take place, a clearing in the imagination. I have been reading Octavio Paz recently, and have been greatly attracted to his far-ranging, often daring speculations on literature and society. This large-minded thinking about poetry and language, about literature and tradition, and about creative life generally, is precisely what we are lacking. And for Paz, criticism offers a way not only into a particular work, but into the process itself. Criticism and creation are one, a total experience, and are not antagonistic at all. It is the condition of thought that is important. Gossip and classification, the two extremes of most literary discussion, do not create understanding, which is surely a major function of intelligent criticism. And to provide us with the kind of understanding we need, criticism should try to work itself clear of a reliance on what some people have conveniently called "the network"—those few who can be expected to listen. They are important, but poetry is, as Paz reminds us, "the search for others, the discovery of otherness." And he speaks of poetry as a fundamental restoration of community; poetry is essentially social, and has always been so.

There are decent, competent poems written today, many of them. They seem good; it is hard to find fault with them in detail. Few of the poems, however, remain in one's mind. They are poems that convey a certain information or mood, a few images, but which read once and understood offer little to return to. They seem meant to be replaced next week or next quarter by others very much like them. If I am at all right about this, it is not preposterous to argue that it is related to what we find in society at large. Everything we are accustomed to having and using is meant to be replaced next season by a new, slightly modified model, one often described as containing startling and revolutionary changes. In fact, it is naive to think that we aren't all affected in many, hardly suspected ways by the planned obsolescence of the material environment. Even human relationships seem to have taken on the same dismaying character.

There is about contemporary poems generally a lack of resonance beyond the page and beyond the self that speaks the poem. For some time I have thought that this might be due partly to the flatness of statement we have grown used to in verse. Our poetry discarded some time ago much of the musical element in verse: regularity of meter, rhyme, and all the little memory aids once so common to poetry. We have grown used to seeing a poem as print, as object on the page, and have lost to some extent the ability to hear, not only the poem as a figure in time, but also the spaces and silences between the words and the syllables where so much can be said.

But there is more to it than this. We have somehow fallen into the notion that one's individual experience in the world is sufficient material to make poetry out of. It is easy to see why so many prefer to think so. We mistrust the received ideas of the past, whether they are stated as philosophy and political theory or are embodied in artistic forms. The mistrust is inevitable, I suppose, since so many of the ideas seem to have failed us when we needed them most. Moreover, the ideas have for the most part not been lived and tested, but inherited as literature, as course material, something to be taught in the classroom and unrelated to everyday life. So we prefer to rely on the illusion of our personal experience, on what can be seen and touched by the individual. This may in fact be a useful way to begin life, but it is not quite enough for poetry.

What makes a poem significant? What makes it memorable? Passion and thought, emotionally charged language, fresh imagery, surprising use of metaphor . . . yes. But also, I think, the very sure sense that the moment we enter the world of the poem we are participating in another episode of the myth-journey of humankind; that a voice has taken up the tale once more. The individual experience as related or presented in the poem renews our deep, implicit faith in that greater experience. A poem remains with us to the extent that it allows us to feel that we are listening to a voice at once contemporary and ancient. This makes all the difference. Innovations in style, strange, disordered syntax, unusual images, idiomatic explosions—these soon pass, or are means to an end. Only that remains which touches us in our deepest, most enduring self. Behind every word is the memory of another, spoken a thousand times; in the intonation of the voice, in the rise and fall of the syllables, memory does its work and reconciles the poet and the reader to a world difficult and strange.

What I have just said may seem ill-defined, but it is directly related to our misuse of, or lack of regard for, the past, what is loosely called "the tradition." I am continually surprised by the number of people in poetry workshops who have read little or no poetry beyond that written during the past five or ten years. Many of them do not read poetry regularly at all, and cannot recognize a familiar passage from Wordsworth, Yeats, Frost, or even Williams. On the other hand, they have perhaps read Creeley and Olson, Plath and Sexton, Hugo and Goldbarth, and a few far lesser people. They are more apt to have read hundreds of recent poems written by younger people influenced by these poets. At worst, they are content to read only each other.

I think this tendency is mistaken. The more one thinks about it, the more mistaken it appears to be. That younger poets should be influenced only by their near or immediate contemporaries seems a very strange notion, and it imposes a serious limitation on the possibilities for growth. Should anyone read Robert Bly, W. S. Merwin, or James Wright, you would think that person would also want to seek out and read the poets *they* learned from. Otherwise, how could anyone come to a firm conclusion about the later work? As Pound used to say, if you really want to learn about an art, you will do best to go back to the earliest things you can find and begin there. Moreover, if there is some quality missing in contemporary work, some defect in it, imitating it will only compound the trouble.

It is amazing to me that anyone with a serious commitment to poetry would not want to seek out the whole of it, to read as much of it as he or she can lay hands on, and to learn from its many forms and voices. Contrary to what many people appear to think, the "tradition" is not something outworn, an empty scaffolding kept more or less intact by English departments, but a living and useful system of values.

One of the strengths of poetry in Spanish in our time is that it has not lost contact with the past. Quevedo and Góngora are still living presences for poets in Spain and South America, as they were for Lorca and others of his generation. Paz has some interesting things to say about this.

> Instead of being a succession of names, works and tendencies, the tradition would be converted into a system of significant relationships: a language. The poetry of Góngora would not be simply something that happened after Garcilaso and before Ruben Darío, but a text related dynamically with other texts. . . . The importance of Quevedo is not exhausted in his work or the conceptualism of the 17th century: we find the sense of his words more fully in some poems of Vallejo, even when, naturally, what the Peruvian says is not identical with what Quevedo said. [*Claude Lévi-Strauss: An Introduction* (New York: Dell, 1974), p. 148]

Elsewhere Paz speaks of historical contexts, saying that they do not serve as examples, but as stimuli. They awaken creative imagination and open up the possibilities of new combinations.

C. M. Bowra, in an essay prefacing *An Anthology of Mexican Poetry* (edited by Octavio Paz, translated by Samuel Beckett [Bloomington, Ind.: Indiana University Press, 1958]), has this to say:

> Traditions are delicate organisms and if they are treated too roughly they cease to do their right work. So if poetry breaks too violently with the past and conducts experiments in too reckless a spirit, it may well hurt itself. Indeed it is difficult not to think that something of this kind has happened in our own time, which has surely been rich in talent but has not quite produced the poetry demanded or deserved by our circumstances.

I suppose Bowra could be criticized for holding too conservative an attitude regarding tradition, but I find his remarks worth thinking about. In significant contrast to his and Paz's beliefs, North American poetry in the past several decades seems to have been marked by a continual burning of bridges, destruction of all links with the past. The result: no past, no tradition, no roots, and finally, perhaps, no poetry.

Our belief in historical continuity has broken down. In the words of someone reviewing a recent Indian history of the American West, ". . . we really don't know who we are, or where we have come from, or what we have done, or why." The meaning of our existence is in doubt. Our confusion takes many forms, and uncertainty about artistic values is only one of them. Beyond literature itself, we can expect to see any number of efforts toward political and economic renovation. We can also look for a revival of traditional religion with the animosities and mistaken boundaries that have warped it through the centuries. And these attempts will have increasingly a spirit of futility and exasperation as we come to feel their inadequacy. People will be turning anywhere for understanding and for solutions. And therein lies a great danger: the search for a rescuer, a hero who will lead us out of our predicament. In the political world this sort of person is not difficult to imagine; we have met him several times before in this century. When the order inherent in social and political structures begins to fail, what we are left with, as Jeffers saw and a hundred fallen kingdoms bear witness to, is power and the struggle for it.

One likely response to this state of things would be mindlessness—an inability or refusal to think at all except in immediate, pragmatic, and self-serving terms. The absence of intelligence in much contemporary writing, the widespread reliance on gut-reaction and crude forms, seems to say that many people have already taken this road and are satisfied to remain on it.

"Our minds are possessed by three mysteries: where we came from, where we are going, and since we are not alone, but members of a countless family, how we should live with one another." This statement of a theme by Edwin Muir seems to me still valid. It evokes for me something of the ancient high seriousness of poetry and storytelling, of instruction in life and death and the continuity of values. It seems to me to be consistent with a remark by Stevens that we can never have great poetry unless we believe that poetry serves great ends. That belief would lie at the heart of our practice of poetry, affecting everything that we do.

Poetry may regain its significance in this country when, in addition to resolving some of the difficulties outlined above, it becomes, as it has in other times and places, a less comfortable occupation; when the writing and publishing of a book of poems will be, as Stevens once described it, "a damned serious matter." This means, of course that, among other things, it will not be written or spoken where there are no others, but where an audience listens and believes.

Donald Hall

Goatfoot, Milktongue, Twinbird
The Psychic Origins of Poetic Form
1973

When we pursue the psychic origins of our satisfaction with poetic form, we come to the end of the trail. It is deep in the woods, and there is a fire; Twinbird sits quietly, absorbed in the play of flame that leaps and falls; Goatfoot dances by the fire, his eyes reflecting the orange coals, as his lean foot taps the stone. Inside the fire there is a mother and child, made one, the universe of the red coal. This is Milktongue.

1. Some Premises

First, in connection with oppositions:

1. Any quality of poetry can be used for a number of purposes, including opposed purposes. Thus, concentration on technique has often been used to trivialize content, by poets afraid of what they will learn about themselves. But concentration on technique can absorb the attention while unacknowledged material enters the language; so technique can facilitate inspiration.

On the other hand, a poet can subscribe to an antitechnical doctrine of inspiration in a way that simply substitutes one technique for another. Surrealism can become as formulaic as a pastoral elegy.

2. When a poet says he is doing *north,* look and see if he is not actually doing *south.* Chances are that his bent is so entirely *south* that he must swear total allegiance to *north* in order to include the globe.

3. Energy arises from conflict. Without conflict, no energy. Yin and yang. Dark and light. Pleasure and pain. No synthesis without thesis and antithesis. Conflict of course need not be binary but may include a number of terms.

4. Every present event that moves us deeply connects in our psyches with something (or things) in the past. The analogy is the two pieces of carbon that make an arc light. When they come close enough, the spark leaps across. The one mourning is all mourning; "After the first death, there is no other." This generalization applies to the composition of poems (writing), and to the recomposition of poems (reading).

5. The way out is the same as the way in. To investigate the process of making a poem is not merely an exercise in curiosity or gossip, but an attempt to understand the nature of literature. In the act of reading, the reader undergoes a process—largely without awareness, as the author was largely without intention—which resembles, like a slightly fainter copy of the original, the process of discovery or recovery that the poet went through in his madness or inspiration.

And then, more general:

6. A poem is human inside talking to human inside. It may *also* be reasonable person talking to reasonable person, but if it is not inside talking to inside, it is not a poem. This inside speaks through the second language of poetry, the unintended language. Sometimes, as in surrealism, the second language is the only language. It is the ancient prong of carbon in the arc light. We all share more when we are five years old than when we are twenty-five; more at five minutes than at five years. The second language allows poetry to be universal.

7. *Lyric poetry, typically, has one goal and one message, which is to urge the condition of inwardness, the "inside" from which its own structure derives.*

2. Form: the Sensual Body

There is the old false distinction between *vates* and *poiein*. It is a boring distinction, and I apologize for dragging it out again. I want to use it in its own despite.

The *poiein*, from the Greek verb for making or doing, becomes the poet—the master of craft, the maker of the labyrinth of epic or tragedy or lyric hymn, tale-teller and spell-binder. The *vates* is bound in his own spell. He is the rhapsode Socrates patronizes in *Ion*. In his purest form he utters what he does not understand at all, be he oracle or André Breton. He is the visionary, divinely inspired, who like Blake may take dictation from voices.

But Blake's voices returned to dictate revisions. The more intimately we observe any poet who claims extremes of inspiration or of craftsmanship, the more we realize that his claims are a disguise. There is no *poiein* for the same reason that there is no *vates*. The claims may be serious (they may be the compensatory distortion which allows the poet to write at all) and the claims may affect the looks of the poem—a surrealist poem and a neoclassic Imitation of Horace *look* different— but the distinction becomes trivial when we discover the psychic origins of poetic form.

I speak of the psychic origins of poetic *form*. Psychologists have written convincingly of the origins of the *material* of arts, in wish-fulfillment and in the universality of myth. We need not go over ideas of the poet as daydreamer, or of the collective unconsciousness. Ernst Kris's "regression in the service of the ego" names an event but does not explain how it comes about. But one bit of Freud's essay on the poet as daydreamer has been a clue in this search. At the end of his intelligent, snippy paper, Freud says that he lacks time now to deal with form, but that he suspects that formal pleasure is related to forepleasure. Then he ducks through the curtain and disappears. Suppose we consider the implications of his parting shot. Forepleasure develops out of the sensuality of the whole body which the infant experiences in the pleasure of the crib and of the breast. The connection between forepleasure and infancy is the motion from rationality to metaphor.

But to begin our search for the psychic origins of poetic form, we must first think of what is usually meant by the word "form," and then we must look for the reality. So often form is looked upon only as the fulfillment of metrical expectations. Meter is nothing but a loose set of probabilities; it is a trick easily learned; anyone can learn to arrange one-hundred-and-forty syllables so that the even syllables are louder than the odd ones, and every tenth syllable rhymes: the object will be a sonnet. But only when you have forgotten the requirements of meter do you begin to write poetry in it. The resolutions of form which ultimately provide the wholeness of a poem—resolutions of syntax, metaphor, diction, and sound—are minute and subtle and vary from poem to poem.

They vary from sonnet to sonnet, or, equally and not more greatly, from sonnet to free verse lyric.

Meter is no more seriously binding than the frame we put around a picture. But the *form* of free verse is as binding and as liberating as the *form* of a rondeau. Free verse is simply less predictable. Yeats said that the finished poem made a sound like the click of the lid on a perfectly made box. One-hundred-and-forty syllables, organized into a sonnet, do not necessarily make a click; the same number of syllables, dispersed in asymmetric lines of free verse, will click like a lid if the poem is good. In the sonnet and in the free verse poem, the poet improvises toward that click, and achieves his resolution in unpredictable ways. The rhymes and line lengths of the sonnet are too gross to contribute greatly to that sense of resolution. The click is our sense of lyric *form*. This pleasure in resolution is Twinbird.

The wholeness and identity of the completed poem, the poem as object in time, the sensual body of the poem—this wholeness depends upon a complex of unpredictable fulfillments. The satisfying resolutions in a sonnet are more subtle than rhyme and meter, and less predictable. The body of sound grows in resolutions like assonance and alliteration, and in near-misses of both; or in the alternations, the going-away and coming-back, of fast and slow, long and short, high and low. The poem—free verse or meter, whatever—may start with lines full of long vowels, glide on diphthong sounds like "eye" and "ay" for instance, move to quick alternative lines of short vowels and clipped consonants, and return in a coda to the long vowels "eye" and "ay." The assonance is shaped like a saucer.

The requirements of fixity are complex, and the conscious mind seldom deals with them. Any poet who has written metrically can write arithmetically correct iambic pentameter as fast as his hand can move. In improvising toward the click, the poet is mostly aware of what sounds right and what does not. When something persists in not sounding right, the poet can examine it bit by bit—can analyze it—in the attempt to consult his knowledge and apply it.

This knowledge is habitual. It is usually not visible to the poet, but it is available for consultation. When you learn something so well that you forget it, you can begin to do it. You dance best when you forget that you are dancing.

Athletics—a tennis stroke, swimming, a receiver catching a football—is full of examples of actions done as if by instinct, which are actually learned procedure, studied and practiced until they become "second nature." So it is with poetry. The literary form of poems is created largely by learning—in collaboration with the unconscious by a process I will talk about later. Possible resolutions of metaphor, diction, and sound are coded into memory from our reading of other poets, occasionally from our reading of criticism, from our talk with other poets, and from our revisions of our own work, with the conscious analysis that this revision sometimes entails. New resolutions are combinations of parts of old ones, making new what may later be combined again and made new again.

When the experienced reader takes a poem in, his sense of fixity comes also from memory. He too has the codes in his head. The new poem fulfills the old habits of expectation in some unexpected way. The reader does not know why—unless he bothers to analyze; then probably not fully—he is pleased by the sensual body of the poem. He does not need to know why, unless he must write about it. The pleasure is sufficient. Since the poet's madness is the reader's madness, the resolution of the mad material is the reader's resolution as well as the poet's. The way in is the same as the way out.

Whatever else we may say of a poem we admire, it exists as a sensual body. It is beautiful and pleasant, manifest content aside, like a worn stone that is good to touch, or like a shape of flowers arranged or accidental. This sensual body reaches us through our mouths, which are warm in the love of vowels held together, and in the muscles of our legs which as in dance tap the motion and pause of linear and syntactic structure. These pleasures are Milktongue and Goatfoot.

There is a nonintellectual beauty in the moving together of words in phrases—"the music of diction"—and in resolution of image and metaphor. The sophisticated reader of poetry responds quickly to the sensual body of a poem, before he interrogates the poem at all. The pleasure we feel, reading a poem, is our assurance of its integrity. (So Pound said that technique is the test of sincerity.) We will glance through a poem rapidly and if it is a skillful fake we will feel repelled. If the poem is alive and honest, we will feel assent in our quickening pulse—though it might take us some time to explain what we were reacting to.

The soi-disant *vates* feels that he speaks from the unconscious (or with the voice of the God), and the *poiein* that he makes all these wholenesses of shape on purpose. Both of them disguise the truth. All poets are *poiein* and *vates*. The *poiein* comes from memory of reading, and the *vates* from memory of infancy. The sensual body of the poem derives from memory of reading most obviously, but ultimately it leads us back further—to the most primitive psychic origins of poetic form.

3. Conflict Makes Energy

People frequently notice that poetry concerns itself with unpleasant subjects: death, deprivation, loneliness, despair, if love then the death of love, and abandonment. Of course there are happy poems, but in English poetry there are few which are happy through and through—and those few tend to be light, short, pleasant, and forgettable. Most memorable happy poems have a portion of blackness in them. Over all— Keats, Blake, Donne, Yeats, Eliot, Shakespeare, Wordsworth— there is more dark than light, more elegy than celebration. There is no great poem in our language which is simply happy.

Noticing these facts, we reach for explanations: maybe to be happy is to be a simpleton; maybe poets are morbid; maybe life is darker than it is light; maybe when you are happy you are too busy being happy to write poems about it and when you are sad, you write poems in order to *do* something. There may be half-truths in these common ideas, but the real explanation lies in the structure of a poem; and, I suggest, in the structure of human reality.

Energy arises from conflict.

A) The sensual body of a poem is a pleasure separate from any message the poem may contain.

B) If the poem contains a message which is pleasurable (a word I have just substituted for "happy"), then the two pleasures walk agreeably together for a few feet, and collapse into a smiling lethargy. The happy poem sleeps in the sun.

C) If the message of the poem, on the whole, is terrifying—that They flee from me, that one time did me seek; that I am sick, I must die; that On Margate Sands / I can connect / Nothing with nothing; that Things fall apart, the center will not hold—then pain of message and pleasure of body copulate in a glorious conflict-dance of energy. This alternation of pleasure and pain is so swift as to seem simultaneous, to *be* simultaneous in the complexity both of creation and reception, a fused circle of yin and yang, a oneness in diversity.

The pain is clear to anyone. The pleasure is clear (dear) to anyone who loves poems. If we acknowledge the pleasure of the sensual body of the poem, we can see why painful poems are best: conflict makes energy and resolves our suffering into ambivalent living tissue. If human nature is necessarily ambivalent, then the structure of the energetic poem resembles the structure of human nature.

The sensual body, in poems, is not simply a compensation for the pain of the message. It is considerably more important, and more central to the nature of poetry. When we pursue the psychic origins of our satisfaction with poetic form, we come to the end of the trail. It is deep in the woods, and there is a fire; Twinbird sits quietly, absorbed in the play of flame that leaps and falls; Goatfoot dances by the fire, his eyes reflecting the orange coals, as his lean foot taps the stone. Inside the fire there is a mother and child, made one, the universe of the red coal. This is Milktongue.

4. Goatfoot, Milktongue, Twinbird

Once at a conference on creativity, a young linguist presented a model of language. Xeroxed in outline, it was beautiful like a concrete poem. I looked for language as used in poems and looked a long time. Finally I found it, under "autistic utterance," with the note that this utterance might later be refined into lyric poetry. It reminded me of another conference I had attended a year or two earlier. A psychoanalyst delivered a paper on deriving biographical information about an author from his fiction. He distributed mimeographed copies of his paper, which his secretary had typed from his obscure handwriting; he began his remarks by presenting a list of errata. The first correction was, "For 'autistic,' read 'artistic' throughout."

The newborn infant cries, he sucks at the air until he finds the nipple. At first he finds his hand to suck by accident— fingers, thumb; then he learns to repeat that pleasure.

Another mouth-pleasure is the autistic babble, the "goo-goo," the small cooing and purring and bubbling. These are sounds of pleasure; they are without message, except that a parent interprets them as "happy": pleasure is happy. Wittgenstein once said that we could sing the song with expression or without expression; very well, he said, let us have the expression without the song. (He was being ironic; I am not.) The baby's autistic murmur is the expression without the song. His small tongue curls around the sounds, the way his tongue warms with the tiny thread of milk that he pulls from his mother. This is Milktongue, and in poetry it is the deep and primitive pleasure of vowels in the mouth, of assonance and of holds on adjacent long vowels; of consonance, mmmm, and alliteration. It is Dylan Thomas and the curlew cry; it is That dolphin-torn, that gong-tormented sea; it is Then, in a wailful choir, the small gnats mourn.

As Milktongue mouths the noises it curls around, the rest of his body plays in pleasure also. His fists open and close spasmodically. His small bowed legs, no good for walking, contract and expand in a rhythmic beat. He has begun the dance, his muscles move like his heartbeat, and Goatfoot improvises his circle around the fire. His whole body throbs and thrills with pleasure. The first parts of his body which he notices are his hands; then his feet. The strange birds fly at his head, waver, and pause. After a while he perceives that there are two of them. They begin to act when he wishes them to act, and since the *mental* creates the *physical*, Twinbird is the first magic he performs. He examines these independent/dependent twin birds. They are exactly alike. And they are exactly unalike, mirror images of each other, the perfection of opposite-same.

As the infant grows, the noises split off partly into messages. "Mmm" can be milk and mother. "Da-da" belongs to another huge shape. He crawls and his muscles become useful to move him toward the toy and the soda cracker. Twinbird flies more and more at his will, as Milktongue speaks, and Goatfoot crawls. But still he rolls on his back and his legs beat in the air. Still, the sister hands flutter at his face. Still, the noises without message fill the happy time of waking before hunger, and the softening down, milktongue full, into sleep. The growing child skips rope, hops, dances to a music outside intelligence, rhymes to the hopscotch or jump rope, and listens to the sounds his parents please him with:

Pease porridge hot
Pease porridge cold
Pease porridge in-the-pot
Five days old.

Or himself learns:

Bah, bah, black sheep
Have you any wool;
Yes, sir, yes, sir,
Three bags full.
One for my master,
One for my dame
And one for the little boy
That lives down the lane.

The mouth-pleasure, the muscle-pleasure, the pleasure of match-unmatch.

But "Shades of the prison house begin to close / Upon the growing boy." Civilized humans try gradually to cut away the autistic component in their speech. Goatfoot survives in the dance, Twinbird in rhyme and resolution of dance and noise. Milktongue hides itself more. It ties us to the mother so obviously that men are ashamed of it. Tribal society was unashamed and worshipped Milktongue in religion and history. Among the outcast in the modern world, Milktongue sometimes endures in language, as it does in the American black world, and in the world of the poor Southern whites. In Ireland where the mother (and the Virgin) are still central, Milktongue remains in swearing and in the love of sweet speech. Probably, in most of the modern world, Milktongue exists only in smoking, eating, and drinking; and in oral sexuality.

But Milktongue and Goatfoot and Twinbird have always lived in the lyric poem, for poet and for reader. They are the ancestors, and they remain the psychic origins of poetic form, primitive both personally (back to the crib) and historically (back to the fire in front of the cave). They keep pure the sensual pleasure that is the dark secret shape of the poem. We need an intermediary to deal with them, for a clear reason:

Goatfoot and Milktongue and Twinbird, like other figures that inhabit the forest, are wholly preverbal. They live before words.

They approach the edge of the clearing, able to come close because the Priestess has no eyes to frighten them with. The Priestess, built of the memory of old pleasures, only knows how to select and order. The Priestess does not know what she says, but she knows that she says it in dactylic hexameter. Goatfoot and Milktongue and Twinbird leave gifts at the edge of the forest. The Priestess picks up the gifts, and turns to the light, and speaks words that carry the dark mysterious memory of the forest and the pleasure.

The poet writing, and the reader reading, lulled by Goatfoot and Milktongue and Twinbird into the oldest world, become able to think as the infant thinks, with transformation and omnipotence and magic. The form of the poem, because it exists separately from messages, can act as trigger or catalyst or enzyme to activate not messages but types of mental behavior. Coleridge spoke of meter as effecting the willing suspension of disbelief. They are the three memories of the body—not only meter; and they are powerful magic—not only suspension of disbelief. The form of the poem unlocks the mind to old pleasures. Pleasure leaves the mind vulnerable to the content of experience before we have intellectualized the experience and made it acceptable to the civilized consciousness. The form allows the mind to encounter real experience, and so the real message is permitted to speak—but only because the figures in the forest, untouched by messages, have danced and crooned and shaped.

The release of power and sweetness! Milktongue also remembers hunger, and the cry without answer. Goatfoot remembers falling, and the ache that bent the night. Twinbird remembers the loss of the brother, so long he believed in abandonment forever. From the earliest times, poetry has existed in order to retrieve, to find again, and to release. In the man who writes the poem, in the reader who lives it again, in the ideas, the wit, the images, the doctrines, the exhortations, the laments and the cries of joy, the lost forest struggles to be born again inside the words. The life or urge and instinct, that rages and coos, kicks and frolics, as it chooses only without choosing—this life is the life the poem grows from, and leans toward.

Robert Hass

One Body
Some Notes on Form
1978

I've been trying to think about form in poetry and my mind keeps returning to a time in the country in New York when I was puzzled that my son Leif was getting up a little earlier every morning. I had to get up with him, so it exasperated me. I wondered about it until I slept in his bed one night. His window faced east. At six-thirty I woke to brilliant sunlight. The sun had risen.

Wonder and repetition. Another morning I was walking Kristin to her bus stop—a light blanket of snow after thaw, the air thick with the rusty croaking of blackbirds so that I remembered, in the interminable winter, the windy feel of June on that hill. Kristin, standing on a snowbank in the cold air, her eyes alert, her face rosy with cold and with some purity of expectation, was looking down the road. It was eight-fifteen. Her bus always arrived at eight-fifteen. She looked down the road and it was coming.

The first fact of the world is that it repeats itself. I had been taught to believe that the freshness of children lay in their capacity for wonder at the vividness and strangeness of the particular, but what is fresh in them is that they still experience the power of repetition, from which our first sense of the power of mastery comes. Though *predictable* is an ugly little word in daily life, in our first experience of it we are clued to the hope of a shapeliness in things. To see that power working on adults, you have to catch them out: the look of foolish happiness on the faces of people who have just sat down to dinner is their knowledge that dinner will be served.

Probably, that is the psychological basis for the power and the necessity of artistic form. I think of our children when they first came home from the hospital, wide, staring eyes, wet mouths, fat, uncontrollable tongues. I thought they responded when I bent over their cribs because they were beginning to recognize me. Now I think it was because they were coming to recognize themselves. They were experiencing in the fluidity of things a certain orderliness: footsteps, a face, the smell of hair and tobacco, cooing syllables. One would gradually have the sense that looking-out-of-the-eyes was a point around which phenomena organized themselves; thinking *this is going to happen* and having it happen might be, then, the authentic source of the experience of being, of identity, that word which implies that a lot of different things are the same thing.

Being and being seen. R. D. Laing says somewhere that small children don't get up at night to see if you're there, they get up to see if *they're* there. It helps me to understand that my first delighted mistaking of the situation—they know who I am!—was natural because I had the same experience as my children. Maybe our first experience of form is the experience of our own formation.

And we have that experience mainly with our mothers. Its roots are in hunger. The infant wants to know that his hunger is going to be satisfied. He cries out, there is a stirring of sensations that begin to be a pattern, and he is fed. The lovely greed of babies: so that the later experience of cognition, of the apprehension of form, carries within it the experience of animal pleasure and the first caressing experience of human affection.

This is clearest in poems of disintegration and return. In Rimbaud's "The Drunken Boat," there is the power of the moment when, in the exhaustion of the impulse of flight, he says: "I dream of Europe and her ancient quays." And Roethke in "The Lost Son"—

> The weeds whined,
> The snakes cried,
> The cows and briars
> Said to me: Die
>
> What a small song. What slow clouds. What dark water.
> Hath the rain a father? All the caves are ice . . .

—returns: "A lively understandable spirit once entertained you." It feels like the first moment after a hard rain. And Pound: "Soshu churned in the sea." The return is so powerful

we are cradled entirely in the form of things, as in that poem
when Gary Snyder's mind leaps from his small fire in the
mountains to the little fires of the summer stars:

> Burning the small dead
>   branches
> broke from beneath
>   thick spreading
>   whitebark pine
>   a hundred summers
> snowmelt rock and air
> hiss in a twisted bough
>   sierra granite:
>   Mt. Ritter—
>   black rock twice as old
> Deneb, Altair
> windy fire

But I am not thinking mainly of poems about form; I'm
thinking of the form of a poem, the shape of its understand-
ing. The presence of that shaping constitutes the presence of
poetry. Not tone, not imagery, however deep or subtle, not
particular qualities of content. It is easiest to say what I mean
by way of example, but almost all the bad examples seem
unfair. This, from last night's reading. "The Sphinx's Riddle
to Oedipus" by Randall Jarrell:

Not to have guessed is better: what is, ends,
But among fellows, with reluctance,
Clasped by the Woman-Breasted, Lion-Pawed.

To have clasped in one's own arms a mother,
To have killed with one's own hands a father
—Is not this, Lame One, to have been alone?

The seer is doomed for seeing; and to understand
Is to pluck out one's own eyes with one's own hands.
But speak: what has a woman's breasts, a lion's paws?

You stand at midday in the marketplace
Before your life: to see is to have spoken.
—Yet to see, Blind One, is to be alone.

The intentions of this poem are completely real. And I learn
things from it: learn from its verbs why Oedipus blinds

himself with Jocasta's clasp, for example. And I see that the sphinx is herself death. But the poem never quite occurs. It can't find its way to its rhythm. In the first line, in the fourth, in the sixth, in the seventh, in the ninth, Jarrell tries, each time in a different way, to find a rhythm. You can feel the poem groping for it, like someone trying to gain admittance to a dance and being each time rebuffed by centrifugal force because he has not got the feel of the center. The last stanza, in his craftsman's hands, gives the poem a structure, but I do not feel the presence of form. That's why the last line sounds portentous and hollow. He has not entered the dance. My guesses about the reasons for this have to do with my reading of the rest of Jarrell's work. He is *sympathizing* with Oedipus and that is a characteristic stance of his poems, to be slightly outside the process sympathizing with someone else, soldiers in the early work, lonely women in the later work. In this poem, he has found an interesting perception, an important perception, but the stance has thrown him off himself. He has not found for himself the form of being in the idea.

Criticism is not especially alert to this matter. It talks about a poet's ideas or themes or imagery and so it treats all the poems of Stevens or Williams equally when they are not equally poems. The result is the curiosity of a huge body of commentary which has very little to do with the art of poetry. And this spills over into university instruction—where, whether we like it or not, an awful lot of the reading and buying of poetry goes on. Students are trained to come away from that poem of Jarrell's thinking they have had an experience of poetry if they can write a four-page essay answering the question. "What has a woman's breasts, a lion's paws?" What gets lost is just the thing that makes art as humanly necessary as bread. Art is an activity of the spirit and when we lose track of what makes an art an art, we lose track of the spirit. It is the form of "Western Wind"—

> Western wind, when wilt thou blow,
> The small rain down can rain.
> Christ, if my love were in my arms
> And I in my bed again!

—that makes life seem lucky, and intense. It is the form of "The White Horse"—

The youth walks up to the white horse to put its halter on,
and the horse looks at him in silence.
They are so silent they are in another world.

—that makes it seem wonderful and solemn.

The connection between gazing and grazing in the Law-
rence poem brings us back to the connection between form,
being, and looking. The best account of this that I know is in
the 1805 *Prelude.* Wordsworth writes:

> Blessed the infant babe
> (For with my best conjectures I would trace
> The progress of our being) blest the babe,
> Nurs'd in his mother's arms, the babe who sleeps
> Upon his mother's breast, who, when his soul
> Claims manifest kindred with an earthly soul,
> Doth gather passion from his mother's eye!
> Such feelings pass into his torpid life
> Like an awakening breeze, and hence his mind
> Even in the first trial of its powers
> Is prompt and watchful, eager to combine
> In one appearance, all the elements
> And parts of the same object, else detached
> And loth to coalesce.

Loth to coalesce. The phrase seems to speak particularly to the
twentieth century, to our experience of fragmentation, of
making form against all odds. It explains something of Picas-
so's cubist nudes which come to form in the insistence of some
previous and violent dismemberment; it glosses Bergman's
borrowings from Picasso in the haunting visualizations of
films like *Persona* and the savage dismemberments of Sylvia
Plath, the strange rachitic birds Charles Simic is likely to see
arising from the shape of a fork. We have been obsessed with
the difficulty of form, of any coherent sense of being, so one
of the values of this passage is that it takes us back to a source:

> Thus, day by day,
> Subjected to the discipline of love,
> His organs and recipient faculties
> Are quickened, are more vigorous, his mind spreads
> Tenacious of the forms which it receives,
> In one beloved presence, nay and more,
> In that most apprehensive habitude

And those sensations which have been derived
From this beloved presence, there exists
A virtue which irradiates and exalts
All objects through all intercourse of sense.
No outcast he, bewilder'd and depressed;
Along his infant veins are interfused
The gravitation and the filial bond
Of nature, that connects him with the world.
Emphatically, such a being lives,
An inmate of this *active* universe . . .

It is this forming, this coming into existence of imagination as a shaping power, that "irradiates and exalts all being" and makes the forms of nature both an echo of that experience and a clue to the larger rhythms of a possible order in which the human mind shares or which it can make. This is also the force of that passage, early in the *Cantos,* when Pound reaches back through a scrap of Chaucer to the origins of poetry in European consciousness:

Betuene Aprile and Merche
    with sap new in the bough
With plum flowers above them
    with almond on the black bough
With jasmine and olive leaf
To the beat of the measure
From star up to the half-dark
From half-dark to half-dark
    Unceasing the measure
Flank by flank on the headland
    with the Goddess' eyes to seaward
By Circeo, by Terracina, with the stone eyes
    white toward the sea
With one measure, unceasing:
    "Fac deum!" "Est factus."
Ver novum!
  ver novum!
Thus made the spring. . . .

And I might just as well summon Stevens on "our old dependency of day and night," on the power of the knowledge that the world is out there:

> Deer walk upon our mountains, and the quail
> Whistle about us their spontaneous cries;
> Sweet berries ripen in the wilderness . . .

It amazes me, the way Wordsworth has come to it:

> From nature largely he receives; nor so
> Is satisfied, but largely gives again,
> For feeling has to him imparted strength,
> And powerful in all sentiments of grief,
> Of exultation, fear and joy, his mind,
> Even as the agent of the one great mind,
> Creates, creator and receiver both,
> Working but in alliance with the works
> Which it beholds—Such, verily, is the first
> Poetic spirit of our human life . . .

though I have none of this assurance, either about the sources of the order of nature or about the absolute continuity between that first nurturing and the form-making activity of the mind. It seems to me, rather, that we make our forms because there is no absolute continuity, because those first assurances are broken. The mind, in the act of recovery, creates.

Louise Glück's "To My Mother" explores this territory and it registers a shock that Wordsworth doesn't:

> It was better when we were
> together in one body.
> Thirty years. Screened
> through the green glass
> of your eye, moonlight
> filtered into my bones
> as we lay
> in the big bed, in the dark,
> waiting for my father.
> Thirty years. He closed
> your eyelids with
> two kisses. And then spring
> came and withdrew from me
> the absolute
> knowledge of the unborn,
> leaving the brick stoop
> where you stand, shading

your eyes, but it is
night, the moon
is stationed in the beech tree
round and white among
the small tin markers of the stars:
Thirty years. A marsh
grows up around the house.
Schools of spores circulate
behind the shades, drift through
gauze flutterings of vegetation.

The power of this poem has to do with the intensity of the
sense of loss, the breaking of myth. The fabulous mother has
become an ordinary woman on a brick stoop, squinting into
the sun. And the assurance of natural process breaks down:
day becomes night, the moon is stationed in the beech, the
stars are tin. There is a strange veering definiteness to the
syntax which moves us from a world of romance to a lost
Chagall-like memory of it. The repeated phrase does not have
the magic of recurrence; it is spoken with a kind of wonder,
but it has the relentlessness of time, of the ways in which time
excludes our own lives and deaths from the magic of recur-
rence. "It is spring!" she says, in another poem, "We are going
to die!" But already something else is at work in the move-
ment; the deliberate writing and the articulation of the syntax
are making a form. When we come to the phrase, "A marsh
grows up around the house," we feel both house and marsh,
the formed and the unformed thing, with equal intensity. In
the title of the book from which the poem comes, the nouns
have been reversed to make an aesthetic commitment: *The
House on Marshland*. The marsh, the shifting ground, gives the
image a terrible pathos. This is a poem about growing up and
it is the marsh, not the house, that grows up. *The mind creates*,
Wordsworth says. The final image is a creation. It makes a
form from all the pathos of loss and dispersal. Spores, gauze
curtains, window, the vegetable world beyond the window are
gathered into a seeing, into the one body of the poem.

One body: it's an illuminating metaphor, and so is the
house, the human indwelling which art makes possible when
it makes forms the imagination can inhabit. I don't think we
have thought about the issue very well. What passes for dis-
cussion of it among younger poets has been an orgy of self-
congratulation because they are not writing metrical poems.

A marginal achievement, since many of us, not having worked at it, couldn't write them competently if we wanted to. The nature of the music of poetry has become an open question and music, the rhythm of poetry, is crucial to its form. Thinking about poetic form has also been complicated by the way we use the word. We speak of the sonnet as "a form," when no two sonnets, however similar their structures, have the same form.

The form of a poem exists in the relation between its music and its seeing; form is not the number or kind of restrictions, conscious or unconscious, many or few, with which a piece of writing begins. A sonnet imposes one set of restrictions and a poem by Robert Creeley with relatively short lines and three- or four-line stanzas imposes another. There are always restrictions because, as Creeley says, quoting Pound, "Verse consists of a constant and a variant." That is, the music of the poem as it develops imposes its own restrictions. That is how it comes to form. When Robert Duncan, in "A Poem Beginning with a Line from Pindar," comes upon all those trochees and dactyls in the names of the presidents—

> Hoover, Roosevelt, Truman, Eisenhower—
> where among these does the power reside
> that moves the heart? What flower of the nation
> bride-sweet broke to the whole rapture?
> Hoover, Coolidge, Harding, Wilson
> hear the factories of human misery turning out commodities

—he has to go with it and then find his way out of that music, which he does, beautifully:

> Garfield, Hayes, Grant, Johnson
> dwell in the roots of the heart's rancor
> How sad "amid lanes and through old woods"
> echoes Whitman's love for Lincoln!

This is a matter of bodily rhythm and the mind's hunger for intelligible recurrence. It applies equally to all verbal music.

I don't think we are in a position yet to understand the reaction against metrical poetry that began in the middle of the nineteenth century. It's an astonishing psychological fact, as if a huge underpinning in the order of things had given way and, where men had heard the power of incantatory repetition before, they now heard its monotony. Or worse. Frost's rhythms use meter in a way that is full of dark, uneasy irony:

> And I keep hearing from the cellar bin
> The rumbling sound
> Of load on load of apples coming in.

And irony, the stresses falling like chains clanking, is very often Robert Lowell's way with meter:

> Our fathers made their world with sticks and stones
> And fenced their gardens with the red man's bones.

The writing seems to accuse not only the fathers but the culture that produced meter and rhyme.

It has always interested me that, if you define meter as the constant, and the rhythmic play of different sounds through meter as the variant, then meter itself can never be heard. Every embodiment is a variation on the meter. One-TWO is a rhythmic variant on the pure iamb and three-FOUR is another. The pure iamb in fact can't be rendered; it only exists as a felt principle of order, beneath all possible embodiments, in the mind of the listener. It exists in silence, is invisible, unspeakable. An imagination of order. A music of the spheres.

Which is how the Renaissance conceived it. All through the Elizabethan period the dance of the order of things is associated with music. And this was the period of the other momentous event in the history of the sound of English-language poetry, the invention of the printing press. In the course of about a hundred years, the printing press tore the lyric poem away from music and left the poet with the sound of his own voice. I think that's why, in the freshness of those writers, in the satires of Wyatt, for example—

> My mother's maids when they do sew and spin,
> They sing a song made of the fieldish mouse ...

or in a prayer in Ben Jonson—

> Good and great God, can I not think on thee,
> But it must straight my melancholy be ...

—meter has the authority of a profound formal order. I think the human voice without music required it; otherwise it was just individual noise in the universe.

Herrick is a fascinating figure in this way. He seems to be a maker of Elizabethan songs, but really he was living by himself fifty years past that time in a country priory in Devonshire, making that music out of his own head. The public occasions of Campion—

> When to her lute Corinna sings

—have become a private music in the mind, a small imagined ordering dance of things. Meter has replaced the lute and become a way of imagining experience, a private artistic vision. It has become form:

> Whenas in silks my Julia goes,
> Then, then, methinks . . .

And meanwhile in London, Denham and Waller were tuning up the new, print-conscious and social sounds of the heroic couplet.

Another clue is the response to Wordsworth's poetry. When he sent one of his books to Charles James Fox, the leader of the liberal faction in Parliament, Fox wrote him a note saying he loved "Goody Blake and Harry Gill" but that he didn't like "Michael" and "The Brothers" because he felt "blank verse inappropriate for such simple subjects." You could write about working people in ballad meters, but not in the lofty riverrun sound of blank verse. That was what bothered people about those poems. They democratized the imagination of spiritual order inside meter.

That's why it's a short leap from Wordsworth to Whitman—or one of the reasons why. It is why free verse appears as part of a consciously democratic poetic program. As long as the feudal class system was a series of mutual obligations, a viable economy, it seemed a natural principle of order. By the time of the French revolution, it had stopped working and society seemed class-ridden. So meter seemed class-ridden. Only it took someone as stubborn as Wordsworth to demonstrate it by introducing the Cumberland beggar to his readers in the spiritual dress of blank verse:

In the sun,
Upon the second step of that small pile,
Surrounded by those wild unpeopled hills,
He sat, and ate his food in solitude:
And ever, scattered from his palsied hands,
That, still attempting to prevent the waste,
Was baffled still, the crumbs in little showers
Fell on the ground; and the small mountain birds,
Not venturing yet to peck the destined meal,
Approached within the length of half his staff.

Once this gesture, or the swollen ankles of a shepherd, was included in the music of the spheres, that music had ceased to have the same function and the ear was prepared for the explosion of "Crossing Brooklyn Ferry":

I too lived, Brooklyn of ample hills was mine,
I too walked the streets of Manhattan Island, and
    bathed in the waters around it,
I too felt the curious abrupt questionings stir
    within me,
In my walks home late at night or as I lay in my
    bed they came upon me,
I too had been struck from the float held forever
    in solution,
I too received identity by my body

And after this moment in the history of the race, in the history of the race's relation to the magic of language, the godhead was scattered and we were its fragments.

So Frost was wrong to say that free verse was like playing tennis without a net. The net was the insistence of the iamb. A lot of William Carlos Williams's individual perceptions are a form of iambic music, but he has rearranged them so that the eye breaks the iambic habit. The phrase—"a dust of snow in the wheeltracks"—becomes

a dust of
snow in
the wheeltracks

and people must have felt: "yes, that is what it is like; not one-TWO, one-TWO. A dust of / snow in / the wheeltracks. That is how perception is. It is that light and quick." The effect depends largely on traditional expectation. The reader had to be able to hear what he was not hearing.

That's probably why Eliot and Pound were so alarmed when Amy Lowell moved in on imagism. Pound records the moment in one of his essays: "At a particular date in a particular room, two authors, neither engaged in picking one another's pocket, decided that the dilution of *vers libre,* Amygism, Lee Masterism, general floppiness, had gone too far and that some countercurrent must be set going. Parallel situation centuries ago in China. Remedy prescribed *Emaux et Camées.* (or the Bay State Hymnbook). Rhyme and regular strophes. Results: poems in Mr. Eliot's *second* volume . . . also 'H. S. Mauberly.' Divergence later."

It does seem to be the case that the power of free verse has had something to do with its revolt against some alternative formal principle that feels fictitious. That was certainly part of the excitement of first reading Creeley and Ginsberg, Duncan and Dorn. They had come back, passionately, to the task of discovering forms of perception. In what Gary Snyder describes as "the spiritual loneliness of the nineteen-fifties," there were all these voices finding their way. And a decade later, when I read them, they still had that intensity.

Now, I think, free verse has lost its edge, become neutral, the given instument. An analogy occurs to me. Maybe it is a little farfetched. I'm thinking of balloon frame construction in housing. According to Gideon, it was invented by a man named George Washington Snow in the 1850s and 1860s, about the same time as *Leaves of Grass.* "In America materials were plentiful and skilled labor scarce; in Europe skilled labor was plentiful and materials scarce. It is this difference which accounts for the differences in the structure of American and European industry from the fifties on." The principle of the balloon frame was simply to replace the ancient method of mortise and tenon—heavy framing timbers carved at the joints so that they locked heavily together—with construction of a frame by using thin studs and nails. It made possible a light, quick, elegant construction with great formal variability and suppleness. For better or worse. "If it had not been for the balloon frame, Chicago and San Francisco could never have arisen, as they did, from little villages to great cities in a single year." The balloon frame, the clapboard house and the Windsor chair. American forms, and *Leaves of Grass* which abandoned the mortise and tenon of meter and rhyme. Suburban tracts and the proliferation of poetry magazines. The difference between a democratic society and a consumer society.

Stanley Plumly has written a very shrewd essay in which he argues that, in contemporary verse, tone has become important in the way that it is important in the dramatic monologues of Browning. Only the poems aren't dramatic monologues, they are spoken by the poets out of their own lives. That is, instead of being an instrument to establish person, tone has become an instrument to establish personality. And the establishment of distinctions of personality by peripheral means is just what consumer society is about. Instead of real differences emanating from the life of the spirit, we are offered specious symbols of it, fantasies of our separateness by way of brands of cigarettes, jogging shoes, exotic food. Once free verse has become neutral, there must be an enormous impulse to use it in this way, to establish tone rather than to make form. Because it has no specific character, we make a character in it. And metrical poetry is used in the same way. When it is strong, it becomes, as it did for Eliot and Pound in the twenties, a personal reaction against cultural formlessness. When it is graceful and elegant, it becomes, as it was in Herrick, a private fiction of civility with no particular relation to the actual social life we live.

Dick Higgins

Seen, Heard, and Understood
1972

I want to defend literature. It's a poor man's art. You can think, even when you can't feel comfortable among the cigarred princes and the knockkneed venerables in miniskirts that run our visual art scene. You can write when you can't afford the fancy pantsy materials to make art-canvas, silk screens and the right kind of paint. You reach people who can't afford to hang De Koonings, Oldenburgs or Sol Lewitts. It's not "by whom ye know shall ye be judged," nowadays, but the intensification of it: "by whom ye know shall ye be hung." The plastic arts are corrupt: that's a commonplace and idiots try to make political capital—or just plain capital—by saying it. But it's come to be that art = money, at least if it's "fine" art. Money is fashionable, therefore art is fashionable, and moves by this or that "look" just like dress design. Whatever happened to the "Gainsborough Look" of the early sixties in women's clothes? And whatever happened to the Abstract Impressionists? It is fashionable to look at things. It is not fashionable to understand them, because that requires the art of thought, which is literature.

Artists and composers are usually poor until they are no longer poor, that is, until they are successful. At least for a season or so. After that they can always un-teach at this or that university, and confuse a sufficient number of students to supply the country with personnel for useless ferment and vacuous bitterness. Poets are never successful in $$$, while art students make wretched photo-offset cameramen, for all their future earning capacity. Poets are what they will, are free to be trained for anything. "Composers"—those trained for the calling—seldom are masters of their trade, however craftsmanly they may be. Composers of the Higher Art can't grind out rock 'n' roll arrangements, usually, because they tell themselves it isn't serious. In college, Stock-

hausen played in a jazz band, but he once wrote to Henry
Flynt that jazz wasn't serious music in the Western sense. Still,
orchestras have to be supported: bread and circuses for the
intelligentsia. But poets are people and can often run
bulldozers. They make good pop musicians too.

Less than 1% of all money given for the arts in the USA is
given for literature in any way. It goes to museums, to display
the past or present fashions. Quite often it goes to flash plastic
artists of one sort or another—especially if they'd like to
spend a year in Rome or Florence or Paris, or some other
living mortuary. It goes to dancers. Dancers are poorer than
plastic artists, richer than composers, but much richer than
writers or poets. Dance is harmless, therefore harmless to
"Our Society." Of course, that's in practice, not in theory. An
attitude of universal dancing and choreography would be
very revolutionary, but dancers would probably call it "too
literary" and dismiss it. The best of new dance is, in fact,
dismissed—Meredith Monk and Kenneth King—as too liter-
ary. Somehow unprofessional. Not sufficiently elegant (read
"remote") to be on a safely high plane. The money goes to
theaters. Not street theaters (too literary, again)—but to pro-
vide the 1600 square feet of wall-to-wall, one-inch-deep pile
carpeting needed by the Beaumont Theater in New York for
their production of *Twelfth Night,* one of my favorite of
sixteenth-century plays. This is not supporting choreographed
literature: it is supporting the tuxedo-rental industry. The
best *Twelfth Night* productions may well happen in sum-
mer camps, high schools in Harlem or in Malibu Beach, and
there is some crazy summer theater in Kimberley Heights
where a bunch of skilled pros just happen to love that play.
You cannot bribe a cast to love Shakespeare, and all the train-
ing of horses never made a performance of *Twelfth Night*
convincing with an all-equine cast. Funny, yes: meaningful,
no. Traditional, illusionistic theater depends on a suspension
of disbelief, and we're a bit more skeptical than the medieval
audiences to whom Ham the Barber could also be Joseph the
Father. If we want illusion at all, we want the illusion to be in
its own spirit and style, and not to seem somehow like wearing
used clothing to a wedding.

Music is in the same fuss. The stage has been made deadly by
its mis-support. Orchestras seem like anachronous mechani-

cal toys, like the puppets that whirl around the clock at the zoo when it's time to feed the animals. Hard to feel modern about orchestras. It would be beautiful if a hundred people could come together to make music, naturally and simply, and it really wouldn't matter what they chose to play. But one is conscious of the over-structured nature of it all. A hundred years ago, Tchaikovsky (on tour in the USA) conducted a thousand musicians in "Yankee Doodle" as an encore. No doubt the aesthetes of the age deplored this, but I'd like to have heard it. Take the freedom out of something, and merely replace it with money, and you get something quite lifeless. Why not invent an Alfred Orch (1585?–1642) after whom the "Orchestra" might have been named? The best American performance of an Earle Brown, ever-so-modern orchestral score was done with an improvised, for-the-occasion ensemble at the Living Theater in 1961. Put him in tails in front of a thoroughly skilled ensemble in a huge concert hall, and you can't hear his structure at all, in spite of his concern about the acoustics, answering of voices, "bumping" in the concept of the score, etc. Not to mention the social element—the musicians seem so darned uncomfortable in their 1890s costumes. Maybe one could alleviate the problem by putting the entire New York Philharmonic in the nude for Earl Brown's piece, but it would still seem somehow anachronistic, I think.

John Cage says his problems are social, not musical: he's right.

The best of art (visual and plastic, I mean) is really about seeing, not about looking at. Music is about hearing, not about listening to. And in the absence of a pure brain wave communication, literature is about understanding, not about mere words, which are a historically derived set—one per language—of materials which follow but are not necessarily in one-to-one correspondence with a similar set of rules called "grammar"—one per language—which stand for the ideas that are the real fundamental of understanding. Play with words, play with grammar, it's still not literature. Play with the look or the sound of words—it's only through those senses that words can be perceived after all—and you still don't have literature. It's only when you have a real interplay between understanding and the mechanical means—words, grammar, heard and seen elements—that literature can begin. Scrap one or another element: it doesn't matter. John Cage is down on grammar: okay. Hanns Helms makes "words" beside the point by writing in six languages at once: okay. Jackson Mac Low tests language poetically by playing with words apart from grammar (in *Stanzas for Iris Lezak*) and in doing so creates a particularly musical poetry. Okay. I use chunks of words grammatically and make an ideational poetry (in *A Book About Love & War & Death*). Okay, though I don't think all work ought to be written that way: this essay isn't for instance. And the concrete poets make words visual: okay. We can be for that too. There's no contradiction, there's value in a thing simply being what is most valuable for it to be. A work determines its own needs.

But look: these kinds of literature include a lot of what's most useful in the plastic arts and in music. In fact, nowadays, everything points to the need for literature because it has been so repressed and de-emphasized by the last half century. Not that good things haven't happened in the vacuum. They have. There's no point in knocking Mallarmé, Arp, Eluard, Brecht, Stramm, Ringelnatz, Rühm, Pound, W. C. Williams, Stein and the more recent people. Literature is a poor man's art: many poor people leave their imprint on history and on our minds, without demanding that we call them by name. In fact, the mere names would ring as hollow as old logs if we misunderstood these writers' work by simply saying what they were about, without having read it, experienced it for ourselves and evolved our own understanding of it. To do this requires placing each work we have come to understand in a matrix of similar experience: and that isn't easy.

Literature and literary understanding isn't something we can do without difficulty in our time. The powers that be, political and social and economic—have seen to that. But any aesthetic communication implies literature: art that is merely looked at is hollow, music that is merely listened to is mood stuff at best. Musical and visual ideas scarcely exist without understanding, except for their cigarships and their ritzy fritzy knocknées.

To summarize, it's not just a matter of words, this literature. You can paint a word, or sculpt it, compose it resonantly as a musician or simply find it and record it: it'll still be raw. But this is merely to use a material incompletely. Fashion be damned (and it's fashion that's afraid of thought), literature is where the thinking artist ends up if he keeps true to his own inner resonances. I'd rather be a mouse in an impoverished mansion than a prince in a velvet bunghole. Literature is the art of thought, call it the lowest common denominator or the highest acting principle: without it, the other arts are trivial.

Towards an Allusive Referential
1977

One of the glories of writing in North American English is that almost every other word can become some other part of speech from what we are accustomed to, a capability which has lessened in most other European languages since the baroque. For instance, "telephone" can be used for "to telephone" or even for "telephone" man. This, perhaps, reflects the delight in multiple identities so typical of our brighter brothers and sisters, and so frightening to the one-track professionals of a generation ago with their Holy Terror of ambiguity. Our identities pun and partake of all the richness of our lives—and this holds true even when we expect it least, both in life and art and verbal art. For instance, without much self-conscious thought, I titled a string of poems I had caught in my mental pond, "deep summer together poem." I thought of the overall concept, not of the individual words. In my head they were fused. But now, looking at my title, I ask myself, does "deep" go with "summer"? Or "together"? Or "poem"? Which modifies which?

Perhaps the units fuse. If so, haven't we transcended the Word and come to the transform, in the Chomskyan sense, as the basic unit of verbal art? The word was sacred to Plato and to the Gnostics—yet it seems so hierarchic, ultimately. If the word is one thing only, then isn't it almost unique in the real world? Words might be taken as, rather, radicals with great polyvalence, capable of entering into a vast variety of identities which are, presumably, difficult to explain hierarchically—in the system, say, of the "tree diagrams" that the old-timers used for diagraming sentences—and yet, as flexible radicals their very ambiguity evokes new meaning. To cite an interchange noted by David Antin, the young black man flirts with the young black woman:

"Mama, you sho is fine!"

And she discourages him with:

"That ain' no way to talk to your mother."

Here dialect is mixed with literate speech, puns are fused with meaning, and, all in all, an element of allusive referential is present which is the very essence of imaginative verbal art.

Allusive referential? What a clumsy phrase! Yet better that than load down our critical tool chest with yet another artificial coinage from Greek or Latin, each user of which must write off to Merriam-Webster to be sure he goes on record as the first user.

What I have in mind is, simply, displacement from the expected over the threshold into the unexpected, not for the sake of novelty, but in order to refer to some additional and relevant element which might otherwise be unevocable. The intuitive leap requires the intuition, and making the reader or listener's intuition effective can be one of the uses of verbal art. One function of literature is that it develops the reader's abilities in his gestalt formation throughout his intellectual experience.

Naturally, in a piece of verbal art, any symbol is in some degree an allusive referential: the semioticians have explored this enough for me not to have to go into this to any great degree. But the psychology of the deliberate use of the allusive referential has not been so well explored.

What it means in art psychology is that: 1) I think *a*. Let us call *a* my "object." 2) As artist, I observe that though I try to think *a* simply, I find that my mind moves on to *b*. I could fight this and insist upon mentioning *a* only. This would cause anxiety, of course, but that might have its uses. However, instead I accept the displacement. *B* now becomes the new object, which I will call a "referential." 3) But I find that when I refer to *b* in my original context, that the sense of *a,* if the intuition has been a close one, remains. *B* is justified by its heightening of the experience of *a*—though a displacement, the allusion (or movement from *a* to *b*) has created a vivid effect in my mind. 4) The reader need not go through the beginning of the process. The reader simply reads *b* and feels *a* (ideally).

Now, this works not merely with the contrast between poetic and purely informational language. I could, here, take some line of Keats and paraphrase it in burocratese: very funny. But here the concept of an allusive referential begins to pay off. Without it, I would have to argue that the poetic language is an imaginative experience for imagination's sake—and then, perhaps, I would go on and say that the meaning of a poem is an unimportant part of it. Or, as that purist of purists, Harold Bloom, puts it, "The meaning of a poem is a poem" (which I object to also because then the critic, as explicator of that meaning, becomes a poet—which is misleading, since we can use both critics and poets separately).

But given an allusive referential, what actually happens is that the meaning is experienced powerfully, particularly when the *b* is mentally matched with the *a* and the intuitive displacement becomes conscious. Discourse is transcended by the displacement.

The poet, then, witnesses life in language: his or her displacement of it is a critique. And the reader or critic's understanding of the poem—and, hopefully, if the reader or critic is active and not passive about these things—integrates the poet's critique with the reader's experience. There is no right or wrong here, though some interpretations may be richer in implications than others. The situation is inherently non-dualistic. It has position and structure, but content and moral values, emotionally and intellectually, develop at a later stage.

As an anglophone, I read a line from Rimbaud's "Mémoire":

Regrets des bras épais et jeunes d'herbe pure!

I translate it—

Regrets of arms thick and young of pure grass!

Perhaps I do not understand. I translate by sound—

The brass regrets in spades, and the Johnnies ate pure herbs!

And the two verbal experiences become fused. I know the meaning of all the words in the French, but find I am less interested in Rimbaud's *a*, his consciously meant object, than in either of my own two intuitive displacements, in both of which I experience complexes of allusive referential. Shall I blame Rimbaud for being unclear? Not at all—I know he is a great poet because I feel these allusive referentials so vividly. Clarity is merely one vivid possibility. To make the work an assemblage of potential meaning is another one. Aleatoric poetry, such as that of John Cage or Jackson Mac Low or, sometimes, myself (and others) requires only an active reader, capable of bringing his or her life experiences to the work: the allusive referential will take care of the rest. A note here might be relevant, though. Mac Low and Cage use the word as the language unit, and they apply chance to it, scrambling it. Others of us find the word rather an arbitrary unit, and try to work with transforms (phrases): when we apply chance to those, we get aleatoric ideas which displace as allusive referentials in larger chunks. There are, then, at least these two basic styles within aleatoric poetry.

But the former sort of aleatoric poetry requires minimal allusive referential for the poet, though maximal for the reader, while the latter sort requires allusive referential for both.

Still, in the present avant-garde, there are three other areas of poetry whose effect, when the poems really work well, are explainable through the allusive referential process—and it is a process, of course, not a principle. I have in mind permutation poetry, concrete poetry, and sound poetry.

Permutation poetry is, at its simplest, poetry that consists of a list (which may or may not have semantic meaning), and the elements of that list are then scrambled. For instance, Brion Gysin's "Junk is no good, baby"—

> no junk is good baby
> good junk is no baby

—etc., just to choose a couple of lines at random. It is a style that has been with us a long time: in fact, in Germany, such pieces are known as "Proteus poems" after a poem by Julius Caesar Scaliger called "Proteus" and published in 1551. The genre has been popular at various times, in German, for instance, in the works of the baroque poets Christian Schade and Quirinus Kühlmann. As always, since art expresses an unchanging human nature, our avant-garde arts have their analogues in the past. Anyway, permutation poetry, whether the components are scrambled aleatorically or systematically (and both possibilities exist) get their effect from the reader's matching of the *b* with the *a* through the allusive referential. The effect may be humorous or serious or, in Kühlmann's case, even ecstatic. All depends on the nature of the object communication, the *a,* and the reader's feelings associated with the displacement to *b.*

Similarly, concrete poetry in its earlier analogues (pattern poems, *carmina figurata,* etc.) got a bad press from critics such as Joseph Addison who minimized the importance of the displacement and stressed the one-track precision of *a* and its expression: for them visual poetries were "false wit." However, when we see a text move into an intermedium between verbal and visual art, and when we feel this displacement as an enrichment of our conceptual experience, we can appreciate the work that has been achieved, and we experience delight (as in the case of Lewis Carroll's "Tail of a Mouse") or even something more profound and less rationally explicable, as in the case of Apollinaire's best *calligrammes* or Ian Hamilton Finlay's "the horizon of holland."

Similarly, sound poetry is an intermedium between verbal art and musical composition, and its roots run from ancient religious formulas through folk nonsemantic passages (from the Navaho Indian "horse songs" to the "nonsense" choruses of English folk songs), through the dada poems of Ball and Hausmann, and into the intuitive poems of Bernard Heidsieck or the technological and electronic manipulative sound poems of Bengt Emil Johnson or Henri Chopin. We feel the displacement move from the traditional media of word or music into the midground which, though essentially simply a new medium (all intermedia become media), can also be the new object, *a*, which is indicated by the allusive referential: this is true of most etude pieces, where the technical aspect is a major part of the artist's intention. The sound in either case becomes a part of the referential, whatever the nature of the actual allusion.

Finally, any language can be part of the allusive referential when it is the language which is being emphasized: and this is notably true, again, in works where the style of the language is more what the artist is concerned with than what he or she is saying in that language. This is true of Joyce's *Finnegans Wake* (at least of some passages of it), of Gertrude Stein's "calligraphic" style texts or the novel *Lucy Church Amiably,* of my own *Book About Love & War & Death,* of Richard Kostelanetz's numerical constructions, etc. All artistic language is, then, a metaphor for experience and an allusive referential for it: strange that most of the semioticians (except for Max Bense and Paul Bouissac) stay so resolutely in their academic closets. And only at great peril can a verbal artist today, when our hunger for the deepened experience that results from an allusive referential is so great—perhaps as an antidote to alienation, perhaps from our need for what the anthropologist Victor Turner calls the "liminal" experiences— only at great peril can an artist use the bland and one-track language of the pretechnological age. Madison Avenue hasn't realized that, but, then, their art is sales, not literature, and they are ciphers in the service of inertia. Most of our academics have only sensed it in the shrinkage of numbers of their literature students and the dropping out of the most gifted ones. They still explain it in terms of the present generation being too pragmatic and antihumanist, since the real educational crisis is several years ahead of us, when the gap between what is thought and written and what is taught will be even more pronounced than it is now.

Finally, the question arises does anything comparable to the allusive referential process exist in the other arts, or is it uniquely a component of the verbal/ideational gestalt formation process. I think it does, though more obviously in the visual arts, where it is a major part of the artist's "vision," than in music. In visual art we see it not only in visual puns and the overall "distortions" which a painter gives us in comparison to what he sees, but it exists also in such places as minimal art works. Obviously not all minimal art works have a powerful impact, any more than all of any other art works do. But when, for instance, George Brecht pastes relief letters "red" on a panel, and paints the letters and panels alike green, it seems to me that the curiously haunting effect that one gets can only be explained in terms of an allusive referential. This is true of a good many other recent art works, especially those of the fluxus movement where, frequently, objects are used in contexts that are utterly different and opposed to their normal ones.

In music the allusive referential is harder to observe. Perhaps it could be argued that in traditional music it is present in the interplay between the expected resolution of harmonies and where, in fact, they go. Voice leading could involve displacement, in other words. But I think it is more evident in concept music and those musics which, in a sense, revive some of the principles of the *Musica speculativa* of Boethius and the ancients—music which, as in the works of John Cage, are either social models or social paradigms, or are conceptual models of reality, in which each musical event happens in a way analogous to how events happen in reality as Cage sees it. The artist (Cage) sees the world and makes each element of his work harmonious with it, concrete with it as opposed to . discrete. The listener, then, hears the sounds or perceives the situations inherent in the performance (scandals, rioting on the part of the audience, graciousness on the part of this or that musician—all these are part of the overall situation), and feels a solidarity between the work and his or her life, thus experiencing an allusive referential.

In theater—in art performances, happenings, group theater improvisations, or group compositions—the situation would be more or less analogous to the situation in music: same in dance. Perhaps in video art and cinema also—where the prevalence of structuralist criticism has tended to reduce the viewer's sensitivity to the obvious and the situational levels which are, equally, a part of the arts.

Enough of this. The tool is now offered to those who want it. It remains to be done to quantitivize its use, classify the variety of its functions, and use it as a component of overall aesthetics and art psychology on the one hand, and to use it to explain the impact and nature of current art works (especially, though it also has uses for older art works too), works of literature and in other media as well.

John Hollander

Uncommonplaces
1976–77

The Way We Walk Now

It was not that there were only the old ways of going from one
chamber to another: we had learned to imitate the noble
walk of those who had built, and dwelt in, the Great Palaces,
moving gravely through the interconnecting rooms; aware
of the painted ceilings and the import of the images there
for their lives, but never needing to look up at them; free
among their footmen; roaming their spaces and yet by no
means imprisoned in the fragile grandeur to which, in the
afternoon light, the rooms had fallen. We had learned
thereafter to mock that stiff way of walking, and after that,
to replace it with our own little dances and gallops; we
roller-skated from room to room, or occasionally bicycled.
Being confined by the layout was not the point, nor was it
what may or may not have happened to the houses—
whether they were indeed in ruins or merely in need
of repair. We had all gone away somewhere: off to
war, or to the city, or had shipped out for the East. And
those of us who returned, or who had stayed wherever it
was, came quite naturally to go about in the field, or among
the hills or through the streets. At first, it was almost with
memorized maps of the ways rooms opened off each other,
and of just what courts it was on which the various windows
gave; after that, with no recollected plan, but always
moving the better for having started out in one of the great
houses.

But then it almost ceased to matter where we were. What had
become necessary that we do by way of amble, or of hop,
skip, and jump, had so taken over power from mere place
that it generated the shapes of space through which it
moved, like a lost, late arrival at the start of a quest who had

178

set out nonetheless, dreaming each new region into which he wandered. Pictures of the old places still had a certain pathos; but they were not of ourselves or of our lives. The distance that had been put between us and the houses crammed full of chambers was utter, like that between the starry heavens above and the text below us, on the opened page.

In the high attic, all the old things had been accumulating meaning. Down in the basement were the pump, the furnace, the oldest masonry, the dark bottles of Pomerol settling slowly toward their prime. The difficulty of living in the house, in all the rooms between these, lay partially in trying to understand how moving up and down stairs between the floors was only a matter of changing levels, not of achieving any real elevation. There were forays made up to all the dusty hangings, the closed chests whose labels themselves, covered with dust, seemed to require labeling, the old pictures that looked somewhat grotesque as opposed to the remembered versions of them with which we were conversant downstairs. When there were descents down the cellar steps, it was because something was wrong, or something was being retrieved; we moved up into the spaces under the eaves, however, when there was nothing else to do. On the floors between, the significance of everything was one with its use.

Stepping out-of-doors—on an October afternoon, perhaps, whose brightness and touches of chill kept the edges of everything very clear—and looking back at the house from outside was something else again: anything it could lead us to conclude would be like a tale told by an abandoned house to some passer-by, who, if he retained any of the whole matter, would remember the interiors, the rooms, the passageways, which he had visualized from the story. He should have forgotten what the house looked like about which he had stopped on his walk to inquire. This is also somehow involved with the problems of living there.

The Sense of Place

That is what it had been about all along, he thought—not as
he drove along West Floral for a mile or so before turning
off, but as he sat, later, still quite alone, pushing the thick
water tumbler, the empty ash-receiver, the crumpled
napkin, the unused fork, around the smooth surface of the
restaurant table. They composed themselves, even without
the legends and roadways of the blue map on the paper
mat, into a nameless region in which the way things were
out of scale hardly mattered. It was as if, with an enormous
dumb wisdom, the parts of the place were aware of his
composing hand and maintaining gaze. And yet it was no
awareness of this on his part which made the place seem so
compelling, which made him feel as if it were beginning to
reach out to him, showing him what there was not,
otherwise, to be seen. The smudged tumbler contained
what had once been the element of water, for example; and
the crumbs in their uncharted constellations were ripe for
new mythologies, tales of the metamorphoses of ruin,
dissolution and dropping. It was with a surprising delight
that he began to realize all this. He would eagerly await the
next place that came to him.

The Boat

It took him away on some nights, its low engine running silently on even until he was too far out to hear it himself. It was as dark as the elements of water and night through which it moved. It was built for one: he was helmsman and supercargo both. It rode so low that he could roll into it from wherever it was tied up, and lie prone, his head perhaps turned to port. It responded surely and delicately to the controls, all accessible from where he lay. It headed out, but never back: he could not remember having come ashore from it. It was out of service for some years, after which he came to realize that his final ride on it, some night, would not be unaccompanied, that the boatman on that voyage would stay aboard, and that he himself would disembark at last.

A View of the Ruins

A short walk up from the hotel brings one to a place more
than half way up, from which the whole site is visible and
the different areas more discernible than from their midst.
Toward the left, an ancient grove will appear to throw
shadows more substantial looking than the trees
themselves. The cool colonnade seems even from such a
height to echo with long-departed footsteps; across from it,
the stoa may be perceived, with its rather boring porch. An
ancient upended tub (to the right of the stoa) is still
inhabited by dogs. Nearby was the tasteful garden. The
whole place was once busy with meaning and the bustle of
life, and when one looks over the whole matter from above,
the various areas can seem to have been plausibly engaged
with the living day. It is only from among the excavations
that the point seems lost—indeed, as the local saying goes,
"The overview, lest nothing be overlooked!" As to what
these ruins have to do with our lives, our problems and
headaches, our terrors and representations, each traveler
will of course determine for himself.

I was young then, of course, and could not know what it all
meant, even though delight and instruction ran joyfully
together along the boulevards, down the dark passages and
out onto the hot, bright, silent squares. Else I should have
recorded the whole journey in all of its continuing life; it
is not, you see, to be revived in any way, and can only
schematically—and perhaps thereby somehow horribly—be
reconstructed from the pictures. (I mean those accom-
plished water-color sketches that travelers would learn
to make, less like snapshots than like guarded time expo-
sures, souvenirs rather than recollections; but no matter.)
What I am left with even now is only the sense of moving
from place to place, savoring each one the while think-
ing of the portion of the journey that yet lay ahead. I
think now—but did not remember at the time—of my
childhood: at the movies on Saturday afternoons, the light
from the screen is reflected on my face, halfway through
the Western, feeling the pleasure of the moment and the
more prudently taken delight in the feeling of the
remainder of the film, the shorts, the gangster movie, all yet
to come, all still unconsumed.

And so it was with this: the high point of beginning at the
place of the clear pools, the color of the sky and of ancient
wisdom. Then the shells of the sounding beach; after that,
the trek inland to the speaking well of the oracle, below the
long, fragrant hill. Then I came, as one usually did, to the
promontory below which lay the long reach of the whole
land—the beautiful hills, the curving plain below that
reached down to the forested area and the hidden mound.
It was never purely the pleasure of the moment, nor the
anticipatory joy of what one would reach next and next
after that. It was the gradually unfolding nature of the
entirety that could make one take so seriously such a
conventional old trip, even though that unfolding would
only be perceived long afterward, when the entirety could
be completed because finally and fully imagined, rescued
from the cold gaol in which failing memory, in her filthy
smock, caressed and clucked over the fractured pieces.

It is because of what one has not found—a tan silo pushing up
beside the gambrel roof of a stone barn; a square, ruined
tower, Frankish, stone, backed on a pine grove and
overlooking the hot sand toward the calm blue water; a
dark, shingled cupola inspecting the wild, gray sea; an
unused wooden water tank atop a penthouse facing
westward beyond the park; an obsolete lighthouse near the
mouth of the bay—of what one has not been able to adapt,
that one has to build. One can plan and plan for years, but
in the end the finished structure will always remain
somewhat surprising: it will have to seem, always, to have
been come upon, in a middle distance, from a dark walk,
the wanderer enwrapped in his study of the failing light
and what arises within it. It will always have to keep its own
distant appearance: even as one looks out, after years of
keeping it, through one after another of the windows—
toward the fire of sunset, out across the noon fields,
into the cold rain dripping from bare boughs—there
must be at least one window, however narrow, out of which
one can see what one looks toward the tower for. One must
be amid all that—dark books shadowing the interior walls,
bright vineyards lying toward the river outside—amid what
has always been, and will be, beyond.

Richard Hugo

Assumptions
1973

Assumptions lie behind the work of all writers. The writer is unaware of most of them, and many of them are weird. Often the weirder the better. Words love the ridiculous areas of our minds. But silly or solid, assumptions are necessary elements in a successful base of writing operations. It is important that a poet not question his or her assumptions, at least not in the middle of composition. Finish the poem first, then worry, if you have to, about being right or sane.

Whenever I see a town that triggers whatever it is inside me that wants to write a poem, I assume at least one of the following:

The name of the town is significant and must appear in the title.

The inhabitants are natives and have lived there forever. I am the only stranger.

I have lived there all my life and should have left long ago but couldn't.

Although I am playing roles, on the surface I appear normal to the townspeople.

I am an outcast returned. Years ago the police told me to never come back but after all this time I assume that either I'll be forgiven or I will not be recognized.

At best, relationships are marginal. The inhabitants have little relation with each other and none with me.

The town is closely knit, and the community is pleasant. I am not a part of it but I am a happy observer.

A hermit lives on the outskirts in a one-room shack. He eats mostly fried potatoes. He spends hours looking at old faded photos. He has not spoken to anyone in years. Passing children often taunt him with songs and jokes.

Each Sunday, a little after 4 P.M., the sky turns a depressing gray and the air becomes chilly.

I run a hardware store and business is slow.

I run a bar and business is fair and constant.

I work in a warehouse on second shift. I am the only one in town on second shift.

I am the town humorist and people are glad to see me because they know I'll have some good new jokes and will tell them well.

The churches are always empty.

A few people attend church and the sermons are boring.

Everybody but me goes to church and the sermons are inspiring.

On Saturday nights everyone has fun but me. I sit home alone and listen to the radio. I wish I could join the others though I enjoy feeling left out.

All beautiful young girls move away right after high school and never return, or if they return, are rich and disdainful of those who stayed on.

I am on friendly terms with all couples, but because I live alone and have no girlfriend, I am of constant concern to them.

I am an eleven-year-old orphan.

I am eighty-nine and grumpy but with enormous presence and wisdom.

Terrible things once happened here and as a result the town became sad and humane.

The population does not vary.

The population decreases slightly each year.

The graveyard is carefully maintained and the dead are honored one day each year.

The graveyard is ignored and overrun with weeds.

No one dies, makes love, or ages.

No music.

Lots of excellent music coming from far off. People never see or know who is playing.

The farmers' market is alive with shoppers, good vegetables, and fruit. Prices are fixed. Bargaining is punishable by death.

The movie house is run by a kind man who lets children in free when no one is looking.

The movie house has been closed for years.

Once the town was booming but it fell on hard times around 1910.

At least one person is insane. He or she is accepted as part of the community.

The annual picnic is a failure. No one has a good time.

The annual picnic is a huge success but the only fun people have all year.

The grain elevator is silver.

The water tower is gray and the paint is peeling.

The mayor is so beloved and kind elections are no longer held.

The newspaper, a weekly, has an excellent gossip column but little or no news from outside.

No crime.

A series of brutal murders took place years ago. The murderer was never caught and is assumed still living in the town.

Years ago I was wealthy and lived in a New York penthouse. I hired about twenty chorus girls from Las Vegas to move in with me. For a year they played out all of my sexual fantasies. At the end of the year my money was gone. The chorus girls had no interest in me once I was poor and they returned to Las Vegas. I moved here where, destitute in a one-room shack on the edge of town, I am living my life out in shame.

One man is a social misfit. He is thrown out of bars and not allowed in church. He shuffles about the street unable to find work and is subjected to insults and disdainful remarks by beautiful girls. He tries to make friends but can't.

A man takes menial jobs for which he is paid very little. He is grateful for what little work he can find and is always cheerful. In any encounter with others he assumes he is wrong and backs down. His place in the town social structure is assured.

Two whores are kind to everyone but each other.

The only whore in town rejected a proposal of marriage years ago. The man left town and later became wealthy and famous in New York.

Cats are fed by a sympathetic but cranky old woman.

Dogs roam the streets.

The schoolhouse is a huge frame building with only one teacher who is old but never ages. She is a spinster and everyone in town was once in her class.

Until I found it, no outsider had ever seen it.

It is not on any map.

It is on a map but no roads to it are shown.

The next town is many miles away. It is much classier, has a nice new movie house, sparkling drive-ins, and better-looking girls. The locals in my town dream of moving to the next town but never do.

The town doctor is corrupt and incompetent.

The town druggist is an alcoholic.

The town was once supported by mining, commercial fishing, or farming. No one knows what supports it now.

One girl in the town is so ugly she knows she will never marry or have a lover. She lives in fantasies and involves herself in social activities of the church trying to keep alive her hopes which she secretly knows are futile.

Wind blows hard through the town except on Sunday afternoons a little after four when the air becomes still.

The air is still all week except on Sunday afternoons when the wind blows.

Once in a while an unlikely animal wanders into town, a grizzly bear or cougar or wolverine.

People stay married forever. No divorce. Widows and widowers never remarry.

No snow.

Lots of rain.

Birds never stop. They fly over, usually too high to be identified.

The grocer is kind. He gives candy to children. He is a widower and his children live in Paris and never write.

People who hated it and left long ago are wealthy and living in South America.

Wild sexual relationships. A lot of adultery to ward off boredom.

The jail is always empty.

There is one prisoner in jail, always the same prisoner. No one is certain why he is there. He doesn't want to get out. People have forgotten his name.

Young men are filled with hate and often fight.

I am welcome in bars. People are happy to see me and buy me drinks.

As far as one can see, the surrounding country is uninhabited.

The ballpark is poorly maintained and only a few people attend the games.

The ballpark is well kept and the entire town supports the team.

The team is in last place every year.

People sit a lot on their porches.

There is always a body of water, a sea just out of sight beyond the hill or a river running through the town. Outside of town a few miles is a lake that has been the scene of both romance and violence.

David Ignatow

The Biggest Bomb
An Impressionistic Essay
1955

It's best to write about things close to one's heart, if one wishes to write accurately. At the very least, the reader derives a sense of urgency and striving for honesty and understanding, even if, in the end, he finds he does not agree with the facts or interpretation of them. He knows, however, that he is being treated with respect as a person by a writer who desires as much in return. Between them they lay a basis for amity and peace, peace in its purest form, in which compassion decides everything.

I despair of myself. I walk around as with a hood over my head, to cloak my identity. Constantly I guard against lifting the hood to laugh. What am I hiding from, I ask, or closer yet, what needs to be shielded from me? Am I a menace in a land of abundant forests, great fertile plains, large calm lakes filled with fish—a country that needs simply to press buttons to feed and clothe itself and to pour its surplus into other hands that are tense with need? How am I a menace, I who simply walk the streets beneath the tallest buildings in the world, in the vicinity of the most powerful and liberal banks in history? I deal with words, I give myself the pleasure of being free with my feelings, my thoughts. I allow them to fall into any shape or color they desire in words. I surround myself with a world that is in my head and nowhere else, and that cannot take possession of anyone without the person's consent. According to our constitution, this is the pure freedom we desire for one another; but emerging from my house to step out into the street, I put my thoughts in order along a certain track that runs side by side with many other tracks and I become as a conductor of my own train, guarding against vagabonds, unpaid passengers, lateness, and unruly behavior on the train. I become a guardian of schedules, rules, and manners. I become my opposite.

Wherein am I a menace to cause distressed looks when I raise my hood or shout through it that I am smothering, that the world around me is mad for forcing me to wear a hood, unless I would risk my life? This feeling for freedom in my poems will make others forget themselves and start on a trail into a forest, as far from city life as possible, as far from the sound and suction of machines as woods can afford, but this is the warning I read in angry looks. My words will evaporate skyscrapers, banks, hotels, housing projects, parks, railroads, clinics for the poor, hospitals for the mentally ill. I am a menace to myself too is what the angry looks warn, since I too have need of skyscrapers, banks, housing projects, benefits of clinics, and hospitals for the mentally ill. Assuming I am ill, where then will I go for treatment? My words are risen from primeval darkness, trailing huge clouds of night with them to blanket the world with chaos. The freedom I write about is for cockroaches, ants, mice, and lice, who have no other life from birth and cannot change. They take their food where they find it, raise their families in shelters where they find them, in holes, cracks, corners, and drainpipes. My words are more dangerous than radioactive dust. Once read, they leave behind life shrunk to the misery of an insect existence. Better dead! Why then, I ask myself, am I allowed to live? I do not dare ask them, but I suspect that my hood is my sign of repentance, guilt, regret. In this condition I make the observer's life meaningful to him. Now he may enjoy his way with zest, free of the guilt which I have taken on myself, perversely. Hurry with the golf clubs, drag out the yacht, open up another bottle of bourbon, the monk is walking by, stifling and sad but who gives pleasure and relief to others with his burden.

So my words, my poems are poisonous and they have poisoned me, with a wish for freedom to speak, to dance, to raise my arms. I am the quintessence of all that is wrong with the natural man. He will not conform to standards, he will not ride the subway with pleasure, he will not sit himself down at a desk in an office with relish, nor take his place at a machine with delight. He arrives at work sorrowfully, he removes his coat slowly, reluctantly, and he complains all day of the conditions and the pay. Toward the end of the working day, he speeds up his activities in order to be finished on time, so that he may hurry home at once to stuff himself with food before he is tempted to dope or drink. Seated in front of his television set, he is unhappy, nothing there on the screen offers him a way out, everything is in praise of things as they are. And they will improve, chortles the advertisement. "Crispy Crunch" will be even more crispy and crunchy next year! Go to bed, despair whispers. Sleep, bury yourself in dreams, in forgetfulness. While the body beside him, that of his wife, is filled too with the languor of his misery. Her body presses up against his for release, but no release can come. Tomorrow she must continue to raise her children in the same conditions as yesterday. But it is criminal to feel this way. It is a threat against the general welfare, it undermines one's confidence in the future, at a time such as this, threatened by atomic havoc from without. He must keep in step, he must set still higher standards of production for himself to avoid disaster. He does want to live, but is it possible this atomic bomb might end for all time production norms? This is criminal thinking of the lowest kind.

Yes, this poet is a menace with his wish for freedom and a need to stretch his arms. He will be obliterated. He has been forced to marry and to raise children, he has been condemned to buying a house in the suburbs, to taking on a large mortgage, to catching his train each morning *on time,* and to relaxing in his garden weekends with a spade and rake, so that he sits down with a deep sigh in front of his television set and welcomes with glazed eyes the torpidity and inanity he sees there as art, entertainment, instruction. No longer does he have strength or will to differentiate or to separate himself, and toward bedtime he pats the heads of his children, wishing them long, prosperous, happy lives, just like his own. So be it. It was foreordained by economics, by the threat of enemies and by the hunger and misery of the rest of the world. Let him give himself unto others! Let him put himself into a can of hash, into drum barrels of oil, into woolen underwear, into soy beans, into cash, credit, loans. Let him spread himself over every part of the earth and never once think of the art of poetry which requires merely a mud hut and tablets of clay. Let him set coins in place of his eyes and a baked bean for a nose and a baked potato for a chin, his mouth will be formed of a string bean. Then the world will approach him with delight and he will be both welcomed and devoured.

The poet is dead, long live the poetry! It will arise from the swamps of its own in the form of alligators, in the cries of victims. Poetry will emerge from the ground itself in the stalks of grain and poison ivy. It will be built into the highways and buildings, good hard asphalt and macadam, steel, stone, brick, and a thirty-two-hour work week. Poetry will be in the workingman who will take himself home, still in possession of his strength and leisure to murder his wife for an imagined wrong. It could even be a real wrong, but the poetry is in the murder and in the reading about it. And the greatest poem of all will be in the biggest bomb.

Donald Justice

Meters and Memory
1978

The mnemonic value of meters seems always to have been recognized. There are, to begin with, the weather saws, counting spells, and the like, which one does more or less get by heart in childhood. But any ornament, however trivial and even meaningless, probably assists the recollection to some degree, if by ornament we mean a device of sound or structure not required by the plain sense of a passage. Repetition obviously functions in this way—anaphora, refrains, even the sort of repetition which involves nothing more than an approximate equivalence of length, as in Pound's Sapphic fragment:

> Spring.......
> Too long.....
> Gongula......

Likewise with such structural features as parallel parts or syllogistic order, whether in verse or prose. For that matter, fine and exact phrasing alone enables the memory to take hold about as well as anything. A friend of mine, at parties, preferred to recite prose rather than verse, usually, as I recall, the opening paragraph of *A Farewell to Arms*.

The purely mnemonic character of a passage, however, contributes very little to its aesthetic power. Often enough rhymes are more effective mnemonically than meters, and occasionally other devices may prove to be. But the meters, where employed at all, are likely to be the groundwork underlying other figurations, hence basic, if not always dominant. Consider a couplet like "Red sky at morning / Sailor take warning." Here the meters cooperate with the rhymes to fit the lines to one another, not only as lines of verse but as linked parts of a perception. It is no more than a slight exaggeration to claim that the couplet becomes fixed in memory by reason of this sense of fittedness. But few devices of sound are enough in themselves to ensure recall. Should, for example, the sky of the couplet be changed from red to blue, although neither rhyme nor meter would be affected, I cannot believe the couplet would survive. Survival in this case has something to do with aptness of observation, with use, that is, as well as cleverness or beauty. The kernel of lore provides a reason for keeping the jingle; the jingle preserves the lore in stable form.

Now all this is to consider memory, as is customary, from the viewpoint of an audience, as if a significant purpose of poetry were simply to put itself in the way of being memorized. For my part, when I am at work on a poem, the memory of an audience concerns me less than my own. While the meters and other assorted devices may ultimately make the lines easier for an audience to remember, they are offering meanwhile, like the stone of the sculptor, a certain resistance to the writer's efforts to call up his subject, which seems always to be involved, one way or another, with memory. (Hobbes somewhere calls imagination the same thing as memory.) In any case, memory is going to keep whatever it chooses to keep not just because it has been made easy and agreeable to remember but because it comes to be recognized as worth the trouble of keeping, and first of all by the poet. The audience will find it possible to commit to memory only what the poet first recalls for himself. Anything can be memorized, including numbers, but numbers that refer to something beyond themselves, as to the combination of a safe, are the easier to keep in mind for that reason. Something other than themselves may likewise be hidden in the meters, and an aptness to be committed to memory might almost be taken as a sign of this other presence. Pattern is not enough. The trivial and insignificant pass beyond recall, no matter how patterned, discounting perhaps a double handful of songs and nonsense pieces, where the pattern itself has somehow become a part of what is memorable (nonsense may be the condition, in any case, to which devices of sound in themselves aspire). But such a result is exceptional. What happens in the more serious and ordinary case is that some recollection of a person, of an incident or a landscape, whatever we are willing to designate as subject, comes to seem worth preserving. The question for the poet is how to preserve it.

One motive for much if not all art (music is probably an

exception) is to accomplish this—to keep memorable what deserves to be remembered. So much seems true at least from the perspective of the one who makes it. Nor should any resemblance to the more mechanical functions of camera and tape recorder prove embarrassing; like a literary text in the making, film and tape also permit editing, room enough for the artist. Let emotion be recollected, in tranquility or turmoil, as luck and temperament would have it. And then what? Art lies still in the future. The emotion needs to be fixed, so that whatever has been temporarily recovered may become as nearly permanent as possible, allowing it to be called back again and again at pleasure. It is at this point that the various aids to memory, and meter most persistently, begin to serve memory beyond mnemonics. Such artifices are, let us say, the fixatives. Like the chemicals in the darkroom, they are useful in developing the negative. The audience is enabled to call back the poem, or pieces of it, the poet to call back the thing itself, the subject, all that was to become the poem.

The transcription of experience represented by the meters ought not to be confused with the experience itself. At best they can perform no more than a reenactment, as on some stage of the mind. This being so, to object to the meters as unnatural because unrealistic is to miss the point. Like the odd mustaches and baggy pants of the old comedians, they put us on notice that we are at a certain distance from the normal rules and expectations of life. The effect has been variously called a distancing or a framing. Wordsworth described it as serving "to divest language, in a certain degree, of its reality, and thus to throw a sort of half-consciousness of unsubstantial existence over the whole composition." The meters signify this much at least, that we are at that remove from life which traditionally we have called art.

Their very presence seems to testify to some degree of plan, purpose, and meaning. The meters seem always faintly teleological by implication, even in company with an anti-teleological argument, as the case may be. They are proof of the hand and ear of a maker (uncapitalized), even in a poetry which otherwise effaces the self. They seem to propose that an emotion, however uncontrollable it may have appeared originally, was not, in fact, unmanageable. "I don't know why I am crying" becomes "Tears, idle tears, I know not what they mean." The difference seems important to me. The poetic line comes to constitute a sort of paraphrase of the raw feeling, which will only get broken back down close to its original state in some future critic's re-paraphrase. The writer in meters, I insist, may feel as deeply as the non-metrical writer, and the choice whether or not to use meters is as likely to be dictated by literary fashion as by depth of feeling or sincerity. Nevertheless, they have become a conventional sign for at least the desire for some outward control; though their use cannot be interpreted as any guarantee of inner control, the very act of writing at all does usually imply an attempt to master the subject well enough to understand it, and the meters reinforce the impression that such an attempt is being made and perhaps succeeding. Even so, the technology of verse does not of itself affirm a philosophy, despite arguments to the contrary. Certain recent critics have argued that even syntax is now "bogus," since the modern world contains no such order as that implied in an ordinary sentence, much less a metrical one. But the imitation theory underlying this argument seems naive and unhistorical, for it was never the obligation of words or of word-order to imitate conditions so reflexively. Syntax deals, after all, primarily with word-order, not world-order, and even the meters, or so it seems to me, can imitate only by convention.

Let me take a simple case. Yvor Winters once offered his line, "The slow cry of a bird," as an example of metrical imitation, not strictly of a birdcall itself but of "the slowness of the cry." The convention would seem to be that two or more strong syllables in succession carry associations of slowness and heaviness, while two or more weak syllables in succession carry contrary associations of rapidity and lightness: melancholy on the one hand, playfulness on the other. But the displacement of a stress from *of* to *cry* in the Winters line, bringing two stresses together, fails to slow the line down, as I hear it. Substitute for this "The *quick* cry of a bird," and the two weak syllables following *cry* can be said to do as much to speed the line up, or as little. But whether the cry is to sound quick or slow, the metrical situation itself remains, practically speaking, identical. If any question of interpretation arises from the reversed foot, the meaning of the reversal must depend on the denotation of the adjective rather than on the particular arrangement of syllables and stresses, for denotation overrides any implication of the meters apart from it.

Though apparently agreed on by generations of poets, the minor convention on which Winters was depending is hardly observed any longer except in criticism or occasionally the classroom. Nor was it, for that matter, observed by Milton in his great melancholy-playful pair, "Il Penseroso" and "L'Allegro," or if observed, then only to be consciously played against. Composers of music for the movies learned early that direct imitation of a visual image through sound was best restricted to comic effects (pizzicati, trombone glissandi, staccato bassoons). Pushed far enough, and that is not very far at all, the results of metrical imitation can seem similarly cartoonlike.

> I sank to the pillow, and Joris, and he;
> I slumbered, Dirck slumbered, we slumbered all three.

In any case, simple imitation by means of rhythm would seem to be more plausible in free verse, with its greater flexibility, and most workable in prose, which is allowed any and every arrangement of syllables. Wordsworth ascribes to the meters a different power, finding in them a "great efficacy in tempering and restraining the passion by an intertexture of ordinary feeling," and, he goes on to add, "of feeling not strictly and necessarily connected with the passion." The meters move along in their own domain, scarcely intersecting the domain of meaning, except in some illusory fashion or by virtue of conventions nearly private. The responsibility they bear to the sense, comic writing aside, is mostly not to interfere. By so effacing themselves they will have accomplished all that they must accomplish in relation to the sense. Speech they can and do imitate, from a little distance, but rarely by quoting, that is to say, by attempting to become speech. Song they perhaps are or can become, their natural inclination; no question in that of imitating anything outside their own nature.

Whether their nature really embodies an imitation of natural processes may be arguable. But I do not think the meters can be, in any such sense, organic. A recognition of this, conscious or not, has been reason enough for their rejection by contemporary organicists, poets and critics both. The meters seem more to resemble the hammer-work of carpenters putting together a building, say, than waves coming in to shore or the parade of seasons. We do inhale and exhale more or less rhythmically, as long as we stay healthy; our hearts do beat without much skipping, for years on end. Breath and heart are the least remote of these similitudes, but any connection between them and the more or less regular alternation of weak and strong syllables in verse seems doubtful to me and, valid or not, need carry no particular prestige. In urban life, far from the Lake Country of 1800, are to be found analogies as appropriate as any from nature, if no more convincing. Signals timed to regulate the flow of traffic not only seem analogous but at times remarkably beautiful, as on a nearly deserted stretch of Ninth Avenue in New York City at 3 A.M., especially in a mild drizzle. If the meters do represent or imitate anything in general, it may be nothing more (or less) than some psychological compulsion, a sort of counting on the fingers or stepping on cracks, magic to keep an unpredictable world under control.

Where the meters are supposed to possess anything of an imitative character, the implicit purpose must be to bring the poetic text closer to its source in reality or nature by making it more "like" the thing it imitates. Such an illusion may be enhanced if the poet's conviction is strong enough to persuade an audience to share his faith, but such conversions are more likely to be accomplished through criticism than through poetry alone. The twin illusions of control and understanding seem more valuable to me than this illusion of the real or the natural, since it is through these, I suspect, that the meters are more firmly connected to memory. To remember an event is almost to begin to control it, as well as to approach an understanding of it; incapable of recurring now, it is only to be contemplated rather than acted on or reacted to. Any sacrifice of immediate reality is compensated for by these new perspectives. The terror or beauty or, for that matter, the plain ordinariness of the original event, being transformed, is fixed and thereby made more tolerable. That the event can recur only in its new context, the context of art, sheers it of some risks, the chief of which may anyhow have been its transitory character.

If for an audience the meters function in part to call back the words of the poem, so for the poet they may help to call the words forth, at the same time casting over them the illusion of a necessary or at least not inappropriate fitness and order. There is a kind of accrediting in the process, a warrant that things are being remembered right and set down right, so long as the meters go on working. In this way the meters serve as a neutral and impersonal check on self-indulgence and whimsy; a subjective event gets made over into something more like an object. It becomes accessible to memory, repeatedly accessible, because it exists finally in a form that can be perused at leisure, like a snapshot in an album. Memory itself tends to act not without craft, but selectively, adding here to restore a gap, omitting the incongruous there, rearranging and shifting the emphasis, striving, consciously or not, to make some sense and point out of what in experience may have seemed to lack either. That other presence of which I spoke earlier—the charge of feeling, let us say, which attaches perhaps inexplicably to the subject, what the psychologist might call its *affect*—is not much subject to vicissitudes and manipulations of this sort, except for a natural enough diminution. It remains, but more than likely beneath the surface.

The meters are worth speculating about because they are so specific to the medium, if not altogether essential. Without them nothing may, on occasion, be lost; with them, on occasion, something may be gained, though whatever that is probably has little or nothing to do with sense or ostensible subject. This, in fact, appears to be the sticking point, that in themselves the meters signify so little. It seems a mistake for a rationalist defender of the meters to insist on too much meaningfulness. Let us concede that the effects of the meters are mysterious, from moment to moment imprecise, often enough uncertain or ambiguous. Like Coleridge's incense or wine, however, their presence may "act powerfully, though themselves unnoticed." To which he adds an interesting comparison to yeast—"worthless," as he says, "or disagreeable by itself, but giving vivacity and spirit to the liquor" in right combination. Meters do accompany the sense, like a kind of percussion only, mostly noise. Over and above syntax, they bind the individual words together, and the larger structural parts as well, over and above whatever appearance of logic survives in the argument; as a result, the words and parts seem to cohere, more perhaps than in plain fact may be the case. How they assist the recollection is by fixing it in permanent, or would-be permanent, form. This, for the poet, may be the large and rather sentimental purpose which gives force to all their various combining and intersecting functions.

X. J. Kennedy

Fenced-In Fields
1972

The larger part of vigorous American poetry in the past ten years has been poetry in free verse. From the work of nearly every young poet of talent, those now in their late twenties or early thirties, meter and rime are now absent. For many young poets, such patterns have come to appear the stalest leavings of a cultural order of the past, in which, as in the society that grew it, they no longer find purpose, or honesty.

We hold, as the saying goes, these truths to be self-evident. Why then do we offer a magazine confined to poems written in meter, or in rime, or in both?

We'll try to state our motives through analogy. This spring in a show of contemporary art at the Boston Museum, we saw a plot of grass with a wooden frame around it. The artist's signature, oddly enough, wasn't that of God, but that of Hymie Glutz (or whoever); and as we stood for a while in contemplation before it, we felt, in spite of ourselves, a certain wonder and doubt. Was not Glutz doing merely what an artist traditionally has done: borrowing something out of nature, lending his own order to it? But the trouble (we realized) was that, by fitting a patch of living grass into a four-board rectangle, the artist wasn't *abstracting* anything from nature, he was lugging in nature itself. And that, it further struck us, was apparently what he wanted to do. There was similar purpose in another disturbing item in the show: an aerial photograph, in color, of the canals of Venice after an artist named Uriburu had poured green dye into the Grand Canal, letting it circulate around the city on the tide. "Art work," proclaimed Uriburu in an accompanying statement, "has no autonomous form anymore. Art work adopts nature form: fluid, dynamic. Art has no place outside of nature . . . its place is inside of nature." The photograph, apparently, was on display for evidence, so

---

Editor's note: This essay introduced the magazine *Counter/Measures*.

that the artist could have something to hang in a museum, and not miss out on his proper notoriety.

Throwing over any distinctions between nature and art may sound like a wow, the best way to pole-vault the wall of one's ego since the discovery of pot—and after all, isn't everything One anyway, when you come right down to it? We wondered, though, what would happen if poets were to work by such an aesthetic. It soon occurred that many contemporary poets already do go according to similar assumptions. Lately we have had the sort of poem made by catching whatever fragments of organic life go whizzing by: the poem made by merely jotting down (or tape-recording) whatever scraps of small talk people utter on walking into the poet's apartment. We have had a single word ("oxygen") sliced out of the lawn of the language and set down, all by itself, in the frame of an empty page. In such an instance, the poet himself hasn't done a lick of making, selecting or arranging. It is odd that he still expects to be given a by-line for it.

We don't for one minute resent those Dadaist sculptors who used to stick a pedestal under a group of gaspipes and call the combination a work of art. At least they were wits, and at best they probably alerted people to the aesthetic satisfactions to be found in just any old gaspipes. And it may be that poems consisting of tape-recorded small talk are supposed to reveal pleasures to be found in small talk of any kind. But often, after reading such a poem, you end in feeling that the talk has remained dismally ordinary. In fact, it may even seem robbed of whatever auditory interest (tone, accent) it may have had before trapped on the poet's tape.

At least, the organic-unity poet might argue, my stuff isn't labored, isn't contrived. O Spontaneity! What put-ons are pulled off in thy name. It's as Renata Adler once said about filmmakers in the Sunday *Times*, about all the "lazy, no-talent celebrities" around:

> Nothing appears more square or less suited to the kind of style and rhetoric that generate fame than working hard. This is not a very puritan moment and all the dreary, life-impoverishing associations of pointless work—lessons learned by rote, overtime hours on the way up, logging time, pedantries, bureaucratic snarl—have cut the romance out of taking pains.

Obviously, a poet has to take pains if he writes in meter and rime. And he might as well admit that by doing so he removes language from that great, fluid stream of organic reality, and works it over, and makes something special from it. He takes (to paraphrase Richard Wilbur) a vaporous genie and claps it into a bottle. Meter is artifice, all right: it has to be striven after. As John Thompson says in his *Founding of English Meter*, "If there is one meaning which the metrical pattern enforces on all language submitted to its influence, it is this: *Whatever else I may be talking about, I am talking also about language itself.*"

Much more so than the aesthetic of fluidity, this disreputably old-fangled view of a work of art as something for the artist to work on and let go of only when he can't further improve on it, seems to us likely to produce valuable poems. Whoever writes in meter and rime offers his poem not as a droplet of the great organic unity, but as something he'll take the blame for, if need be, and not just the credit: a thing more or less achieved, a thing made.

We don't mean to damn free verse poets in general as lazy louts, or charlatans. There's no doubt in our minds that a Gary Snyder or a Robert Creeley works hard at his trade; that indeed, he may be attempting something more difficult and more demanding than the task of writing a formal iambic ode. But it is clear that, in the present poetic climate, when practically anything at all is tolerated and there isn't much searching criticism, when readers never say "uncle" because there aren't any readers, or very few, bad poetry threatens to drive good poetry out of circulation—both metrical and nonmetrical kinds. Many writers of poetry have tried to find sanction for their urges to spew by referring to the late Charles Olson's theories. Olson, we believe, was a noble thinker and a generous man—even (in occasional moments) a startling poet. The one time we met him, he greeted us heartily, and, recalling some skeptical remarks against his theory of prosody we had made in a magazine, he said, "Well you didn't understand what I was driving at very good, did you?" Despite our lasting admiration for the man, we remain unable to accept his theory of breathing as form. Moreover, to claim that white space and indentations counted with the spacebar of a typewriter can possibly denote with any accuracy the subtleties of the human breath-process is like claiming that a bucket of housepaint can capture the blush of the rose.

Olson's revolution has succeeded. In fact, so thoroughly has it overpowered the crumbling empire of the New Criticism that it is in danger of giving way to a police state, with an orthodox church every bit as doctrinaire as the Empire's used to be. Here and there, it is true, you see pockets of elder conservatives still in power. But it is open form (whether derived from Olson's thinking or from elsewhere) that prevails among most citizens. It has become practically an act of civil disobedience to write a sonnet. Opt for the villanelle and you cringe, waiting for the rap of the nightstick at your door. To write in meter and rime these days is to give yourself a permanently suspect credit rating. In effect, some of the possibilities of poetry are today forbidden, or at least officially disliked.

To deny poetry any of its possibilities is mistaken, we believe. We could quote a long, depressing catalogue of recent pontifications by critics and poets to the effect that meter and rime are worn out, and don't matter. It isn't that we greatly mind seeing these patterns attacked by people who couldn't scan a nursery rime if they tried. What saddens us still more is that the attack has been carried on by many skilled, literate poets who, in the act of turning from their earlier fondness for pattern, have thought it necessary to preach the destruction of the entire metrical tradition—like suicides who want to take along the whole airliner. In such an age, we are grateful for the common sense of Robert Lowell, whose own practice has not been conditioned solely by theory, and who remarked (in Mezey and Berg's antimetrical anthology *Naked Poetry*) that he couldn't see how any poet who had written both metered and unmetered poems could settle for one of them and abandon the other.

We are cautioned by the new orthodoxy that the old measures no longer correspond to the nervous, staccato rhythms of our civilization. Perhaps there is truth in that assertion. But why poets should want to be faithful to the cadences of this particular civilization anyhow, is more than we can see. Kooky as it may sound to affirm this, there are still, after all, rhythms perceptible in the seasons and tides, in the succession of daylight and dark, in the beating of the blood against heart-valve and artery. Such facts make us wonder whether, in identifying the *irregular* with the natural and organic, proponents of open field poetry aren't taking a limited view. Granted, the cadences that most of us live by aren't particularly natural ones: the start-and-stop of rush-hour traffic, the cut-zoom-cut of the TV commercial. Invited to listen to the pulse-beat of a meter, we have a hard time standing still and concentrating long enough. Meter walks with its measured stride, when we want to gun our engines. The time and patience required to write a poem in a rime-scheme are apparently more than most contemporary poets can offer. (*Rhythm*, by the way, is a notion widely misapprehended. As the term has long been used by most people, *rhythm* means a pattern established through a recurrence: of night and day, of spring and fall, of metrical stress and nonstress. In this sense, free verse doesn't have any "rhythms" to it—not for more than a line or so, although it may arrange its stresses interestingly.)

We are warned that to write a poem in the pattern, say, of a Shakespearean sonnet is to force words into a chain gang against their will. A true poem (so goes the theory) has to be written in organic form, discovering its individual nature as it goes along. Such a discovery, we are told, can't ever be made by the writer of a sonnet. Such dogmas rest upon a couple of unexamined assumptions. One is the assumption that a sonnet is nothing but a hollow box to be stuffed full of verbiage. Another is the assumption that a sonnet can't possibly begin unknown to itself, that it can't possibly discover its proper organic form while (and only while) its poet is writing it. But many a poet has discovered that he didn't plan to write a sonnet when he started out. To his surprise, he finds the thing turning out in fourteen lines, as it naturally hankers to be. Oh, no doubt the poet has read a bale of other people's sonnets in his time, and once he gets writing along and finds the first eight lines gravitating into an octave, he can't help remembering them. Is that bad? But a good sonnet, far from being a vacuum to be filled, dutifully and mechanically and joylessly, is (if worth anything) a sonnet-sized explosion in the mind.

Recently, the young poet Hale Chatfield wrote provocatively:

If meter is at best secondary in importance, it cannot be of primary importance to take a stand for or against metrical poetry. Perhaps the issue today is more properly whether or not a poem is sufficiently *physical*. Perhaps much of the skillful verse in the quarterlies fails to affect us because it has abandoned the body in favor of the body's shadows.

Precisely, but that's where we disagree. We see a return to meter (for poets who care for it) as a means to break through again into the physical. To recall that heartbeat it abstracts from, that physical pulse.

Some will object, with Chatfield, that to try to separate patterned poetry from nonpatterned is unimportant, or even wrong. They will say (with some good reason) that in deciding which poems to print, any editor's consideration ought to be excellence. In the light of eternity, we have to agree with that; and already, in picking out poems for this issue, we have felt at times slightly foolish in going over the poet's lines with our patented meter-measurer—not to see that he didn't depart from his pattern, Lord knows, since only bad poets (like writers of greeting cards) stick to metrical patterns with perfect fidelity; but to see if there was any pattern there. We have done so because this magazine has a point to make. In truth, we can think of few things less engaging than the scansion (in the abstract, without any words) of an iambic pentameter line. We are mindful that it is foolish to adore form (whether traditional or organic) as an entity to itself. The pattern of a poem, to our minds, is no more than the stick with which the Zen master drubs his pupil into awakening. Poets are their own masters, we reckon, and when the enlightenment—the true poem—comes, then the stick might as well be snapped and the pieces thrown away. It isn't as though to draw a line between patterned poetry and nonpatterned poetry is arbitrary. Any poem, after all, makes that distinction very clearly in its opening words, or lines. Either it invites us to play a certain riming or metrical game, or it lets us know that there is no game, that we must watch for other satisfactions.

It need not put rime and meter in a sinister light to declare that they have gamelike elements. (Huizinga, our favorite historian, has shown in *Homo Ludens* how profoundly the element of game informs most human activities.) We can risk a guess, too, why most American poets in the late 1950s and early 1960s abruptly picked up their money and declared "no dice." If riming and metrical games no longer seemed to them worth playing, that may have been because they wanted to talk directly about themselves, and their immediate experience. Aware of social evils that cried out to be castigated, they wanted their poems to get at them; and to write in meter would have made it harder to speak out.

But passionate language tends to fall into meter, and meter, far from being a bookish artifice, is modeled after a tendency in the spoken language: the tendency to fall roughly into iambs, more or less. To think it something bookish and artificial, something imposed on speech (rather than something perceived IN speech) is to miss the point. "We can cuss in meter, and do," people say in the Tidewater, Maryland (according to James M. Cain). We once heard a sailor from Texas chewing out another man, "Why, you piss-complected puddle o' puke, I could pass through you like a dose o' salts!" Perhaps our ears for the metrical tendencies of speech have grown blunted, here in America. Think of the most *feelingful* and musical talkers you know: chances are they're old people. While we haven't the evidence to say for sure, the editors had a definite impression during a recent year spent living in England that the English—especially milkmen, plumbers, carpenters, and old women who frequent pubs—talked more vigorously, with a greater rise and fall of intonation than most Americans, who don't (for all our endless gab) especially take joy in hearing ourselves talk. As Robert Louis Stevenson observed a long time ago,

> In our canorous language, rhythm is always at the door. But it must not be forgotten that in some languages that element is almost, if not quite, extinct, and that in our own it is probably decaying. The even speech of many educated Americans sounds the note of danger.

If Stevenson was right, how much further the decline must have proceeded since his time.

We are content to believe that most American poets who abandoned meter in the 1960s may have had good reason to do so, reasons of their own. In several cases, their retreats from pattern gained them victories. From the recent *Collected Poems* of James Wright, it looks as though Wright was a good poet to begin with, but venturing into open fields, he became bolder, stranger, wiser, more penetrating. Denise

Levertov wrote an early book, published in England, full of the most godawful drab stanzaic verse. Once she discovered Dr. Williams, however, her work improved tremendously. Donald Hall, to name only one other, wrote a highly uneven *tour de force* of a first book, displaying his command of many traditional forms. As you can tell from his selected poems, *The Alligator Bride,* his move into free (or syllabic) forms was the best move he ever made. Sadly, not all who shed metrical patterns had such good fortune. Several prominent poets, their corsets loosened, decomposed themselves far and wide. W. S. Merwin, ever a technician and a craftsman, hasn't improved, but has managed to hold his own. Since Merwin's essential theme has always been the very form of his poem itself, his switch from obvious stanzaic patterns to subtle free verse has caused the brief poems in his last two volumes, as brilliant as ever, to hang like wisps of cigaret smoke in some lunar sea of desolation.

An unfashionable truth, that you won't learn from certain new anthologies, is that many American poets still choose to write in meter and rime. Like Wilbur, they have stuck to their lonely posts with great integrity. It might appear that all pattern vanished from American poetry with the advent of *Howl* and of *Life Studies*; yet, in the 1960s and early 1970s, we have seen the appearance of Roethke's *Collected Poems* and *The Far Field* (by no means all of it naked poetry); *Berryman's Sonnets* and the loosely blank verse *Dream Songs;* new books by Cummings, Frost, Hecht, Snodgrass, Daniel Hoffman and Edgar Bowers; three collections by Wilbur; Lowell's nearly metrical *Notebooks*; Sylvia Plath's *Ariel*; much of the work of Anne Sexton, Elizabeth Bishop, Robert Watson, Richard Eberhart, James Merrill, and Paul Goodman (none of them always bound to pattern, or lack of it). We have had the ballads of Robert Duncan and Helen Adam; the many songlike lyrics of Creeley; James Camp and Keith Waldrop's songs. There have been Stanley Kunitz's striking accentual poems in his new book *The Testing Tree;* first collections by Richard Moore, Louise Glück, L. E. Sissman, Turner Cassity, Raphael Rudnick, and George P. Elliott; volumes of poems new and selected by such middle-aged or even older figures as Allen Tate, William Jay Smith, Robert Fitzgerald, William Meredith, Louise Bogan, Howard Nemerov, Reed Whittemore, John Crowe Ransom, and Howard Moss. Cunningham's collected poems appeared, and Jarrell's and Auden's; Nims revised his translation of St. John of the Cross and Ciardi completed his version of the *Divine Comedy*. This is to note only a small part of the harvest, not even to mention Canadian poetry, nor other vital developments overseas.

Another fact (which we don't yet know what to make of) is that the best-loved poetry of young auditors—that vast majority who haven't heard of Olson—has been the rimed and metrical lyric all along. Most rock song lyrics don't happen to be poetry, but a significant few of them do. When asked to explain this, most people who swear by organic form (but who also want to believe in Bob Dylan) start to hem and haw and shuffle, and maybe say, "Well, rock songwriters aren't *really* writing in rime and meter, don't you know—it's actually something new: like speech rhythms." What we hope to consider, among other questions in *Counter/Measures* is: just what *has* happened in popular song over the past few years, and how significant is it for bookish poetry?

Don't get us wrong. We have no desire to emulate Stanton A. Coblentz, that conservative critic who dismisses T. S. Eliot as a fake; nor the now-defunct Legion for Sanity in Poetry, which sought to take poetry back to the Pre-Raphaelites, in practically every way. We are just praying, too, that all those blue-haired little old ladies with trunkfuls of yellowing sonnets won't find out about us, and we beg our readers not to sic them upon us—unless, of course, they're as wonderful as Abbie Huston Evans. You never know.

Evidently, it is neither possible nor desirable for rimed metrical poetry to retreat to the strategies of Thomas Hardy, nor to rewrite Emily Dickinson. Poets working in patterns these days may find that in order to survive they may have to shed certain reticences, to venture forth more joyously, more boldly, and more adventurously. They may try their hands at songwriting, if they wish; or try speaking in breakneck measures with a little of Sylvia Plath's reckless urgency. They can look back past the Renaissance to the accentuals of Old English (any number of syllables, a fixed number of stresses to each line). They can read Yeats, whose great discoveries—seemingly wild but calculated departures from metrical norms—have had few enough takers. There are fine metrical poets in other languages still waiting for translators. Far from having run up against a dead end, poets of a mind to work in patterns have light-years still ahead of them.

And so, we have no quarrel with any poet who seriously practices the difficult craft of honest open verse. He will have read this magazine through a foggy glass who thinks that it claims that all poems ought to have meter and rime. A poet, thank God, can do anything he likes in the universe, provided he can get away with it. But he has to love words, in a physical sense—has to love the weight and heft and motions of them. Like Catholics aware that their faith is under attack and willing to make peace with Protestants, we invite friendship with any poet—whatever his persuasion—who still cares that stresses fall meaningfully upon his words. For the sake of fruitful argument, though, we won't print free verse. Besides, we are essentially lazy souls, and by not publishing the kind of poetry now predominant, we hope to receive a leaner mail than do most poetry magazines. *Counter/Measures* will continue to appear until we believe its point has been made, or until it withers from malnutrition. We aren't greatly afraid that meter and rime are dying, but if in fact we're wrong, at least we'll provide a respectful convoy to the cemetery.

Bliem Kern

Sound Poetry
1976

o

be

be   o

be

be   beoo

be

before the event of the printed page   be

man lived and communicated his thoughts

feelings and perceptions in the realm of

be

phonetic space   as a result of the Gutenberg press

the oral heritage of man has been transformed

through the visual traditions

o

of language and literature   be

the dynamics of the technology of   press

twentieth century man are dissolving

these traditional forms of knowledge

be   through the telegraph radio

film   television and video disk

man is returning

o   to the intimacy

and immediacy   disk

of oral

communication

be   on

un

o   un

be. o un

disk

x

be   on   213

```
        o                           o
                  archangel
                    o               o
        ba                                   b
                         olo
                              a
        a rama mara      prana   pet her  sesa      aramu muru
  christ      agni       hierarchy  sun ra    silver              buddha
      adi   disk   red   horse     yoga          tigris euphrates   atma
                         atom    venus    manu    wand  shamballa
          khephra
  shan-gri-la          zoom      earth    heru ha        blue white
          isis                   stars    viveka    atlantis
      lemuria         twelve                      philadelphia  zoom
  green          rain          fohat                pentacle   light
        new york       cup     form    ali kita
    embah
          raja       dream    gold    sarasana   chaldean  invisible
      peru       invisible wind  oah    harpocrates      bhut    tibet
            lisbon                                   violet
        death          air  brihaspati   chant                pluto
                  guru  gokula ua   space   mu leya        ray
        numbers
                       mercury seven    ashemu per suka
                  amen  gods     salt   moola

                  deva   sound   noun  senzar
                  color   yama   three

                     fire   xeper  zoom
                  vakra  seventy-eight  spirits

                     verbs  smell  azolta
                  kumbha   kona  moon

                  aah  ba  pushpaka
                  indu  baiu

                     ba  i

                      u


            your karma   is revealed   maya chance
        sacred mysteries   invisible brahma   egyptian olo
      thought  thoth  will   feeling   out   self discovery  primordial
  language   substance   between   humans   animals   plants   minerals
        objects   spirits   of environment   beforeafter   signs
            symbols   of our language   initiate sounds
              others follow  touching is
                  important
```

```
                  oa
          o
                      oa
              ur

          ea      ur      o
          each our own
          a place to start
          speech for the gods
          from whom poems and paintings are a gift
   gift language our tool of communication
          voice our instrument    initiate light
              from invisible    nouns verbs
                  the power of language
              diction form imagery rhythmn
                  the elements of a poem
              line form color space texture
                  the elements of painting
          phonemes vowels consonants dipthongs olo
                  the elements of phonetics
                      phonetic space the
                  space world of primordial man
              sound poetry world language ritual
                  the origins of poetry
                      o        p
                          r        o
                                   i
                                      e

                                  g
                                      t
                                  i n

                      the              s  r
                    origins              o
                    of poetry              f
                                              y
                  sacred knowledge
              wisdom past on orally by            poetry
              priests magicians  shamans          poetry
          oracles  hierophants  meditations      poetry
      incantations  spells  chants  logos  charms  senzar
   mantras  prayers  songs  hymns  libations  scriptures
   m          primordial meditations  an offering sacrifice
   m                to the gods  earth  sun  moon  stars
          m    planets  invisible world for birth
   m    m            death rebirth prosperous crops
                  beauty  truth  peace
                      understanding
                      love
                  return through
              a return through
          a return through return through
```

```
                           a
                        return
                    a return through
                  return through return
               return through return through return
       return through return through return through
       return through    babylon
       return through    anu    hea    bel
       return through    chaldean
       return through    ishtar    gilgamesh    nebu
       return through    scandinavian
       return through    jumala    ukko    akka    paiva    ku    ilama
       return through    chinese
       return through    fu-shi    ti    yao    yu    li    yi king
       return through    egyptian
       return through    thoth    ra    isis    osiris    pot amun
       return through    persian
       return through    mithra    magi    ahur mazda
       return through    indian
       return through    indra    agni    varuna    maruts
       meditations primordial meditations
          speech visions for the gods
          sound poetry my daily ritual
    a indwelling in the spiritual in preparation for
        the eminent destruction of the material
          natures rebellion upon itself
             a cleansing of the soul
             result of its own karma
              mans selfish thinking
             must get worse before it
                can get better
          a search for beauty and truth
          a unity of these my sacred sounds
       with signs and symbols of the visual plane
          sound poetry    sound painting
        perfection of my self knowledge wisdom
            a quest joining with the
       external universal world knowledge wisdom
          development of ritual sound
         development of painting with sound
         development of sound philosophy
       a return to old sacred knowledge wisdom
          from which we can build new forms
             new forms a return to new
               forms a return to
                a return to
                a return
                   a
```

```
                    a
                                re
              b           tu
           fu

              future
           return to future
        return to return to return
     return to return to return to return
return to return to    return to return to
return to future to return to future to return
return to future    oral heritage of man
return to future    new forms in art and literature
return to future    pagan beauty and truth in nature
return to future    healing power of sound and color
return to future    mysteries of primordial man
return to future    inherent self respect of the soul
return to future    unity of astral etheric physical mental body
return to future    clairvoyant consciousness of atlantis
return to future    companionship between man and gods
return to future    wisdom of invisible influences
return to future    harmony in the spirit of man
return to future    return of the christ
return to future    harmony of ego
return to future    future to return
        to future    future to
           ure    future too
        a quest for truth
      and beauty beyond chance
     which is part of it also
    a harmony between inner being
  inner worlds of self knowledge wisdom
   and outer universal knowledge
      wisdom of external
           worlds
       there are not
     accidents this i know
  in my writing i am translating
 the oral into the visual through
the use of language    in performing
  my poetry i am translating
    the visual into the oral
       through sound
        speech visions
         sound poetry
        sound painting
        my life work
         my life
         my i
          y

               y

                   y

               y
```

m

e d

it

ta

t

i o n

s

meditationsmeditationsmeditations
primordialprimordialprimordial
meditationsmeditationsmeditations
meditation
a word farm
merêe doon ar zint
a chance selected chance voyage
into self discovery an attempt towards
pre language inner dialogues with myself before
i learned the signs symbols of our language funneled
through my reincarnated life experience
till now touching is important
i initiate sounds others follow
no audience performer audience is performer
each our own   speech for the gods
primordial ritual of sound
philosophy of life
lost language
senzar
found language
a look forward for both
man and woman to an age of peace
and love for all until the death of the sun
almighty god of the heavens   this is what it is to me
it can be anything to you

kee kee kee albọ albọ albọ albọ

Bliem Kern   6:25 pm new moon February 29, 1976 new york city

Galway Kinnell

Poetry, Personality, and Death
1971

In this little poem by Stephen Crane, I find an image which stands as the portrait of us all:

> In the desert
> I saw a creature, naked, bestial,
> Who squatting upon the ground,
> Held his heart in his hands,
> And ate of it.
> I said, "Is it good, friend?"
> "It is bitter—bitter," he answered;
> "But I like it
> Because it is bitter,
> And because it is my heart."

The poetry of this century is marked by extreme self-absorption. So we have been a "school" of self-dissection, the so-called confessional poets, who sometimes strike me as being interested in their own experience to the exclusion of everyone else's. Even Robert Lowell, in *Life Studies*—that rich, lively book which remains more fascinating than all but a few of the books of its time—puts me off somewhat by the strange pride—possibly the pride by which the book lives—that he takes in his own suffering.

I was on a bus some years ago, when a man suddenly spoke up in a loud, pained voice: "You don't know how I suffer! No one on this bus suffers the way I do!" Somebody in the back called out, "Rent a hall!" Someone else said, "Do you want to borrow my crutches?" and actually produced a pair of crutches and offered them across the aisle. The man tapped his knee and looked out the window with an exasperated expression, as if to say, "I wish there weren't so many nuts riding the busses." What I would like to find in poetry, as on that bus, is one who could express the pain of everyone.

Robert Bly's poems often seem liberated from this self-absorbed, closed ego. In his first two books Bly avoids specific autobiographical detail almost entirely. Though he speaks in the first person about intimate feelings, the self has somehow been erased. The "I" is not any particular person, a man like the rest of us, who has sweated, cursed, loathed himself, hated, envied, been cold-hearted, mean, frightened, unforgiving, ambitious, and so on. Rather it is a person of total mental health, an ideal "I" who has more in common with ancient Chinese poets than with anyone alive in the United States today. This would be a blessing for all of us if Bly had really succeeded in "transcending" personality in his poetry. But I think he has not. He simply has not dealt with it. He has been vehement about getting rid of old poeticisms, and this he has done: his poetry is, indeed, contemporary; it is his role as poet he has borrowed out of old literature.

This borrowed self, this disguise, may be deliberate, the consequence of a theory of impersonality. It seems to spring, too, from a compulsive need for secrecy, from the poet's reluctance to reveal himself in his poems. Consider this poem, "The Busy Man Speaks":

Not to the mother of solitude will I give myself
Away, not to the mother of love, nor to the mother of conversation,
Nor to the mother of art, nor the mother
Of tears, nor the mother of the ocean;
Not to the mother of sorrow, nor the mother
Of the downcast face, nor the mother of the suffering of death;
Not to the mother of the night full of crickets,
Nor the mother of the open fields, nor the mother of Christ.

But I will give myself to the father of righteousness, the father
Of cheerfulness, who is also the father of rocks,
Who is also the father of perfect gestures;
From the Chase National Bank
An arm of flame has come, and I am drawn
To the desert, to the parched places, to the landscape of zeros;
And I shall give myself away to the father of righteousness,
The stones of cheerfulness, the steel of money, the father of rocks.

The individual lines are strong; yet the poem as a whole leaves me unsatisfied, as do all poems which divide men into two kinds. Someone less unwilling to reveal himself might have reversed the positives and negatives. But if Bly had said,

"To the mother of solitude will I give myself / Away, to the mother of love . . . ," then he would, perhaps, have been obliged, in the second stanza, to say, "And yet I give myself, also, to the father of righteousness. . . ." Speaking in his own voice, the voice of a complicated individual, he would have been forced to be lucid regarding his own ambiguous allegiances. Bly stumbles as if through fear into setting up this simplified *persona,* the "busy man."

A *persona* has its uses, and also its dangers. In theory, it would be a way to get past the self, to dissolve the barrier between poet and reader. Writing in the voice of another, the poet would open himself to that person. All that would be required would be for the reader to make the same act of sympathetic identification, and, in the *persona,* poet and reader would meet as one. Of course, for the poem to be interesting, the *persona* would have to represent a central facet of the poet's self; the kind of thing Browning's dramatic monologues do very well, prose fiction does much better.

In the voice of J. Alfred Prufrock, Eliot expressed his own sense of futility and his own wish to die. Without the use of the *persona* Eliot might not have been able to express this at all, for isn't it embarrassing for a young man to admit to feeling so old? The *persona* makes it OK. For the same reason, it is an evasion. As he develops his character, even Eliot forgets that this sense of futility and this wish to die are his own, as well as Prufrock's. The *persona* makes it unnecessary for him to confront the sources of these feelings or to explore their consequences in himself. It functions like the Freudian dream, fictionalizing what one does not want to know is real.

The problem is similar in James Dickey's "The Firebombing," the most famous *persona* poem of recent years. In his attack on the poem—an attack almost as famous as the poem—Robert Bly says:

> If the anguish in this poem were real, we would feel terrible remorse as we read, we would stop what we were doing, we would break the television set with an axe, we would throw ourselves on the ground sobbing.

Oddly enough, Dickey, in the poem, accuses his *persona* of just that indecent coldness of which Bly accused Dickey, and in much the same terms:

> My hat should crawl on my head
> in streetcars, thinking of it,
> the fat on my body should pale.

Over and over in the poem, Dickey makes clear the moral limits of his *persona,* that exfirebomber whose aesthetic relish in his exploits was a function of his lack of imagination, his inability to conceive of the persons he killed, and who lives ever after in confusion and unresolved guilt.

The poem is not about the pleasure of war, but about the failures of character which make war, or mechanized war, possible. And yet, Bly's criticism is not irrelevant. I, too, find something in this poem which makes me uneasy, something which has to do, I think, with the evasions permitted by the use of the *persona.*

In an essay James Dickey wrote on the *persona* in poetry, he says,

> A true poet can write with utter convincingness about "his" career as a sex murderer, and then in the next poem with equal conviction about tenderness and children and self-sacrifice.

This is true. Even a poet who does not write "dramatic" poetry, who writes only about himself, must experience all manner of human emotions, since he uses the words which express these emotions. As Whitman says,

> Latent in a great user of words, must be all passions, crimes, trades, animals, stars, God, sex, the past, might, space, metals, and the like—because these are the words, and he who is not these, plays with a foreign tongue, turning helplessly to dictionaries and authorities.

I admire James Dickey for exposing the firebomber within himself—particularly since the firebomber does appear to be a central facet of Dickey's makeup. It is a courageous act. Few poets would be as willing to reveal their inner sickness, and we can be sure that many poets seem healthier than Dickey only because they tell us less about themselves.

Yet revelation alone is not sufficient. In the same essay on the *persona*, Dickey has this curious sentence—curious for what it fails to say:

> The activity [of poetry] gives the poet a chance to confront and dramatize parts of himself that otherwise would not have surfaced.

Between "confront" and "dramatize," aren't certain crucial verbs missing? If Dickey does feel as close to his *persona* as he seems to, if he feels within himself a deadness of imagination regarding those whom he hurts, if he himself even vicariously takes aesthetic pleasure in killing, can't we expect him, as a poet, to explore this region of himself—not merely to dramatize it as though it belonged to another? We don't ask that he suppress the firebomber within; on the contrary, we want him to try to find out what it means in his own life. Thoreau said, "Be it life or death, we crave only reality." Dickey does not accept the risk of this search, the risk that in finding reality we may find only death; that we may find no sources of transfiguration, only regret and pain. Instead, he uses a *persona* as a way out, in much the same way Eliot does.

In *Earth House Hold,* Gary Snyder points out that

> The archaic and primitive ritual dramas, which acknowledged all sides of human nature, including the destructive, demonic, and ambivalent, were liberating and harmonizing.

Neither liberation nor harmony can result from "The Firebombing," for the drama it enacts has no protagonist: now it is the poet, now it is someone else invented to bear the onus the poet does not care to take on himself. As a result, this poem trying to clarify the sources of war adds to our confusion.

* * *

We can't understand this phenomenon in poetry—this closed, unshared "I"—unless we look at its source, the closed ego of modern man, the neurotic burden which to some degree cripples us all. I mean that ego which separates us from the life of the planet, which keeps us apart from one another, which makes us feel self-conscious, inadequate, lonely, suspicious, possessive, jealous, awkward, fearful, and hostile; which thwarts our deepest desire, which is to be one with all creation. We moderns, who like to see ourselves as victims of life—victims of the so-called absurd condition—are in truth its frustrated conquerors. Our alienation is in proportion to our success in subjugating it. The more we conquer nature, the more nature becomes our enemy, and since we are, like it or not, creatures of nature, the more we make an enemy of the very life within us.

Alchemy, the search for the philosopher's stone, was, on the surface, an attempt to master nature, to change base metals into gold; secretly, however, it was a symbolic science, and its occult aim was to propitiate the sexual, creative forces in nature, and to transfigure the inner life. When a chemistry finally overthrew alchemy, in the seventeenth century, it was a decisive moment, among all the other decisive moments of that century. Overtly a quest for pure knowledge, chemistry derives its enormous energy from the desire to subdue and harness.

This is the case, of course, with the whole scientific and technological enterprise. The fatal moment was when the human mind learned the knack of detaching itself from what it studied, even when what it studied was itself. The mind became pure will: immaterial, unattached, free of the traumas of birth and death. Turned on any natural thing, the eye trained to scientific objectivity and glowing with the impersonal spirit of conquest becomes a deathray. What it kills is the creative relationship between man and thing. In the science fiction stories that scientists sometimes write on the side, they often reveal the fantasies of cosmic hostility which lurk unobserved in their learned treatises.

Not long ago it was commonly supposed that the scientific spirit would solve our social ills. We heard talk of a "cultural lag," according to which we had gained control over nature but not yet over ourselves. Science was to cure that. We now know that science is the trouble. I cannot forget how, in those days when our involvement in Vietnam was just beginning, so many social scientists blithely stepped forward to defend our madness. They were not bloodthirsty men; for the most part they were polite, mild, and well-meaning. But they saw Vietnam in geopolitical terms, as an objective, technological problem, to be dealt with by technological and social-scientific means. The United States undertook this most stupid of wars, during which so many have died, die, and will die for nothing, in exactly the same spirit in which it undertakes the exploration of space—as a challenge to our technology: *Can we do it?* Did I say, "die for nothing?" That is not quite it. They died for science.

One might have thought the Americans would be more likely to die for material gain. But no, America is not a materialist country. Perhaps there has never existed a people who cared less for material. We despise it. The effort of our technology is to turn us into nearly immaterial beings who live in a nearly immaterial world. Our most pervasive invention, plastic, is an antimaterial; it puts up no resistance, it never had its own form, it is totally subject to our will, and relative to organic materials, which return to the life cycle, it is immortal. We spend billions of dollars trying to render our bodies acceptable to our alienated condition: as odorless, hairless, sanitary and neutral as plastic. Americans who are white feel that the black man with his greater physical grace, spontaneity, and "soul" resides closer to nature, and therefore regard him as a traitor to mankind, and fear him.

This attempt to transcend materiality is, of course, a worldwide phenomenon, involving all countries and all races. It is only that the white American has taken the lead. He is the one marked and transfigured by the technological age—and I mean "transfigured" literally. What else can one make of the changes that have come over the European face after it migrated to technological America? Contrast the ancestral faces one still sees in Europe, contrast the faces in old paintings and photographs. Is it just in my imagination that the American chin has thickened, its very bones swollen, as if to repel what lies ahead? And those broad, smooth, curving, translucent eyelids, that gave such mystery to the eyes—is it my private delusion that they have disappeared, permanently rolled themselves up, turning the eyes into windows without curtains, not to be taken by surprise again? And that the nose, the feature unique to man, the part of him which moves first into the unknown, has become on our faces a small, neat bump? Maybe only healthily large teeth cause the lips to protrude, giving the all-American mouth its odd, simian pucker.

That the human face has changed at all is, of course, a question. I have perceptive friends who assure me the American face differs in no way from its European sources. These things are all guesses, and guessing itself can make it so. But Max Picard so loved the human face, so carefully meditated on it, that I have to believe something of his sense of its fall. He writes—and I choose a passage from *The Human Face* almost at random:

> In our day, it seems sometimes that were eternity but to touch it, the face of a man must fall apart, even as a ghost collapses at the touch of holy reality. . . .

> In such a face there is a fear that it may be the last. It is timorous, lest from it be taken, and it cowers within itself, it holds itself tightly, it becomes sharp and shiny. Such a face is like polished metal. It is alike a metallic model: cold. It is fashioned to endure, but not based upon eternity as were the faces of olden days. Such a face watches constantly over itself. It even fears to rest at night, so mistrustful is it of its very own sleep.

I spent a year not long ago in Southern California. There I saw men with these changed faces willing to do anything— pollute, bulldoze, ravage, lay waste—as long as it made money. That seemed in character. What surprised me was that they were willing to do it even if it didn't make money. California matters because it represents the future of the rest of us; it is a huge mirror set up on the western shore of what we shall become, just as the United States mirrors the future of the world. The Asians, too, appear to adore our technology—some of them doubtless worshiping it even while it burns them to death.

* * *

Yet one sees signs around us of the efforts to reintegrate ourselves with life. One sees it in poetry, perhaps particularly in poetry. For poetry has taken on itself the task of breaking out of the closed ego. To quote from Gary Snyder again:

> Of all the streams of civilized tradition with roots in the paleolithic, poetry is one of the few that can realistically claim an unchanged function and a relevance which will outlast most of the activities that surround us today. Poets, as few others, must live close to the world that primitive men are in: the world, in its nakedness, which is fundamental for all of us— birth, love, death; the sheer fact of being alive.

The first important poem of this new undertaking is Allen Ginsberg's "Howl." It is the first modern poem fully to break out, fully to open itself. It is a poem which *consists* of autobiography, just as confessional poetry does; yet at the same time it transcends autobiography and speaks on behalf of everyone. "Howl" has become the most famous poem of its time less by its "style" or "subject matter" than by this inner generosity.

"Howl" suffers the self, it does not step around it. It gets beyond personality by going through it. This is true of much of the interesting poetry of today. It is one reason that Robert Bly's prose poems are so moving. For the first time in his poetry, Bly in *The Morning Glory* speaks to us—and for us—in his own voice. As one reads, the "I" in the poem becomes oneself.

> I am in a cliff-hollow, surrounded by fossils and furry shells. The sea breathes and breathes under the new moon. Suddenly it rises, hurrying into the long crevices in the rock shelves, it rises like a woman's belly as if nine months has passed in a second; rising like milk to the tiny veins, it overflows like a snake going over a low wall.

> I have the sensation that half an inch under my skin there are nomad bands, stringy-legged men with firesticks and wide-eyed babies. The rocks with their backs turned to me have something spiritual in them. On these rocks I am not afraid of death; death is like the sound of the motor in an airplane as we fly, the sound so steady and comforting. And I still haven't found the woman I loved in some former life—how could I, when I loved only once on this rock, though twice in the moon, and three times in the rising water. Two spirit-children leap toward me, shouting, arms in the air. A bird with long wings comes flying toward me in the dusk, pumping just over the darkening waves. He has flown around the whole planet, it has taken him centuries. He returns to me the lean-legged runner laughing as he runs through the stringy grasses, and gives back to me my buttons, and the soft sleeves of my sweater.

The poem is personal yet common, open yet mysterious. For the moment of the poem, I, too, have loved "only once on this rock, though twice in the moon, and three times in the rising water."

We move toward a poetry in which the poet seeks an inner liberation by going so deeply into himself—into the worst of himself as well as the best—that he suddenly finds he is everyone. In James Wright's "The Life," whatever is autobiographical—and the reference in the first stanza must have its origin in something very personal and particular in Wright's life—is transmuted, opens out as the inner autobiography of us all:

> Murdered, I went, risen,
> Where the murderers are,
> That black ditch
> Of river.
>
> And if I come back to my only country
> With a white rose on my shoulder,
> What is that to you?
> It is the grave
> In blossom.
>
> It is the trillium of darkness,
> It is hell, it is the beginning of winter,
> It is a ghost town of Etruscans who have no names
> Any more.
>
> It is the old loneliness.
> It is.
> And it is
> The last time.

That poem, and the following passage from John Logan's poem, "Spring of the Thief," are among the great, self-transcending moments of contemporary poetry.

> Ekelof said there is a freshness
> nothing can destroy in us—
> not even we ourselves.
> Perhaps that
> Freshness is the changed name of God.
> Where all the monsters also hide
> I bear him in the ocean of my blood
> and in the pulp of my enormous head.
> He lives beneath the unkempt potter's grass
> of my belly and chest.

> I feel his terrible, aged heart
> moving under mine . . . can see the shadows
> of the gorgeous light
> that plays at the edges of his giant eye . . .
> or tell the faint press and hum
> of his eternal pool of sperm.
> Like sandalwood! *Like sandalwood!*
> *the righteous man*
> *perfumes the axe that falls on him.*

The selflessness in these passages is the result of entering the self, entering one's own pain and coming out on the other side, no longer only James Wright or John Logan, but all men. The voice is a particular recognizable voice; at the same time it mysteriously sheds personality and becomes simply the voice of a creature on earth speaking.

If we take seriously Thoreau's dictum, "Be it life or death, we crave only reality," if we are willing to face the worst in ourselves, we also have to accept the risk I have mentioned, that probing into one's own wretchedness one may just dig up more wretchedness. What justifies the risk is the hope that in the end the search may open and transfigure us. Many people feel one shouldn't poke under the surface—that one shouldn't tempt the gods or invite trouble, that one should be content to live with his taboos unchallenged, with his repressions and politenesses unquestioned; that just as the highest virtue in the state is law and order, so the highest virtue of poetry is formality and morality—or if immorality, then in the voice of a *persona*—and on the whole cheerful, or at least ironic, good humor. In Tacoma, Washington, once, after a reading in which I read certain poems that exposed my own wretchedness, a woman came up and handed me a poem she had written during the reading. There was a little hieroglyph for the signature. Under it, it said, "If you want me, ask." The poem went like this:

> Galway Kinnel
> Why
> Are you in love with blood?
> What
> Dark part of your soul
> Glories so
> To wallow in gore?

Deep in your mind there lies
Despair, disgust, disease.
When
Did the beauty of life
Go from your desolate soul?
How
Can life be sweet to you
Who hold a wondrous gift
And use it for
Depravity?
Your voice too is false
Your comments cruel
As the depths of your heart
Exalt in ugliness
And dwell
In death
Here
In the midst of life
You
Are a sickness.

I laughed later that night, when I read it. But the laughter died quickly. For a long time I kept the poem pinned to the wall above my desk, as a *memento mori*. It *is* a risk: it is possible we will go on to the end feeding, with less and less relish, on the bitter flesh of our heart. The worst is that we ourselves may be the last to know that this is how we spent our life.

* * *

If much stands to be lost, however, it is true that everything stands to be gained. What do we want more than that oneness which bestows—which *is*—life? We want only to be more alive, not less. And the standard of what it is to be alive is very high. It was set in our infancy. Not yet divided into mind and body, our mind still a function of our senses, we laughed, we felt joyous connection with the things around us. In adult life don't we often feel half-dead, as if we were just brains walking around in corpses? The only sense we still respect is eyesight, probably because it is so closely attached to the brain. Go into any American house at random, you will find something—a plastic flower, false tiles, some imitation paneling—*something* which can be appreciated as material only if apprehended by eyesight alone. Don't we go sightseeing in cars, thinking we can experience a landscape by looking at it through glass? A baby takes pleasure in seeing a thing, yes, but seeing is a first act. For fulfillment the baby must reach out, grasp it, put it in his mouth, suck it, savor it, taste it, manipulate it, smell it, physically be one with it. From here comes our notion of heaven itself. Every experience of happiness in later life is a stirring of that ineradicable memory of once belonging wholly to the life of the planet.

Somehow it happened that the "mind" got separated from the rest of us. It got specified as the self. In reality, the mind is only a denser place in the flesh. Might we not just as well locate our center in the genitals, or in the solar plexus? Or even in that little shadow which Hesse describes, that goes from the shoulder to the breast? We have to learn anew to take delight in the physical life.

> If I worship one thing more than another it shall
>   be the spread of my own body, or any part of it,
> Translucent mould of me it shall be you!
> Shaded ledges and rests it shall be you!
> Firm masculine colter it shall be you!
> Whatever goes to the tilth of me it shall be you!
> You my rich blood! your milky stream pale strippings
>   of my life!
> Breast that presses against other breasts it shall
>   be you!
> My brain it shall be your occult convolutions!
> Root of wash'd sweet-flag! timorous pond-snipe! nest
>   of guarded duplicate eggs! it shall be you!
> Mix'd tussled hay of head, beard, brawn, it shall be you!
> Trickling sap of maple, fibre of manly wheat, it shall
>   be you!
> Sun so generous it shall be you!
> Vapors lighting and shading my face it shall be you!
> You sweaty brooks and dews it shall be you!
> Winds whose soft-tickling genitals rub against me it
>   shall be you!
> Broad muscular fields, branches of live oak, loving
>   lounger in my winding paths, it shall be you!
> Hands I have taken, face I have kiss'd, mortal I have
>   ever touch'd, it shall be you.
>
> I dote on myself, there is that lot of me and all
>   so luscious . . .

The great thing about Whitman is that he knew *all* of our being must be loved, if we are to love any of it. I have often thought there should be a book called *Shit*, telling us that what comes out of the body is no less a part of reality, no less sacred, than what goes into it; only a little less nourishing. It's a matter of its moment in the life cycle: food eaten is on the cross, at its moment of sacrifice, while food eliminated is at its moment of ascension. There is a divine madness, remember; and if you dismiss the exuberance of self-love, you may be left with an impeccable reasonableness, but a dead body.

In the tale of Dr. Jekyll and Mr. Hyde, the vicious, animal half of the man escapes the control of the civilized, rational half and destroys it. The story is a Victorian fantasy which plays out the dread of nature; it is also a true myth of repression and its consequences. I wonder if the tale shouldn't be rewritten, with a happy ending? How would it be if, in his nightly cruising, Mr. Hyde should discover the possibility of tender love? What would happen if he came back to the fearful, overly mental, puritan, self-enclosed Dr. Jekyll and converted him, so that they went out cruising together; or else, if he came back and seduced him? This conjectural version of the story would assume that the blame for their disharmony lay more with Dr. Jekyll than with Mr. Hyde, and it would look primarily to Mr. Hyde for their salvation.

Many ancient stories tell of the mating of man and animal—the Dr. Jekyll and Mr. Hyde of nature. It seems always to be a female human and a male animal who mate, never the reverse. Of course, around farms men have always copulated with animals, and it would be difficult to render this act into an instructive myth, since the men use the animals, if not rape them. In Colin Wilson's *Encyclopedia of Murder,* he records the case of a man who preliminary to killing someone would fuck a goose, or after fucking a goose would kill someone, however you like to look at it—the basic pathology is clear. But the basic reason is that women—at least in the imagination of men—reside closer to nature, feel less threatened by it, are more willing to give themselves up to it. Leda undoubtedly knows terror as she lies under the swan—for in matings between beings so alien there must be an element of rape—but she also knows exaltation, as she gives herself to the natural life. Therefore men always depict the

Muse as female; and in this sense the poet knows himself to be of a more feminine disposition than the banker.

> Muses resemble women who creep out at night to give themselves to unknown sailors and return to talk of Chinese porcelain—porcelain is best made, a Japanese critic has said, where the conditions of life are hard—or of the Ninth Symphony— virginity renews itself like the moon—except that the Muses sometimes form in those low haunts their most lasting attachments.

So wrote Yeats. If one chooses, one can think of the muse in less fanciful terms, as Gary Snyder does:

> Widely speaking, the muse is anything other that touches you and moves you. Be it a mountain range, a band of people, the morning star, or a diesel generator. Breaks through the ego-barrier. But this touching-deep is as a mirror, and man in his sexual nature has found the clearest mirror to be his human lover.

Let me turn for a moment, then, to that widely used—or perhaps not so widely used—sentence, "I love you." Who is the "I?" Who is the "you?" Everyone except people who make scientific studies of love admits that love is a force of a kind which transcends person and personality. Wasn't Gatsby's most devastating put-down of the love between Tom and Daisy to say that it was "only personal?" Plato was eloquent in persuading us that love is a transcendent force, but in his dream, the loved person, and indeed the whole realm in which love takes place, turn into rubble. For the Christians, too, love transcended person and personality; it was not the man or woman, but the image of God in the person, that one loved. The Christians, unfortunately, were unable to permit this love to include sexual love, for it was too much for them to conceive of God as having sexual intercourse with himself through the instrumentality of his images.

D. H. Lawrence wrote an odd little poem on the subject:

> I wish I knew a woman
> who was like a red fire on the hearth
> glowing after the day's restless draughts.

So that one could draw near her
in the red stillness of the dusk
and really take delight in her
without having to make the polite effort of loving her
or the mental effort of making her acquaintance.
Without having to take a chill, talking to her.

It isn't always easy to know when Lawrence is serious and
when he is joking. As a rule of thumb, probably serious. But
this union deeper than personality, as Lawrence of course
knew, is not to be had that way. As with poetry, so with love: it
is necessary to go through the personality to reach beyond it.
Short of a swan descending from heaven, the great moments
of sexual love are not between strangers, but between those
who know and care for each other, and who then pass beyond
each other, becoming nameless creatures enacting the primal
sexuality of all life.

It is curious that sexual love, which is the only sacred ex-
perience of most lives on this earth, is a religion without a
Book. Even the *Kama Sutra* is too much like a sex manual. It is
a religion that has many poems, though, and I would like to
quote two of them, the first D. H. Lawrence's "River Roses," a
matchless account of the casting off of selves:

By the Isar, in the twilight
We were wandering and singing,
By the Isar, in the evening
We climbed the huntsman's ladder and sat swinging
In the fir-tree overlooking the marshes,
While the river met with river, and the ringing
Of their pale-green glacier water filled the evening.

By the Isar, in the twilight
We found the dark wild roses
Hanging red at the river; and simmering
Frogs were singing, and over the river closes
Was savour of ice and of roses; and glimmering
Fear was abroad. We whispered: "No one knows us.
Let it be as the snake disposes
Here in this simmering marsh."

The separate egos vanish; the wand of cosmic sexuality rules.

The following poem, section 5 from "Song of Myself,"
though not ostensibly a love poem, obviously has its source in

a love experience. It is the kind of poem Dr. Jekyll would write, after his seduction by Mr. Hyde.

> Loafe with me on the grass, loose the stop from your
>   throat,
> Not words, not music or rhyme I want, not custom or
>   lecture, not even the best,
> Only the lull I like, the hum of your valvéd voice.
>
> I mind how once we lay such a transparent summer
>   morning,
> How you settled your head athwart my hips and gently
>   turn'd over upon me,
> And parted the shirt from my bosom-bone, and plunged
>   your tongue to my bare-stript heart,
> And reach'd till you felt my beard, and reach'd till
>   you held my feet.
>
> Swiftly arose and spread around me the peace and knowledge
>   that pass all the argument of the earth,
> And I know that the hand of God is the promise of my
>   own,
> And I know that the spirit of God is the brother of my
>   own,
> And that all the men ever born are also my brothers, and
>   the women my sisters and lovers,
> And that a kelson of the creation is love,
> And limitless are leaves stiff or drooping in the fields,
> And brown ants in the little wells beneath them,
> And mossy scabs of the worm fence, heap'd stones, elder,
>   mullein and poke-weed.

* * *

The death of the self I seek, in poetry and out of poetry, is not a drying up or withering. It is a death, yes, but a death out of which one might hope to be reborn more giving, more alive, more open, more related to the natural life. I have never felt the appeal of that death of self certain kinds of Buddhism describe—that death which purges us of desire, which removes us from our loves. For myself, I would like a death that would give me more loves, not fewer. And greater desire, not less. Isn't it possible that to desire a thing, to truly desire it, is a form of having it? I suppose nothing is stronger than fate—if fate is that amount of vital energy allotted each of us—but if anything were stronger, it would not be acquiescence, the coming to want only what one already has, it would be desire, desire which rises from the roots of one's life and transfigures it.

This Navajo night-chant, which is no more than an expression of desire, gives whoever says it with his whole being, at least for the moment of saying it, and who knows, perhaps forever, everything he asks.

> Tse'gihi.
> House made of dawn.
> House made of evening light.
> House made of the dark cloud.
> House made of male rain.
> House made of dark mist.
> House made of female rain.
> House made of pollen.
> House made of grasshoppers.
> Dark cloud is at the door.
> The trail out of it is dark cloud.
> The zigzag lightning stands high upon it.
> Male deity!
> Your offering I make.
> I have prepared a smoke for you.
> Restore my feet for me.
> Restore my legs for me.
> Restore my body for me.
> Restore my mind for me.
> This very day take out your spell for me.
> Your spell remove for me.
> You have taken it away for me.
> Far off it has gone.
> Happily I recover.
> Happily my interior becomes cool.
> Happily I go forth.
> My interior feeling cool, may I walk.
> No longer sore, may I walk.
> Impervious to pain, may I walk.
> With lively feelings may I walk.
> As it used to be long ago, may I walk.
> Happily may I walk.
> Happily, with abundant dark clouds, may I walk.
> Happily, with abundant showers, may I walk.
> Happily, with abundant plants, may I walk.

Happily, on the trail of pollen, may I walk.
Happily may I walk.
Being as it used to be long ago, may I walk.
May it be beautiful before me.
May it be beautiful behind me.
May it be beautiful below me.
May it be beautiful above me.
May it be beautiful all around me.
In beauty it is finished.

Richard Kostelanetz

"Avant-Garde"
1973–78

The term *avant-garde* refers to those out front, forging a path that others will take. Initially coined to characterize the shock troops of an army, the epithet passed over into art. Used precisely, it should refer, first, to work that satisfies three discriminatory criteria: it transcends current conventions in crucial respects, establishing a discernible distance between itself and the mass of current practices; it will necessarily take considerable time to find its maximum audience; and it will probably inspire future, comparably advanced endeavors. Only a small minority can be avant-garde, for once the majority has caught up to something new, the avant-garde, by definition, will have gone someplace else. The term has the same meaning in English as in French and thus need not be italicized. Problems notwithstanding, it remains a critically useful category.

As a temporal term, avant-garde characterizes art that seems to be "ahead of its time"—that is beginning something—while "decadent" art, by contrast, stands at the end of a prosperous development. "Academic" refers to art that is conceived according to rules that are learned in the classroom; it is temporally postdecadent. Whereas decadent art is created in expectation of an immediate sale, the academic artist expects approval from his superiors. Both are essentially opportunistic, desiring immediate profit, even at the cost of likely disappearance in the near future from the corpus of art that survives by being remembered.

Avant-garde art has been defined as "whatever artists can get away with." However, this is true only in time—only if the invention contributes to an ongoing perceptible tendency or challenges an acknowledged professional issue. The exact same brand-new creation that might seem innovative at one time will seem irrelevant, if not decadent, at another.

Past art can still legitimately be called avant-garde, if it was

238

innovative at its debut. Such works comprise the history of avant-garde art in modern times.

The vanguard, the leading edge of art, is the front of the train; the derrière-garde, the caboose. Most artists ride cars in the middle.

One secondary characteristic of avant-garde art is that, in the course of entering new terrain, it violates entrenched rules—it makes current "aesthetics" seem irrelevant; it seems to descend from "false premises" or "heretical assumptions." For instance, Suzanne Langer's theory of symbolism, so prominent in the forties, is hardly relevant to the past two decades' new art—the music of John Cage, say, or Milton Babbitt, the painting of Frank Stella, the choreography of Merce Cunningham—where what you see is most, if not all, of what there is. This sense of irrelevance is less a criticism of Langer's theories than a measure of drastic difference.

One explanation for why avant-garde works should be initially hard to comprehend is not that they are intrinsically inscrutable but that they challenge the perceptual procedures of artistically educated people; they forbid easy access or easy acceptance. An audience perceives them as different, if not as forbiddingly revolutionary. Nonetheless, if the audience learns to accept an innovative work, it will stretch their perceptual capabilities, affording them kinds of perceptual experience unknown before. Edgard Varèse's *Ionization* (1931), for instance, taught a generation of listeners about the possible beauty and coherences in what they had previously perceived as percussive "noise."

A closely related characteristic is that avant-garde art usually offends people, especially serious artists, before it persuades. It strikes most of us as "wrong" before we acknowledge it as, possibly, "right"; it "fails" but still *works*.

Its author would prefer that his creation be disreputably unforgettable than commendably forgotten. (Art that offends but does not advance into new terrain is also likely to disappear.)

The "past" that the avant-garde aims to surpass is not the tradition of art but the currently decadent fashions. Harold Rosenberg has said: "Avant-garde art is haunted by fashion."

Those most antagonized by the avant-garde are not the general populace, which does not care, but the guardians of culture, who do, whether they be cultural bureaucrats, established artists, or their epigones, because *they* feel, as they sometimes admit, "threatened."

Those works that veterans dismiss and new artists debate are usually avant-garde.

Though vanguard activity may dominate discussion among professionals, it never dominates the general making of art. Most work created at any time, in every art, honors long-passed models. Even today, in the United States, most of the fiction written and published and reviewed has in form scarcely progressed beyond the early twentieth century; most poetry today is similarly decadent.

Because avant-gardes are customarily regarded as succeeding each other, they are equated with the world of fashion, in which styles also succeed each other. However, in both origins and function, the two are quite different. *Fashion* relates to the sociology of lucrative taste; *avant-garde* to the history of art. In essence, avant-garde artistic activity has a dialectical relationship with fashion, for the emerging lucrative fashions can usually be characterized as a synthesis of advanced elements, whose purposes are antithetical to those of fashion, with more familiar stuff. Though fashion imitates the tone of innovation and exploits the myth of its value, the aim of fashion is standardization; the goal of fashion's creators is a successful formula. The avant-garde artist, by contrast, is interested in discovery and self-transcendence. When an avant-garde invention becomes fashionable—as, say, collage in visual art or associational syntax in poetry has—then it begins to seem decadent, and the genuine vanguard artist feels in his gut that this new fashion is a milestone he is obliged to transcend.

Whenever the current state of an art is generally perceived as decadent or expired, a new avant-garde is destined to arise.

The aesthetic avant-garde ("left") does not coincide with the political vanguard (also "left"), the former regarding the latter as culturally insensitive and humanly exploitative, and the latter regarding the former as individualistic and politically inept. Each thinks the other is naive about cultural change; and needless to say perhaps, each is right.

The term *avant-garde* can also refer to individuals creating such path-forging art; but even by this criterion, the work itself, rather than the artist's intention, is the measure of the epithet's legitimacy. Thus, an artist or writer is avant-garde only at crucial points in his creative career, and only his most advanced works will be considered genuinely avant-garde. The phrase may also refer to artistic groups, if and only if most of its members are crucially contributing to an authentically exploratory activity.

The term is sometimes equated with cultural antagonism, for it is assumed that the "avant-garde" leads artists in their perennial war against the philistines. However, this philistine antagonism is a secondary characteristic, as artists' social position and attitudes descend from the fate of their creative efforts, rather than the reverse.

Certain conservative critics have recently asserted that "the avant-garde no longer exists," because, as they see it, the suburban public laps up all new art. However, it is both false and ignorant to use a secondary characteristic in lieu of a primary definition; and if an art critic in particular fails to use "avant-garde" as primarily an art-historical term, then he is exploiting the authority of his position to spread needless confusion. The fact that the avant-garde is widely discussed, as well as written about, scarcely makes it fashionable or lucrative.

The conservative charge is factually wrong as well, as nearly all avant-gardes in art are ignored by the middle-class public (and its agents in the culture industries), precisely because innovative work is commonly perceived as "peculiar," if not "unacceptable." Indeed, the commonness of those perceptions is, of course, a patent measure of the work's being art-historically ahead of its time.

It is also erroneous to think of all current avant-gardes as necessarily extending or elaborating previous avant-gardes. It is misleading, for instance, to classify the painter Jasper Johns as only a descendant of Dada, for implicit in his best art is a conceptual leap that reflects Dada and yet moves beyond it. Partial resemblances notwithstanding, Johns's work is done for other reasons, out of other interests, from other assumptions. Indeed, the term *avant-garde* is most appropriate when it is applied to work which is so different in intention and experience that it renders the old classifications irrelevant.

Since the avant-garde claims to be prophetic, the ultimate judge of current claims will be a future cultural public; a future-sensitive critic can only try to posit tentative estimates.

One reason why the artistic innovations of the future cannot be described today is that the avant-garde, by definition, transcends prediction.

Originality

It is untrue to say that, "There is nothing new under the sun," for always there have been and always there will be certain works that are formally so original that, were they presented to a jury of twelve experts, the sages would unanimously agree that that kind of work had not been done before.

Nonetheless, even innovative art resembles more conservative work in revealing the influence of one or another work of previous art, but what separates the two is the extent of difference. Though Stephan Mallarmé's "Un Coup de Dés" (1897) reflected certain preoccupations of earlier French poetry, it was also drastically different in certain respects, such as the disjunctiveness of its syntax and its use of the entire available space of the printed page. Few literate people have ever denied the spectacular originality of James Joyce's *Finnegans Wake*.

> Well, you know or don't you kennet or haven't I told you every telling has a taling and that's the he and the she of it. Look, look, the dusk is growing! My branches lofty are taking root. And my cold cher's gone ashley. Fieluhr? Filou! What age is at? It saon is late. 'Tis endles now senne eye or erewone last saw Waterhouse's clogh. They took it asunder, I hurd thum sigh. When will they reassemble it? O, my back, my back, my bach! I'd want to go to Aches-les-Pains. Pingpong! There's the Belle for Sexaloitez!

Distinct originality is one way of insuring that a work will be noticed and thus be remembered. Other purposes notwithstanding, every artist ultimately wants to make something that will be remembered—that will stand out from the mass of art that bombards the audience interested in it. The overwhelming bulk of current art makes the audience's perception of originality a crucial element in contemporary artistic experience.

Much original art initially strikes us as incredible. It is hard for the spectator to believe that human beings made such works as the *Wake,* Simon Rodia's Watts Towers, Charles Ives's Fourth Symphony, Pound's *Cantos,* etc. This sense of incredulity is an emotion that must be aesthetic, because it is not anything else.

Sometimes this incredible originality is entwined with an offensive quality. How dare anyone claim there is art in the utter simplicity of minimal sculpture, the elliptical style of *Naked Lunch,* the restricted vocabulary of Dick Higgins's "Structure" (1970)?

```
structure (for cary and linda)
pearls, pearls of pearls
    pearls, pearls of garlic
        pearls, pearls of leaves
pearls, garlic of pearls
    pearls, garlic of garlic
        pearls, garlic of leaves
pearls, leaves of pearls
    pearls, leaves of garlic
        pearls, leaves of leaves

garlic, pearls of pearls
    garlic, pearls of garlic
        garlic, pearls of leaves
garlic, garlic of pearls
    garlic, garlic of garlic
        garlic, garlic of leaves
garlic, leaves of pearls
    garlic, leaves of garlic
        garlic, leaves of leaves

leaves, pearls of pearls
    leaves, pearls of garlic
        leaves, pearls of leaves
leaves, garlic of pearls
    leaves, garlic of garlic
        leaves, garlic of leaves
leaves, leaves of pearls
    leaves, leaves of garlic
        leaves, leaves of leaves
```

The more familiar we become with such work, the less offensive its originality becomes. Eventually, even the conservative's skepticism about it disappears.

Extremism in politics may be a vice, but in art it is usually a virtue.

Pound speaks of literary inventors as "men who found a new process, or whose extant work gives us the first known example of a process." By these criteria, Pound himself was an inventor; so were Faulkner, Beckett, and Gertrude Stein at crucial points in their creative lives. Invention, in technology as in art, is the creation of something decisively unlike anything that went before.

Originality of this kind is, to repeat, indubitably verifiable; indeed, it is almost measurable.

Eccentricity defines personal peculiarity; originality exists outside one's self. On rare occasions, the two coincide. Originality that is not avant-garde is ultimately eccentric.

By common consent the community of art bestows a kind of patent upon genuine invention. Thus, the artist who uses it without either change or acknowledgement is customarily accused of "plagiarism." If a later artist turns the innovation to personal uses, then his or her work is initially characterized as *imitative* or *derivative*. Such reminders do not invalidate new work; instead, they give it an art-historical definition.

One factor distinguishing the present art audience from the past is the value that contemporaries place upon innovation. Because everyday life is characterized by recurrence and predictability, we turn to art for invention and surprise.

If we take the regimentation of response to be humanly pernicious, then the interruption of expectation is morally superior. Furthermore, given the fact of historical change, our perception of art, like our awareness of reality, must continually be updated. On this level, original art can be socially useful without undermining its own integrity.

Experimental

Avant-garde writing resembles experimental science in that both incorporate, to quote my *Webster's*, "an action or process undertaken to discover something not yet known." In a broad sense, all imaginative writing could be considered "experimental," as writers are continually making literature that, short of plagiarism, does not already exist.

However, only those forays that courageously court the unknown—that go well beyond established conventions—

finally deserve the honorific epithet. Francis Bacon, the father of experimental science, noted in *The New Organon* (1620): "It would be unsound and self-contradictory to expect things which have never been done can be done except by means which have never been tried."

Bertolt Brecht once said: "Only new contents permit new forms," but it is more true to say that new forms permit, as well as generate, new contents—only with new media, with new methods, can the poet or the scientist discover new ends. Indeed, new contents are better presented in older forms, precisely because unfamiliar experiences are more easily understood and communicated in familiar formats. Conversely, if a writer wants to experiment with unfamiliar forms, it might be wise to choose a familiar subject.

Art and science also share the principle that the most consequential experiments are those which are acknowledged by at least some peers, who comprise the initial audience for both experimental science and experimental art; and one practical measure of the value of a current experiment is its capacity to inspire further experiment.

At first I planned to echo the familiar sentiment that, "An artistic experiment may be successful on its own terms, but irrelevant to any larger contents, simply because it fails to generate any further exploration." However, on further thought, I was unable to think of any step-ahead artistic experiment that did not eventually have some sort of perceptible impact upon future art.

Some artistic experiments are based upon personal incompetence. When Arnold Schoenberg told his pupil John Cage that he had no talent for harmony, the young man disregarded harmony in his musical experiments; when Gertrude Stein was told her writing was often ungrammatical, she made her principal experiment the possibilities of ungrammatical English. In our time, experiments with insufficiency are more interesting, more heroic, than the exploitation of virtuosity.

One measure of "success" in literary creation is whether the language of a work creates its own world—whether it is stylistically consistent within itself—and one measure of experimental success is whether or not this language has appeared in print before. Ideally, an experimental writer reinvents language anew for every work or every phase of his artistic life. One factor that makes Gertrude Stein more significant than Thomas Wolfe, say, is that she invented not one style but several.

In both art and science, there is no future in doing what has already been done. Pound commented: "Willingness to experiment is not enough, but unwillingness to experiment is mere death."

Marcel Duchamp's reputation is based upon the quality not of his craftsmanship but of his inventions.

Pound observed that "The scientist does not expect to be acclaimed a great scientist until he has discovered something."

Historically, the great experiments *and* thus the great discoveries in literature focused upon technique rather than content.

"Forming the habit of experimental observation," Thomas Munro writes, "one learns to adjust one's apperceptive habits to new kinds of sensory effect, new meanings and arrangements." Not only artists but the audience for art also resemble scientists in making new discoveries through experimental processes, developing perceptual capacities—powers of mind—that were previously dormant.

The aim of art in our time is the creation not of "beauty" but of rare experience; the effect of art is not "pleasure" but unusual perception.

Life of Forms

Biological metaphors appropriately characterize the career of innovative forms. That is, a form is born, it grows and matures before passing through a period of senility which ushers in its eventual death. Once this process has begun, it may be opposed; but it cannot be reversed.

In serious writing, naturalistic fiction is as dead as rhymed verse, Shavian theater is as indisputably dead as linear detective fiction.

Collage, which was probably the single greatest formal invention of twentieth-century art, reached its artistic demise in the sixties. That is not to say that collage disappeared—quite the contrary is true—but that recent works indebted to collage techniques were no longer as strikingly original. What initially made collage so fertile was not just the enormous number of possibilities but its usefulness in all the arts. Once artists discovered the principle of splicing materials that would not normally be found together, the potential for realizing pointed juxtapositions seemed limitless. As the syntax of collage became familiar, it was popularized in posters, ads, and even popular music. Almost anyone with a pair of scissors and a taste for incongruity could facilely do it.

However, the time came when collage could no longer generate original art; it could no longer instill the sense of awesome surprise that even sophisticated viewers experience in the presence of something new. I estimate that this moment occurred around 1960, because I cannot think of a single experimental work, composed since then in any art, that is formally based upon collage.

The last great use of collage in poetry, for instance, occurred in Pound's *Cantos,* whose own history recapitulated the evolution of its primary form—innovative when Pound began it (1915), and yet by its end (1970), becoming as a compendium of ways in which poetry need no longer be written. The last major collage in fiction was William Burrough's *Naked Lunch* (1958); in essaying, Michel Butor's *Mobile* (1962). The last successful collages in visual art were Robert Rauschenberg's three-dimensional combines of the late fifties.

In my temporal judgment, associational syntax in poetry is as senile as the "confessional" voice; the first-person narrator in fiction seems as depleted as chronological narrative; reportage of nonsequential vignettes seems as artistically hopeless as a theater of social representation. Perhaps the surest index of spectator sophistication is the experience of discovering that something that was once shockingly original (and "unacceptable") is now utterly familiar (and, alas, acceptable). Certainly, the spectator today admiring a Braque collage appreciates it not as contemporary art but as art history.

In art, unlike life, death is one symptom of success.

Scientific Revolutions

One of the most inadvertently illuminating essays about avant-garde art is Thomas S. Kuhn's *The Structure of Scientific Revolutions* (1962), because it provides a neat and accurate model for understanding a radical change in artistic style. As Kuhn notes, a certain "paradigm" dominates a scientific field at a particular time, and by *paradigm* he means "universally recognized scientific achievements that for a time provide model problems and solutions to a community of practitioners."

By analogy, representationalism in painting and diatonic tonality in music were paradigms, while rhyme and meter in verse had a similar function within the community of poetry. Not only does this dominant paradigm characterize certain dimensions of all endeavors within an intellectual field, but it also offers general guidelines for deploying the materials of an art.

Into a settled field comes a new work that is so radically different—so revolutionary—that it conflicts with the reigning paradigms. The prime example in scientific history was the Copernican revolution in astronomy, replacing the Ptolemaic image of the universe. As Kuhn describes this process, a revolutionary work is one that "necessitated the community's rejection of one time-honored scientific theory in favor of another incompatible with it. Each produced a consequent shift in the problems available for scientific scrutiny and . . . each transformed the scientific imagination in ways that we shall ultimately need to describe as a transformation of the world within which scientific work was done." In astronomy, the prototypical revolutionary was Copernicus. In modern painting, two analogues to a scientific revolution were, of course, cubism and collage; in music, two revolutions were dissonant counterpoint and Schoenberg's twelve-tone system; in poetry two paradigms are free verse and then associational syntax, where images and perspectives are strung together, rather than developed in a step-by-step linear fashion.

It is Kuhn's thesis that the history of science does not follow a cumulative and linear path, where contributions inevitably follow upon each other. Rather, each field of science has witnessed a discontinuous series of drastic reorientations.

The histories of modern art and writing have, of course, the same structural shape, not only because every genuine artistic advance incorporates at least one prior aesthetic heresy, but also because every innovation attracts, almost as a measure of its success, both a squadron of followers and a squadron of detractors. One reason for their similarity is that both artists and scientists comprise international, self-conscious communities based upon a good deal of professional communication, especially in the form of specialized journals.

As Michael Kirby observed, "Like the scientist, the avant-garde artist is working [initially] for a very limited audience whose experience, understanding of historic developments and current concepts in the field, and interest make it possible for it to appreciate points that are unavailable to a general audience." Kirby continues elsewhere, "In art as in science, it is the new that gives the field its significance."

The arts do not evolve in the sense of becoming more complex or more refined, or in building progressively upon prior achievements; but change indeed they do. Nonetheless, change in the arts has no more direction, and ultimately no more "progress" than change in science.

As Baudelaire said, the chief task of artistic genius is the invention of a paradigm.

Denise Levertov

An Admonition
1964

And indeed what are the heavens, the earth, nay, every creature, but Hiero-
glyphis and Emblems of his glory?

Francis Quarles

You cannot crack a myth as you can crack Minoan. In hieroglyphic the meaning
is embodied in the figure itself.

Elizabeth Sewell, in *The Orphic Voice*

Deliberately to encode knowledge so as to hide it from the vulgar is the task of
cipher but never of myth or poetry. . . . "This stands for that" . . . is cipher and
not myth.

Ibid.

"No ideas but in things" does not mean "No ideas." Nor does
it specify:
"No ideas but in everyday things,
          modern things,
               urban things." No! It means that:
poetry appears when meaning is embodied in the figure.

Written for the magazine *things* (No. 1, Fall, 1964), in response to a
manifesto sent me by the editors, which said in part: "The title [of
the magazine] is from a line in W. C. Williams's *Paterson:* ' . . . no
ideas but in things.' It reflects our awareness that literature should be
direct and particular, grounded in the concrete events of contempo-
rary life. It should be literature of assertion rather than analysis,
statement rather than criticism. . . . The language . . . cannot be that
of 'humanist' literature. . . . Allusions to Actaeon do not speak to us
of pain and terror. . . . We shall not . . . publish lyrics about Love,
because each experience of love differs from every other experience.
We will publish poems which relate specific love experiences in the
metaphor of the world we recognize and live in. . . . The essays we
publish will present human facts not sociological generalizations."

Language is not the dress but the incarnation of thought.

Wordsworth

Life is no less complex and mysterious than it has always been. That we dwell in enormous cities, and invent and use astonishing machinery, does not simplify it, but continually reveals the dissolution of limit after limit to physical possibility. Our still tentative awareness of the great gulfs of the unconscious, in constant transformation like the marvelous cloudscapes one sees from a jet plane, must surely lead to awe, not to supposed simplicity. Therefore if our poetry is to seek truth—and it must, for that is a condition of its viability, breath to its lungs—then it cannot confine itself to what you, the editors of *things,* in your prospectus, have called *direct statement,* but must allow for all the dazzle, shadow, bafflement, leaps of conjecture, prayers, and dream-substance of that quest.

"Allusions to Actaeon do not speak to us of pain and terror," you say. I know there have been many poems on mythological themes written by subject-seeking poets not seriously engaged with the life of art. Right. But if a poet within himself identifies with Actaeon; or has felt the hand of any god on his shoulder; or has himself been steeped in the cosmogony and mythological history of any place and time; then (if he *is* a poet) he can write of it so that his pain and terror, or delight, will be felt by the reader whether or not that reader's education has given him specific clues to the allusion. Or rather, yes, you are right, *allusions* tell one nothing: Actaeon (or any other personage of the imagination) must be present in the poem. It is that *presentness* that is the "direct statement" I *do* believe in; not the banishment of Actaeon. "*A poetry denies its end in any* descriptive *act, I mean any act which leaves the attention outside the poem,*" Robert Creeley wrote in *To Define.* (And this—the attention being put or left outside of the work: given allusions, references, only, to things not present in the substance of the work—is not the same as having the attention *led to awareness* of things that though not named, not visible, exist within the universe of the work.)

"We shall not publish lyrics about Love, because each experience of love differs from every other experience." But the idea of Love, the seeking to understand it, may be a passion in

DENISE LEVERTOV / 251

a man. Will you write off Dante, will you write off George Herbert? Will you write off Robert Duncan today, when he writes for instance,

> for I went down into the end of all things
> to bring up the spirit of Man before me
> > to the beginnings of Love

or:

> > The light that is Love
> rushes on toward passion. It verges upon Dark.
> > Roses and blood flood the clouds.
> Solitary first riders advance into legend.

or:

> > It is life
> > that tenders   green shoots of
> > hurt and healing

> we name Love.

"We shall look for innovation in the content and language of a poem, not in its form. There are no new forms: free verse is merely another vehicle available to capable craftsmen." This intention reveals a basic misunderstanding of the nature of form. Form exists only *in* the content and language. The visual shape of a poem is not its form but a result of the notation of its form. Oh, not to quibble, it is true that the set forms exist abstractly, too; sonnet, sestina, etc., have their rules, and one can invent rules for new "forms" in this sense ad infinitum. But this is a rudimentary view. In fact—and not only in organic poetry and "free verse"—form is the total interactive functioning of content and language, including every contributing element. The form of a man is not that he has two legs, two arms, a head and body and no tail, but the sum of his anatomical, physiological, mental, textural, moral, motor, etc., structure. And the form of a poem comprises all the equivalent components you can think of.

"Form is never more than the extension of content." At the Vancouver poetry conference this summer (1963) I proposed to Robert Creeley, the originator of this now famous formula, that it should be changed to read: "Form is never more than the *revelation* of content" (to which he agreed).

Against the editorial statement that "there are no new forms: free verse is merely another vehicle," etc., I pose my belief that the poet, not the poem, is a vehicle.

All poetry is experimental poetry.

Wallace Stevens

Robert Duncan (in *The Day Book,* part of a work in progress centered in a study of the poetry of H.D.) has pointed out how the poets and critics of the school of Rational Imagination—and we still have them with us—have regarded words "not as powers but as counters." A misinterpretation of "No ideas but in things" can lead to a similar stance. But the poem leaves the room the moment the poet begins to use its fallen eyelashes, its nail-parings, its frozen tears, its drops of blood, and eventually its fingers and toes in his checker game. No sir.

"Ornament does not interest us." Here again you oversimplify. The "ornaments" in a harpsichord piece show how ornament can be functional. A lapel without a buttonhole, a buttonhole without a flower, are no more virtuous than those whose hole invites a flower, whose flower invites a smile.

We need a poetry not of *direct statement* but of *direct evocation:* a poetry of hieroglyphics, of embodiment, incarnation; in which the personages may be of myth or of Monday, no matter, if they are of the living imagination.

You asked for my "moral support," and how could I *not* give it to a magazine that takes its title from *Paterson,* and from a line that has always meant so much to me? You will know, I think, that it is given with genuine interest, just because, not in spite of, its being in the form of admonition.

Origins of a Poem
1968

Some time in 1960 I wrote "The Necessity," a poem which has remained, for me, a kind of testament, or a point of both moral and technical reference, but which has seemed obscure to some readers. Since I don't think its diction or its syntax really are obscure, it seems to me their difficulties with it must arise from their unawareness of the ground it stands on, or is rooted in; or to put it another way, the poem—any poem, but especially a poem having for the poet that character of testament—is fruit, flower, or twig of a tree, and is not to be fully comprehended without some knowledge of the tree's nature and structure, even though its claim to *be* a poem must depend on internal evidence alone. What I propose to do here is not to paraphrase or explicate "The Necessity," which I assume to be a poem, but to provide and explore some of the attitudes and realizations to which it is related.

I keep two kinds of notebooks: one is a kind of anthology of brief essential texts, the other a journal that includes meditations or ruminations on such texts. In drawing from these sources, as I propose to do here, I am not implying that all of them are literally antedecents, in my consciousness, of this particular poem. In fact, although most or all of the sources—the quotations I shall be making from other writers—were probably familiar to me by 1960, and in many instances long before, and had been copied out by then into my private anthology, the reflections on them written in my journals are of later date. I am therefore not speaking of simple sequence but of habitual preoccupations, which accrue and which periodically emerge in different forms.

One such preoccupation forms itself as a question. What is the task of the poet? What is the essential nature of his work? Are these not questions we too often fail to ask ourselves, as we blindly pursue some form of poetic activity? In the confusion of our relativistic age and our eroding, or at least rapidly changing, culture, the very phrase, "the task of the poet," may seem to have a nineteenth-century ring, both highfalutin and irrelevant. Our fear of the highfalutin is related to the salutary dislike of hypocrisy; but I believe we undercut ourselves, deprive ourselves of certain profound and necessary understandings, if we dismiss the question as irrelevant, and refuse, out of what is really only a kind of embarrassment, to consider as a task, and a lofty one, the engagement with language into which we are led by whatever talent we may have. And precisely this lack of an underlying conception of what the poet is doing accounts for the subject-seeking of some young poets—and maybe some old ones too—and for the emptiness, flippancy, or total subjectivity of a certain amount of writing that goes under the name of poetry.

Years ago, I copied out this statement by Ibsen in a letter.

> The task of the poet is to make clear to himself, and thereby to others, the temporal and eternal questions. . . .

In 1959 or 1960, I used these words as the subject of one of "Three Meditations." The three formed one poem, so that in referring to this one alone certain allusions are lost; but it makes a certain amount of sense on its own:

> Barbarians
> throng the straight roads of
> my empire, converging
> on black Rome.
> There is darkness in me.
> Silver sunrays
> sternly, in tenuous joy
> cut through its folds:
> mountains
> arise from cloud.
> Who was it yelled, cracking
> the glass of delight?
> Who sent the child
> sobbing to bed, and woke it
> later to comfort it?
> I, I, I, I.
> I multitude, I tyrant,

> I angel, I you, you
> world, battlefield, stirring
> with unheard litanies, sounds of piercing
> green half-smothered by
> strewn bones.

My emphasis was on asking oneself the questions, internalizing them, on coming to realize how much the apparently external problems have their parallels within us. (Parenthetically, I would suggest that man has to recognize not only that he tends to project his personal problems on the external world but also that he is a microcosm within which indeed the same problems, the same tyrannies, injustices, hopes, and mercies act and react and demand resolution.) This internalization still seems to me what is essential in Ibsen's dictum: what the poet is called on to clarify is not answers but the existence and nature of questions; and his likelihood of so clarifying them for others is made possible only through dialogue with himself. Inner colloquy as a means of communication with others was something I assumed in the poem but had not been at that time overtly concerned with, though in fact I had already translated a Toltec poem that includes the line, "The true artist / maintains dialogue with his heart."

What duality does *dialogue with himself, dialogue with his heart,* imply? "Every art needs two—one who makes it, and one who needs it," Ernst Barlach, the German sculptor and playwright, is reported to have said. If this is taken to mean *someone out there* who needs it—an audience—the working artist is in immediate danger of externalizing his activity, of distorting his vision to accommodate it to what he knows, or supposes he knows, his audience requires, or to what he thinks it ought to hear. Writing to a student in 1964, I put it this way:

> . . . you will find yourself not saying all you have to say—you will limit yourself according to your sense of his, or her, or their, capacity. In order to do *all that one can* in any given instance (and nothing less than all is good enough, though the artist, not being of a complacent nature, will never feel sure he *has* done all) one must develop objectivity: at some stage in the writing of a poem you must dismiss from your mind all special knowledge (of what you were *intending* to say, of private allu-

sions, etc.) and read it with the innocence you bring to a poem by someone unknown to you. If you satisfy yourself as *reader* (not just as "self-expressive" writer) you have a reasonable expectation of reaching others too.

This "reader within one" is identical with Barlach's "one who needs" the work of art. To become aware of him safeguards the artist both from the superficialities resulting from overadaptation to the external, and from miasmic subjectivities. My reference above to "self-expression" is closely related to what I believe Ibsen must have meant by "to make clear to himself." A self-expressive act is one which makes the doer feel liberated, "clear" in the act itself. A scream, a shout, a leaping into the air, a clapping of hands—or an effusion of words associated for their writer at that moment with an emotion—all these are self-expressive. They satisfy their performer momentarily. But they are not art. And the poet's "making clear," which Ibsen was talking about, *is* art: it goes beyond (though it includes) the self-expressive verbal effusion, as it goes beyond the ephemeral gesture; it is a construct of words that *remains* clear even after the writer has ceased to be aware of the associations that initially impelled it. This kind of "making clear" engages both the subjective and objective in him. The difference is between the satisfaction of exercising the power of utterance as such, of *saying,* of the clarity of action; and of the autonomous clarity of *the thing said,* the enduring clarity of the right words. Cid Corman once said in a broadcast that poetry gives us "not experience thrown as a personal problem on others but experience as an order that will sing to others."

The poet—when he is writing—is a priest; the poem is a temple; epiphanies and communion take place within it. The communion is triple: between the maker and the needer within the poet; between the maker and the needers outside him—those who need but can't make their own poems (or who do make their own but need this one too); and between the human and the divine in both poet and reader. By divine I mean something beyond both the making and the needing elements, vast, irreducible, a spirit summoned by the exercise of needing and making. When the poet converses with this god he has summoned into manifestation, he reveals to others the possibility of their own dialogue with the god in themselves. Writing the poem is the poet's means of summoning the divine; the reader's may be through reading the poem, or through what the experience of the poem leads him to.

Rilke wrote in a letter:

> . . . art does not ultimately tend to produce more artists. It does not mean to call anyone over to it; indeed, it has always been my guess that it is not concerned at all with any effect. But while its creations, having issued irresistibly from an inexhaustible source, stand there strangely quiet and surpassable among things, it may be that involuntarily they become somehow exemplary for *every* human activity by reason of their innate disinterestedness, freedom, and intensity. . . .

It is when making and needing have a single point of origin that this "disinterestedness" occurs. And only when it does occur are the "freedom and intensity" generated which "involuntarily become exemplary"—which do, that is, communicate to others outside the artist's self. That is the logic of Ibsen's word "thereby" ("to make clear to himself and *thereby* to others").

I'd like to take a closer look at this word *need*. The need I am talking about is specific (and it is the same, I think, that Rilke meant when in the famous first letter to the Young Poet he told him he should ask himself, "*Must* I write?"). This need is the need for a *poem;* when this fact is not recognized, other needs—such as an undifferentiated need for self-expression, which could just as well find satisfaction in a gesture or an action; or the need to reassure the ego by writing something that will impress others—are apt to be mistaken for specific poem-need. Talent will not save a poem written under these misapprehensions from being weak and ephemeral.

For years I understood the related testimony of Jean Hélion, the contemporary French painter, only as it concerned "integrity" and as an affirmation of the *existence* of an "other" within oneself, when he wrote in an English art magazine of the 1940s:

> Art degenerates if not kept essentially the language of the mysterious being hidden in each man, behind his eyes. I act as if this hidden being got life only through the manipulation of plastic quantities, as if they were his only body, as if their growth were his only future. I identify him with his language.

> Instead of a description, an expression, or a comment, art becomes a realization with which the urge to live collaborates as a mason.

But when I reconsidered this passage in relation to how the transition from the inner world, inner dialogue, of the artist, to communication with any external other, is effected, I came to realize that Hélion is also implying that it is through the sensuous substance of the art, and only through that, that the transition is made.

The act of realizing inner experience in material substance is in itself an action *toward others,* even when the conscious intention has not gone beyond the desire for self-expression. Just as the activity of the artist gives body and future to "the mysterious being hidden behind his eyes," so the very fact of concrete manifestation, of paint, of words, reaches over beyond the world of inner dialogue. When Hélion says that then art becomes a realization, he clearly means not "awareness" but quite literally "real-ization," making real, substantiation. Instead of description, expression, comment—all of which only refer to an absent subject—art becomes substance, entity.

Heidegger, interpreting Hölderlin, says that to be human is to *be a conversation*—a strange and striking way of saying that communion is the very basis of human living, of *living humanly.* The poet develops the basic human need for dialogue in concretions that are audible to others; in listening, others are stimulated into awareness of their own needs and capacities, stirred into taking up their own dialogues, which are so often neglected (as are the poet's own, too often, when he is not actively *being* a poet). Yet this effect, or result, of his work, though he cannot but be aware of it, cannot be the *intention* of the poet, for such outward, effect-directed intention is self-defeating.

Man's vital need for communion, his humanity's being rooted in "conversation," is due to the fact that since living things, and parts of living things, atrophy if not exercised in their proper functions and since man does contain, among his living parts, the complementary dualities of Needer and Maker, he must engage them if they are not to deteriorate. That is why Hélion speaks of "the urge to live collaborating as a mason" in the realization of art. The two beings are one being, mutually dependent. The life of both depends not merely on mutual recognition but on the manifestation of that recognition in substantial terms—whether as "plastic quantities" or as words (or in the means of whatever art is in question). The substance, the means, of an art, is an incarnation—not reference but phenomenon. A poem is an indivisibility of "spirit and matter" much more absolute than what most people seem to understand by "synthesis of form and content." That phrase is often taken to imply a process of will, craft, taste, and understanding, by which the form of a work may painstakingly be molded to a perfect expression of, or vehicle for, its content. But artists know this is *not* the case—or only as a recourse, a substitute in thin times for the real thing. It is without doubt the proper process for certain forms of writing—for exposition of ideas, for critical studies. But in the primary work of art it exists, at best, as a stepping-stone to activity less laborious, less linked to effort and will. Just as the "other being" of Hélion's metaphor is *identified,* in process, with his language, which is his "only body, his only future," so *content,* which is the dialogue between him and the "maker," *becomes* form. Emerson says, "insight which expresses itself by what is called Imagination *does not come by study,* but by the intellect being *where and what it sees,* by sharing the path or circuit of things through forms, and so making them translucid to others" (emphasis added). Goethe says, "moralists think of the ulterior effect, about which the true artist troubles himself as little as Nature does when she makes a lion or a hummingbird." And Heidegger, in "Hölderlin and the Essence of Poetry," writes:

> Poetry looks like a game and is not. A game does indeed bring men together, but in such a way that each forgets himself in the process. In poetry, on the other hand, man is reunited on the foundation of his existence. There he comes to rest; not indeed to the seeming rest of inactivity and emptiness of thought, but to that infinite state of rest in which all powers and relations are active.

"Disinterested intensity," of which Rilke wrote, then, is truly exemplary and affective intensity. What Charles Olson has called a man's "filling of his given space," what John Donne said of the presence of God in a straw—"God is a straw in a straw"—point toward that disinterest. The strawness of straw, the humanness of the human, is their divinity; in that intensity is the "divine spark" Hasidic lore tells us dwells in all created things. "Who then is man?" Heidegger asks. "He who must affirm what he is. To affirm means to declare; but at the same time it means: to give in the declaration a guarantee of what is declared. Man is *he* who he *is,* precisely in the affirmation of his own existence."

Olson's words about filling our given space occur in a passage that further parallels Heidegger:

> . . . a man, carved
> out of himself, so wrought he
> fills his given space, makes
> traceries sufficient to
> others' needs . . .
> here is
> social action, for the poet
> anyway, his
> politics, his
> needs . . .

Olson is saying, as Heidegger is saying, that it is *by* being what he is capable of being, *by* living his life so that his identity is "carved," is "wrought," *by* filling his given space, that a man, and in particular a poet as a representative of an activity peculiarly human, *does* make "traceries sufficient to others' needs" (which is, in the most profound sense, a "social" or "political" action). Poems bear witness to the manness of man, which, like the strawness of straw, is an exiled spark. Only by the light and heat of these divine sparks can we see, can we feel, the extent of the human range. They bear witness to the *possibility* of "disinterest, freedom, and intensity."

"Therefore dive deep," wrote Edward Young, author of the once so popular, later despised, "Night Thoughts,"

> dive deep into thy bosom; learn the depths, extent, bias, and full fort of thy mind; contract full intimacy with the stranger within thee; excite and cherish every spark of intellectual light and heat, however smothered under former negligence, or scattered through the dull, dark mass of common thoughts; and collecting them into a body, let thy genius rise (if genius thou hast) as the sun from chaos; and if I then should say, like an Indian, Worship it (though too bold) yet should I say little more than my second rule enjoins, *viz.,* Reverence thyself.

What I have up to now been suggesting as the task of the poet may seem of an Emersonian idealism (though perhaps

Emerson has been misread on this point) that refuses to look man's capacity for evil square in the eyes. Now as perhaps never before, when we are so acutely conscious of being ruled by evil men, and that in our time man's inhumanity to man has swollen to proportions of perhaps unexampled monstrosity, such a refusal would be no less than idiotic. Or I may seem to have been advocating a Nietzschean acceptance of man's power for evil, simply on the ground that it is among his possibilities. But Young's final injunction, in the passage just quoted, is what, for me, holds the clue to what must make the poet's humanity *humane*. "Reverence thyself" is necessarily an aspect of Schweitzer's doctrine of Reverence for Life, the recognition of oneself as *life that wants to live* among other *forms of life that want to live*. This recognition is indissoluble, reciprocal, and dual. There can be no self-respect without respect for others, no love and reverence for others without love and reverence for oneself; and no recognition of others is possible without the imagination. The imagination of what it is to *be* those other forms of life that want to live is the only way to recognition; and it is that imaginative recognition that brings compassion to birth. Man's capacity for evil, then, is less a positive capacity, for all its horrendous activity, than a failure to develop man's most human function, the imagination, to its fullness, and consequently a failure to develop compassion.

But how is this relevant to the practice of the arts, and of poetry in particular? Reverence for life, if it is a necessary relationship to the world, must be so for all people, not only for poets. Yes; but it is the poet who has language in his care; the poet who more than others recognizes language also as a *form of life* and a common resource to be cherished and served as we should serve and cherish earth and its waters, animal and vegetable life, and each other. The would-be poet who looks on language merely as something to be used, as the bad farmer or the rapacious industrialist looks on the soil or on rivers merely as things to be used, will not discover a deep poetry; he will only, according to the degree of his skill, construct a counterfeit more or less acceptable—a subpoetry, at best efficiently representative of his thought or feeling—a reference, not an incarnation. And he will be contributing, even if not in any immediately apparent way, to the erosion of language, just as the irresponsible, irreverent farmer and industrialist erode the land and pollute the rivers. All of our common resources, tangible or intangible, need to be given to, not exclusively taken from. They require the care that arises from intellectual love—from an understanding of their perfections.

Moreover, the poet's love of language must, if language is to reward him with unlooked-for miracles, that is, with poetry, amount to a passion. The passion for the things of the world and the passion for naming them must be in him indistinguishable. I think that Wordsworth's intensity of feeling lay as much in his naming of the waterfall as in his physical apprehension of it, when he wrote:

> ... The sounding cataract
> Haunted me like a passion....

The poet's task is to hold in trust the knowledge that language, as Robert Duncan has declared, is not a set of counters to be manipulated, but a Power. And only in this knowledge does he arrive at music, at that quality of song within speech which is not the result of manipulations of euphonious parts but of an attention, at once to the organic relationships of experienced phenomena and to the latent harmony and counterpoint of language itself as it is identified with those phenomena. Writing poetry is a process of discovery, revealing *inherent* music, the music of correspondences, the music of inscape. It parallels what, in a person's life, is called individuation: the evolution of consciousness toward wholeness, not an isolation of intellectual awareness but an awareness involving the whole self, a *knowing* (as man and woman "know" one another), a touching, a "being in touch."

All the thinking I do about poetry leads me back, always, to Reverence for Life as the ground for poetic activity; because it seems the ground for Attention. This is not to put the cart before the horse: some sense of identity, at which we wonder; an innocent self-regard, which we see in infants and in the humblest forms of life; these come first, a center out of which Attention reaches. Without Attention—to the world outside us, to the voices within us—what poems could possibly come into existence? Attention is the exercise of Reverence for the "other forms of life that want to live." The progression seems clear to me: from Reverence for Life to Attention to Life, from Attention to Life to a highly developed Seeing and Hearing, from Seeing and Hearing (faculties almost indistinguishable for the poet) to the Discovery and Revelation of Form, from Form to Song.

There are links in this chain of which I have not spoken, except to name them—the heightened Seeing and Hearing that result from Attention to any thing, their relation to the discovery and revelation of Form. To speak intelligibly of them would take more time and space than I have. But I hope that I have conveyed some idea of the true background of a poem, and have helped to define for others much that they have already intuited in and for their own labors, perhaps without knowing that they knew it:

The Necessity

From love one takes
petal to *rock* and *blesséd*
away towards
descend,

one took thought
for frail tint and spectral
glisten, trusted
from way back that stillness,

one knew
that heart of fire, rose
at the core of gold glow,
could go down undiminished,

for love and
or if in fear knowing
the risk, knowing
what one is touching, one does it,

each part
of speech a spark
awaiting redemption, each
a virtue, a power

in abeyance unless we
give it care
our need designs in us. Then
all we have led away returns to us.

On the Function of the Line
1979

Not only hapless adolescents, but many gifted and justly esteemed poets writing in contemporary nonmetrical forms, have only the vaguest concept, and the most haphazard use, of the line. Yet there is at our disposal no tool of the poetic craft more important, none that yields more subtle and precise effects, than the line-break if it is properly understood.

If I say that its function in the development of modern poetry in English is evolutionary I do not mean to imply that I consider modern, nonmetrical poetry "better" or "superior" to the great poetry of the past, which I love and honor. That would obviously be absurd. But I do feel that there are few poets today whose sensibility naturally expresses itself in the traditional forms (except for satire or pronounced irony), and that those who do so are somewhat anachronistic. The closed, contained quality of such forms has less relation to the relativistic sense of life which unavoidably prevails in the late twentieth century than modes that are more exploratory, more open-ended. A sonnet may end with a question; but its essential, underlying structure arrives at *conclusion.* "Open forms" do not necessarily terminate inconclusively, but their degree of conclusion is—structurally, and thereby expressively—less pronounced, and partakes of the open quality of the whole. They do not, typically, imply a dogmatic certitude; whereas, under a surface, perhaps, of individual doubts, tn4the structure of the sonnet or the heroic couplet bears witness to the certitudes of these forms' respective epochs of origin. The forms more apt to express the sensibility of our age are the exploratory, open ones.

In what way is contemporary, non-metrical poetry exploratory? What I mean by that word is that such poetry, more than most poetry of the past, incorporates and reveals the *process* of thinking/feeling, feeling/thinking, rather than focusing more exclusively on its *results;* and in so doing it explores (or can explore) human experience in a way that is not wholly new but is (or can be) valuable in its subtle difference of approach: valuable both as human testimony and as aesthetic experience. And the crucial precision tool for creating this exploratory mode is the line-break. The most obvious function of the line-break is rhythmic: it can record the slight (but meaningful) hesitations between word and word that are characteristic of the mind's dance among perceptions but which are not noted by grammatical punctuation. Regular punctuation is a part of regular sentence structure, that is, of the expression of completed thoughts; and this expression is typical of prose, even though prose is not at all times bound by its logic. But in poems one has the opportunity not only, as in expressive prose, to depart from the syntactic norm, but to make manifest, by an intrinsic structural means, the interplay or counterpoint of process and completion—in other words, to present the dynamics of perception *along with* its arrival at full expression. The line-break is a form of punctuation *additional* to the punctuation that forms part of the logic of completed thoughts. Line-breaks—together with intelligent use of indentation and other devices of scoring—represent a peculiarly *poetic*, a-logical, parallel (not competitive) punctuation.

What is the nature of the a-logical pauses the line-break records? If readers will think of their own speech, or their silent inner monologue, when describing thoughts, feelings, perceptions, scenes or events, they will, I think, recognize that they frequently hesitate—albeit very briefly—as if with an unspoken question—a "what?" or a "who?" or a "how?"—before nouns, adjectives, verbs, adverbs, none of which require to be preceded by a comma or other regular punctuation in the course of syntactic logic. To incorporate these pauses in the rhythmic structure of the poem can do several things: for example, it allows the reader to share more intimately the experience that is being articulated; and by introducing an a-logical counter-rhythm into the logical rhythm of syntax it causes, as they interact, an effect closer to song than to statement, closer to dance than to walking. Thus the emotional experience of empathy or identification plus the sonic complexity of the language structure synthesize in an intense aesthetic order that is different from that which is received from a poetry in which metric forms are combined with logical syntax alone. (Of course, the management of the line in *metrical* forms may also permit the recording of such a-logical pauses; Gerard Manley Hopkins provides an abundance of evidence for that. But Hopkins, in this as in other matters, seems to be "the exception that proves the rule"; and the alliance of metric forms and the similarly "closed" or "complete" character of logical syntax seems natural and appropriate, inversions notwithstanding. Inversions of normal prose word order were, after all, a stylistic convention, adopted from choice, not technical ineptitude, for centuries; although if utilized after a certain date they strike one as admissions of lack of skill, and indeed are the first signs of the waning of a tradition's viability.) It is not that the dance of a-logical thinking/feeling in process *cannot* be registered in metric forms, but rather that to do so seems to go against the natural grain of such forms, to be a forcing of an intractable medium into inappropriate use—whereas the potential for such use is implicit in the constantly evolving nature of open forms.

But the most particular, precise, and exciting function of the line-break, and the least understood, is its effect on the *melos* of the poem. It is in this, and not only in rhythmic effects, that its greatest potential lies, both in the exploration of areas of human consciousness and in creating new aesthetic experiences. How do the line-breaks affect the melodic element of a poem? So simply that it seems amazing that this aspect of their function is disregarded—yet not only student poetry workshops but any magazine or anthology of contemporary poetry provides evidence of a general lack of understanding of this factor; and even when individual poets manifest an intuitive sense of how to break their lines it seems rarely to be accompanied by any theoretical comprehension of what they've done right. Yet it is not hard to demonstrate to students that—given that the deployment of the poem on the page is regarded as a score, that is, as the visual instructions for auditory effects—the way the lines are broken affects not only rhythm but pitch patterns.

Rhythm can be sounded on a monotone, a single pitch; melody is the result of pitch patterns combined with rhythmic patterns. The way in which line-breaks, observed, respectfully, as a part of a score (and regarded as, say, roughly a half-comma in duration), determine the pitch pattern of a sentence, can clearly be seen if a poem, or a few lines of it, is written out in a variety of ways (changing the line-breaks but nothing else) and read aloud. Take, for instance, these lines of my own (picked at random):

> Crippled with desire, he questioned it.
> Evening upon the heights, juice of the pomegranate:
> who could connect it with sunlight?
>
> From "4 Embroideries: II, Red Snow"

Read them aloud. Now try reading the same words aloud from this score:

> Crippled with desire, he
> questioned it. Evening
> upon the heights,
> juice of the pomegranate:
> who
> could connect it with sunlight?

Or

> Crippled
> with desire, he questioned
> it. Evening
> upon the heights, juice
> of the pomegranate:
> who could
> connect it with sunlight?

The intonation, the ups and downs of the voice, involuntarily change as the rhythm (altered by the place where the tiny pause or musical "rest" takes place) changes. These changes could be recorded in graph form by some instrument, as heartbeats or brain waves are graphed. The point is not whether the lines, as I wrote them, are divided in the best possible way; as to that, readers must judge for themselves. I am simply pointing out that, read naturally but with respect for the line-break's fractional pause, a pitch pattern change *does occur* with each variation of lineation. A beautiful example of expressive lineation is William Carlos Williams's well-known poem about the old woman eating plums.

> They taste good to her.
> They taste good
> to her. They taste
> good to her.
>
> "To a poor old woman"

First the statement is made; then the word *good* is (without the clumsy overemphasis a change of typeface would give) brought to the center of our (and her) attention for an instant; then the word *taste* is given similar momentary prominence, with "good" sounding on a new note, reaffirmed—so that we have first the general recognition of well-being, then the intensification of that sensation, then its voluptuous location in the sense of taste. And all this is presented through indicated pitches, that is, by melody, not by rhythm alone.

I have always been thrilled by the way in which the musicality of a poem could arise from what I called "fidelity to experience," but it took me some time to realize what the mechanics of such precision were as they related to this matter of pitch pattern. The point is that, just as vowels and consonants affect the music of poetry not by mere euphony but by expressive, significant interrelationship, so the nuances of meaning apprehended in variations of pitch create *significant, expressive melody,* not just a pretty "tune" in the close tone-range of speech.

One of the ways in which many poets reveal their lack of awareness about the function of the line-break is the way in which they will begin a line with the word "it," for instance, even when it is clear from the context that they don't want the extra emphasis—relating to both rhythm and pitch—this gives it. Thus, if one writes,

> He did not know
> it, but at his very moment
> his house was burning,

The word "it" is given undue importance. Another example is given in my second variant of the lines from "Red Snow." The "it" in the third line is given a prominence entirely without significance—obtrusive and absurd. When a poet places a word meaninglessly from the sonic point of view it seems clear that he or she doesn't understand the effect of doing so—or is confusedly tied to the idea of "enjambment." Enjambment is useful in preventing the monotony of too many end-stopped lines in a metrical poem, but the desired variety can be attained by various other means in contemporary open forms; and to take away from the contemporary line its fractional pause (which, as I've said, represents, or rather manifests, a comparable minuscule but affective hesitation in the thinking/feeling process) is to rob a precision tool of its principal use. Often the poet unsure of any principle according to which to end a line will write as if the real break comes after the first word of the next line, e.g.,

> As children in their night
> gowns go upstairs . . . ,

where *if one observes the score* an awkward and inexpressive "rest" occurs between two words that the poet, reading aloud, links naturally as "nightgowns." X. J. Kennedy's definition of a run-on line is that "it does not end in punctuation and therefore is read with only a *slight pause* after it," whereas "if it ends in a full pause—usually indicated by some mark of punctuation—we call it *end-stopped*" (my italics on "slight pause"). Poets who write nonmetrical poems but treat the line-break as nonexistent are not even respecting the traditional "slight pause" of the end-stoppped line. The fact is, they are confused about what the line is at all, and consequently some of our best and most influential poets have increasingly turned to the prose paragraph for what I feel are the wrong reasons—less from a sense of the peculiar virtues of the prose poem than from a despair of making sense of the line.

One of the important virtues of comprehending the function of the line-break, that is, of the line itself, is that such comprehension by no means causes poets to write like one another. It is a *tool,* not a style. As a tool, its use can be incorporated into any style. Students in a workshop who grasp the idea of accurate scoring do not begin to all sound alike. Instead, each one's individual voice sounds more clearly, because each one has gained a degree of control over how they want a poem to sound. Sometimes a student scores a poem one way on paper, but reads it aloud differently. My concern—and that of his or her fellow students once they have understood the problem—is to determine which way the author wants the poem to sound. Someone will read it back to him or her as written and someone else will point out the ways in which the text, the score, was ignored in the reading. "Here you ran on," "Here you paused, but it's in the middle of a line and there's no indication for a 'rest' there." Then the student poet can decide, or feel out, whether he or she wrote it down wrong but read it right, or vice versa. That decision is a very personal one and has quite as much to do with the individual sensibility of the writer and the unique character of the experience embodied in the words of the poem, as with universally recognizable rationality, though that may play a part, too. The outcome, in any case, is rather to define and clarify individual voices than to homogenize them; because *reasons* for halts and checks, emphases and expressive pitch changes, will be as various as the persons writing. Comprehension of the function of the line-break gives to each unique creator the power to be more precise, and thereby more, not less, individuated. The voice thus revealed will be not necessarily the recognizable "outer" one heard in poets who have taken Olson's "breath" theory all too literally, but rather the inner voice, the voice of each one's solitude made audible and singing to the multitude of other solitudes.

Excess of subjectivity (and hence incommunicability) in the making of structural decisions in open forms is a problem only when the writer has an inadequate form sense. When the written score precisely notates perceptions, a whole—an inscape or gestalt—begins to emerge; and the gifted writer is not so submerged in the parts that the sum goes unseen. The sum is objective—relatively, at least; it has presence, character, and—as it develops—needs. The parts of the poem are instinctively adjusted in some degree to serve the needs of the whole. And as this adjustment takes place, excess subjectivity is avoided. Details of a private, as distinct from personal, nature may be deleted, for example, in the interests of a fuller, clearer, more communicable whole. (By private I mean those which have associations for the writer that are inaccessible to readers without a special explanation from the writer which does not form part of the poem; whereas the personal, though it may incorporate the private, has an energy derived from associations that are shareable with the reader and *are* so shared within the poem itself.)

Another way to approach the problem of subjective/objective is to say that while traditional modes provide certain standards for objective comparison and evaluation of poems as effective structures, (technically, at any rate) open forms, used with comprehension of their technical opportunities, *build unique contexts* which likewise provide for such evaluation. In other words, though the "rightness" of its lines can't be judged by a preconceived method of scansion, each such poem, if well written, presents a composed whole in which false lines (or other lapses) can be heard by any attentive ear—not as failing to conform to an external rule, but as failures to contribute to the grace or strength implicit in a system peculiar to that poem, and stemming from the inscape of which it is the verbal manifestation.

The *melos* of metrical poetry was not easy of attainment, but there were guidelines and models, even if in the last resort nothing could substitute for the gifted "ear." The *melos* of open forms is even harder to study if we look for models; its secret lies not in models but in that "fidelity to experience" of which I have written elsewhere; and, in turn, that fidelity demands a delicate and precise comprehension of the technical means at our disposal. A general recognition of the primary importance of the line and of the way in which rhythm relates to melody would be useful to the state of the art of poetry in the way general acceptance of the bar line and other musical notations were useful to the art of music. A fully adequate latitude in the matter of interpretation of a musical score was retained (as anyone listening to different pianists playing the same sonata, for instance, can hear) but at the same time the composer acquired a finer degree of control. Only if writers agree about the nature and function of this tool can readers fully cooperate, so that the poem shall have the fullest degree of autonomous life.

John Logan

On Poets and Poetry Today
1971

Poets and poetry today. Yes, but where is poetry itself? Or as Cummings might ask, "Who is poetry, anyway?" Poetry is existentially first among the great genres because, thinking of poetry as lyric contrasted to tragic and epic and agreeing with Yeats that out of our quarrels with ourselves we make poetry, we can say that this thing, poetry, is the expression in literature of the narrowest or first circle of encounter, the circle of one's self, whereas tragedy is the expression of encounter with the immediate community, the community of family, and epic the expression of encounter with the larger community of the nation or the race. Under this view the novel is a mixed form of poetry which may be primarily lyric as in Proust, primarily tragic as in Dostoevsky and Faulkner or primarily epic as in Tolstoy. But given this manner of definition, with its increasingly large circles of encounter, one expects the larger circles to include the smaller, so that one anticipates in tragedy certain lyric moments as in Claudius's monologue at prayer in *Hamlet* and one expects in epic both the lyric moment (as in Achilles' soliloquy by the sea) as well as certain tragic figurings (as that of Achilles and Patroclus in the *Iliad*).

The question arises rather naturally why lyric poets die so young—i.e., why they do not survive to surmount tragic encounters and reach the larger circle of epic involvements (or as we might say political involvement): Keats, Shelley, Byron, Hart Crane, Dylan Thomas, the latter remaining a little longer, Rimbaud a little less long, having abandoned as a teenager any powerful production of words and surviving only to write domestic or business letters.

I would like to expand my definitions in a different direction to include comedy in order to say what I think about it. There are two tragic moments allied to levels of personal maturity or (looked at from inside the hero) as rites of passage: the tragedy of the young man, of Hamlet or Oedipus Rex who moves from young manhood to maturity, and the tragedy of the older man, of Lear or Oedipus at Colonus (or in a certain reading of Willy Loman) who moves from maturity to sanctity or *superior* manhood. The first is a movement embracing life as the fulfillment of youth and the other is a movement embracing death as a fulfillment of life. Oedipus must leave Thebes in order to make himself available to other states. Christ must leave us locally, he says, in order to be really with us. Hamlet died for us.

Between these two tragic moments lies comedy, which is the moment of wedding, as in *Twelfth Night,* comedy par excellence, where three couples marry at the close, or in *Ulysses* which ends with Molly Bloom's powerful yea saying to the idea of renewed honeymoon. It is at the moment of wedding where the young tragic problem is solved: the encounter with the family is reconciled by one's stepping out of the family he is born into in order to found his own. But this healing action involves love and love must be learned. The source of tragic conflict is ambivalence and the problem of learning to love is the problem of learning to exorcise the ambivalence in one's relationship with another. Language enters the discussion at the point because we are all stutterers in the face of love; all of us then are country bumpkins who must learn to speak, to utter our love without ambivalence. Thus all of us, as poor lovers, identify with the mute or inarticulate heroes, the Benjys, the jongleurs, the lonely hunters of the heart. "We fog bound people are all stammerers," O'Neill says.

The final moment of inarticulation is the moment of silence, the moment of late tragedy as the other inarticulation is the moment of young tragedy. In the later inarticulateness one hears this "Be still and know that I am God." It is the silence of Hamlet (who moves so swiftly from the one tragic moment to the other, combining the acceptance of life with the acceptance of death) as opposed to the self-castrating silence of Iago. Wovon man nicht sprechen kann daruber muszt man schweigen. (Wittgenstein: "Whereof man cannot speak of this he must remain silent.") As distinct from these two moments of inarticulation the very first such moment of which I shall speak later is that of infancy. To say a paradox: Man's inarticulations mark the joints in his life.

Now as it is practically impossible to rid ourselves utterly of ambivalence, so at the time of wedding we still stutter and the comedy is imperfect, thus tragicomedy is the most existential dramatic form, the one closest to the truth of the human situation, and Beckett knew acutely what he was about when he used this genre.

"I suppose the easiest part of the production of art is the suffering," I have written elsewhere.

> Artists have not minded pain so long as they could keep it from killing them and get their work done: so long as the mad man, the beast, and the angel Dylan Thomas found inside himself or the boy, the man, and the woman James Joyce found in himself, did not crack the china skull in which they sprouted so dangerously together.

But many poets have chosen death rather than to continue their work and some poets (I have mentioned Rimbaud) have been able to survive only if they did not write but committed instead the symbolic castration of the murder of the gift, the excision of power in themselves. The trauma of continued life for a poet is I believe allied to the problem of continuing to build what we call "the body of work" a man forms. The word body ("corpus") is important. One of my colleagues at State University of New York has found that Sylvia Plath's work shows a fantasy of building the body of the father, the *Colossus* of her title—that her poems are fragments of this body and that her suicide coincides with the inability to continue such work. This exactly corroborates for the female poet what I have suggested for the male lyric poet: that he builds in his work the body of his mother—that he wishes to give birth to her as she has done for him. In building the body of the parent of the opposite sex through his work the poet establishes a sexual relationship with his own work and dramatizes at the lyric level (the battle with himself, that is) the tragic battle (the battle with the parent). Thus he plays out within himself the primal scene, one part of himself taking the feminine role, another the masculine. It is because of this fact, that one forms a body with his poetry, that we must demand of poetry a surface of sensual beauty.* The poet must conjure

---

*In my opinion the poets who most show this in my time are James Wright, Galway Kinnell, and Robert Bly.

the vision of the mother and he must make her sing to him (and, in narrative poetry, tell him "a story").

The fact that so many lyric poets die young, or, in Dante's phrase, "midway through life" (Hart Crane was nearly thirty-three) suggests that they cannot duplicate in their work the lower half of the mother's body, the part that *takes* as well as giving, with the upper part. A poet who survives may find himself, like Yeats, writing poetry which is more sexually oriented in his later years. I find it significant here that one's breaking into syntax, an advance which makes poetry possible, comes about rather suddenly, as another acquaintance of mine has found, in connection with attempts to deal with the separation from the mother at about the age of one-and-a-half. Separated from the breast the poet begins to rebuild that portion of the mother's body with the mouthing of his poetry, having already as a child rebuilt her face in another way into that of his dolls or his toy animals (on the significance of the doll, see the work of Zelda Teplitz, M.D.). But oftentimes the poet would rather die than face the sexuality of the mother (and hence, of the parents together), which keeps him separated from her in the tragic fashion. He chooses death over the tragic encounter, remaining a lyric poet, holding onto his melancholy for dear life, as it were, and falling far short of the true comic moment, the moment of wedding free of ambivalence (the wedding which on the other hand is so often also the wake [as in Shakespeare, Joyce, and Faulkner]).

This concern of the poet with the mother's body as I see it helps me to understand why New York School poetry is so unfeeling. Whether Kenneth Koch writes about "The Pleasures of Peace" or whether he writes about "Sleeping with Women" all feeling is leveled, and one is left with brilliant ratiocination and with a bastard comedy which has somehow short-circuited the moment of the truly comic, the moment, I repeat, of wedding. Perhaps we laugh at this poetry for the same reason we laugh at jokes, because we are spared the expenditure of energy necessary to deal with anxieties roused by feelings, and this excess of energy can emerge in the smile. It is easy to see why Koch is such a great teacher of children. There is no body of the mother and no scene of the parents in New York School poetry and so this poetry shows its kinship with abstract painting, which it grew up with. Abstract painting has got rid of the human figure and thus got rid of erotic feeling, for Kenneth Clark has pointed out that there is erotic feeling present at the base of the use of the nude in painting. All figures painted (once undressed in the eye of the beholder) lead to the nude and hence to the primal scene. The audience as voyeur is spared sexual anxiety in abstract painting. However it is a self-defeating movement for, as Plato pointed out in the *Meno,* where there is color there shape goes also, and wherever there is shape I add there lurks finally (to "rorshock" us) the figure of the parent and its display in the primal scene. The figure finds its way back into pop art and pop poetry only through the elaboration of the child's comic strip (I now see "comic strip" as an unconscious pun) with its curious pointillist composition which visualizes the minute bullets the TV gun shoots us with to form its images. Or again pop art (should I call it mom art also?) elevates into totem status the baked goods and the cans of the kitchen or tubes of the bathroom and so uses figures which hide again the parents and their scene together.

As painting shows erotic concern at its root (a painter paints with the brush of his penis, said D. H. Lawrence) so does poetry both at the fantasy level of the body of the work and also at the level of immediate presence, for in poetry there is always breath, the breath of the mouth, and behind it of moist, hidden organs, with their enactment of expulsions. To use an earlier myth one might say that every breathing of a poem is an expulsion from the garden of Eden, which by the poem's content and by its ritual rhythms, its yearnings, tries to dramatize our return to that garden. Here, however, I am more directly concerned with genital expulsion out of the mouth—I am more concerned with the displacement upward from that "other mouth" which the man and woman know, and with the expelling itself, which looked at from the masculine point of view, is ejaculation, while looked at from the feminine it is giving birth. (While as an image common to male and female it might be seen as displaced anal activity.)

The aggressive poetry of hatred, or warmongering or antiwarmongering, of racism or antiracism, tries to hide behind the skirts of the poet's mouth to say that the poet is only masculine (and this whether the mouth speaks feminist content or not). I am not saying there is no place in poetry for militancy, the politically persuasive, the feminist or the masculinist. I am saying that what makes something poetry in the first place is its musical quarrel with the self, its lyricism. Without that there *is* no poetry though there may well be something else. David Ray once asked me to write a poem about the Hungarian Revolution and I told him all my poetry was about the Hungarian Revolution. "Out of our quarrels with others we make rhetoric," Yeats said. "And out of our quarrels with ourselves we make Poetry." "The spiritual combat," Rimbaud told us, "is more bloody than any human battle." And he should know for he died a slow death of it. Some poets brandish their swords to make us forget they are using words and that words are of the mouth, of the mother and to make us forget that poetry is learned first as a way of separating from the mother's breast, as a way of realizing, through the pain of weaning the radical separateness, the identity indeed, of the self. So Robert Bly in his Deep Image School as it is sometimes called writes brilliant, strong poetry of the war (against it to be sure) as in "The Teeth Mother Naked at Last," but reminds us in discussion that the true job of the poet is to lead the masculine, aggressive function back a certain way toward the wings of the feminine function. (I may say here that I am mildly suspicious of how successful Bly's aesthetic is at exorcizing the aggressive element, for in an essay he speaks of "dipping down into the unconscious" when this active procedure can in fact scarcely work. One does not dip down into the unconscious, one finds a method of allowing it to well up into one's poem.)

To return, when I spoke of the poet's leading "the masculine aggressive function back a certain way toward the wings of the feminine function" I was not basically using a theatrical image, but I might do that: the poet comes out on the stage in the masculine light of day, under the sun, sometimes too much "I' the sun" indeed, having emerged from the dark belly of Jonah's whale onto the shore or, in my present image, having just emerged from the wings. But he must return there, to the belly or the wings, in order to recoup and nourish himself so that he can nourish us, feed us bread, not stones.

Returning from the wings onto the stage the poet may well lead his brothers, the members of his school, and one thinks first here of the school coming out of the shadow of Black Mountain. I may say that this celebration of brothers too is a way of short-circuiting the tragic encounter with the parents with their primal scene and their judgmental function. One needn't deal with the parents if one keeps in touch primarily with the brothers. Insofar as paternal figures are relevant for the Black Mountain group they indeed seem more maternal or matriarchial than patriarchial even though they be sexually male (Olson and Williams), for there is more concern in this group with its members being of the same earth than with a judgmental hierarchy of first and second sons or daughters, but I am particularly concerned here with the following fact: in showing us what good brothers and sisters they are the Black Mountain poets deny the *fight* with the brothers. Now Melanie Klein in her analysis of youngsters has found that sibling battles dramatize the primal scene. The Black Mountain poets thus deny their involvement in that. I know that fraternity is more important for instance to Duncan than hierarchy for when I wrote him in 1961 or 1962 at the time of the beginning of my poetry magazine *Choice* and asked him for poems (having stated that I did not believe in schools because schools tended to elevate lesser talents in the same swim and to ignore greater talents not in the same swim), Robert replied that he did not agree with the policy of printing the best wherever you could find it and thought it much more important to print members of a group. I also know that fraternity is very important not only to the Black Mountain School as such but to the San Francisco Beat group as well, which constantly talk about one another in their poems and have their pictures taken and published together. The two schools often overlap and give readings or workshops together. I remember a wonderful quotation from Ginsberg who was being interviewed in San Francisco after he, Creeley, Levertov, and Duncan had given a workshop together in Vancouver. "Mr. Ginsberg," asked the interviewer, "I understand you and Miss Levertov and Mr. Duncan taught the craft of verse up at UBC in Vancouver." "No," said Ginsberg, "Denise and Robert and I did not teach the craft of verse. We were all emotionally bankrupt and went around weeping and asking our students for love."

He is right about that. We must love one another or die said Auden, and before him a character in *Brothers Kara-mazov*. Poets say they want everybody to love everybody but they (we) mainly want you the audience to care about us, and so we do what we can to make you feel that we care about you. The poet is an anonymous lover, I believe, and his poetry is an anonymous reaching out, which occasionally becomes personal—when there are those present who care to listen. At the personal moment a mysterious thing happens, which reminds us of magic, and hence of the power of Orpheus: the loneliness each of us feels locked inside his own skin, and the anonymous reaching each of us does therefore, becomes a *bond* and hence we are neither alone nor anonymous in the same sense as we were before.

I for my part am a loner, not a member of a school. I want to help others discover their own voices in workshops and I want others upon hearing my work to hear their own voices echoing inside themselves.

Does this allow me to say I have escaped the flight from the primal scene somehow? That I have faced it and stood alone, having earned the right to wear a necklace of "the bad mother's" teeth, having come away from them unbidden and unbitten? Or that I have watched the primal scene untraumatized and been enabled to move on without the support of sisters and brothers? I might wish it did, but in fact it does not, for in some ways I am jealous of the brotherhoods of poets which do not number me among them. And as a loner reaching out to you, the audience, with the long penis of my tongue of poems, showering the sperm of my syllables and breathing on you with the passion of my warm breath, I have only recently learned to look at you as you are looking at me. (It is easier for me to imagine that I am an exhibitionist in the spotlight than that I am a voyeur, which is probably closer to the truth, wanting to peer into the curtained windows of your inmost heart to see what I may be fertilizing there.) In other words I too displace the battle of the primal scene and in still another way: for it takes place between you and me which is (in my terms) more tragic than lyric, for it is the displacement of relationships from my own parents and siblings, with whom I am not at ease. Why do we so much fear that primal scene? Why do poets go to such great lengths (my phrase) to displace, dramatize and (right word) *embody* it? Perhaps because otherwise we would have to see that we are as gods: that we have the power and thus the responsibility to give life or to withhold it, to love or to murder, engender or destroy.

Though this be true for poet and nonpoet alike the poet feels it especially: for, unable to account for the gift he possesses, he has already begun to suspect for this other reason that he may be a god. Such anointment, such mixed blessings brings special, powerful guilt. As I have said in another place and still deeply believe and repeat: "It's not the skeleton in the closet we are afraid of, it's the god."

Audre Lorde

Poems Are Not Luxuries
1977

The quality of light by which we scrutinize our lives has direct bearing upon the product which we live, and upon the changes which we hope to bring about through those lives. It is within this light that we form those ideas by which we pursue our magic and make it realized. This is poetry as illumination, for it is through poetry that we give name to those ideas which are, until the poem, nameless and formless—about to be birthed, but already felt. That distillation of experience from which true poetry springs births thought as dream births concept, as feeling births idea, as knowledge births (precedes) understanding.

As we learn to bear the intimacy of scrutiny, and to flourish within it, as we learn to use the products of that scrutiny for power within our living, those fears which rule our lives and form our silences begin to lose their control over us.

For each of us as women, there is a dark place within where hidden and growing our true spirit rises, "Beautiful and tough as chestnut / Stanchions against our nightmare of weakness" and of impotence. These places of possibility within ourselves are dark because they are ancient and hidden; they have survived and grown strong through darkness. Within these deep places, each one of us holds an incredible reserve of creativity and power, storehouse of unexamined and unrecorded emotion and feeling. The woman's place of power within each of us is neither white nor surface; it is dark, it is ancient, and it is deep.

When we view living, in the european mode, only as a problem to be solved, we rely solely upon our ideas to make us free, for these were what the white fathers told us were precious. But as we become more in touch with our own ancient, black, noneuropean view of living as a situation to be experienced and interacted with, we learn more and more to cherish our feelings, to respect those hidden sources of our power from where true knowledge and therefore lasting action comes. At this point in time, I believe that women carry within ourselves the possibility for fusion of these two approaches as a keystone for survival, and we come closest to this combination in our poetry. I speak here of poetry as the revelation or distillation of experience, not the sterile word play that, too often, the white fathers distorted the word *poetry* to mean—in order to cover their desperate wish for imagination without insight.

For women, then, poetry is not a luxury. It is a vital necessity of our existence. It forms the quality of the light within which we predicate our hopes and dreams toward survival and change, first made into language, then into idea, then into more tangible action. Poetry is the way we help give name to the nameless so it can be thought. The farthest external horizons of our hopes and fears are cobbled by our poems, carved from the rock experiences of our daily lives.

As they become known and accepted to ourselves, our feelings, and the honest exploration of them, become sanctuaries and fortresses and spawning grounds for the most radical and daring of ideas, the house of difference so necessary to change and the conceptualization of any meaningful action. Right now, I could name at least ten ideas I would once have found intolerable or incomprehensible and frightening, except as they came after dreams and poems. This is not idle fantasy, but the true meaning of "It feels right to me." We can train ourselves to respect our feelings and to discipline (transpose) them into a language that catches those feelings so they can be shared. And where that language does not yet exist, it is our poetry which helps to fashion it. Poetry is not only dream or vision, it is the skeleton architecture of our lives.

Possibility is neither forever nor instant. It is also not easy to sustain belief in its efficacy. We can sometimes work long and hard to establish one beachhead of real resistance to the deaths we are expected to live, only to have that beachhead assaulted or threatened by canards we have been socialized to fear, or by the withdrawal of those approvals that we have been warned to seek for safety. We see ourselves diminished or softened by the falsely benign accusations of childishness, of nonuniversality, of self-centeredness, of sensuality. And who asks the question: Am I altering your aura, your ideas, your dreams, or am I merely moving you to temporary and reactive action? (Even the latter is no mean task, but one that must rather be seen within the context of a true alteration of the texture of our lives.)

The white fathers told us, "I think therefore I am," and the black mothers in each of us—the poets—whisper in our dreams, "I feel therefore I can be free." Poetry coins the language to express and charter this revolutionary awareness and demand—the implementation of that freedom. However, experience has taught us that the action in the now is also always necessary. Our children cannot dream unless they live, they cannot live unless they are nourished, and who else will feed them the real food without which their dreams will be no different from ours?

Sometimes we drug ourselves with dreams of new ideas. The head will save us. The brain alone will set us free. But there are no new ideas still waiting in the wings to save us as women, as human. There are only old and forgotten ones, new combinations, extrapolations and recognitions from within ourselves, along with the renewed courage to try them out. And we must constantly encourage ourselves and each other to attempt the heretical actions our dreams imply and some of our old ideas disparage. In the forefront of our move toward change, there is only our poetry to hint at possibility made real. Our poems formulate the implications of ourselves, what we feel within and dare make real (or bring action into accordance with), our fears, our hopes, our most cherished terrors.

For within structures defined by profit, by linear power, by institutional dehumanization, our feelings were not meant to survive. Kept around as unavoidable adjuncts or pleasant pasttimes, feelings were meant to kneel to thought as we were meant to kneel to men. But women have survived. As poets. And there are no new pains. We have felt them all already. We have hidden that fact in the same place where we have our power. They lie in our dreams, and it is our dreams that point the way to freedom. They are made realizable through our poems that give us the strength and courage to see, to feel, to speak, and to dare.

If what we need to dream, to move our spirits most deeply and directly toward and through promise, is a luxury, then we have given up the core—the fountain—of our power, our womanness; we have given up the future of our worlds.

For there are no new ideas. There are only new ways of making them felt, of examining what our ideas really mean (feel like) on Sunday morning at 7 A.M., after brunch, during wild love, making war, giving birth; while we suffer the old longings, battle the old warnings and fears of being silent and impotent and alone, while tasting our new possibilities and strengths.

Thomas McGrath

Language, Power, and Dream
1980

"The history of all hitherto existing society is the history of class struggles." And the history of history is language, and *in* language. There are the fossils (even from the time before class struggle) that are benign. There are others, later, like the Homeric "honor," like seventeenth century "honor," "honor" among thieves, the white confederate "honor" of Jefferson Davis—these fossils contain poisons that are still active and some deadly. There are words like *moon* and *labor* which, if we look inside, contain more rings of growth than even the oldest tree.

Language is, perhaps, only a moment of the growth of what became consciousness and will go beyond it, but it is our machine for separating ourselves from the world in order to create it (as Adam did by naming the beasts and herbs). In creating the world we also *appropriate* it. The world then is internalized. Now we can make maps; the demons of the four cardinal compass points (Cham to Amaymon) are born and the Age of Exploration (external and internal) begins.

Any of these roads would take us back or forward to Eden, but the class struggle in the form of the Angel blocks the way back with a flaming sword. There would still be no problem if language *still and only* belonged to the workers—we would simply shove the sword up the ass of the angel and march on in. But with *division*—so important in separating ourselves from the world in order to see it, know it, and, finally, change it—that same necessitous Angel, who symbolizes also the class struggle, has put up signs: *Eden—Detour 3 miles sòuth by way of route 66.* Or: (to put it in another way:) if direction is discovered, misdirection becomes possible, i.e., the tree blazed on the wrong side, newspapers, education-with-Ph.D. theses-on-Marxist-poets, foxfire, "the book with one thousand false addresses"—a general production of false consciousness even by men who think they are men of good will.

"Make it new," said Pound. But Pound, like Eliot and Yeats, was essentially a pre-nineteenth-century man and his thinking was, in part at least, that of an even earlier ruling class. The language of these poets generates (among other things) a fog of false consciousness in which platoons of professors are still wandering, sending out plaintive cries about the "depth," the "profundity" of the bogs they have fallen into. But, it is true, there *is* something there: pain, above all. About which the old masters were never wrong, or so we have been told. Their pain is of the loss of the "centre" of "tradition" of "virtue" and *virtu*—a loss of aristocratic values already knocked in the head by the bourgeoisie. These "modernists" are really belated medieval writers—they followed the signs out of their own century. But that is why they have such a modern sound. The strategies, the successes and failures, of this holy trinity, point to the reasons why we have not yet had a great *bourgeois* poem of the twentieth century. In English. And never will have.

To go back to the Angel. The law is: the owners will put up the signs and most of them will point in the wrong direction. If language can delude, it will first delude the user. We must try to remember the revolutionary axiom: In the beginning was the *world!*

* * *

Everyone wants to reform language. Reformers can be dangerous: they begin by wanting to purify the language of the tribe but may end (as Shaw had it) slaughtering multitudes over an extra vowel. Things turn to their opposites. The liberating purification of language which begins with Wordsworth becomes constrictive, becomes protectionist, buys guard dogs and chainlink fences, wants law and order, is in favor of high tariffs. Or to take examples from our own times—either Pound or Williams will do—they begin as revolutionaries, knocking down the inflated and bankrupt language of the American survivors of Victorianism. And indeed it *was* liberating to see those apparitional faces, and interesting to see the chickens and the red wheelbarrow, though the "so much" that is said to depend upon them turns out to be not (as Williams supposed) the validity of the whole visible world of objects but merely the temporality of a consumer society.

THOMAS McGRATH / 287

Metaphysical consumerism! As the Williams tradition runs down in the work of the less talented of his followers, the object becomes All, becomes the One. Things (but not goods) are hypostatized and so any thing is as good as anything else and a beer can equals the Mona Lisa. This mock materialism is essentially puritan. Feelings are muted or excised and objects proliferate. This is what Freud called anal and Marx called petty bourgeois or commodity fetishism and it is where the search for purity has led a lot of poets and novelists: to things rather than feelings about them, to situations without people, to aesthetics pretending to be politics.

Out of so much of this temporary "war politics" rises a terrible spiritual smell which signals to the enemy: "I'm not really like this. Just stop bombing Hanoi and I will go back to my primary interests: flowers, early cockcrow, the Holy Ghost, wheelbarrows, the letter G, inhabitable animals, the sacred mysteries of the typewriter keyboard, and High Thought including the Greater, the Lesser, and High, Low, Jack-and-the-goddam-game mysticism." Worthy enough subjects in themselves. . . .

* * *

Language is always a little out of date and so it always needs reforming: because the world changes; because the real landscape that underlies the landscape of the poem erodes and alters; because our consciousness changes to catch up with the changes in the world; because the world is never adequate to our needs and desires and so we must change it—and by doing so change our needs and desires. The best poets find the new words for this new world of change and need. They may not be understood or felt until we see that the world is changing and "filling in" their words. Then "illusion" is transformed into "reality."

The search for purity and limit in language is often a hedge against anxiety—anxiety that results from a glimpse of the flux and change that is the world. A poet feeling this often sets up a metaphysical system of absolutes, values derived from picking the bones of various systems, to set against the flux. Or, if less honest, he buries his absolutes. His poems, like the pointer on a compass, always turn to these magnets. True North is always under his feet! He has found the still point of the turning world and there, locked in the chastity belt of "purified" language, he remains.

I prefer the impure. There is, after all, in our time, another tradition of language—that leading from Hart Crane and others. What we want and need, in my view, *now,* is not this questionable purity but a language, to paraphrase Louis Simpson, like the belly of a shark, a language that can digest *anything.*

Language is part of the forces of production for the poets—it is what they use to create their poetic "goods." The language chosen by or given to some poets, like certain kinds of machines, can produce variety: "aphorisms, epigrams, songs, songlike poems and so on" as Roethke had it, the tremendous range of "impure poetry" in Neruda's term. Alas, our time tends toward specialization. But if you want to make wood for the winter a chain saw is better than a stone axe.

If we continue the analogy we will see that even more important than the forces are the *relations* of production. If the poet thinks he *owns* the means of production (that language factory where the private vision must be socialized into the public myth) when in fact he only uses what has been given to him (*any* tradition within the bourgeois limit) he will produce a consciousness that is at least in part false. The American worker thinks he is free, but he is chained to the machine. So "politics must be in command." We must try to find our real relationship to things.

* * *

Language gives us perception and orientation—which includes the possibility of lying signposts, false consciousness. Through language we appropriate the world and our selves, existence creating essence in a process that can never be complete. History—that is, class struggle—begins with alienation and exile when we were cast out of Eden. History *is* alienation as it appears to consciousness. It is the sense of division, of duality, which the fig leaves symbolized, the pain of being incomplete. When we return to Eden we will possess full consciousness and alienation will end.

Satori, those "mystical" returns to what was and will be, can only be realized individually. They are returns to the Eden of the time before the snake. They are brief because Eden is not big enough for all of us and complete consciousness cannot be merely *personal*—the appropriation and internalization of the world through action, art, and language is a social process. What we feel now is the pain of duality and conflict: man vs. the world (which is men struggling with themselves, nature and other men). In the beginning was the world. But in transcendence subject and object will become the Word: Mannature. Then love must change its form—when the Flesh is made Word—and death, for the unalienated, will have to be reinvented. . . .

* * *

Somebody writes to ask: "Are you still working on that long poem about North Dakota?" But I'm not writing a poem about North Dakota as such, though there is a lot in the poem that involves experiences, past and present, from places *in* North Dakota.

"North Dakota is everywhere," the poem says. This provoked indignation in an English reviewer, who seemed appalled at the idea. But the line was written in Skyros, was set off by the suicide of an impoverished and destroyed fisherman, and referred to a *condition*. And North Dakota is a condition, or a part of one. North Dakota—or Montana or New Mexico or wherever, so long as it is not the East, the city—is an experience which many poets are now having. If the experience could be easily described perhaps it would not be necessary for us to write about it in poems. But the poems are discovering the experience, creating it, destroying false consciousness, creating the new. . . .

What is in that experience? Here are two reactions to the West from the November 21, 1971, issue of the *New York Times Book Review*. The first is from Shirley Schoonover, writing from Nebraska. What is Nebraska? Once, she notes, there were buffalo and Indians; now there are beef and farmers. The state is physically beautiful, she says, and she responds to the terrific weather. As for culture, "Insurance companies have made cement monuments where long ago the Indians came to talk peace or war." (*That* is right on, but she can't see where it leads.) Art "is fine for covering that crack over the fireplace." The Nebraska football team has a huge coliseum but the University Theater goes begging. Etc., etc. (It's still

Mainstreet, seen at this level.) As for the lot of writers "I've already indicated that the three most famous Nebraska writers went East and stayed there. That should tell you a lot." The writers she refers to are Willa Cather, Mari Sandoz, and Wright Morris. She is getting out herself. "That's Nebraska. Beautiful but killingly lonely for the writer."

Perhaps she is doing the right thing—I don't know her work and maybe there is nothing she could learn from the Genius of the place, even if she could get in contact with that restless spirit. But loneliness can be greatly valuable—surely it was valuable to Cather and Morris. And in any case the three writers *took the place along with them*—Nebraska is everywhere. Miss Schoonover noticed a few blazes that might have led to something interesting, but in general she seems to have seen only real estate. The author's note says that she now lives in Rochester, New York.

The second reaction is that of William Eastlake, from Arizona. The piece is a fanciful dialogue between Eastlake and "my Indian writer friend, Many Bitter Songs." It is full of jokes, but some things seem to be said with considerable seriousness. Many Bitter Songs asks why Eastlake writes in the West:

"Because, as you said, the West has never been written about. Never until your time. The West is just being discovered," I said.

"There have been several white geniuses in America. Why didn't they write about the West?"

"Because," I said, "they were cowards. They could not face the horrors of the West. The extermination of the Indian, the murder of the land. The terrific beauty. They sat in New York and polished old sayings... America is too terrible a subject for an American...."

"Then we can forget the West."

"No, no. We cannot forget the West. There is no America outside the West, and there never will be. It is the dream, and that dream is the only hope. No, we cannot forget the West. Where all the races meet in a place of beauty, not in a place of blood. The land cannot grant amnesty."

That meeting in a place of beauty rather than of blood has to be in "the dream." The time surely has not arrived yet. It won't be arrived at either until we come to terms with "the extermination of the Indian," until we understand the exploitations and rip-offs that have been practiced against all ethnic groups, until we can square these rip-offs and those against the working class as well. This must enter—and is entering—our consciousness and our politics. All this great "West" is a place of wounds. All of *America* is such a place, but the East has paved over them. If we see this, "Nebraska" can be intensely dramatic for a writer. We certainly don't want an art to "cover that crack over the fireplace." *Do not bandage these wounds!*

* * *

What is there, out here on the edge, that makes our experience different from that of the city poet? First there is the land itself. It has been disciplined by machines but it is still not dominated. The plow that broke the plains is long gone and the giant tractor and the combine are here, but the process of making a living is still a struggle and a gamble—it is not a matter of putting raw materials in one end of a factory and taking finished products out of the other. Weather, which is only a nuisance in the city, takes on the power of the gods here, and vast cycles of climate, which will one day make all the area a dust bowl again and finally return it to grass, make all man's successes momentary and ambiguous. Here man can never think of himself, as he can in the city, as the master of nature. Like it or not he is subject to the ancient power of seasonal change; he cannot avoid being *in* nature; he has a heroic adversary that is no abstraction. At a level below immediate consciousness we respond to this, are less alien to our bodies, to human and natural time.

The East is much older than these farther states, has more history. But I believe that that history no longer functions, has been forgotten, has been "paved over." In the East man begins every day from himself. Here, the past is still alive and close at hand—the arrowheads we turn up may have been shot at our grandfathers. I am not thinking of any romantic frontier. The past out here was bloody, and full of injustice, though hopeful and heroic. It is very close here—my father took shelter with his family at Fort Ransom during an Indian scare when he was a boy. Later he heard of the massacre at Wounded Knee. Most of us are haunted by the closeness of that past, and by the fact that we are only a step from the Indian, whose sense of life so many of the younger people are trying to learn.

* * *

Not long ago, if one wanted to be an artist of any kind, it was necessary to leave these parts. Lenin spoke of "the idiocy of the villages," and in the nineteenth and early twentieth centuries if one wanted to experience his own time he *had* to go to the cities. The city was, in fact, being remade—out of factory production, class struggle, the growth of the city working class, the rise of revolutionary politics. And of course, even if the artist was unaware of these vast and radical social changes, the city was the repository of art and culture. So the artist *had* to go to the city, where he/she was successful, or failed and disappeared, or returned defeated.

That old pattern has changed. The young would-be artist may still go to the city; but more and more frequently now he returns—to Nebraska or Arizona or wherever. Part of this is the result of our "affluence" and "mobility." If he wants to make another run to San Francisco or Seattle (would-be *poets* from west of Chicago never seem to go to New York any more) he can always do so. The result of this "return" (a part of all initiation rites) is only now being felt. God knows what will come of it, but the waste places are being populated by long-haired poets, and little magazines turn up like toadstools after a rain.

Why do they return? In part, I think, because they find the unknown lands in which they were born dramatic for the reasons I have tried to sketch out above. Also, I think, they are reacting against the deracination they feel in the city artist, who, unless he is a revolutionary or third world person, must find his materials in that very deracination (a field well worked for a century) or in the frayed remnants of a cosmopolitan tradition. What does the young writer need? The central experience of his time, whatever it may be. Beyond that, books and talk with others in his craft. These he can now find as easily out in the backlands as in the city—and not just young poets like himself but older ones like Bly, or Stafford, or Hugo, who have been in the city and left it. The result will be, I think, a poetry which, for a time at least, finds the city irrelevant. But, since these poets have had their wanderjahre and are not parochial or simply regional, it will be a poetry which is both local *and* international.

> Without a terrain in which, to which, I belong,
> language itself is my one home, my Jerusalem. . . .

This is Denise Levertov in her generous and courageous poem "To Stay Alive." It is a terrifying idea, because language has a history, can never be up in the air—the very "Jerusalem" she refers to is not just that spiritual home and terminal of longing: it is also now a particular city within the system of international imperialism. History has added a new meaning to the word. It is hard to see this if we try to make language itself our home, and perhaps it is some realization of this which leads more and more poets to a sense of the necessity of place: a place to turn around in, ground under our feet, a base to operate from, a blaze on a tree that lets us locate ourselves on the map of ourselves and our time.

I think this is our "Yenan" period, (I'm *not* using the term in the way that James Moore has used it recently) and that it will be necessary to reenter the city. Supposing he already knows the facts of life and the class struggle, the poet has nothing to learn from the city. Where once it was a liberating place, it is now a stultifying one. Only in the ghettos is something "happening," as the great proliferation of black, Chicano, and Indian poetry shows. For such poets the ghettos are a source of strength. But the white poet can enter the ghetto only with great difficulty and in any case the ghettos are only beginning to work through to revolutionary politics. At the moment they are still involved (with important exceptions) in cultural and political nationalism, dead ends which it seems must be explored before a serious politics becomes possible. When that time comes the cities will again be the place of the central experience of the time and the poets will have to go back. But when that time comes, a new revolutionary consciousness will have solved many old problems and created new ones.

The point is to find, during these years of "wandering in

the desert," the link with the revolutionary past in order to create, invent, rescue, restructure, resurrect that past. This may be our gift to the city. But we cannot find that "place we went wrong" without a knowledge of the ground under our feet. So place is important.

* * *

And for me, two places. Where I began—still there and still changeless, the little river and the coulee hills, enduring under the accumulating strata of change and history. To quote Joseph Smeall, "Of the purgative and cathartic emotions that are a chief business of poetry, Aristotle says, that they start amid near things."

So I begin with that place and my life. But, again I say, not my *personal life as such.* All of us live twice at the same time— once uniquely and once representatively. I am interested in those moments when my unique personal life intersects with something bigger, when my small brief moment has a part in "fabricating the legend."

So there has to be a second "place" and it is anywhere *outside this window* where I am writing, i.e., the world in large. The writing itself is part of the subject of the poem, the act, impossible to accomplish, of bringing the two masks of the world into line, of solving the social, personal, and political riddles I see all around. Looking out that window, I see that North Dakota *is* everywhere.

Jackson Mac Low

Poetry, Chance, Silence, Etc.
1961; cor., with added note, 1980

I

Poems in which meaning & connections are left entirely (or for the most part) unspecified, in which appearances & concatenations of words happen because of an objective chance-operational method, not thru the immediate choice of the poet (intuitional or rational),—such poems are not vehicles merely of the vision of the individual poet but constructions or event-series which allow each reader or hearer to be visionary himself rather than the passive receiver of the poet's vision. Confronted by this kind of poem, the sympathetic reader or hearer (& the poet himself as he watches the product of his chance-operational actions appear) addresses his attention primarily to each word or series of words as it happens, without attempting consciously to find meanings beyond those obviously belonging to the words themselves, or to connect the words more than they are already connected. Nevertheless, some layer of his mind will be, to some extent, providing meanings & connections of which he may be only dimly aware. (Or he may be quite aware of them.) In this way, poem & audience interpenetrate with a minimum of interference by the poet, whose own action consists of inventing the chance-operational system used, making what choices are necessary to initiate its actions, & carrying thru the actions required by it to produce the poem. In this situation one may say that the poet, & the word-sources, the audience & the world (as chance in action & as environment) are transparently & unobstructedly interpenetrating.

Such interpenetration is most apparent in chance-composed poems wherein single words or series of them are separated by silences longer than customary caesurae or punctuational pauses. In these intervals the hearer becomes occupied with the ambient noises &/or with his own thoughts, feelings, volitions & sensations. These are of course always present but are likely to come strongly into the foreground when the speaker falls silent for appreciable lengths of time. Such silences in the midst of words (with or without other sounds produced by performers) arouse annoyance—even, I have been told, anguish—in audiences, mostly, I think, because people do not want to abandon their passivity or habitual activity. To be asked to shift their attention from the speaker to the rest of their environment &/or themselves is, it seems, even more outrageous than to be asked to bring their own meanings & connections to words upon which, purposely, the poet has refused to impose his own.

A different kind of experience is provided by poems wherein the poet has improvised connective tissue between nuclei provided by chance operations. In these the poet's own vision, as aroused by the series of chance-given nuclei, is conveyed by the poem. Here the hearer is less free to provide or discover his own meanings & connections, unless the poet's are ambiguous &/or shifting enough to provide opportunities for real activity in the hearer (or reader).

Plays in which the performers must improvise speeches &/or actions from chance-given nuclei make the performers the primary visionaries. It is now they who provide, as they see fit, more or less meaning &/or connection. Those in which words, their delivery &/or actions are strictly determined by chance operations may (as in the Living Theater's production of *The Marrying Maiden*) become to some extent vehicles of the director's vision, as aroused by the chance-given words, &c., as well as that of the performers, but may still arouse the audience to unaccustomed activity. Accustomed to disguising their own provision of meanings & connections to ambiguous modern plays as a search for the author's meanings, when audiences are called upon to do so openly, to be visionaries— it inevitably arouses resentment &/or bewilderment. They don't want to be co-producers, only consumers. (The same, of course, is true of hearers & readers of poems.)

Maybe it is wrong or cruel to require such activity from the public. I think it's not wrong but the greatest necessity to arouse people to activity (as did—in another, but far from unconnected, sense—Brecht) & if this is cruel (this which one would think were the greatest of kindnesses) did not the visionary of modern theater, Antonin Artaud, call precisely for a Theater of Cruelty?

The works calling for the greatest activity are the indeterminate asymmetries. In these, schemata & methods of realisation are provided from which the reader may construct his own poems. Why shdnt he simply write his own poems & forget about my schemata & methods? If he can, good—but if he wd like to try using what I provide, he may experience other visions than those now available to him.

II

After beginning chance composition of music in about 1953, I began to compose poetry by chance operations in 1954. First were the 5 *biblical poems*, constructed entirely by chance operations except that the source book, the Jewish *Holy Scriptures* in the JPS translation, was chosen spontaneously. In these poems I first used silences (each the duration of *any* word, & thus indeterminate) & stanzaic forms consisting of lines each containing a chance-specified number of words &/or silences. Also I conceived the (optional) use of non-verbal sounds, musical or otherwise, to indicate line endings, since silences occurred *within* lines. In the *5th biblical poem*, which is also my 1st chance-composed play, I first used simultaneous speech: it is written for 3 simultaneous, indeterminately juxtaposed, readers. Subsequently the other 4 were seen to be also performable as simultaneous poetry as well as solos.

Between 1954 & 1961 I composed by chance operations many types of poems, stanzaic & non-stanzaic, with & without long silences, simultaneous &/or solo poems. Some incorporated non-verbal sounds as well as words & silences, & in some the loudness &/or the speed of delivery were regulated.

The characters, scene divisions & speeches of the play *The Marrying Maiden* were chance-composed in Summer 1958; the source (both of words & of some of the chance operations used in the composition) was the *I Ching*, or *Book of Changes*, a Chinese classic translated by Richard Wilhelm & Cary Baynes. During the subsequent year, the speed, loudness & manner (emotional, dialectal, &c.) of delivering the words were specified by chance-composed regulatory notations. In Winter 1960 a pack of about 1200 cards with actions written on them was composed to be used in the play (later hand-lettered on playing cards by Iris Lezak) & in June 1960 the play was produced in New York by The Living Theater. It was directed by Judith Malina with scenery, costumes, & interscene movie by Julian Beck, lights by Nicola Cernovich, & music by John Cage: a magnetic tape composed of the words of the play, re-randomized with silences but otherwise unmodified, which was turned on at random intervals simultaneously with the scenes, & 6 other tapes composed of the same words electronically modified, which were played between scenes.

In 1960 also, some of the simultaneous poems were performed at Pratt Institute (Brooklyn), Carnegie Recital Hall, on 2 different programs at The Living Theater & at the Phase 2 Coffee House (with mimes). Two 3-hour programs of my chance music, solo & simultaneous chance poems, & a new chance play, *Verdurous Sanguinaria,* occurred in April, 1961, at Yoko Ono's studio on Chambers St., & 4 other programs (presenting new plays, solo & simultaneous poems, music & magnetic tapes) were given during Summer, 1961, at the AG Gallery. Various poems (solo & simultaneous) were also performed in 1960–61 at the Tenth Street & Les Deux Mégots coffee houses & in July 1961 I read at the latter a large number of my non-chance poems (1938–1959) interspersed with 1961 chance-&-improvisational music.

In Summer, 1960, the stanzaic forms (some of which consist of so many *words* per line in corresponding lines of each stanza, others of numbers of phrases, sentence endings, sentences, syllables, word-fragments &c., & of mixtures of various of these) reached a final efflorescence in the *Stanzas for Iris Lezak,* a series of nearly 100 stanzaic poems, the separated stanzas of which may be (& were in several programs) read as a simultaneous poem wherein any stanzas of any of the poems may occur together. In the simultaneous performances speed & loudness of delivery, & durations of silence are regulated by cards, & line endings often are indicated by musical sounds or noises.

After Summer, 1960, asymmetrical verse forms, & improvisation by performers as well as other types of indeterminacy, became incorporated increasingly in my poems, plays & music. After 1958, & especially in 1961, the distinction between poetry, music & drama tended to disappear in many of the works. Alternative methods of performance made such poems as the group of 501 *Asymmetries* (Oct 1960–April 1961) solo poetry, simultaneous poetry, non-verbal musical works or combinations of any 2 or all 3 of these. Free connection of chance-given series of nuclei occurred in prose works of 1960 & poems & plays of 1961. The 1st completely indeterminate asymmetries were composed in Jan 1961 as part of the group of 501.

III

Underlying chance composition are the Taoist ideal of *Wu-Wei* (non-action, letting the Way do it); the Buddhist conception of egolessness; the Zen Buddhist conception of the No-mind, the Way subsisting as unconscious Mind, below both the individual ("Freudian") unconscious & (if it exists) the collective ("Jungian") unconscious, & producing all phenomena, subjective &/or objective; the Zen Buddhist realisation that Nirvana (enlightenment) & Samsara (the ordinary round of birth, life, death & rebirth), the universal & the individual, the subjective & the objective, are *not* 2, & that close attention to *any* phenomenon or experience can lead to the abrupt realisation of this not-twoness; the Kegon Buddhist realisation that all individuals unobstructedly interpenetrate & are interpenetrated by each other & the whole; & the *I Ching*'s assumption of the significance underlying or embodied in any simultaneously occuring events.

The possibility & validity of the use of chance operations, appreciable durations of silence & indeterminacy were brought to my attention in the early 1950's by the musical works & conversation of John Cage. (The first poem in which I encountered a silence longer than an ordinary caesura was "Hands: birds." by Mary Caroline Richards. The silence between the 2 words is about as long as a traditional sonnet.) However, I was predisposed to chance, silence, indeterminacy, etc., by previous (since 1944) acquaintance with Taoism & Buddhism, & came to understand more about it while studying Zen & Kegon Buddhism in the Columbia University classes (1954?–1957) of Dr. D. T. Suzuki as well as in his books & those of other Buddhists. Similarly, I became acquainted with the *I Ching* early in the 1950's soon after its publication by the Bollingen Foundation, & used it both as oracle & wisdom book for 2 or 3 years before I began chance composition, which is akin to the methods used to consult it as an oracle. Also I had long been influenced (in my non-chance poetry) by Mallarmé, & was especially fascinated by his last completed poem. *Un coup de dés jamais n'abolira le hasard* (A throw of dice never will abolish chance). It seemed natural to me when, in the late 1950's, I learned from Cage that Mallarmé's last work, *Le Livre*, which was not published until 1953, was an elaborate, unfinished & highly determinate chance project.

Note (4 December 1980)

When Donald Hall asked to reprint the above essay (written 28 September 1961), I remembered it as needing considerable change. However, when I found the time to locate my copy of *Nomad/New York* and reread the essay, I found remarkably little that I would change now. I decided only to correct typos, solecisms, etc., and add this note.

Probably at present I'd eschew such terms as "vision" and "visionary" and write "larger meaning" or "meaning of the work as a whole" rather than "vision" and "provider of meanings" rather than "visionary." Thus: "the meanings (or intentions) of the individual poet" and "allow each reader or hearer to be a provider of meaning," and so on.

Mainly, this is because "vision" and "visionary" have acquired such soft edges—especially during the 1960s—but I'm afraid they've always had too much of the phoney-baloney about them for my taste. My use of them in this essay is fairly atypical of me.

Besides, the terms are both too wide and too narrow. The kinds of meanings that will come into perceivers' minds as they read or hear aleatoric verbal works will range from the vaguest to the most precise, may be shades of emotion, clear or unclear images, or ideas at various levels of abstraction. They may "add up" or flicker in and out of perceivers' minds, become clearly conscious or imprecisely so or occur semiconsciously. "Vision" and "visionary" are both too grand and pretentious and too imprecise to deal with aleatoric verbal work and perceivers' responses thereto.

Also, of course, I'd now eschew the generic "he/him." I might write "he or she" or (more probably) use "the singular 'they,'" as I advocated in an appendix to the recent 3rd edition of *The Pronouns—A Collection of 40 Dances—For the Dancers* (Barrytown, NY: Station Hill, 1979)—or rewrite the sentences to allow for the plural "they."

In addition, I'm not as sure now that perceivers of aleatoric verbal works *will* become active in providing meanings, etc. Sometimes they may just pay attention to each word or string as it goes by, or sometimes not pay attention at all—attention will flicker in and out, even in well-disposed perceivers.

Also, after more experience and study of Buddhism, I'm a little diffident now about advancing the connection between aleatoric art and Buddhism, but on the whole, I don't reject that connection. It may not subsist exactly as I thought it did in 1961, but Buddhist attitudes and meditative experiences certainly find counterparts in experiences of serious aleatoric work.

Again, I think I used to believe more strongly in the nonegoic nature and origin of aleatoric art than I do now. However, there's certainly a real sense in which the artist's ego is held partly in abeyance when chance operations, performers' choices, etc., provide the details or even the structures of artworks. But the artist's motivation is inevitably mixed, at best—and the ego's not really evadable. Besides, nothing would get done—the work would never get written or performed—if the artist's ego—including, of course, the body—didn't get it done.

Also, I think the "interpenetration" of poet, sources, audience, and world mentioned in the first paragraph *does* take place, but I realize now that only in optimum situations can it ever be said to be "transparent" and "unobstructed"—except insofar as all things in the world so interpenetrate with each other and the whole. Those Kegon Buddhist adjectives *do* apply—but when it comes to aleatoric art, they must be hedged about with qualifiers like "sometimes," "often," "now and then," etc.

Finally, a bibliographical note: *Stanzas for Iris Lezak,* written in 1960, was published by Something Else Press in Barton, Vt. in 1972, and over half of the 501 Asymmetries written in 1960-61 have just been published by Printed Editions (New York) as *Asymmetries 1–260.* (I have copies of both available for those who are interested.)

W. S. Merwin

On Open Form
1968

What is called its form may be simply that part of the poem that had directly to do with time: the time of the poem, the time in which it was written, and the sense of recurrence in which the unique moment of vision is set.

Perhaps this is why in much of the poetry of the high Middle Ages the form seems transparent. Both the role of time in the poem and the role of the poem in time doubtless seemed clear and simple to the Arcipreste de Hita, Dante, Guillaume de Lorris and Chaucer. We can be sure of neither, and we cannot even be certain whether the pretense to such certainty that characterizes some later periods of society (in particular certain phases of neoclassicism) is one of the absurd disguises that can help an art to survive, or merely one of the shrouds that are hardly more than wasted efforts to lend decency to its burial.

The invention of a new form of stanza was a matter of genuine poetic importance to the troubadours. To us it would probably seem scarcely a matter for much curiosity. For the troubadours the abstract form (which certainly they did not hear as an abstract thing) was unquestionably related to that part of the poem that was poetic. For us it is hard to remain convinced that the form, insofar as it is abstract, is not merely part of what in the poem is inescapably technical. For us, for whom everything is in question, the making keeps leading us back into the patterns of a world of artifice so intricate, so insidious, and so impressive, that often it seems indistinguishable from the whole of time.

In a world of technique *motions* tend to become methods. But the undependable life that appears on occasion as poetry would rather die, or so it seems, than follow this tendency, and when a poet himself follows it farther than the source of his gift warrants, his gains of technical facility are likely to render him the helpless master of mere confection.

And yet neither technique nor abstract form can be abandoned, finally. And no doubt neither is dangerous in itself as long as each is recognized as no more than a means, and is not made into an idol and loved for itself. (But it seems to be characteristic of a technological age that means come to dwarf and eclipse or destroy their ends.)

And certainly neither of them automatically excludes or implies the other.

* * *

In an age when time and technique encroach hourly, or appear to, on the source itself of poetry, it seems as though what is needed for any particular nebulous unwritten hope that may become a poem is not a manipulable, more or less predictably recurring pattern, but an unduplicatable resonance, something that would be like an echo except that it is repeating no sound. Something that always belonged to it: its sense and its conformation before it entered words.

* * *

At the same time I realize that I am a formalist, in the most strict and orthodox sense. For years I have had a recurring dream of finding, as it were in an attic, poems of my own that were as lyrically formal, but as limpid and essentially unliterary as those of Villon.

* * *

Much of what appears, or appeared, as great constructive energy in the poetic revolutions of the first half of this century must have been in part energy made available by the decomposition of a vast and finally antipoetic poetic organism that had become a nuisance even to itself. The original iconoclasts have reared up other antipoetic poetic monsters that have achieved senility far more quickly since their shapes were less definite and their substance more questionable from the start.

* * *

A poetic form: the setting down of a way of hearing how poetry happens in words. The words themselves do not make it. At the same time it is testimony of a way of hearing how life happens in time. But time does not make it.

* * *

To recur in its purest forms (whether they are strict, as in Waller's "Go, Lovely Rose," or apparently untrammelled, as in The Book of Isaiah in the King James Version) poetry seems to have to keep reverting to its naked condition, where it touches on all that is unrealized.

Our age pesters us with the illusion that we have realized a great deal. The agitation serves chiefly to obscure what we have forgotten, into whose limbo poetry itself at times seems about to pass.

* * *

What are here called open forms are in some concerns the strictest. Here only the poem itself can be seen as its form. In a peculiar sense if you criticize how it happens you criticize what it is.

* * *

Obviously it is the poem that is or is not the only possible justification for any form, however theory runs. The poem is or it is not the answer to "why that form?" The consideration of the evolution of forms, strict or open, belongs largely to history and to method. The visitation that is going to be a poem finds the form it needs in spite of both.

* * *

The "freedom" that precedes strict forms and the "freedom" that follows them are not necessarily much alike. Then there is the "freedom" that accompanies poetry at a distance and occasionally joins it, often without being recognized, as in some proverbs. ("God comes to see without a bell." "He that lives on hope dances without music.")

Frank O'Hara

Personism
A Manifesto
1959

Everything is in the poems, but at the risk of sounding like the poor wealthy man's Allen Ginsberg I will write to you because I just heard that one of my fellow poets thinks that a poem of mine that can't be got at one reading is because I was confused too. Now, come on. I don't believe in god, so I don't have to make elaborately sounded structures. I hate Vachel Lindsay, always have, I don't even like rhythm, assonance, all that stuff. You just go on your nerve. If someone's chasing you down the street with a knife you just run, you don't turn around and shout, "Give it up! I was a track star for Mineola Prep."

That's for the writing poems part. As for their reception, suppose you're in love and someone's mistreating (*mal aimé*) you, you don't say, "Hey, you can't hurt me this way, I *care!*" you just let all the different bodies fall where they may, and they always do may after a few months. But that's not why you fell in love in the first place, just to hang onto life, so you have to take your chances and try to avoid being logical. Pain always produces logic, which is very bad for you.

I'm not saying that I don't have practically the most lofty ideas of anyone writing today, but what difference does that make? they're just ideas. The only good thing about it is that when I get lofty enough I've stopped thinking and that's when refreshment arrives.

But how can you really care if anybody gets it, or gets what it means, or if it improves them. Improves them for what? for death? Why hurry them along? Too many poets act like a middle-aged mother trying to get her kids to eat too much cooked meat, and potatoes with drippings (tears). I don't give a damn whether they eat or not. Forced feeding leads to excessive thinness (effete). Nobody should experience anything they don't need to, if they don't need poetry bully for them, I like the movies too. And after all, only Whitman and Crane and Williams, of the American poets, are better than the movies. As for measure and other technical apparatus, that's just common sense: if you're going to buy a pair of pants you want them to be tight enough so everyone will want to go to bed with you. There's nothing metaphysical about it. Unless, of course, you flatter yourself into thinking that what you're experiencing is "yearning."

Abstraction in poetry, which Allen recently commented on in *It is,* is intriguing. I think it appears mostly in the minute particulars where decision is necessary. Abstraction (in poetry, not in painting) involves personal removal by the poet. For instance, the decision involved in the choice between "the nostalgia of the infinite" and "the nostalgia *for* the infinite" defines an attitude towards degree of abstraction. The nostalgia *of* the infinite representing the greater degree of abstraction, removal, and negative capability (as in Keats and Mallarmé). Personism, a movement which I recently founded and which nobody yet knows about, interests me a great deal, being so totally opposed to this kind of abstract removal that it is verging on a true abstraction for the first time, really, in the history of poetry. Personism is to Wallace Stevens what *la poésie pure* was to Béranger. Personism has nothing to do with philosophy, it's all art. It does not have to do with personality or intimacy, far from it! But to give you a vague idea, one of its minimal aspects is to address itself to one person (other than the poet himself), thus evoking overtones of love without destroying love's life-giving vulgarity, and sustaining the poet's feelings towards the poem while preventing love from distracting him into feeling about the person. That's part of personism. It was founded by me after lunch with LeRoi Jones on August 27, 1959, a day in which I was in love with someone (not Roi, by the way, a blond). I went back to work and wrote a poem for this person. While I was writing it I was realizing that if I wanted to I could use the telephone instead of writing the poem, and so Personism was born. It's a very exciting movement which will undoubtedly have lots of adherents. It puts the poem squarely between the poet and the person, Lucky Pierre style, and the poem is correspondingly gratified. The poem is at last between two persons instead of two pages. In all modesty, I confess that it may be the death of literature as we know it. While I have certain regrets, I am still glad I got there before Alain Robbe-Grillet did. Poetry being quicker and surer than prose, it is only just that poetry finish literature off. For a time people thought that Artaud was going to accomplish this, but actually, for all its magnificence, his polemical writings are not more outside literature than Bear Mountain is outside New York State. His relation is no more astounding than Dubuffet's to painting.

What can we expect of Personism? (This is getting good, isn't it?) Everything, but we won't get it. It is too new, too vital a movement to promise anything. But it, like Africa, is on the way. The recent propagandists for technique on the one hand, and for content on the other, had better watch out.

Alicia Ostriker

The Nerves of a Midwife
Contemporary American Women's Poetry
1977

> I am obnoxious to each carping tongue
> Who says my hand a needle better fits.

Thus briskly wrote the pilgrim mother Anne Bradstreet in a "Prologue" to her book of poems, first published in 1650, and thus meekly two stanzas later the first woman poet in America apologized:

> Men have precedency and still excel...
> Men can do best and women know it well.
> Preeminence in each and all is yours;
> Yet grant some small acknowledgment of ours.

A fraction over three centuries later, Erica Jong observed in "Bitter Pills for the Dark Ladies" (1968) just how small the acknowledgment could be:

> If they let you out it's as Supermansaint
> & the ultimate praise is always a question of nots:
> viz. not like a woman
> viz. "certainly not another poetess"
> meanin'
> she got a cunt but she don't talk funny
> & he's a nigger but he don't smell funny
> & the only good poetess is a dead.

The "certainly not another poetess" remark was Robert Lowell's at the advent of Sylvia Plath's *Ariel*, and Plath, who certainly did not want to be another poetess, might well have been pleased by it. But Plath and Jong have in fact both contributed to an extraordinary tide of poetry by American women poets since the late 1950s* which shows no sign of abating. An increasing proportion of this work is explicitly female in the sense that the writer has consciously chosen not to "write like a man" but to explore experiences central to her sex, to find the style necessary to express such experiences, and therefore, at least at first, often to invite the scorn of conventional literary critics, editors, and male poets.

In the 1970s, dozens of little magazines and presses have sprung up which print only women's poetry. Universities across the country run series of women's poetry readings, as do, on a more modest level, coffeehouses; conferences of women poets occur and recur. The audience upon which these activities depend takes its poetry avidly and personally. One young woman poet I know calls the work of other women "survival tools." Another writes me:

> About women poets. I like them and read them because I think they're writing more exciting poetry than most men. Their poetry is about discovery and breaking new ground and it feels more like life to me . . . like work that comes to grips with what I feel is essential in all arts—what are we doing in our lives? Why do we do it? How do we see each other? How can we change what we have into what we want?

Among commercial and university presses, good women poets are widely published and recognized for their individual voices. Their books on the whole receive thoughtful reviews, written with clearer understanding and less condescension every year.

Anthologies of women's poetry fare differently from books of poems by individual women. I read *Parnassus* for enlightened, stimulating criticism of poetry and poetics, and am seldom disappointed. But in the Spring/Summer 1975 *Parnassus* I find a review which spends six lines on Segnitz and Rainey's *Psyche: An Anthology of Modern American Women Poets*

---

*Among the breakthrough volumes initiating this period are Adrienne Rich, *Snapshots of a Daughter-in-Law: Poems 1954–62* (published 1963), Muriel Rukeyser, *The Speed of Darkness* (1960), Anne Sexton, *To Bedlam and Part Way Back* (1960) and *All My Pretty Ones* (1962), Denise Levertov, *The Jacob's Ladder* (1961) and *O Taste and See* (1963), Diane Wakoski, *Inside the Blood Factory* (1962), Carolyn Kizer, *Pro Femina* (1963), Sylvia Plath, *Ariel* (1963).

and calls it "petite" (it is 256 pages, or about the same size as Donald Hall's *Contemporary American Poetry*, which for years was a standard volume). "The twenty poets are good," says the reviewer, but does not name one, or quote one line; and then proceeds to six encomiastic pages on Rothenberg and Quasha's *America A Prophecy*, finding it "a big anthology." That is rather extreme old-school. Yet the Fall/Winter issue of the same year contains a review of two other women's anthologies, in which the reviewer, though far more conscientious and detailed in analysis—he distinguishes intelligently between the two volumes, argues soundly against the editorial polemic of one of them while allowing the justice of its essential points, and appreciates excellence in the poems of both— nevertheless confesses discomfort with the existence of such anthologies. He praises Levertov for "triumphing on tiptoe over biology and destiny," Rich for "the emotional distance that enables her to perfect aesthetic form," and gives his opinion that many of the poets "would prefer to be read as women second, as poets first." What causes him, I wonder, to think so? Must we prefer one of those terms to the other?

True, instead of "certainly not another poetess," the highest praise in some circles is "certainly not another feminist," but even this is changing.

What has not changed is that most critics and professors of literature, including modern literature, deny that "women's poetry," as distinct from poetry by individual women, exists. Many women writers agree. Some will not permit their work to appear in women's anthologies.

The superficial plausibility of this position rests on the undeniable fact that women writers are a diverse lot, adhering to no single set of beliefs, doctrines, styles, or subjects. Yet would anyone deny the usefulness of the term "American poetry" (or "French poetry" or "Brazilian poetry") on the grounds that American (or French, or Brazilian) poets are diverse? Should we call Whitman, Frost, Pound, and Stevens "poets" but not "American poets"? Did T. S. Eliot's rejection of America make him any less quintessentially an American poet? In all these cases, the poet's nationality is central to his work; we might even argue that the more deeply an artist represents a nation, the more likely that artist is to represent humanity. Shakespeare was thoroughly English, Dante thoroughly Italian, and so on.

Because of the critical assumption that poetry has no gender, we have not learned to see women poets generically, or to discuss the ideas, apart from the temporary ideologies, that the flowering of their poetry generates. In what follows, I make the assumption that "women's poetry" exists in much the same sense that "American poetry" exists, and that from it we should discover not only more of what it means to be a woman but also more of what it means to be human. Although we may not be able to guess just which poems or poets from the present lively moment will in the long run endure, we can reasonably expect that whatever is shallow will evaporate by itself, and that whatever is profound and strong will ultimately enrich the mainstream of letters. Here I would like to touch, speculatively, on four elements in women's poetry which seem to me original, important, and organically connected with one another. These are the quest for autonomous self-definition; the intimate treatment of the body; the release of anger; and what I call, for want of a better name, the contact imperative. Each of these themes appears in the work of many more writers than I will be able to quote, and some of those I quote will be familiar names while some will not, precisely because the ideas, the feelings, are not merely the property of individuals. I will also say a few hesitating words about stylistic and formal considerations in women's poetry, and how they may correlate with certain emotional requirements.

First of all, then, it appears that to define oneself as authentically as possible from within has become the major female enterprise in poetry. "No more masks!" is a line from Muriel Rukeyser and the title of an anthology. Not what our fathers and mothers told us, not what our teachers expected, not what our lovers suppose, nor necessarily what literature and mythology, however beautiful and compelling, tells us: what are we then? As soon as the question is asked, certain typical rifts appear. Denise Levertov in the poem "In Mind" discovers two incompatible selves: one a woman

> of innocence, unadorned but
> fair-featured, and smelling of
> apples or grass. She wears
> a utopian smock . . .
> > And there's a
> turbulent moon-ridden girl

or old woman, or both,
dressed in opals and rags, feathers
and torn taffeta . . .

The first "is kind" but lacks imagination. The second "knows strange songs" but is not kind. A self approved by others, modest, decorous, and humanistically valuable (it has written, I think, Levertov's poems of social and political compassion), stands against a darker, more mysterious and dangerous self. Both are natural—it is not a question of one being real, one hypocritical—although the latter might perhaps better be called preternatural. Levertov, perhaps the sweetest and most life-celebratory of poets writing today, nevertheless writes of a "coldness to life," an inner-directedness which seems "un-womanly" because insufficiently nurturing of others. Or she writes of cherishing a "madness . . . blue poison, green pain in the mind's veins" though she has always been the sanest of her friends, the one they came to for comfort. The split is a central one in Levertov, and many young women warm to her work because it expresses both clearly and gently a dilemma they find in themselves. More flamboyantly, Diane Wakoski in "Beauty" parades a self something like Levertov's moon-ridden girl, asking:

and if I cut off my long hair,
if I stopped speaking,
if I stopped dreaming for other people about parts of the car,
stopped handing them tall creamy flowered silks,
and loosing the magnificent hawks to fly in their direction . . .
if I stopped crying for the salvation of the tea ceremony,
stopped rushing in excitedly with a spikey bird-of-Paradise,
and never let them see how accurate my pistol-shooting is,
who would I be?

The dilemma in Wakoski, and again it is a common one, is a sense of overpowering pride, vitality, and imaginative energy crossed by a self-destructive dependence on others for its confirmation. "Where is the real me I want them all to love," she asks self-mockingly, as she swings from one father-lover figure to another—George Washington whom she excoriates at one end of her pendulum, Beethoven to whom she clings at the other, and the easy riders whom she invites to make her life hard in between.

Not only roles and temperaments may come into question, but sexual identity itself, as it does in Adrienne Rich:

> I do not know
> if sex is an illusion
>
> I do not know
> who I was when I did those things
> or who I said I was
> or whether I willed to feel
> what I had read about
> or who in fact was there with me
> or whether I knew, even then
> that there was doubt about these things
>
> "Dialogue"

> If I am flesh sunning on rock
> if I am brain burning in fluorescent light
>
> if I am dream like a wire with fire
> throbbing along it
>
> if I am death to man
> I have to know it
>
> "August"

I have to know it. That is the unspoken theme behind the self-regard which dominates many women's work, whether the work is a delicate blend of feeling, sensation, and thought like Levertov's, passionately exhibitionistic like Wakoski's, or essentially intellectual like Rich's. The fact that the question of identity is a real one, for which the thinking woman may have as yet no satisfactory answer, may turn her resolutely inward. It may also make her poetry urgent and emotional, insofar as feelings initially inhibited, whether from within or without, have permission to erupt into the poem—and she will not know who she is until she lets them. In such work, academic distinctions between art and life, or between the self and what we in the classroom call the speaker or the persona of a poem (persona, recall, means "mask"), move to vanishing point.

A good deal of the confusion felt by some readers confronted with women's poetry may be a simple matter of fashion. Our present critical milieu expects and rewards the maintenance of low profiles in poetry: "reticence," for example, is the term Richard Howard employs to recommend Ammons's *Sphere*, and Ashbery's *Self-Portrait in a Convex Mirror* enjoys a *succès d'estime* for implying that a distorting lens tells us all we know and all we need to know about the self. "Control" and "distance" make good buzzwords on any book-jacket, while the phrase "confessional poetry" has become equivalent to wrinkling up one's nose as at a nasty odor, something vulgar. But when a woman poet says "I" she is likely to mean the actual "I" as intensely as her verbal skills permit, much as Wordsworth or Keats did—or Blake, or Milton, or John Donne of the *Holy Sonnets,* before Eliot's "extinction of personality" became the mandatory twentieth-century initiation ritual for young American poets.

Another problem is that the woman poet who seeks herself puts trivial material, that is, the material of her own daily life and feelings, into poems. "Some women marry houses," begins Anne Sexton's terse and deadpan "Housewife":

> It's another kind of skin; it has a heart,
> a mouth, a liver and bowel movements.
> The walls are permanent and pink.
> See how she sits on her knees all day,
> faithfully washing herself down.
> Men enter by force, drawn back like Jonah
> into their fleshy mothers.
> A women *is* her mother.
> That's the main thing.

Or, again, "They say women are too personal. We are not personal enough," begins Penelope Schott, in a poem which speaks of insufficient empathy with other women, who push baby carriages she has grown free of. She remembers how it felt to push the baby carriages, laden with groceries, down curbstones. She remembers that her mother lied to her about growing pubic hair, and about the pain of childbirth, and that "I have already lied to my daughter." To tell the truth to our daughters requires that we acknowledge it ourselves. The poem becomes the tribunal where a persona will not suffice; it is oneself who will be found innocent or guilty.

As the two poems just quoted already indicate, one subject that all women have in common to tell the truth about is anatomy; not, perhaps, as destiny but as priority, especially since in a world where perhaps not much is to be trusted, "the body does not lie." *Tota mulier in utero,* says the Latin, although until recently anatomy was not a subject for women's pens. While Lawrence, Joyce, and Henry Miller wrote and let censorship be damned, Virginia Woolf in a lecture on "Professions for Women" recalled her impulse, when young, to describe "something about the body . . . which it was unfitting for her as a woman to say. Men, her reason told her, would be shocked. . . . For though men sensibly allow themselves great freedom in these respects, I doubt that they realize or control the extreme severity with which they condemn such freedom in women." In the 1970s, descriptions of bodily experiences have become the most common sign of female identification in poetry. Tactility and orality abound—Sexton and Jong are particularly oral, for example, their poems filled with images of food, eating, sucking, licking. Sex receives graphic treatment hot and cold—Lynn Lifshin is probably the silkiest siren among the Wife of Bath's daughters, Elizabeth Sargent and Alta the lustiest. Looking at and touching oneself, dressing and adorning oneself, menstruation, pregnancy and birth, abortion, rape, the surgeon's knife, the process of aging, the handling of children—because women have traditionally been defined by and confined to the secret gardens of their physical selves, while being forbidden to talk in mixed company about them, they now have much to say. The abundance and variety of body images in women's poetry presently outweighs that of men's, as does the nonairbrushed intimacy of focus.

The range of attitudes women take toward the body is also startling. At one extreme, which would be medieval were it not so modern, Sylvia Plath perceives the flesh as infinitely and fascinatingly vulnerable. "I am red meat," she realizes in "Death & Co.," and her poems form a *totentanz* of the body's subjection to laceration, mutilation, disease, paralysis, rendered in chillingly vivid images of passivity and pain:

They have propped my head between the pillow and the sheet-cuff
Like an eye between two white lids that will not shut.
Stupid pupil, it has to take everything in . . .
My husband and child smiling out of the family photo;
Their smiles catch onto my skin, little smiling hooks.

The world of Plath's imagination is bounded by the brutal destruction of flesh in the Nazi holocaust and the everyday brutality of "The butcher's guillotine that whispers 'How's this, how's this?'" More recently, the young poet Ai depicts a rural Southwest in which men and women alike exist at a level of ruthless bodily hungers. When a man beats a runaway woman:

> The corner of your mouth bleeds
> and your tongue slips out, slips in.
> You don't fight me, you never do.

When a midwife does her job:

> A scraggy, red child comes out of her into my hands
> like warehouse ice sliding down the chute.

The bondage of a female body takes another form in poems which deal with the ambivalence of beauty. To cosmetize or not to cosmetize? This is a subgenre in itself, opening a rich vein of comic possibilities. Carolyn Kizer in *Pro Femina* remarks on "Our masks, always in peril of smearing or cracking," attention to which keeps a woman from serious work, neglect of which keeps her without a love life, catching up on her reading. Honor Moore's "My Mother's Mustache" gives the pros and cons of depilatories. Karen Swenson worries about a bosom less ample than Monroe's. "It's a sex object if you're pretty / love and no sex if you're fat," observes Nikki Giovanni. Jong writes a hilarious poem on "Aging," with a surprise happy ending. These poems are as undignified as they are funny—we are off the pedestal—and of course, like all good clowning, work of this sort spins from a painful core. Raised up to be narcissists, which is a game every woman ultimately loses, we must laugh that we may not weep.

Also among the poems just beginning to be written are some which treat the female body as a power rather than a liability. In Sharon Barba's "A Cycle of Women," the poet evokes

> that dream world Anaïs speaks of
> that dark watery place
> where everything is female,

and imagines a new Venus emerging from it, "a woman big-hipped, beautiful and fierce." Sexton writes "In Celebration of my Uterus," comparing "the central creature and its delight" to a singing schoolgirl, a spirit, a cup, "soil of the fields . . . roots," and hyperbolically declares:

> Each cell has a life.
> There is enough here to feed a nation . . .
> Any person, any commonwealth would say of it,
> "It is good this year that we may plant again
> and think forward to a harvest."

Robin Morgan's long "Network of the Imaginary Mother" recounts the poet's conversion from loathing to loving her own body, precipitated by the baptismal experience of nursing her dying mother, and defines her biological capacities in terms of goddess-figures representing a triumphant will to love and nurture, opposed to the killing abstractions of technology. Muriel Rukeyser has developed a language similarly rooted in gender and ramifying into politics, which envisions radical social change impelled by principles of maternity. The power of the maternal drive to transform even the most intimate grief and guilt into strength appears in Lucille Clifton's "The Lost Baby Poem:"

> the time i dropped your almost body down
> to meet the waters under the city
> and run one with the sewage to the sea
> what did i know about waters rushing back
> what did i know about drowning
> or being drowned . . .
>
> if i am ever less than a mountain
> for your definite brothers and sisters
> let the rivers pour over my head
> let the sea take me for a spiller
> of seas let black men call me stranger
> always for your never named sake

And for Adrienne Rich, in the difficult yet triumphant close to "The Mirror in Which Two Are Seen as One," it is ourselves to whom we must heroically give birth:

> your mother dead and you unborn
> your two hands grasping your head

> drawing it down against the blade of life
> your nerves the nerves of a midwife
> learning her trade.

It will be interesting to see whether such female metaphors will come to take their place alongside more conventional metaphors for heroism. Meanwhile, whether engaged or not in ideology, it would be difficult to find a woman poet writing today who does not treat the facts of her and our physical experience as essential material for poetry.

If we turn to sexual politics in the sense coined by Kate Millett, we find less pleasure, more anger, and a striking development of poems about violence, although (or because) neither violence nor anger has been a traditionally acceptable mode of expression for women. When women perceive themselves as victims, suppressed, confined, their strengths denied and their weaknesses encouraged under the collective and personal system feminists have come to call patriarchy, they write self-pity poems, mad-housewife poems, off-our-back poems, all of which are interesting at least symptomatically. The most interesting of them are those which generalize, or make generalization possible, by plunging to the principles which animate persons.

One recalls Plath's archetypally authoritarian male figure in "Lady Lazarus," the composite Doctor-Nazi-sideshow manager, "Herr God, Herr Lucifer." In the eyes of this figure the poet is, she knows, an object to be manipulated, a freak, "your jewel . . . your valuable." In Mona Van Duyn's complex and witty "Death by Aesthetics," the same unpleasant figure appears as a physician-lover, probably also psychoanalyst, an icy Doctor Feelgood:

> His fluoroscope hugs her. Soft the intemperate girl
> disordered. Willing she lies while he unfolds
> her disease, but a stem of glass protects his fingers
> from her heat, nor will he catch her cold . . .
>
> He hands her a paper. "Goodbye. Live quietly,
> make some new friends. I've seen these stubborn cases
> cured with time. My bill will arrive. Dear lady,
> it's been a most enjoyable diagnosis."

In vain the patient begs:

meet me, feel the way my body feels,
and in my bounty of dews, fluxes and seasons,
orifices, in my wastes and smells
see self.

He has already gone, saying "Don't touch me," and his pre-
scription reads "Separateness."

The experimental playwright and poet Rochelle Owens, in
the ironically titled "The Power of Love: He Wants Shih," has
composed a sadistic fantasy for a practitioner of martial arts.
The hero explains that a woman's love for him is his weapon,
that as her feeling increases, his disappears:

It's heaven's will, shua hsi!
In my mind I smear the mucus
from my nose on her breasts . . .
& drop ants into her two mouths . . .
I fill up all her orifices—
I'm very generous . . .
& she calls me the divinity
of mountains & streams &
I think of how it would be
to piss on her!

May Swenson's "Bleeding" takes the form of a dialogue between
a cut and a knife, the former apologetic, the latter angry about
being made "messy with this blood." Similarly grim is the
dialogue in Marge Piercy's "The Friend," in which a man
across the table tells a woman to cut off her hands because
they poke and might touch him, to burn her body because it is
"not clean and smells like sex." She agrees and says she loves
him. He says he likes to be loved and asks her if she has cut off
her hands yet.

Such poems, it seems to me, probe deeply into the sources
of male-female misery, directing one's horror almost equally
against the hypocrite male's inaccessibility to emotion, and the
female's compliance in her victimization. Men, in poems
about male domination, are always authority figures as-
sociated with technology, abstract and analytical thinking in-
stead of feeling, a will to exercise control, and a gluttonous
demand for admiration. But the women are helpless petition-
ers: all they need is love, they make no demands, they will do
anything and permit anything to be done to them, they are all

too ready to obey. Nor is it an accident that the scenes of these poems are all intimately physical. The presumably male idea of the uncleanness of flesh, and of women's flesh in particular, which we inherit with the rest of our Judeo-Christian dreamlife baggage (e.g., Tertullian, "Woman is a temple over a sewer"), is one that perhaps few women themselves evade. Self-disgust is a strong drink, and to the passive woman an intoxicant: "Every woman adores a fascist / The boot in the face."

One need not believe that individual men necessarily fill the role which so many women's poems have men play, that of aggressive or impassive villain; or that women themselves are universally innocent of such vices. Some men mop the floor. Some women are bitches. One of the excellences of a poem like Swenson's is that it assigns no explicit gender to the cut and the knife—the masochistic cut in fact sounds very much like Shakespeare's Shylock. Such games can be played by persons of any sex, in any combination; compare Ginsberg's "Master" in *The Fall of America*. But this does not invalidate the individual suffering in the poems, or the generic applications implied by them. We know the bleeding cut feels feminine, we know the knife which wants to be hard and shiny feels masculine.

What follows, then, at any rate in a significant number of poems, is the fantasy of vengeance. Plath imagines a ritual slaying of the father she loves and hates in "Daddy," and a return from the grave to devour men in "Lady Lazarus." Rich in "The Phenomenology of Anger" dreams of becoming an acetylene torch, to burn away the lie of her enemy, the killer of babies at My Lai, the defoliator of fields. She desires, she says, to leave him a new man, yet one cannot escape the sense of her compulsion to punish. In her more down-to-earth manner, Diane Wakoski dedicates *The Motorcycle Betrayal Poems* "to all those men who betrayed me at one time or another, in hopes they will fall off their motorcycles and break their necks." In one of the poems of that volume, Wakoski imagines shooting a lover in the back with a Thompson Contender, and watching him topple over once for every man—from her father to the President—who has neglected her. In "They Eat Out," Margaret Atwood punctures, with a fork, a self-important gentleman friend. Grisliest of the lot, perhaps, is Cynthia Macdonald's "Objets d'Art." Having been told by a stranger in a railway station that she was "a real ball-cutter," she thinks it over, goes into the business, finds that freezing is the best method of preservation—and is interested, of course, only in volunteers:

> It is an art like hypnosis
> Which cannot be imposed on the unwilling victim,

which brings us full circle on the fine line between fear and need in human motivation.

But if the release of anger is a major element in women's poetry, so, to an even greater degree, is the release of a contrary passion, which in part explains the vehemence of women's rage. The superiority of male over female (or the mind over the body, or the impersonal over the personal) appears to be the more intolerable to many women poets because of intense cravings for unity, for a sense of relationship which escapes the vertical grid of dominance and submission altogether. Mutuality, continuity, connection, identification, touch: this theme in women's work is one which we might call the contact imperative, and it strongly affects the way women write about love, time, history, politics, and themselves.

In love poetry, the contact imperative means goodbye to the strong silent type. "I like my men / talky and / tender," says Carol Bergé, and in poem after poem describing gratified desire, those lovers and husbands are praised who are most gentle and warm; i.e., who release rather than suppress their "feminine" qualities. Conversely, the poets seem best satisfied with themselves when they quit passivity and take some form of initiative, like Nikki Giovanni in "The Seduction," forthrightly undressing her man while he lectures on about the revolution. Domestically, women tend to envision love as something natural, normal, and shared, as in Lisel Mueller's "Love Like Salt." To explain ecstasy, women consistently seem to employ the idea of interpenetration between two lovers, the dissolving of boundaries between individual selves, and at especially blissful moments, the elimination of distinctions between human and nonhuman existence. A couple makes love in a bedroom, and then there is

> the hot joy spilling
> puddles on the bed, the rug,

the back yard, the earth
happy with us, needing our joy.

"Anybody could write this poem," insists Alta in her title. "All you have to say is Yes." Again, in Maxine Kumin's "We Are," the lovingly developed metaphor for a pair of lovers is that of a pond, complete with frogs whose legs open like very small children's, skimmed by waterbugs, surrounded by blackberry bushes: "We teem, we overgrow." Still again, in Daniela Gioseffi's quasi-surrealistic, quasi-pornographic "Paradise Is Not a Place," the lovers sail the seas on their mattress, and ultimately fuse into a giant Mount Androgynous which becomes a permanent tourist attraction in the mid-Pacific. One would think of Donne's "The Canonization," except that for Gioseffi, as for women love poets in general, love does not signify transcendence of carnality or mortality, nor does it involve trials, tests, obstacles. The images are of relaxation and immanence rather than strenuousness. The motion of love is down, not up: down toward the earth, down into the flesh, easily.

The need for connection can also express itself in terms of exploring continuities between generations. Daughters write of parents or grandparents, mothers write of children. Women write of continuities from one writer to another (not, *pace* Harold Bloom, on the Oedipal model of killing and superseding, but on the Demeter-Kore model of returning and reviving), or the love-and-support relationships (sexual or not) generated and reinforced by the feminist movement.

Among politically radical writers such as Rich, Piercy, and Morgan, desire for personal affection assumes the status of a nonnegotiable demand. Intimacies between friends and lovers become a model for the conduct of political life. What resists the self-surrender of love in the microcosm of private relationships is also what resists it in Vietnam, Biafra, Harlem, and these poets want to break that resistance, tear off the armor, and liberate the willing lover at the core of the unwilling enemy. Thus an embrace is a "guerrilla tactic" in Piercy's "Agitprop," and the woman who inflicts it on an unresponding man is sending his deeper self "promises . . . of interim relief / and ultimate victory."

These are also the writers who make poems for and from the lives of lost women, the insulted and injured of present and past history, and an occasional heroine. Working-class girls appear in several of Piercy's poems, and Piercy has done a fine lament for Janis Joplin. The lives of frontierwomen are celebrated and mourned in Rich's "From an Old House in America"; Rich has also written about Marie Curie and Caroline Herschel. Morgan's "Network of the Imaginary Mother" includes a recital of the names of witches executed, or tortured and executed, up until the eighteenth century. Susan Griffin writes equally of welfare mothers, her own middle-class alcoholic one, and Harriet Tubman. Judy Grahn writes a sequence of poems entitled "The Common Woman," concluding with Marilyn Monroe. One of the most powerful statements about the personal and social dimensions of women's love for women is Grahn's *A Woman Is Talking to Death*. To extract quotations from this work is to mutilate it, but Grahn should be better known. The following passage is from a mock interrogation:

What about kissing? Have you kissed any women?

I have kissed many women.

When was the first woman you kissed with serious feeling?

The first woman ever I kissed was Josie, who I had loved at such a distance for months. Josie was not only beautiful, she was tough and handsome too. Josie had black hair and white teeth and strong brown muscles. Then she dropped out of school unexplained. When she came back she came back for one day only, to finish the term, and there was a child in her. She was all shame, pain and defiance. Her eyes were dark as the water under a bridge and no one would talk to her, they laughed and threw things at her. In the afternoon I walked across the front of the class and looked deep into Josie's eyes and I picked up her chin with my hand, because I loved her, because nothing like her trouble would ever happen to me, because I hated it that she was pregnant and unhappy, and an outcast. We were thirteen.

You didn't kiss her?

How does it feel to be thirteen and having a baby?

You didn't actually kiss her? . . .

In a later section of the poem, Grahn is knocked down in a diner by a Spanish-speaking youth who calls her "queer." Counterman and police prove indifferent. Weeks later it occurs to her that this might be Josie's son. In a still later section, she and her "pervert" friends encounter a fifty-five-year-old Chinese woman who has been raped by a cabdriver and left bleeding in the snow. They kiss and try to reassure her, knowing it is not enough. Grahn burns with desire to rule the city with this woman, but she lets her go in the ambulance with the bored policemen, guiltily unable to enact her defiance, to "get the real loving done."

Within the symposium of the self, a number of women poets evidently wish to reverse Yeat's dictum that from the quarrel with ourselves we make poetry. They struggle rather to make poetry about coming to peace with ourselves by reconciling internal antimonies. Coleridge, Rimbaud, and Woolf are invoked for the idea of the androgynous being who combines both intellect and emotion, strength and gentleness. Rukeyser, in a poem on Kathe Kollwitz, quotes Kollwitz' testimony that her own work required a masculine element. Rich, in "Diving into the Wreck," discovers as she descends to the depths of personal and communal history, "I am he . . . I am she." Although Rich has since repudiated the ideal of androgyny, it remains attractive to others, and perhaps is responsible for the tough-but-tender style of a writer like Grahn.*

I believe that it is the contact imperative which finally accounts for the confessional or diarist mode in women's writing, because of the intimacy this mode imposes on the audience. One cannot read, for example, a Wakoski or a Sexton poem with feeling that the ordinary objectivity of readership comes under severe attack, and the same is true, if

---

*An exception that seems to me to prove the rule of women's concern for unifying relationships is Margaret Atwood. Atwood is an important poet, most of whose work seems to express a steely and mistrustful avoidance of, rather than desire for, human closeness. On the other hand, the "Circe-Mud Poems" which conclude her recent *You Are Happy* appear to move toward the possibility, at least in imagination, of transcending isolation and hoping for harmony of male and female in the natural world, as is also the case with the heroine of her novel, *Surfacing.*

to a less breathtaking degree, with many other women poets. "No more masks" means something for reader as well as writer. As the poet refuses to distance herself from her emotions, so she prevents us from distancing ourselves. We are obliged to witness, to experience the hot breath of the poem upon us. Or perhaps we want to wrestle loose. The poem is impolite, crude, it imposes too much. In either case, we have been obliged to some degree to relinquish our roles as readers, and to respond personally. That, evidently, has been the aim of the poet. In a sense beyond what Plath intended, these are disquieting muses.

Having said this much, I do not suppose I have exhausted the themes and modes of contemporary women's poetry, any more than I have mentioned all the "good" women writers. I suspect, for example, that the need to define presocial strata in female nature is producing a revival of mythology in poetry, much as the compulsion to explore nonrational human passions led Coleridge to the supernatural, Keats and Shelley to classical Greek myth, Blake to a self-invented mythology, Yeats to occultism, Eliot to *The Golden Bough*. I would not be surprised to find that certain traditional images and symbols reveal new facets for women artists. Water, in women's poetry, seems to function as an image not of chaos and danger, but of security and a potential for rebirth. Another instance is the symbol of the flower, which in women's poetry today repeatedly signifies vitality, power, sensuousness to an almost predatory degree, much as in the visual imagery of Georgia O'Keeffe or Judy Chicago. Still another is blood, which becomes in many poems an image for creativity.

Nor do I suppose that the issues I have been outlining are the exclusive property of women writers. Poets like Ginsberg, Duncan, and Bly work intensively on some of the same problems that beset women, and in fact each of these men has identified his concerns as symbolically female. Theodore Roethke's profound sensuousness and discomfort with abstractions had a feminine cast (although through most of his career his explicit self-identifications were emphatically with plants and animals, and his treatment of women thoroughly conventional). Paul Goodman's poetry shares many antiauthoritarian ideas with that of the radical feminist poets, including the idea of congruence between the body and the body politic. Galway Kinnell dives faithfully into his own wreck, and his essay on "Poetry, Personality, and Death" eloquently discusses the limitations of impersonality in poetry, pointing out that while a persona may enable a writer to dramatize otherwise hidden aspects of his own personality, it may also release him from the painfulness of a full examination. The poet, Kinnell remarks, "knows himself to be of a more feminine disposition than the banker." To a greater or lesser extent, such writers defy the dominant "modern" mode of weary irony which has characterized English and American poetry for fifty years, deviations from which have usually been antiacademic, grassroots movements of one sort or another. Yet at the present moment, the flying wedge of dissent and quest is composed mainly of women, who collectively are contributing an extraordinary intellectual, emotional, and moral exhilaration to American poetry, and who may be expected to have an impact on its future course.

Ron Padgett

Three Poems
1971–72

Ladies and Gentlemen in Outer Space

Here is my philosophy:
Everything changes (the word "everything"
has just changed as the
word "change" has: it now
means "no change") so
quickly that it literally surpasses my belief,
charges right past it
like some of the giant
ideas in this area.
I had no beginning and I shall have
no end: the beam of light
stretches out before and behind
and I cook the vegetables
for a few minutes only,
the fewer the better. Butter
and serve. Here is my
philosophy: butter and serve.

Poetic License

This license certifies
That Ron Padgett may tell whatever lies
His heart desires
Until it expires

Louisiana Perch

Certain words disappear from a language:
their meanings become attenuated
grow antique, insanely remote or small,
vanish.
       Or become something else:
transport. Mac
the truck driver falls for a waitress
    where the water flows. The

great words are those without meaning:
  from a their or
  Or the for a the
  The those

The rest are fragile, transitory
  like the waitress, a

beautiful slender young girl!
I love her! Want to
marry her! Have hamburgers!
Have hamburgers! Have hamburgers!

Robert Pinsky

Poetry and the World
1981

i.

In dealing with my topic, I want to consider "poetry" in its broadest definition, to include such forms as the short story; and to consider "the World" in a relatively narrow definition. I have in mind the world of worldliness: the social world, but more particularly the social world in its alternate glamour and squalor, its almost identical powers to divert us and to jade us. It is what Ben Jonson could embody by saying "the Court"; and indeed, in his great poem "To the World: A Farewell for a Gentlewoman, Virtuous and Noble," Jonson does seem to use "the World" as if it and "the Court" were synonymous.

To assert the existence of such a worldly world implies that there is also a different, distinct world which is other, a spiritual world. English verse, with the dual, linked courtly and devotional traditions of its first great flowering, has often involved the problem of an orientation to these two worlds. I would like to use this topic as the occasion for talking about a wide, perhaps eccentric range of works. It has occurred to me that many of my favorite works, recent and historical, involve a bridge or space between the worldly and the spiritual. Poetry itself suggests such a dualism, related in ways I can't unravel. That is, the medium of words is social, yet it can also be the fabric of the most rarefied, introspective ideas; and the sensuousness of poetry is to give elegance and significance to the sounds that breath makes vibrating in the mouth and throat, animating by art those bodily noises of communication. In such ways poetry seems to have a special, enigmatic relation to the worldly world. On a more immediate level, it is worth inquiring into the role of the worldly in contemporary poems: what role does "the World" in this sense play in the new poem one is about to write or to read?

The first example, however, is from the sixteenth century, Thomas Campion's "Now Winter Nights Enlarge":

> Now winter nights enlarge
> The number of their hours,
> And clouds their storms discharge
> Upon the airy towers.
> Let now the chimneys blaze
> And cups o-erflow with wine;
> Let well-tuned words amaze
> With harmony divine!
> Now yellow waxen lights
> Shall wait on honey love
> While youthful revels, masques and Courtly sights,
> Sleep's leaden spells remove.
>
> This time doth well dispense
> With lovers' long discourse;
> Much speech hath some defence,
> Though beauty no remorse.
> All do not all things well;
> Some measures comely tread,
> Some knotted riddles tell,
> Some poems smoothly read.
> The summer hath his joys,
> And winter his delights;
> Though love and all his pleasures are but toys
> They shorten tedious nights.

The poem celebrates with the utmost relish the scenes and diversions which it puts in their proper place. While it can seem superficially a charming song about hardly anything at all, it is about that proper place, the idea of decorum. What is startling is that the stuffy idea of decorum can be treated with such energy and ebullience, an omnivorous verve that extends its appetite to flirtations, poems, riddles, dance-steps, wine-cups, the miniature honey-comb of lights and the massive, fantastic storm.

Yvor Winters has used Campion's opening lines—"Now winter nights enlarge / The number of their hours"—as a *locus classicus* for the effective use of connotative, or supra rational effects in language: the word "enlarge" denotes rationally only the relative number of hours in a winter night, but its aura magnifies and enhances the large scale of the charming, almost Disneyesque storm and towers. In a similar vein, Winters points out the pleasing connotative harmony of "waxen lights" with "honey love": the castle with its comb of cells becomes a cozy, mysteriously sunny beehive in the thick of winter.

Such "harmony" and "amazement," to borrow Campion's own terms, are so egregious in the poem that Winters found them convenient examples of certain rhetorical effects. The harmony and amazement, blending the golden with the leaden, and blazing discharge of energy with well-tuned spells, by being made so prominent perform for us Campion's relation to these aristocratic, intoxicating worldly pastimes. The amazing, harmonious blending of air and architecture, wine and words, enlargement of space and time, rests on a sense of limit.

This idea of limit is quite explicit in the second stanza: the prolix, amoral rituals of courtship are limited by being assigned, with a smile, to the season of long, cold nights. And then, in a marvelous line, "All do not all things well": lovemaking, dancing, riddle setting, the performance of poems—individuals are limited by their skills at these diversions; and the diversions themselves are limited, implicitly by their collocation and explicitly by the affectionate, but diminutive terms of the last two lines:

> Though love and all his pleasures are but toys
> They shorten tedious nights.

For a good poem to end with a brief summarizing moral statement violates a creative writing slogan; but that is another example of the sense of limit on which Campion's song founds its success. It is a shrewd, oddly detached praise of both pleasure, and pleasure's limits.

ii.

Pleasure, especially the linked pleasures of art and sexual attraction, is the primary and perhaps the quintessential attraction of the worldly. In some of the stories by the great Russian writer Isaac Babel, pleasure plays a central role in a fictional questioning of the worldly world, and its reality. Perhaps the odd comparison comes to mind because the idea of "the Court" persists in Babel, making possibly one of its last nonarchaic appearances in literature. Needless to say, Campion's relation to "Courtly sights" is less complex than Babel's politically, and possibly in every other way, too. But though we can only gesture a little in the direction of such complexities, a brief attempt may suggest some comparative terms for the ways a contemporary poet stands in relation to the attractions and limits of the world.

In Babel's story "An Evening at the Empress's," the narrator is a hungry young poet, rather knowing and flippant in his narrative manner, drifting through the streets of Petersburg on a cold night in the early years of the Russian Revolution:

> I needed a place to shelter. Hunger was plucking at me like a clumsy kid playing a fiddle. I went over in my mind all the apartments abandoned by the bourgeoisie. The great squat hulk of the Anichkov Palace heaved into my line of vision. That was the place for me.

He slips into the empty entry hall and through the uninhabited palace, to find himself in the private library of the Dowager Empress Maria Fyodorovna—the mother of the late Nicholas II, and born a Princess of the Danish Court. An old German, functionary under People's Commisar for Enlightenment Lunacharsky, is about to go to bed:

> My luck was really kissing me on the lips; I knew this German. I had once typed for him, free of charge, a declaration about his lost identity papers. He belonged to me with all his honest, sluggish guts. We decided that I had come to see Lunacharsky and was just waiting for him in the library.

I quote Max Hayward's translation (from *You Must Know Everything*, ed. Nathalie Babel), the tone of which one is inclined to trust, because this youthful, bohemian-wise-guy toughness of speech modulates into a poignant, important contrast.

After eating his rough ration bread from an ancient Chinese lacquer table, while snow falls harshly on the granite city, the young writer takes down some of the Empress's books, on which a warm light falls in "lemon cascades." His response—the story's response—to these books has a peculiar, subtle flavor. I think that it touches upon the conflict between pleasure and time, the Court-World's splendor and the cruel limits imposed upon it by another world; the way Babel mingles nostalgia and irony seems to me like an effort to pin down those limits, to define the relation between the body's craving for comfort and ease on one side, and the cold truths of the soul on the other. The medium for all this is supplied by the elegant, pathetic old books:

> The books, their pages moldering and scented, carried me far away to Denmark. More than half a century ago they had been presented to the young princess as she set out from her small, sedate country for savage Russia. On the austere title pages, in three slanting lines of faded ink, were farewell good wishes from the ladies of the court who had brought her up ... her tutors, parchment faced professors from the Lycée; the King, her father, and her weeping mother, the Queen. On the long shelves were small, fat books with gold edges now gone dark, ink-stained children's Bibles with timid blots and awkward, homemade prayers to the Lord Jesus, small morocco-bound volumes of Lamartine and Chénier with withered flowers crumbling to dust. I turned over these thin pages, snatched from oblivion; the images of an unknown country, a succession of unusual days passed before me—low walls around the royal gardens, dew on the close-cropped lawns, sleepy emeralds of canals, and the tall King with chocolate-colored sideburns ...

I think that this is no mere elegy, just as (on a different plane) Campion was not writing mere party music.

One of the ways in which it is not merely elegy has to do with the context: the sudden, absurdly luxurious roosting place of the Revolutionary-era poet. His historical, political and cultural perspective allows him, in the next paragraph, to speak of the former Danish princess as "A small woman with powder worked into her skin, a shrewd schemer driven by a tireless urge to exercise authority, a fierce female among the Preobrazhensky Grenadiers, a merciless but attentive mother who met her match in the German woman"—that is, in her daughter-in-law the Czarina. The imaginative sympathy and amused judgment, the stylization and intimacy join other disparate elements of Babel's work, held together by his mysterious urgency of vision.

His work, in general, meditates the grace and energy of the actual world, and the horrible deficiency of order in the distribution of grace and energy. A brutal soldier, an exploitative regime, or imbecile fate itself, like a pig unwittingly gobbling a live chick or a pearl necklace, may be the vessel of the attractive force or elegance. The pleasure of the world is splattered about insanely, unpredictably, or embalmed in the dusty atmosphere of books.

Yet the stories, dramatizing this mess with their mingled appetite and horror, seem by their jangling of contexts to insist that a decorum, a limiting boundary, must prevail ultimately. I think that part of what makes Babel a great artist is that he does not glibly propose an ultimate order to be embodied merely by "art itself." On the contrary, there is something like the respectful but limiting tone of Campion's phrase "Some poems smoothly read," in the way the narrator's cockiness and the library's "ghosts with their bloodied heads"—the young artist and the old culture—chastise and expose one another. Neither of them feels quite as real as the relation between them, the historical violence and possibility that brings them strangely together.

This sense of limit and proportion emerging from violent disparities underlies the wry, anarchic grin of Babel's final sentence: "Let those who have fled it know," says the young man, who after recovering at the Palace sleeps the night in the train station, "that in Petersburg there are places where a homeless poet can spend an evening." The energy of the story centers not on the two places, nor even on the contrast between them, but on the Petersburg that brings them to the poet on a single night.

The lost, worldly pleasures of the Danish or Czarist court, and the crude worldly wants of the young poet whose luck kisses him on the lips, complement and then negate one another: they are not all that there is. Somewhere in the narrative intelligence that encompasses both of these disproportionate realms is a value above them. This value is implicit, perhaps, in the fact that the back-currents of Revolution have brought the young drifter to this room, and in the more remarkable, more absurd fact that he can read and respond to the pathetic books in the room. The last sentence is ironic and comic about the historical swirl and confusion that brings a half-frozen young scribbler to dine on coarse bread in a palace, and to sleep in a train station; but there is in the sentence, too, a kind of pride or pleasure, a need for things to work out in Petersburg, and a germ of justification for that need.

That germ makes Babel's story more than an elegiac contrast of past and present worlds. Though one must call it political, it gives the story the spiritual force of a critique of both those worlds.

If we ask how the Campion song manages the balance needed to celebrate a world of elegant diversions and sexual pleasure, while confidently asserting the limits of such "toys," the answer would have to do with an implicit context. To avoid any embarrassing intellectual-historical cliches, let us say about the context simply that it is the kind of cultural and intellectual context on which such limits and judgments might rest. That is, Campion's imagined soirée implies a cultural frame in which worldly pleasures have their place within a distinct hierarchy. I think that in a more complex way, Babel's sense of balance in relation to the pleasures of the Anichkov Palace depends on a sense of another, higher, more stringent world. His willingness to be hopeful or exhilarated, in his strange historical moment, is as invisible and implicit as the Chain of Being (and so forth) in "Now Winter Nights Enlarge."

This idea of a kind of metaphysical political hope—or if not a hope, a sense of possibility, however desperate or ironic—embodies what I mean by another world. The idea's presence and importance in Babel's story is heightened, I think, by Babel's reworking of this same material in a later story, "The Road There" (as translated by Andrew R. MacAndrew). In this version, Babel in a way turns up the volume of all elements: the poet is also a soldier, leaving the collapsed front of 1917 for the city. On the train, an idealistic Jewish schoolteacher and his young wife, carrying papers signed by Minister of Enlightenment Lunacharsky, fall asleep together "whispering about educational methods that would produce well-rounded citizens"; then, this couple become the victims of murderous brutality at the hands of a detachment of anti-semitic peasants who check papers at a stop. The soldier-poet nearly has his frozen feet amputated, and spends some time in a hospital before getting to the Anichkov palace. There, he not only eats, but is bathed, spends the night, is given the Czar's dressing gown and cigars by the official in charge, who is a former comrade-in-arms. The nostalgic, funereal elegy, going over "Nicholas II's toys . . . Bibles, volumes of Lamartine's poetry" is also expanded and intensified.

Though in some ways the story is less successful in this more explicit version, the idea of a beleaguered hope, expressing itself through the limits of the worldly, is more clear. "He's one of us," the old comrade announces, and the narrator is made a translator in the Commissariat.

> I set about translating the depositions made by various diplomats, *provocateurs,* and spies.
>
> Within a day, I had everything—clothes, food, work, and friends, friends loyal in life and in death, such as can be found in no other country but ours.
>
> That was how, thirteen years ago, my great life, full of ideas and joy, began.

The young Jewish schoolteacher on the train was shot in the mouth, his genitals cut off and pushed into the wife's mouth; the male nurse who bandaged the narrator's feet quoted Engels on the abolition of nations, but disagreed with Engels, asking the narrator in effect "What are you Jews after?" All of this material, narrated abruptly and without comment, heightens the irony in this final reference to "my great life"; but it also heightens the importance of the wish to believe that the loyalty, comfort, place in the world are true. The escape from history, though political in means, is for Babel unworldly and spiritual in its pained essence.

iii.

The elegance of the world, and its appalling cruelty, may be represented by the "harmony divine" of well-tuned words and the "savage Russia" of historical reality. Both elegance and cruelty are forced by the works of art to recede a certain amount into perspective. The pleasure of divine harmony is ultimately just a "toy"; the savagery of Russia is a fluid, violent amalgam of brutality and exalting possibility. In both poem and story, the social world, with its pleasures, limits, horrors, is put firmly in its place.

The pair of recent poems I have in mind might be said to proceed in the opposite direction, trying to locate the part of life that is not social, not of the World. These poems are the first two in Elizabeth Bishop's book *Geography III*. In a peculiar way, they recall Ben Jonson's poem, the "Farewell to the World" I alluded to at the outset. Jonson's noblewoman addresses the world:

> Do not once hope that thou canst tempt
>   A spirit so resolved to tread
> Upon thy throat, and live exempt
>   From all the nets that thou canst spread.
> I know thy forms are studied arts,
>   Thy subtle ways be narrow straits,
> Thy courtesy but sudden starts,
>   And what thou call'st thy gifts are baits.

The brilliant line about courtesy, and the one about forms, anticipate the later lines where this militant posture is pretty clearly directed toward the Court, as epitome of the World at its best and worst:

> Then, in a soil hast planted me
>   Where breathe the basest of thy fools;
> Where envious arts professed be,
>   And pride and ignorance the schools;
> Where nothing is examined, weighed
>   But as tis rumored, so believed;
> Where every freedom is betrayed,
>   And every goodness taxed or grieved.

The embattled contempt (superbly driven home by the rhymes) yields to a somewhat different, perhaps surprising variety of "scorn," tempering the conventional theme of *contemptus mundi* with a peculiar, almost sweet note of resignation:

> But what we're born for, we must bear:
>   Our frail condition, it is such
> That, what to all may happen here,
>   If it chance to me, I must not grutch;
> Else I my state should much mistake
>   To harbor a divided thought
> From all my kind—that for my sake,
>   There should a miracle be wrought.
> No, I do know that I was born
>   To age, misfortune, sickness, grief:
> But I will bear them with that scorn
>   As shall not need thy false relief.

> Nor for my peace will I go far,
>   As wanderers do, that still do roam,
> But make my strengths, such as they are,
>   Here in my bosom, and at home.

The military nobility of "resolved to tread / Upon thy throat" has become an equally stern, but more controlled, inward, even domestic kind of defiance: to "make my strengths, such as they are, / Here in my bosom, and at home." The words, "I my state should much mistake / To harbor a divided thought / From all my kind" are especially affecting because they contradict the poem's inner direction and amend the "noble gentlewoman's" main response to the World. That response, her final moral resource, is isolation.

Isolation is a starting place and a central concern in Bishop's *Geography III*. The opening poem, "In the Waiting Room," portrays a seven-year-old child's realization that she is in a world of people and artifacts—and, even more terrifying, is a part of that world. That is, she is among the "grown-up people, arctics and overcoats, lamps and magazines," "Osa and Martin Johnson dressed in riding breeches," "a dead man slung on a pole—'Long Pig,' the caption said," "black naked women with necks wound round and round with wire," the "shadowy gray knees" and "different pairs of hands lying under the lamps"—all the grotesque, manifold contents of the *National Geographic* magazine or of the waiting room. But more, she is a member of that world, part of the contents, without having decided to be, and an all-but-anonymous part of the swirl:

> I felt: you are an *I*,
> you are an *Elizabeth*,
> you are one of *them*.
> *Why* should you be one too?

And:

> What similarities—
> boots, hands, the family voice
> I felt in my throat, or even
> the *National Geographic*
> and those awful hanging breasts—
> held us all together

or made us all just one?
How—I didn't know any
word for it—how "unlikely" . . .
How had I come to be here,
like them . . .

It is hard to picture a more explicit, graphic version of a self
needing to isolate itself from the social, worldly world, in
order not to be lost in it. From the moment the child realizes
this situation, a conflict begins. As the poem says: "The War
was on."

"Crusoe in England" is (among other things) an allegory of
the solitary, inner life in relation to the engulfing, numbing
World. The poem's genius and originality stem partly from
the moral insight that makes the solitary inner life something
quite far from a paradise. It is an "other" world; and it is the
object of affection (to be precise, of nostalgia)—but it is no
heaven: "my poor old island," with its "fifty-two miserable,
small volcanoes," hissing, and its hissing turtles, "cloud-
dump" sky, waterspouts, one kind of berry, goats. Taken as
an allegorical self-portrait of one's inward life, it has the wit to
be neither flattering nor flatteringly self-accusing. It is in-
teresting, harsh, strange.

Correspondingly, the social world, the World itself, the
other island of England to which the solitary has now re-
turned, is not presented in trite or literary terms as sinister,
monstrously huge, malevolently controlling, dramatically un-
just. Rather, it is dwindling, numbing, rather cozy as well as
depriving; it is where one lives if the sense of another, per-
sonal world has flagged:

Now I live here, another island,
that doesn't seem like one, but who decides?
My blood was full of them; my brain
bred islands. But that archipelago
has petered out. I'm old.
I'm bored too, drinking my real tea,
surrounded by uninteresting lumber.
The knife there on the shelf—
it reeked of meaning, like a crucifix.
It lived. How many years did I
beg it, implore it, not to break?
I knew each nick and scratch by heart,

the bluish blade, the broken tip,
the lines of wood-grain on the handle . . .
Now it won't look at me at all.
The living soul has dribbled away.
My eyes rest on it and pass on.

In the conflict between the isolated world of the self and the communal world of England, the knife is a charmed artifact, a sacred weapon—but only in its primal context. On the terrain of the worldly, it becomes like a poem written years ago, when the World was not an enveloping, suffusing mass: when the maker was isolated from it.

That isolation is presented as onerous as well as sacred, an occasion for pathetic melancholy as well as for pride. Is it a matter of accomplishment, a matter, even, of volition? Bishop treats that question with a marvelous combination of comedy and cruelty:

I often gave way to self-pity.
"Do I deserve this? I suppose I must.
I wouldn't be here otherwise. Was there
a moment when I actually chose this?
I don't remember, but there could have been."
What's wrong with self-pity anyway?
With my legs dangling down familiarly
over a crater's edge, I told myself
"Pity should begin at home." So the more
pity I felt, the more I felt at home.

Her Crusoe questions whether the life apart from the World—the life of a castaway—is an imposed circumstance, or a product of the will. He does not directly raise the question of its value, but "pity" is only one of the products of his "island industries." He also creates home brew, dreams, a philosophy, a parasol and trousers, a home-made flute, a baby goat dyed bright red with berry-juice—suggesting that the world of isolation is the world of compulsive, sometimes trivial or frightful art-making. Crusoe's dancing, flute-playing, drinking, dressing-up constitute a kind of court-life of one. His nightmare is of other islands—other people and their own isolate, demanding, particular selves, each "an *I*" if not "an *Elizabeth*." If self-pity begins at home, could sympathy ever extend to the grotesquely multiple other-worlds of humanity at large?

> I'd have
> nightmares of other islands
> stretching away from mine, innnities
> of islands, islands spawning islands,
> like frog's eggs turning into polliwogs
> of islands, knowing that I had to live
> on each and every one, eventually,
> for ages, registering their flora,
> their fauna, their geography.

This idea of a kind of Christian love—"self-pity" extended as a principle of acceptance to the whole swarm of isolate souls—is too appalling. Better to settle for the aggregate island of England and the World, or to be grateful for the saving exception of Friday.

It seems to me that in its way "Crusoe in England" treads upon the throat of the mere World, treads too on the World's trite expectations about the other world, about the "inner life" in this case of "an artist." Nor does Bishop exactly "harbor a divided thought" from the rest of us. The "other islands" have their flora, fauna, geography; the author of this poem simply does not know anything about them, is made sick by the thought of needing to know about them. Compared to Campion's benign, confident categorizing of "love and all his pleasures" as "but toys" within a divine harmony, Bishop's other world of the isolated self, and the isolated, mortal relationship ("my dear Friday") seems rather a desert plant: harsh, sturdy, vigorous on minimal terms. Even Babel's version of the worldly pleasures and diversions of a lost court or a luxurious room is less severe than the almost monastic calm of Bishop's protagonist.

But what is inspiring to me in these poems by Bishop is the insistent, credible enactment of a human soul that is in the World, but not entirely of it, outside of the World, but not entirely apart from it. Her poems suggest that when we write, we need not be limited merely to the spinning out of the filaments of memory and autobiography, on the one hand, or on the other hand merely to idly shifting the diverting kaleidoscope of imagination. Without neglecting the pleasures, interests, urgencies of the communal realm, she stays true to the way the mind itself craves something beyond that realm. And she does that without sanctifying either realm.

In fact, like Campion in his poem and Babel in his story,

Bishop seems deliberately and explicitly to tease our easy responses about the holiness or specialness of art, especially in its relation to the World. The Court, nowadays, has been replaced as the repository of human elegance and creation by other official institutions: the archive, the performance center, the museum:

> The local museum's asked me to
> leave everything to them:
> the flute, the knife, the shrivelled shoes,
> my shedding goatskin trousers
> (moths have got in the fur),
> the parasol that took me such a time
> remembering the way the ribs should go.
> It still will work but, folded up,
> looks like a plucked and skinny fowl.
> How can anyone want such things?
> —And Friday, my dear Friday, died of measles
> seventeen years ago come March.

In Bishop's allegory of the World and the individual artist, the memorabilia and leftovers—not just the manuscripts and diaries and letters perhaps, but the work itself as well as the desk and materials—embody a pointless husk, the visible shell of a flown, invisible and untractable form of life.

Why do we want such things? How can anyone get pleasure from them? For the artist, the actual anniversary of a particular death may mean far more. But for the world, the comical, laborious parasol and the pathetic, decomposing goatskin trousers are charged with meaning and mysterious force. "All do not all things well." The gift of the makers, the ornament of skill, provides an elegant diversion from long nights, or from atrocities of history; and beyond that, it is a gift that suggests by its origin that there is another place than this one—though it be as small, hard and isolated as the island of a single soul.

Adrienne Rich

When We Dead Awaken
Writing as Re-vision
1971

The Modern Language Association is both marketplace and funeral
parlor for the professional study of Western literature in North
America. Like all gatherings of the professions, it has been and re-
mains a "procession of the sons of educated men" (Virginia Woolf): a
congeries of old-boys' networks, academicians rehearsing their
numb canons in sessions dedicated to the literature of white males,
junior scholars under the lash of "publish or perish" delivering pa-
pers in the bizarrely lit drawing rooms of immense hotels: a ritual
competition veering between cynicism and desperation.

However, in the interstices of these gentlemanly rites (or, in Mary
Daly's words, on the boundaries of this patriarchal space),* some
feminist scholars, teachers, and graduate students, joined by feminist
writers, editors, and publishers, have for a decade been creating
more subversive occasions, challenging the sacredness of the gen-
tlemanly canon, sharing the rediscovery of buried works by women,
asking women's questions, bringing literary history and criticism
back to life in both senses. The Commission on the Status of Women
in the Profession was formed in 1969, and held its first public event
in 1970. In 1971 the Commission asked Ellen Peck Killoh, Tillie
Olsen, Elaine Reuben, and myself, with Elaine Hedges as moderator,
to talk on "The Woman Writer in the Twentieth Century." The essay
that follows was written for that forum, and later published, along
with the other papers from the forum and workshops, in an issue of
College English edited by Elaine Hedges ("Women Writing and
Teaching," 34, no. 1 [October 1972]). With a few revisions, mainly
updating, it was reprinted in *American Poets in 1976*, edited by
William Heyen (New York: Bobbs-Merrill, 1976). That later text is
the one published here.

The challenge flung by feminists at the accepted literary canon, at
the methods of teaching it, and at the biased and astigmatic view of
male "literary scholarship," has not diminished in the decade since

---

*Mary Daly, *Beyond God the Father* (Boston: Beacon, 1971), pp.
40–41.

the first Women's Forum; it has become broadened and intensified more recently by the challenges of black and lesbian feminists pointing out that feminist literary criticism itself has overlooked or held back from examining the work of black women and lesbians. The dynamic between a political vision and the demand for a fresh vision of literature is clear: without a growing feminist movement, the first inroads of feminist scholarship could not have been made; without the sharpening of a black feminist consciousness, black women's writing would have been left in limbo between misogynist black male critics and white feminists still struggling to unearth a white women's tradition; without an articulate lesbian/feminist movement, lesbian writing would still be lying in that closet where many of us used to sit reading forbidden books "in a bad light."

Much, much more is yet to be done; and university curricula have of course changed very little as a result of all this. What *is* changing is the availability of knowledge, of vital texts, the visible effects on women's lives of seeing, hearing our wordless or negated experience affirmed and pursued further in language.

Ibsen's *When We Dead Awaken* is a play about the use that the male artist and thinker—in the process of creating culture as we know it—has made of women, in his life and in his work; and about a woman's slow struggling awakening to the use to which her life has been put. Bernard Shaw wrote in 1900 of this play:

> [Ibsen] shows us that no degradation ever devized or permitted is as disastrous as this degradation; that through it women can die into luxuries for men and yet can kill them; that men and women are becoming conscious of this; and that what remains to be seen as perhaps the most interesting of all imminent social developments is what will happen "when we dead awaken."[1]

It's exhilarating to be alive in a time of awakening consciousness; it can also be confusing, disorienting, and painful. This awakening of dead or sleeping consciousness has already affected the lives of millions of women, even those who don't know it yet. It is also affecting the lives of men, even those who deny its claims upon them. The argument will go on

1. G. B. Shaw. *The Quintessence of Ibsenism* (New York: Hill & Wang, 1922), p. 139.

whether an oppressive economic class system is responsible for the oppressive nature of male/female relations, or whether, in fact, patriarchy—the domination of males—is the original model of oppression on which all others are based. But in the last few years the women's movement has drawn inescapable and illuminating connections between our sexual lives and our political institutions. The sleepwalkers are coming awake, and for the first time this awakening has a collective reality; it is no longer such a lonely thing to open one's eyes.

Re-vision—the act of looking back, of seeing with fresh eyes, of entering an old text from a new critical direction—is for women more than a chapter in cultural history: it is an act of survival. Until we can understand the assumptions in which we are drenched we cannot know ourselves. And this drive to self-knowledge, for women, is more than a search for identity: it is part of our refusal of the self-destructiveness of male-dominated society. A radical critique of literature, feminist in its impulse, would take the work first of all as a clue to how we live, how we have been living, how we have been led to imagine ourselves, how our language has trapped as well as liberated us, how the very act of naming has been till now a male prerogative, and how we can begin to see and name—and therefore live—afresh. A change in the concept of sexual identity is essential if we are not going to see the old political order reassert itself in every new revolution. We need to know the writing of the past, and know it differently than we have ever known it; not to pass on a tradition but to break its hold over us.

For writers, and at this moment for women writers in particular, there is the challenge and promise of a whole new psychic geography to be explored. But there is also a difficult and dangerous walking on the ice, as we try to find language and images for a consciousness we are just coming into, and with little in the past to support us. I want to talk about some aspects of this difficulty and this danger.

Jane Harrison, the great classical anthropologist, wrote in 1914 in a letter to her friend Gilbert Murray:

> By the by, about "Women," it has bothered me often—why do women never want to write poetry about Man as a sex—why is

Woman a dream and a terror to man and not the other way
around? . . . Is it mere convention and propriety, or something
deeper?[2]

I think Jane Harrison's question cuts deep into the myth-
making tradition, the romantic tradition; deep into what
women and men have been to each other; and deep into the
psyche of the woman writer. Thinking about that question, I
began thinking of the work of two twentieth-century women
poets, Sylvia Plath and Diane Wakoski. It strikes me that in
the work of both Man appears as, if not a dream, a fascination
and a terror; and that the source of the fascination and the
terror is, simply, Man's power—to dominate, tyrannize,
choose, or reject the woman. The charisma of Man seems to
come purely from his power over her and his control of the
world by force, not from anything fertile or life-giving in him.
And, in the work of both these poets, it is finally the woman's
sense of *herself*—embattled, possessed—that gives the poetry
its dynamic charge, its rhythms of struggle, need, will, and
female energy. Until recently this female anger and this furi-
ous awareness of the Man's power over her were not available
materials to the female poet, who tended to write of Love as
the source of her suffering, and to view that victimization by
Love as an almost inevitable fate. Or, like Marianne Moore
and Elizabeth Bishop, she kept sexuality at a measured and
chiseled distance in her poems.

One answer to Jane Harrison's question has to be that his-
torically men and women have played very different parts in
each others' lives. Where woman has been a luxury for man,
and has served as the painter's model and the poet's muse, but
also as comforter, nurse, cook, bearer of his seed, secretarial
assistant, and copyist of manuscripts, man has played a quite
different role for the female artist. Henry James repeats an
incident which the writer Prosper Mérimée described, of how,
while he was living with George Sand,

> he once opened his eyes, in the raw winter dawn, to see his
> companion, in a dressing-gown, on her knees before the
> domestic hearth, a candlestick beside her and a red *madras*

---

2. J. G. Stewart, *Jane Ellen Harrison: A Portrait from Letters* (London:
Merlin, 1959), p. 140.

round her head, making bravely, with her own hands the fire that was to enable her to sit down betimes to urgent pen and paper. The story represents him as having felt that the spectacle chilled his ardor and tried his taste; her appearance was unfortunate, her occupation an inconsequence, and her industry a reproof—the result of all which was a lively irritation and an early rupture.[3]

The specter of this kind of male judgment, along with the misnaming and thwarting of her needs by a culture controlled by males, has created problems for the woman writer: problems of contact with herself, problems of language and style, problems of energy and survival.

In rereading Virginia Woolf's *A Room of One's Own* (1929) for the first time in some years, I was astonished at the sense of effort, of pains taken, of dogged tentativeness, in the tone of that essay. And I recognized that tone. I had heard it often enough, in myself and in other women. It is the tone of a woman almost in touch with her anger, who is determined not to appear angry, who is *willing* herself to be calm, detached, and even charming in a roomful of men where things have been said which are attacks on her very integrity. Virginia Woolf is addressing an audience of women, but she is acutely conscious—as she always was—of being overheard by men: by Morgan and Lytton and Maynard Keynes and for that matter by her father, Leslie Stephen.[4] She drew the language out into an exacerbated thread in her determination to have her own sensibility yet protect it from those masculine presences. Only at rare moments in that essay do you hear the passion in her voice; she was trying to sound as cool as Jane Austen, as

---

3. Henry James, "Notes on Novelists," in *Selected Literary Criticism of Henry James*, ed. Morris Shapira (London: Heinemann, 1963), pp. 157–58.

4. A. R., 1978: This intuition of mine was corroborated when, early in 1978, I read the correspondence between Woolf and Dame Ethel Smyth (Henry W. and Albert A. Berg Collection, The New York Public Library, Astor. Lenox and Tilden Foundations); in a letter dated June 8, 1933, Woolf speaks of having kept her own personality out of *A Room of One's Own* lest she not be taken seriously: " . . . how personal, so will they say, rubbing their hands with glee, women always are; *I even hear them as I write*" (emphasis added).

Olympian as Shakespeare, because that is the way the men of the culture thought a writer should sound.

No male writer has written primarily or even largely for women, or with the sense of women's criticism as a consideration when he chooses his materials, his theme, his language. But to a lesser or greater extent, every woman writer has written for men even when, like Virginia Woolf, she was supposed to be addressing women. If we have come to the point when this balance might begin to change, when women can stop being haunted, not only by "convention and propriety" but by internalized fears of being and saying themselves, then it is an extraordinary moment for the woman writer—and reader.

I have hesitated to do what I am going to do now, which is to use myself as an illustration. For one thing, it's a lot easier and less dangerous to talk about other women writers. But there is something else. Like Virginia Woolf, I am aware of the women who are not with us here because they are washing the dishes and looking after the children. Nearly fifty years after she spoke, that fact remains largely unchanged. And I am thinking also of women whom she left out of the picture altogether—women who are washing other people's dishes and caring for other people's children, not to mention women who went on the streets last night in order to feed their children. We seem to be special women here, we have liked to think of ourselves as special, and we have known that men would tolerate, even romanticize us as special, as long as our words and actions didn't threaten their privilege of tolerating or rejecting us and our work according to *their* ideas of what a special woman ought to be. An important insight of the radical women's movement has been how divisive and how ultimately destructive is this myth of the special woman, who is also the token woman. Every one of us here in this room has had great luck—we are teachers, writers, academicians; our own gifts could not have been enough, for we all know women whose gifts are buried or aborted. Our struggles can have meaning and our privileges—however precarious under patriarchy—can be justified only if they can help to change the lives of women whose gifts—and whose very being— continue to be thwarted and silenced.

My own luck was being born white and middle-class into a house full of books, with a father who encouraged me to read and write. So for about twenty years I wrote for a particular man, who criticized and praised me and made me feel I was indeed "special." The obverse side of this, of course, was that I tried for a long time to please him, or rather, not to displease him. And then of course there were other men— writers, teachers—the Man, who was not a terror or a dream but a literary master and a master in other ways less easy to acknowledge. And there were all those poems about women, written by men: it seemed to be a given that men wrote poems and women frequently inhabited them. These women were almost always beautiful, but threatened with the loss of beauty, the loss of youth—the fate worse than death. Or, they were beautiful and died young, like Lucy and Lenore. Or, the woman was like Maud Gonne, cruel and disastrously mistaken, and the poem reproached her because she had refused to become a luxury for the poet.

A lot is being said today about the influence that the myths and images of women have on all of us who are products of culture. I think it has been a peculiar confusion to the girl or woman who tries to write because she is peculiarly susceptible to language. She goes to poetry or fiction looking for *her* way of being in the world, since she too has been putting words and images together; she is looking eagerly for guides, maps, possibilities; and over and over in the "words' masculine persuasive force" of literature she comes up against something that negates everything she is about: she meets the image of Woman in books written by men. She finds a terror and a dream, she finds a beautiful pale face, she finds La Belle Dame Sans Merci, she finds Juliet or Tess or Salomé, but precisely what she does not find is that absorbed, drudging, puzzled, sometimes inspired creature, herself, who sits at a desk trying to put words together.

So what does she do? What did I do? I read the older women poets with their peculiar keenness and ambivalence: Sappho, Christina Rossetti, Emily Dickinson, Elinor Wylie, Edna Millay, H. D. I discovered that the woman poet most admired at the time (by men) was Marianne Moore, who was maidenly, elegant, intellectual, discreet. But even in reading these women I was looking in them for the same things I had found in the poetry of men, because I wanted women poets to be the equals of men, and to be equal was still confused with sounding the same.

I know that my style was formed first by male poets: by the men I was reading as an undergraduate—Frost, Dylan Thomas, Donne, Auden, MacNiece, Stevens, Yeats. What I chiefly learned from them was craft.[5] But poems are like dreams: in them you put what you don't know you know. Looking back at poems I wrote before I was twenty-one, I'm startled because beneath the conscious craft are glimpses of the split I even then experienced between the girl who wrote poems, who defined herself in writing poems, and the girl who was to define herself by her relationships with men. "Aunt Jennifer's Tigers" (1951), written while I was a student, looks with deliberate detachment at this split.[6]

> Aunt Jennifer's tigers stride across a screen,
> Bright topaz denizens of a world of green.
> They do not fear the men beneath the tree;
> They pace in sleek chivalric certainty.
>
> Aunt Jennifer's fingers fluttering through her wool
> Find even the ivory needle hard to pull.
> The massive weight of Uncle's wedding band
> Sits heavily upon Aunt Jennifer's hand.
>
> When Aunt is dead, her terrified hands will lie
> Still ringed with ordeals she was mastered by.
> The tigers in the panel that she made
> Will go on striding, proud and unafraid.

In writing this poem, composed and apparently cool as it is, I thought I was creating a portrait of an imaginary woman. But this woman suffers from the opposition of her imagination, worked out in tapestry, and her life-style, "ringed with ordeals she was mastered by." It was important to me that Aunt Jennifer was a person as distinct from myself as possible—distanced by the formalism of the poem, by its objective, ob-

---

5. A. R., 1978: Yet I spent months, at sixteen, memorizing and writing imitations of Millay's sonnets: and in notebooks of that period I find what are obviously attempts to imitate Dickinson's metrics and verbal compression. I knew H. D. only through anthologized lyrics; her epic poetry was not then available to me.

6. A. R., 1978: Texts of poetry quoted herein can be found in A. R., *Poems Selected and New: 1950–1974* (New York: Norton, 1975).

servant tone—even by putting the woman in a different generation.

In those years formalism was part of the strategy—like asbestos gloves, it allowed me to handle materials I couldn't pick up bare-handed. A later strategy was to use the persona of a man, as I did in "The Loser" (1958):

A man thinks of the woman he once loved: first, after her wedding, and then nearly a decade later.

I
I kissed you, bride and lost, and went
home from that bourgeois sacrament,
your cheek still tasting cold upon
my lips that gave you benison
with all the swagger that they knew—
as losers somehow learn to do.

Your wedding made my eyes ache; soon
the world would be worse off for one
more golden apple dropped to ground
without the least protesting sound,
and you would windfall lie, and we
forget your shimmer on the tree.

Beauty is always wasted: if
not Mignon's song sung to the deaf,
at all events to the unmoved.
A face like yours cannot be loved
long or seriously enough.
Almost, we seem to hold it off.

II
Well, you are tougher than I thought.
Now when the wash with ice hangs taut
this morning of St. Valentine,
I see you strip the squeaking line,
your body weighed against the load,
and all my groans can do no good.

Because you are still beautiful,
though squared and stiffened by the pull
of what nine windy years have done.
You have three daughters, lost a son.
I see all your intelligence
flung into that unwearied stance.

My envy is of no avail.
I turn my head and wish him well
who chafed your beauty into use
and lives forever in a house
lit by the friction of your mind.
You stagger in against the wind.

I finished college, published my first book by a fluke, as it seemed to me, and broke off a love affair. I took a job, lived alone, went on writing, fell in love. I was young, full of energy, and the book seemed to mean that others agreed I was a poet. Because I was also determined to prove that as a woman poet I could also have what was then defined as a "full" woman's life, I plunged in my early twenties into marriage and had three children before I was thirty. There was nothing overt in the environment to warn me: these were the fifties, and in reaction to the earlier wave of feminism, middle-class women were making careers of domestic perfection, working to send their husbands through professional schools, then retiring to raise large families. People were moving out to the suburbs, technology was going to be the answer to everything, even sex; the family was in its glory. Life was extremely private; women were isolated from each other by the loyalties of marriage. I have a sense that women didn't talk to each other much in the fifties—not about their secret emptinesses, their frustrations. I went on trying to write; my second book and first child appeared in the same month. But by the time that book came out I was already dissatisfied with those poems, which seemed to me mere exercises for poems I hadn't written. The book was praised, however, for its "gracefulness"; I had a marriage and a child. If there were doubts, if there were periods of null depression or active despairing, these could only mean that I was ungrateful, insatiable, perhaps a monster.

About the time my third child was born, I felt that I had either to consider myself a failed woman and a failed poet, or to try to find some synthesis by which to understand what was happening to me. What frightened me most was the sense of drift, of being pulled along on a current which called itself my destiny, but in which I seemed to be losing touch with who-ever I had been, with the girl who had experienced her own will and energy almost ecstatically at times, walking around a city or riding a train at night or typing in a student room. In a poem about my grandmother I wrote (of myself): "A young girl, thought sleeping, is certified dead" ("Halfway"). I was writing very little, partly from fatigue, that female fatigue of suppressed anger and loss of contact with my own being; partly from the discontinuity of female life with its attention to small chores, errands, work that others constantly undo, small children's constant needs. What I did write was unconvincing to me; my anger and frustration were hard to acknowledge in or out of poems because in fact I cared a great deal about my husband and my children. Trying to look back and understand that time I have tried to analyze the real nature of the conflict. Most, if not all, human lives are full of fantasy—passive daydreaming which need not be acted on. But to write poetry or fiction, or even to think well, is not to fantasize, or to put fantasies on paper. For a poem to coalesce, for a character or an action to take shape, there has to be an imaginative transformation of reality which is no way passive. And a certain freedom of the mind is needed—freedom to press on, to enter the currents of your thought like a glider pilot, knowing that your motion can be sustained, that the buoyancy of your attention will not be suddenly snatched away. Moreover, if the imagination is to transcend and transform experience it has to question, to challenge, to conceive of alternatives, perhaps to the very life you are living at that moment. You have to be free to play around with the notion that day might be night, love might be hate; nothing can be too sacred for the imagination to turn into its opposite or to call experimentally by another name. For writing is renaming. Now, to be maternally with small children all day in the old way, to be with a man in the old way of marriage, requires a holding back, a putting aside of that imaginative activity, and demands instead a kind of conservatism. I want to make it clear that I am *not* saying that in order to write well, or think well, it is necessary to become unavailable to others, or to become a devouring ego. This has been the myth of the masculine artist and thinker: and I do not accept it. But to be a female human being trying to fulfill traditional female functions in a traditional way *is* in direct conflict with the subversive function of the imagination. The word traditional is important here. There must be ways, and we will be finding out more and more about them, in which the energy of creation and energy of relation can be united. But in those years I always felt the conflict as a failure of love in myself. I had thought I was choosing a full life: the life available to most men, in which sexuality, work, and parenthood could coexist. But I felt, at twenty-nine, guilt toward the people closest to me, and guilty toward my own being.

I wanted, then, more than anything, the one thing of which there was never enough: time to think, time to write. The fifties and early sixties were years of rapid revelations: the sit-ins and marches in the South, the Bay of Pigs, the early antiwar movement, raised large questions—questions for which the masculine world of the academy around me seemed to have expert and fluent answers. But I needed to think for myself—about pacifism and dissent and violence, about poetry and society, and about my own relationship to all these things. For about ten years I was reading in fierce snatches, scribbling in notebooks, writing poetry in fragments; I was looking desperately for clues, because if there were no clues then I thought I might be insane. I wrote in a notebook about this time:

> Paralyzed by the sense that there exists a mesh of relationships—e.g., between my anger at the children, my sensual life, pacifism, sex (I mean sex in its broadest significance, not merely sexual desire)—an interconnectedness which, if I could see it, make it valid, would give me back myself, make it possible to function lucidly and passionately. Yet I grope in and out among these dark webs.

I think I began at this point to feel that politics was not something "out there" but something "in here" and of the essence of my condition.

In the late fifties I was able to write, for the first time, directly about experiencing myself as a woman. The poem was jotted in fragments during children's naps, brief hours in a library, or at 3:00 A.M. after rising with a wakeful child. I despaired of doing any continuous work at this time. Yet I began to feel that my fragments and scraps had a common consciousness and a common theme, one which I would have been very unwilling to put on paper at an earlier time because I had been taught that poetry should be "universal," which meant, of course, nonfemale. Until then I had tried very much *not* to identify myself as a female poet. Over two years I wrote a ten-part poem called "Snapshots of a Daughter-in-Law" (1958–60), in a longer looser mode than I'd ever trusted myself with before. It was an extraordinary relief to write that poem. It strikes me now as too literary, too dependent on allusion; I hadn't found the courage yet to do without authorities, or even to use the pronoun "I"—the woman in the poem is always "she." One section of it, No. 2, concerns a woman who thinks she is going mad; she is haunted by voices telling her to resist and rebel, voices which she can hear but not obey.

2.
Banging the coffee-pot into the sink
she hears the angels chiding, and looks out
past the raked gardens to the sloppy sky.
Only a week since They said: *Have no patience.*

The next time it was: *Be insatiable.*
Then: *Save yourself; others you cannot save.*
Sometimes she's let the tapstream scald her arm,
a match burn to her thumbnail,

or held her hand above the kettle's snout
right in the woolly steam. They are probably angels,
since nothing hurts her anymore, except
each morning's grit blowing into her eyes.

The poem "Orion," written five years later, is a poem of reconnection with a part of myself I had felt I was losing—the active principle, the energetic imagination, the "half-brother" whom I projected, as I had for many years, into the constellation Orion. It's no accident that the words "cold and egotistical" appear in this poem, and are applied to myself.

Far back when I went zig-zagging
through tamarack pastures
you were my genius, you
my cast-iron Viking, my helmed
lion-heart king in prison.
Years later now you're young

my fierce half-brother, staring
down from that simplified west

your breast open, your belt dragged down
by an oldfashioned thing, a sword
the last bravado you won't give over
though it weighs you down as you stride

and the stars in it are dim
and maybe have stopped burning.
But you burn, and I know it;
as I throw back my head to take you in
an old transfusion happens again:
divine astronomy is nothing to it.

Indoors I bruise and blunder,
break faith, leave ill enough
alone, a dead child born in the dark.
Night cracks up over the chimney,
pieces of time, frozen geodes
come showering down in the grate.

A man reaches behind my eyes
and finds them empty
a woman's head turns away
from my head in the mirror
children are dying my death
and eating crumbs of my life.

Pity is not your forte.
Calmly you ache up there
pinned aloft in your crow's nest,
my speechless pirate!
You take it all for granted
and when I look you back

it's with a starlike eye
shooting its cold and egotistical spear
where it can do least damage.
Breathe deep! No hurt, no pardon
out here in the cold with you
you with your back to the wall.

The choice still seemed to be between "love"—womanly, ma-
ternal love, altruistic love—a love defined and ruled by the
weight of an entire culture; and egotism—a force directed by
men into creation, achievement, ambition, often at the ex-
pense of others, but justifiably so. For weren't they men, and

wasn't that their destiny as womanly, selfless love was ours? We know now that the alternatives are false ones—that the word "love" is itself in need of re-vision.

There is a companion poem to "Orion," written three years later, in which at last the woman in the poem and the woman writing the poem become the same person. It is called "Planetarium," and it was written after a visit to a real planetarium, where I read an account of the work of Caroline Herschel, the astronomer, who worked with her brother William, but whose name remained obscure, as his did not.

Thinking of Caroline Herschel, 1750–1848, astronomer, sister of William; and others

A woman in the shape of a monster
a monster in the shape of a woman
the skies are full of them

a woman   "in the snow
among the Clocks and instruments
or measuring the ground with poles"

in her 98 years to discover
8 comets

she whom the moon ruled
like us
levitating into the night sky
riding the polished lenses

Galaxies of women, there
doing penance for impetuousness
ribs chilled
in those spaces   of the mind

An eye,
    "virile, precise and absolutely certain"
    from the mad webs of Uranisborg

                              encountering the NOVA

every impulse of light exploding
from the core
as life flies out of us
        Tycho whispering at last
        "Let me not seem to have lived in vain"

What we see, we see
and seeing is changing

the light that shrivels a mountain
and leaves a man alive

Heartbeat of the pulsar
heart sweating through my body

The radio impulse
pouring in from Taurus

      I am bombarded yet   I stand

I have been standing all my life in the
direct path of a battery of signals
the most accurately transmitted most
untranslateable language in the universe
I am a galactic cloud so deep so invo-
luted that a light wave could take 15
years to travel through me And has
taken   I am an instrument in the shape
of a woman trying to translate pulsations
into images   for the relief of the body
and the reconstruction of the mind.

In closing I want to tell you about a dream I had last sum-
mer. I dreamed I was asked to read my poetry at a mass
women's meeting, but when I began to read, what came out
were the lyrics of a blues song. I share this dream with you
because it seemed to me to say something about the problems
and the future of the woman writer, and probably of women
in general. The awakening of consciousness is not like the
crossing of a frontier—one step and you are in another coun-
try. Much of woman's poetry has been of the nature of the
blues song: a cry of pain, of victimization, or a lyric of seduc-
tion.[7] And today, much poetry by women—and prose for that
matter—is charged with anger. I think we need to go through
that anger, and we will betray our own reality if we try, as
Virginia Woolf was trying, for an objectivity, a detachment,

---

7. A. R., 1978: When I dreamed that dream, was I wholly ignorant of
the tradition of Bessie Smith and other women's blues lyrics which
transcended victimization to sing of resistance and independence?

that would make us sound more like Jane Austen or Shake-speare. We know more than Jane Austen or Shakespeare knew: more than Jane Austen because our lives are more complex, more than Shakespeare because we know more about the lives of women—Jane Austen and Virginia Woolf included.

Both the victimization and the anger experienced by women are real, and have real sources, everywhere in the environment, built into society, language, the structures of thought. They will go on being tapped and explored by poets, among others. We can neither deny them, nor will we rest there. A new generation of women poets is already working out of the psychic energy released when women begin to move out toward what the feminist philosopher Mary Daly has described as the "new space" on the boundaries of pat-riarchy.[8] Women are speaking to and of women in these poems, out of a newly released courage to name, to love each other, to share risk and grief and celebration.

To the eye of a feminist, the work of Western male poets now writing reveals a deep, fatalistic pessimism as to the pos-sibilities of change, whether societal or personal, along with a familiar and threadbare use of women (and nature) as a re-demptive on the one hand, threatening on the other; and a new tide of phallocentric sadism and overt woman-hating which matches the sexual brutality of recent films. "Political" poetry by men remains stranded amid the struggles for power among male groups; in condemning U.S. imperialism or the Chilean junta the poet can claim to speak for the oppressed while remaining, as male, part of a system of sexual oppression. The enemy is always outside the self, the struggle somewhere else. The mood of isolation, self-pity, and self-imitation that pervades "nonpolitical" poetry suggests that a profound change in masculine consciousness will have to precede any new male poetic—or other—inspiration. The creative energy of patriarchy is fast running out; what remains is its self-generating energy for destruction. As women, we have our work cut out for us.

---

8. Mary Daly, *Beyond God the Father: Towards a Philosophy of Women's Liberation* (Boston: Beacon, 1973).

Michael Ryan

On the Nature of Poetry
1980

On a steamy night last week, after a rare Vermont day when it had been hot enough to lightning, I drove home from my office through a deep fog. It was nearly midnight; there was almost no light from the sky. I parked my car in the driveway, and began to sense my way to the front door, when I looked up and saw an enormous, black shape in the yard: the ninety-foot tree which I had watched in the sunlight with great pleasure now seemed awesome. Darker than the darkness, it was numinous, and impossibly huge, like a god. I came inside feeling stirred, feeling I had been touched beneath rationality, and since I was working on this talk and having a hard time writing it, I felt I had been instructed. I don't think my experience of the tree can be explained, and yet such experiences, in solitude and with others, are surely part of our lives; some people feel them as the most important part, informing the rest. I said that I had been touched beneath rationality, which I believe is true, but I would take it farther than that to say that I had been touched beneath personality; it was as if this profound feeling had nothing to do with me, personally, at least in the daily ways I think about myself.

Jung might have called this an experience of the archetype:

> Do we ever understand what we think? We understand only such thinking as is mere equation and from which nothing comes out but what we have put in. That is the manner of working of the intellect. But beyond that there is thinking in primordial images—in symbols that are older than historical man; which have been ingrained in him from earliest times, and, eternally living, outlasting all generations, still make up the groundwork of the human psyche.

Jung, Neumann, Joseph Campbell and many others have demonstrated the recurrence of essential primordial images in the art and myth of cultures that could not have known of one another. Bastian called this phenomenon "elementary ideas," always rendered by way of local ethnic forms: Freud, while listening to his European and American patients speak out their anguish and fantasies, stared at an array of African carvings of gods. Whatever the metaphor—and for Jung the archetypes are not only images but a process, "persons" living in our personalities—much of our psyche seems to be beneath or beyond individual intellect; as human beings we share what Jung called the "collective unconscious," an impersonal personality, even if we have difficulty understanding it in itself or how it works in us individually.

This difficulty may arise not from its inherent obscurity but from our removal from it. We think of ourselves as rational beings, and ostensibly conduct the business of society according to rational premises, but our evolution as a species occurred over a long time before the evolution of rational intelligence. Just how long is shown by the calendar that compresses the fifteen-billion-year life-in-progress of the universe into a single year. On that calendar, the earth is formed about September 25, hominids appear at approximately 10:30 P.M. on December 31, and the whole of recorded human history takes place during the last ten seconds. This dramatizes both our recent arrival and the elements of our nature: there is much that made us that we don't know about. It's amazing to imagine a "thoughtless" world, and easy to forget that we are thoroughly creatures of the universe, formed in the ooze for four billion years before we were able to write down how it feels to be human; the oldest specimens of written language date back only five thousand years, barely a moment in terms of evolution.

Lewis Thomas says in *The Lives of a Cell:*

Man is embedded in Nature . . . The uniformity of the earth's life, more astonishing than its diversity, is accountable by the high probability that we derived, originally, from some single cell, fertilized in a bolt of lightning as the earth cooled . . . We still share genes around, and the resemblance of enzymes of grasses to those of whales is a family resemblance.

And:

A good case can be made for our non-existence as entities. We are not made up, as we had always supposed, of successfully enriched packets of our own parts. We are shared, rented, occupied. At the interior of our cells, driving them, providing the oxidative energy that sends us out for the improvement of each shining day, are the mitochondria, and in a strict sense they are not ours. They turn out to be little separate creatures, the colonial posterity of migrant prokaryocytes, probably primitive bacteria that swam into ancestral precursors of our eukaryotic cells and stayed there. Ever since, they have maintained themselves and their ways, replicating in their own fashion, privately, with their own DNA and RNA quite different from ours. They are as much symbionts as the rhizobial bacteria in the roots of beans. Without them, we would not move a muscle, drum a finger, think a thought.

It might be argued, through Thomas, that Jung's archaic remnants are a physiological fact; as further evidence, Joseph Campbell, in *The Masks of God,* describes innate releasing mechanisms in animals—how a baby chick responds to the shadow of a hawk even before it's all the way out of the shell—and one could also cite the encoded transfer of genetic messages from generation to generation. But whether we live the archetypes, or the archetypes "live us" (as James Hillman says), this nonrational, primitive *stuff* reaches into everything we do and think and feel, perhaps powerfully enough at times to make contact directly: beneath rationality, beneath personality. We may not be able to understand it through analysis, which Hillman maintains is "a late manifestation of the Western, Protestant, scientific, Apollonic ego," but we experience it in the primordial image, in poetry and music and myth. With Freud and Jung, we call it the unconscious (*unbewusst,* which also translates as "unaware, involuntary, instinctive"); it informs our sense of shape and all nonlinear, affective modes, which is most of what we are and cannot say. The problem with talking about it is the same as with defining God: one tends toward either tautology or mysticism. Yet those four billion years, if they are contained in the presence of a huge tree on a foggy night or the magnetism of an attractive stranger, must also be part of language.

This seems undeniable: language, in conjunction with consciousness, is an evolutionary development (unless one day it suddenly appeared on earth); if so, its underlayers are that from which it evolved, for which we have only negative terms: the preliterate and unconscious. This is implied by Chomsky's notion that the fact of many languages does not deny a unity at the depth of the species, a unity which manifests itself in universal language capability and the formal properties of language.

In making poetry, and in reading it, we give the formal properties of words, their sound and arrangement, a kind of attention we usually do not give them, because we are usually intent on the meaning of the words alone. As a result, something extraordinary may happen to the language: its shape becomes palpable, its cadence becomes definite, its meaning may range from common sense to the edge of intelligibility and hover there, and the whole arrangement of words is felt as a solid that shifts and changes.

I think if there is anything in us that is purely preliterate and unconscious, it is rhythm. We are subject to its influences incessantly, and our lives depend on it, our sense of timing. Night and day; the seasons; the beat of the ocean against the shore; the internal clocks which determine, among other things, the stages of sleep and dreaming; our heartbeats; our brain waves in alternating states of excitation and inhibition: these are just a few of the countless rhythms we are in the midst of, outside and within. Because they are so various and pervasive and deeply internal, they escape our attention, even as they enter our thoughts, our feelings, and our language.

I've never taught a poetry writing class that has not suffered my reiteration of Duke Ellington's line: "It don't mean a thing if it ain't got that swing." How can you describe the feeling of reading a Roethke poem, any one really, but especially the late poems in stanza forms such as "In A Dark Time" or "The Sequel," when the rhythm is so palpable it is as if the poem could be cupped in your hands? Those poems move great distances in meaning between sentences and yet they hold together, largely because of the sound. The same thing is operating in a song that makes you want to get up and dance. From the poet's point of view, the rhythm helps the poem to get written; the poet feels the right word, its sound tugging against its meaning, and doesn't *think* of it, at least in the ways we usually think of thinking. Rhythm and sound and arrangement—the formal properties of words—allow the poet to get beyond thought, or beneath it.

In the earliest poetry, rhythm was believed to indicate the presence of the divine. There's little doubt that what we write today would not be recognized by the ancients as poetry; theirs was much closer to song or chant. The Homeric bards would go into a trance as they recited hundreds of dactylic hexameter lines; it was said of Archilochus that he could provoke suicide through the power of his iambic abuse. Julian Jaynes says

> The association of rhythmical or repetitively patterned utterance with supernatural knowledge endures well into the later conscious period. Among the early Arabic peoples the word for poet was *sha'ir*, "the knower," or a person endowed with knowledge by the spirits; his metered speech in recitation was the mark of its divine origin. The poet and divine seer have a long tradition of association in the ancient world, and several Indo-European languages have a common term for them. Rhyme and alliteration too were always the linguistic province of the gods and their prophets.

Jaynes is interested in early poetry as evidence of what he calls the bicameral mind, essentially a separation between right- and left-hemisphere brain functions, rhythm being a right-hemisphere function and, according to Jaynes, the crucial ingredient of the language in which gods dictated their wills to men. The poet was the shaman-healer, the most important member of the tribe, and even as late as ancient Greece the poet was given great respect as the bearer of the preliterate roots of the race. The way he was able to say extraordinary things was through entering rhythm, and thus his words harked back to the beginning even if plain talk did not. Because of this, the poet was an authority dangerous to civilization, in which language is to be used according to the dictates of reason, to formulate the moral agreements institutionalized as laws that will insure good order if the citizenry understands them and agrees to them. So it's no accident that Plato, in constructing his idea of a civilized society, devotes the last book of the *Republic* to banishing the poet from the state. Rhythm, rhyme, alliteration—the formal properties of words—allow the gods to speak because, as impulses, they deflect the tyranny of reason as the sole criterion for word-choice. Their speech is prerational, preliterate and compelling; their wills are capricious, their power absolute.

Emily Dickinson said, "If I feel physically as if the top of my head were taken off, I know this is poetry." The poem begins and ends in the body, all those years inside us. And yet, paradoxically, it's because of language that we can't feel the world purely physically, immediately—as Stanley Burnshaw says—"seamlessly." Language makes its own relationship to the world and interacts with our physicality; this enmeshed mode of perception and thought and feeling is still unique among the beasts, despite Lana's and Washoe's linguistic inventions and the communication system of dolphins, though perhaps they will be the next race of poets. Language is linkage: the word-as-thing. But it's also not-the-thing or, more exactly, a thing-in-itself. Thus an iconic theory of language can't account for our linguistic capacity, because of the room in language for seemingly infinite flexibility, discovery, and self-reference—in short, for a great variety of play, just to see what it will do.

Perhaps the inclination to play, common to mammals, derives from the desire to reproduce in small the randomness-into-form and variations-within-form that are the fifteen billion years of our generation; recreation: *re-creation*. The first act of poetry seems to come from entering this "playful" relationship to language, when the writer learns how, in Mallarmé's phrase, to "yield the initiative to the words." Early in my introductory poetry writing classes, I try to help my students break down their accustomed way of using language—rationally, as reference, as an indicator which disappears once the intended meaning is communicated. I try to get them to listen to the words, to hear their music, to feel their arrangement, to "lose control," if necessary, in order that the language itself jar them into new meanings they could not have "thought" of otherwise.

Their success at doing this depends on a feeling for form that can be awakened but can't be taught; it seems to me a genetic endowment that is probably, as Stanley Kunitz says, a "prehensile thing." Julian Jaynes writes:

> As you listen to an address, phonemes disappear into words and words into sentences and sentences disappear into what they are trying to say, into meaning. To be conscious of the elements of speech is to destroy the intention of the speech.

Yet at climactic moments of real or rhetorical passion, a speaker may enact the cadence with his hands and arms and body, as if he would call upon all the resources of the language. The form of verse is an announcement to both the writer and the reader of precisely that intention—that words will be used here in all their richness, not only for reference and meaning, as linkage, but also for their formal properties, as things-in-themselves.

Of course, the form of the poem is more than an announcement; it allows the interaction of formal properties, the play of the language to take place, without everything getting out of hand or nothing happening at all. This is why Frost thought writing free verse is like playing tennis with the net down: without form there is no game, no order, no possibility for discovery.

But form need not mean conventional or received forms, and the Modernist distrust of them, or more precisely Pound's and Eliot's distrust during their Imagist phase, derives from the conviction that conventional forms allow only certain kinds of poems to be written, the kinds of poems that are the monuments of English literature and which had fallen into decadence at the beginning of this century. It's fascinating to imagine a psychology inherent in the iambic pentameter line, in which some 70 percent of English poetry has been composed: why that duration, that specific number of beats, to tighten the formal attention? Or to speculate why a fourteen-line, strictly end-rhymed verse with a contextual turn (the volte) between the octave and sestet seems to be an apt form for lyric utterance, especially directed to a human or divine beloved. The advantage of conventional forms is obvious: they insist that there be an interaction of the formal properties of the words used, even if that insistence is as gentle as a ten-syllable pattern of predominantly alternate stress; therefore, theoretically at least, they push the poem away from talk or prose cut into lines, and try to influence some slight jarring into new meaning. Their disadvantage, from our vantage in literary history, is even more obvious: conventional forms cannot accommodate all formal impulses; or—to look at it from another angle, the angle of the poem's generation—the interaction of formal properties of words is too multifarious to be standardized. In Pound's view (about 1912), conventional forms promoted bad writing because they didn't allow the writer to say what he would "in the stress of some emotion, actually say." As with the Romantics, most of the complicated formal innovations of the Modernists were based on the simple need to reform poetic diction. Yeats, partially due to Pound's influence, changed his diction, but rhyme and meter were to him invaluable aids to composition; he could write no poetry without the forms of verse.

Frost was right in thinking free verse is a contradiction in terms; as Delmore Schwartz said of Williams's prosodic notion of a variable foot, it's like an elastic inch. Good "free verse" is really formal improvisation. The words interconnect and interact formally every bit as thoroughly as in the strictest sonnet. The difference is that no pattern of interaction, however slight, is set at the beginning, to allow for a greater richness of formal interaction, not a lesser, to allow for a greater instrumentality of the language.

The fact that this is usually not the result of "permissiveness" has no bearing on the potential for an unmetered but rhythmical, unrhymed but sound-linked form of poetry. Many of the best poems of this century have been written in this "free verse" form. There's no reason why poems can't continue to be written in conventional forms as well—in fact, some that now aren't probably should be—but I doubt that we will ever go back to a time when all of them are. Historically, in terms of form, poets have never been in a better position, though such adages of contemporary poetry as the one Charles Olson attributed to Robert Creeley—"form is never more than an extension of content"—are simplistic and misleading. The form of the poem is the way the poem tells the poet what it wants to be; the poet, once he has absorbed this way of feeling language and responding to its form, may stand as a kind of censor, rejecting the impulses that aren't *right* in every possible way, in meaning as well as sound and arrangement. Auden, thinking mostly about content, wanted to extend the Censor to a Censorate including "a sensitive only child, a practical housewife, a logician, a monk, an irreverent buffoon and even, perhaps, hated by all the others and returning their dislike, a brutal, foul-mouthed drill sergeant who considers all poetry rubbish." One begins writing poems as program notes to his personality, and maybe they should always retain that early ardor of self-expression; but a poet cares about the poem as a made thing as much as about what it says, and to him the two are as inseparable as a word from its sound.

Whether we are aware of them or not, the formal prop-
erties of language make their own complex patterns which
are followed and, to some extent, fulfilled in all language
usage, even in discursive prose. The most scholarly article,
researched and outlined in advance, will probably come out
with a few surprises in it for the writer; writing at the top of
page one, he can't predict the exact words he will use at the
bottom of page two. E. M. Forster has the old lady exclaim
"How can I know what I think until I see what I say?" This is
one source of the joy of using language, but for the writer it's
the source of no end of fretting as well.

The poet, released from most of the responsibilities of the
scholar, in the end has others that are much more onerous. As
Frost said, "The poem begins in delight and ends in wisdom."
That is a large demand. On another occasion, Frost put the
same formula in different terms: "Poetry begins in trivial
metaphors, pretty metaphors, 'grace' metaphors, and goes on
to the profoundest thinking that we have." Like many of
Frost's remarks about poetry, both of these emphasize the
writing as a journey of discovery, but "the profoundest think-
ing that we have" *is* metaphorical thinking and it is taking
place as soon as the poem begins. For the act of making
metaphor is inherent in the linguistic act, as well as in all of
our most important operations of mind. I'm astonished when
I think of how many of the foundation-blocks of our under-
standing are metaphors (as is the term foundation-blocks):
chemical "bonding," the properties of light as "waves" and
"particles," the "conscious" and "unconscious" (a term that
did not exist in any language until the eighteenth century).
The words we use are the results of particular historical cur-
rents ("currents")—we can hardly speak without metaphor.
Yet we act as if these words refer to real things because of our
habit of using language-as-linkage, and we even use them to
explain metaphor itself when in fact they are themselves
metaphors.

In this way, language can become self-referential and
jargon-ridden; too much inbreeding causes it to lose vitality.
The significance of metaphor, Stevens argued in *The Necessary
Angel*, always derives from its reference to reality. The root of
metaphor—*metapherein*—means "carry over" or "bear across,"
and implies a conceptual movement, a translation between

worlds: at its most profound, perhaps, a translation from the world of our wordless origins into our own.

That first world resides in all of us. Mnemosyne, the goddess of memory, is the mother of the muses. Poetry puts wordlessness into words. Blake exhorted us to "cleanse the doors of perception": not the windows, the doors, that which allows exit and entrance. Physiologically, we see more with our brain than with our eyes, according to expectation and habituation; the same might be said of metaphorical seeing with the brain of cultural expectation and linguistic habit.

"No surprise for the writer, no surprise for the reader"; we want the poem to change our way of seeing. Yet, for the sake of survival, the brain programs itself to limit vision, in both senses. One of the symptoms of schizophrenia is sensory overload; the brain can't process all the data presented to it by the body. It functions properly more by exclusion than inclusion—like art, through a selection of detail. But there always remains the central human and aesthetic question about *what* is being excluded. Auden said, "A poem may fail in two ways: it may exclude too much (banality), or attempt to embody more than one community at once (disorder)."

If Richard Leakey is right in *Origins,* that language arose out of the need to communicate shared tasks in order to survive, then its original function was to exclude from attention what was unimportant to the task at hand, thereby providing an ordering of the experience of the world. That exclusion, which characterizes rationality and discursiveness, is also necessary and useful to poetry, because it is in the balance between order and inclusion that poems are made. As Stevens said, "The poem must resist the intelligence *almost* successfully." The rage for order must win in the end because it is that rage that allows us to survive. However, if the battle against it—by the world, by nature, by the unconscious and preliterate, by the sound and rhythm of the words—is not a raging battle, the poem will not embody the richness and strife of our origins.

At the same time that we are a part of nature, we are *apart* from it because of our consciousness of it and of ourselves. It's significant that one of the first things Adam does in Eden is to name the animals: that act of naming distinguishes us. It's as amazing to imagine a languageless world as a thoughtless world, since the two are so intimately connected in us, but one can picture the psychological change when the hunters are able to plan the hunt. Suddenly, there is a future; and with it, leisure; and with leisure, play; and with play, culture.

But a future also brings anxiety and a foreknowledge of death. All Occidental mythologies include some notion of the Fall, and trace the human condition to a separation from God and his Perfection. Of course, that separation is a metaphor for birth; the rubric of the myth parallels our experience of the first nine months of life, when our needs are met immediately and presumably we feel no isolation or desire. In the womb we are languageless, not having developed the cortical tissue that performs linguistic functions. But even if language were possible it would not be necessary, if it's tied to survival and consciousness of the self as distinct from the world. Language promotes self-consciousness, and vice versa; the bite of the apple from the Tree of Knowledge is the source both of human ingenuity and human anguish.

Perhaps this is one reason why so many of the greatest poets are poets of isolation (such as Dickinson, Frost, and Stevens, to name three Americans): at the heart of the linguistic act is self-consciousness and separation from the world. And visionary poetry, that would articulate our nonrational identity with the universe, may be difficult to write successfully for the same reason; such articulation would elude language if it is designed to delineate, define, and exclude.

But even if we can't imagine what the hominids thought or felt during those four million years or so before they began recording how they lived, much less what the cells that formed their structure thought or felt for the four billion years before that, all that time inside us has at least as much weight and influence on our psyche as the five thousand years we know about. Language is creative in this sense; it continuously, amazingly extends its province, even to precede its origin. All myths of origin, of both East and West, point back to a preliterate time, when the world was womb and life was an eternal moment, the *in illo tempore* of primitive sacred rites. Erich Neumann, in *The Origins and History of Consciousness*, calls this primal image of origin the uroborus.

In Egypt as in New Zealand, in Greece as in Africa and India, the World Parents, heaven and earth, lie on top of the other in the round, spacelessly and timelessly united, for as yet nothing has come between them to create duality out of this original unity. The container of the masculine and feminine opposites is the great hermaphrodite, the primal creative element, the Hindu *purusha* who combines the poles in himself.... This perfect state of being, in which the opposites are contained, is perfect because it is autarchic. Its self-sufficiency, self-containment, and independence of any "you" and any "other" are signs of its self-contained eternality.... The perfection of that which rests in itself in no way contradicts the perfection of that which circles in itself. Although absolute rest is something static and eternal, unchanging and therefore without history, it is at the same time the place of origin and the germ cell of creativity. Living the cycle of its own life, it is the circular snake, the primal dragon of the beginning that bites its own tail, the self-begetting uroborus.

The impulse to poetry is the same as the impulse to myth: to construct an image of the discursively unknowable. In ritual, the myth is enacted, and the participants go through the sacred movements in order to feel the myth and know its way of knowing. When a dancer puts on the mask of a god, he *is* that god; there is no pretending about it. Language has that same function when used to tell mythic tales; the reality it communicates is to primitive people more genuine than that which can be seen and touched. The mythic world infuses the physical world, and both physical and metaphorical vision are informed by it. The result is an animistic world, in which looking at the tree one sees its spirit. The roots of poetry are in this way of using language; the whole enterprise is "as if," but there is finally no "as if" about it. Poetry, as Stevens believed, is a way of knowing the world.

The uroborus is the oldest mythic image we have. For Judeo-Christian culture, the beginning was the Word, but the uroborus is before the Word, both in the historical sequence of creation myths and in our psyche. It addresses the preliterate, the psychology in the womb, the experience of pattern joined to the sequential-linear-analytical mode that dominates our culture, our way of using language, and our seeing.

The thesis of Stanley Burnshaw's *The Seamless Web* is that the primary human drive, manifesting itself in art and poetry as well as in myth and religion, is to recover this "seamlessness," this "primary organic unity with the rest of creation."

It's a wonderful book and everyone interested in poetry and language should read it. But Burnshaw's thesis seems to me slightly off center. Whether or not this "primary organic unity" was ever an actual historical condition (as the calendar of the life of the universe implies) and is now a physiological remnant (as argued by Thomas's *The Lives of a Cell*), the drive to consciousness is also intimately connected to our survival, and therefore to our being, as a species. The joy of learning is a physical pleasure of growth; new engrams are formed in the brain as ideas connect, which allow that electrical path to be traveled more easily in the future. We desire consciousness, as well as seamlessness, and would not give up its pleasures and benefits; otherwise, civilization and its cultures could never have developed. Although Neumann's model of human nature is the same as Burnshaw's, he takes exactly the opposite tack:

> Fixation in unconsciousness, the downward drag of its specific gravity, cannot be called a desire to remain unconscious; on the contrary, *that* is the natural thing. There is, as a counteracting force, the desire to become conscious, a veritable instinct impelling man in this direction.

In poetry, the drives for seamless organic unity and for consciousness exist hand in hand, enriching rather than contradicting each other. As in myth, which presents terms for human nature at its depths, poetry enacts its marriage of these drives as "a balance or reconcilement of opposite or discordant qualities," whereas elsewhere we feel their collision and entanglement as conflict and ambiguity. The poem brings the previously unknown and unformed to consciousness. It communicates, in the root sense of that word (to make common), as fully as any discourse, while it embodies the manifold patterning which characterizes the preliterate, nonrational mode of the psyche. Poems proceed in two ways at once: in time, insofar as the first word is read first, the second word second, and so on; and *in illo tempore*, as a pattern being filled in as we read the words. This is indicated by our sense of closure—as Yeats said, "The poem comes right with a click like a closing box"—we feel a sequence and pattern join and complete itself. So each word must not only promote its own interest, to stir us out of our linguistic habits into new vision, but it must also engage us in the pattern emerging. This may be why we are unsatisfied by a string of brilliant images, no matter how amazing or amusing each is in itself, if that's all the poem is; and are at least as unsatisfied by poems whose individual moments are predetermined by an obvious logic, whose pattern seems mechanical or static. We want richness, evocation, connections too various for analysis. We want to feel the poem as we feel the atmosphere when entering a room where so many things are happening we can't possibly isolate them. We aren't smart enough to do this by ourselves. The poem does it through the instrumentality of the language used in profound conjunction, not just according to the dictates of logic: conjunction made possible by form. The mode of logic, or discursiveness, as Burnshaw points out, is only one mode that a poem may include within it; there is an opportunity for "plurality of modes of thought" and "both common and uncommon sense together." As Hart Crane said, every poem makes a "new word," a joining of language and psyche which then becomes a public fact of language and culture, a "making common," a communication.

In closing, I want to return to the first two sentences of the passage from Jung I quoted at the beginning:

> Do we ever understand what we think? We understand only such thinking as is mere equation and from which nothing comes out but what we have put in.

In this isolation and ignorance is one of the difficulties of being human. But the form of poetry allows us to enter language, as language enters us, and gives us a way of thinking beneath and beyond thought that returns much more than we are able to put in: "a momentary stay against confusion," which is embodied and which we may fully understand.

> Ramon Fernandez, tell me, if you know,
> Why, when the singing ended and we turned
> Toward the town, tell why the glassy lights,
> The lights in the fishing boats at anchor there,
> As the night descended, tilting in the air,
> Mastered the night and portioned out the sea,
> Fixing emblazoned zones and fiery poles,
> Arranging, deepening, enchanting night.

Oh! Blessed rage for order, pale Ramon,
The maker's rage to order words of the sea,
Words of the fragrant portals, dimly-starred,
And of ourselves and of our origins,
In ghostlier demarcations, keener sounds.

Ron Silliman

The New Sentence*
1979

Literary criticism ought to serve as a corrective. Unlike philosophy, it is a discourse with a clearly understood material object. Like philosophy, it is centuries old as a discipline. In addition, it is fortunately situated in western societies, where literature is treated in the schools as a natural extension of language learning.

As Jonathan Culler cautions in *Structuralist Poetics,* literary criticism is the study of reading, not writing. If a theory of the sentence is to be found in poetics, it won't necessarily be of great use to writers. However, it might function as the basis on which to create such a theory.

I want to look first at the New Critics, partly because they were so dominant that, until recently, all other critical tendencies were defined by the nature of their opposition. The New Critics were strongly influenced by the British philosophical tradition, with I. A. Richards, for example, playing a major role in both communities. In addition, René Wellek was a product of the Prague school of linguistics, and as such was thoroughly familiar with the work of Saussure on the one hand, and Shklovsky on the other, both of whom are cited with approval in the *Theory of Literature,* written by Wellek and Austin Warren in 1949.

These influences already suggest that the *Theory of Literature* is not going to contain a coherent theory of the sentence. The Saussurian model of linguistics is implicit in this famous statement:

> Every work of art is, first of all, a series of sounds out of which arises the meaning. In some literary works, this stratum of

---

*An abridgement. Earlier, looking at modern linguistics (Chomsky, Saussure, Ivic, Ries, Voloshinov, Potter, Moskowitz, Hjelmslev, Bloomfield) and philosophy (Derrida, Wittgenstein, Ayer, Quine) Silliman finds no consensus as to the definition of the sentence.

sounds is minimized in its importance; and it becomes, so to speak, diaphanous, as in most novels. But even there the phonetic stratum is a necessary precondition of the meaning. The distinction between a novel by Dreiser and a poem like Poe's "The Bells" is in this respect only quantitative and fails to justify the setting up of two contrasting kinds of literature, fiction and poetry.

A definition as generalized as this will have a limited explanatory capacity. The differences between an oral poem composed within a preliterate society and a novel such as Judith Krantz's *Scruples,* intended even by its author to be sold at the checkout counter of supermarkets, are more than just quantitative.

Formally, this statement represents a reduction, a mode of analysis heavily influenced by the practice of philosophy, based in turn on logic, itself based on mathematics. The desire of Wellek and Warren is to construct a science of literature, with precisely the prestige of science.

What is the reduction? Literature is equal to language, which in turn means phonetic linguistics. Everything which has already been said criticizing modern linguistics, and particularly the work of Saussure, can be brought to bear on this reduction. Wellek and Warren are aware of this also, and defend themselves with a little sleight of hand, arguing that:

A... common assumption, that sound should be analysed in complete divorce from meaning, is also false.

This does not, as it might have, lead them toward an examination of syntax—let alone sentences. But it does put them in the enviable position of defending a point of view from which their own assertion—which equates phonemes, the units of sound, with morphemes, the units of meaning—could easily have been attacked.

The *Theory of Literature* is not a theory of writing. In part, this is due to the very accurate perception that not all literature is written. Nonetheless, Wellek and Warren fail to address the specific changes which occur once literature is submitted to the process of writing. They justify this gap by arguing that the written text is never the "real" work:

That the writing on the paper is not the "real" poem can be demonstrated by another argument. The printed page contains a great many elements which are extraneous to the poem: the size of the type, the sort of type used (roman, italic), the size of the page, and many other factors. If we should take seriously the view that a poem is an artifact, we would have to come to the conclusion that every single copy or, at least, every differently printed edition is a different work of art. There would be no a priori reason why copies in different editions should be copies of the same book. Besides, not every correct printing is considered by us, the readers, a correct printing of the poem. The very fact that we are able to correct printers' errors in a text which we might not have read before . . . shows that we do not consider the printed lines as the genuine poem.

Thirty years after it was written, this sounds half obvious and half presumptuous—the authority of a reader to be the judge of what is or isn't a "correct printing of a poem," is the sort of prerogative that comes easily to one who prepares Variorum Editions of the dead.

But the importance of the argument is that it allows Wellek and Warren not only to devalue the text as arbiter of the work, but to put aside any consideration of the impact of printing on literature, beyond the most banal acknowledgement of its existence.

Viktor Shklovsky notes the importance of this consideration in an interview in the Winter 1978–79 issue of the *Soviet Review*, when he says:

At one time only poetry was recognized, and prose was regarded as something second class, for it seemed a counterfeit; for a long time it was not admitted into high art. It was let in only when they started printing books.

If we argue—and I am arguing—that the sentence, as distinct from the utterance of speech, is a unit of prose, and if prose as literature and the rise of printing are inextricably interwoven, then the impact of printing on literature, not just on the presentation of literature, but on how writing itself is written, needs to be addressed. This would be the historical component of any theory of the sentence.

But Wellek and Warren avoid any such discussion. Instead,

they divide literature into a binary scheme, one side devoted to character and plot construction, the other devoted to wordplay. Generally speaking, these become the axes of fiction and poetry. This also parallels Saussure's division of language into a paradigmatic and a syntagmatic axis. And it also parallels the strategies of Structuralism.

Now this wordplay, the paradigmatic axis of poetry, could go itself toward an investigation of the sentence, but it doesn't. The realms Wellek and Warren carry it to are image, metaphor, symbol and myth: successively broader groupings of referentiality.

Like New Criticism, Structuralism—and here I mean structuralist poetics—is founded on the model of linguistics first constructed by Saussure and later codified by Louis Hjemslev and Roman Jakobson. However, it has several practical advantages over New Criticism: it is not heavily influenced by the British school of philosophy; it has not identified itself with the conservative movement in literature; and it is at least conscious of the critique of Saussurian linguistics posed by Derrida.

Structuralism has come closer to a recognition of the need for a theory of the sentence than any tendencies we have thus far examined.

But this doesn't mean one has been developed. The most recent classic of French Structuralism to be translated into English is Pierre Machery's *Theory of Literary Production*. Following a division made by Wellek and Warren of discourse into three broad categories—everyday, scientific, and literary—Machery proposes that everyday discourse is ideological, scientific discourse is empirical, and literary discourse moves back and forth between these two poles. This model echoes the one made by Zukofsky of his work having a lower limit of speech and an upper one of music. Machery's revision makes a real distinction and moves it well towards something that could be put into a contextualized theory of utterance such as that proposed by Voloshinov in *Marxism and the Philosophy of Language*. But Machery's divisions are inaccurate.

Everyday discourse is purely ideological, but so too is all specialized discourse. The constraints posed on all modes of professional jargon and technical language, whether scientific, legal, medical, or whatever, communicate class in addition to any other object of their discourse. There is no such thing as a nonideological or value-free discourse.

Tzvestan Todorov's *The Poetics of Prose* actually addresses the function of the sentence, for about two paragraphs. Todorov defines meaning according to the formula of Emile Beneviste: "It is the capacity of a linguistic unit to integrate a higher-level unit." This definition of meaning is central to Todorov's work. It is based on an observation by Valery:

> Literature is, and can be nothing other than, a kind of extension and application of certain properties of language.

Todorov demonstrates his understanding of the importance of the question of integration, both in *The Poetics of Prose* and in a brief lecture he gave along with Roland Barthes at Johns Hopkins in 1966. I'm quoting from the talk:

> While in speech the integration of units does not go beyond the sentence, in literature sentences are integrated again as part of larger articulations, and the latter in their turn into units of greater dimension, and so on until we have the entire work. . . . On the other hand, the interpretations of each unit are innumerable, for their comprehension depends on the system in which it will be included.

I want to give an example of how meaning shifts as units are integrated into successively higher levels. Here are three sentences from *Tjanting:*

> Someone calld Douglas. Someone calld Douglas over. He was killed by someone calld Douglas over in Oakland.

Roland Barthes, of course, is the most celebrated of Structuralist critics. He also has been the most explicit in calling for a theory of the sentence. In the same symposium with Todorov, he goes so far as to say:

> The structure of the sentence, the object of linguistics, is found again, homologically, in the structure of works. Discourse is not simply an adding together of sentences; it is, itself, one great sentence.

This statement has the glaring flaw that the sentence is not the object of linguistics, and Barthes is deliberately being audacious in the way he states this. But there is an important insight here, which is that the modes of integration which carry words into phrases and phrases into sentences are not fundamentally different from those by which an individual sentence integrates itself into a larger work. This not only gives us a good reason for demanding a theory of sentences, but also suggests that such a theory would lead us toward a new mode of analysis of literary products themselves.

In *S/Z,* Barthes demonstrates how a structuralist interpretation of a specific story ought to proceed. He takes Balzac's "Sarrasine" and analyzes it according to several different codes. In a sense, he goes word by word through the text, but he does *not* break his analysis into sentences. Instead, he uses what he calls lexias, anywhere from one word to several sentences long. Barthes himself describes the selection of lexias as being "arbitrary in the extreme," although he treats them as "units of reading."

His earliest work, *Writing Degree Zero,* which is also the one most widely quoted in conjunction with so-called language writers, does address the question, but in a highly metaphoric style and with a certain primitiveness, really only a reflection of the other work which had been done in this area in the past twenty-five years.

Classical language does not reach the functional perfection of the relational network of mathematics: relations are not signified, in it, by any special signs, but only by accidents of form and disposition. It is the restraint of the words themselves, their alignment, which achieves the relational nature of classic discourse. Overworked in a restricted number of ever-similar relations, classical words are on the way to becoming an algebra.

Modern poetry, since it must be distinguished from classical poetry and from any type of prose, destroys the spontaneously functional nature of language, and leaves standing only its lexical basis. It retains only the outward shape of relationships, their music, but not their reality. The Word shines forth above a line of relationships emptied of their content, grammar is bereft of its purpose, it becomes prosody and is no longer anything but an inflexion which lasts only to present the Word.

Barthes is here casting against the temporal plane of history a proposition originally proposed by Roman Jakobson for all poetry:

> The poetic function projects the principle of equivalence from the axis of selection into the axis of combination.

Jakobson's formula suggests the primacy of the paradigmatic to the extent that it imposes itself on the supposed value-free combinations of the syntagmatic.

Barthes suggests that the Jakobsonian projection of the paradigm is not a constant, but that history has seen the movement from a syntagmatic focus to a paradigmatic one, and that a break has occurred at a point when some critical mass—not specifically identified by Barthes—renders it impossible for units to continue to integrate beyond grammatical levels, e.g., the sentence.

Barthes is, I believe, wrong in this. What has occurred is that printing has made literature and literacy more available across a progressively more stratified scale of social classes and that the poles of paradigm and syntagm have become more and more identified with the limits, respectively, of high and low art.

Writing occurs in every literate class, although only a fraction ever gets into print. Each class which has writing also has a range of literary art extending from high to low. This is obscured by the presentation of literature as a unified body of work without internal class markers. Helen Adam represents an instance of high lumpen art, although from the idealized and imaginary point of view of a unified literature, she is often taken as an example of how poetry can still aspire to the condition of low art without being, by virtue of that, bad writing.

How do sentences integrate into higher units of meaning? The obvious first step here is toward the paragraph, and here I want to quote Voloshinov one last time:

> ... in certain crucial respects paragraphs are analogues to exchanges in dialogue. The paragraph is something like a vitiated dialogue worked into the body of a monologic utterance. Behind the device of partitioning speech into units,

which are termed paragraphs in their written form, lie orientation toward listener or reader and calculation of the latter's possible reactions.

The definition here is not that radically different from partitioning strategies in some current work, such as David Bromige's essay poems. David Antin, in his talk at 80 Langton Street, described his own work in just Voloshinov's terms, as a vitiated dialogue.

Ferrucio Rossi-Landi, the Italian semiotician, focuses on this problem more closely, when he argues that the syllogism is the classic mode of above-sentence integration. For example, the sentences "All women were once girls" and "Some women are lawyers" logically lead to a third sentence or conclusion, a higher level of meaning: "Some lawyers were once girls." Literature proceeds by suppression, most often, of this third term, positing instead chains of the order of the first two. For example:

> He thought they were a family unit. There were seven men and four women, and thirteen children in the house. Which voice was he going to record?
> > "Plasma," Barrett Watten

But this integration is, in fact, a presumption by the reader. In the next paragraph, Watten plays with the reader's recognition of this presumptiveness:

> That's why we talk language. Back in Sofala I'm writing this down wallowing in a soft leather armchair. A dead dog lies in the gutter, his feet in the air.

Whereas two paragraphs before, the separation of the sentences was so large as to suppress integration altogether:

> The burden of classes is the twentieth-century career. He can be incredibly cruel. Events are advancing at a terrifying rate.

Rossi-Landi also gives us a final means of looking at the importance of the sentence. *Linguistics and Economics* argues that language use arises from the need to divide labor in the community, and that the elaboration of language systems and of labor production, up to and including all social production, follow identical paths. In this view, the completed tool is a sentence.

A hammer, for example, consists of a face, a handle, and a peen. Without the presence of all three, the hammer will not function. Sentences relate to their subunits in just this way. Only the manufacturer of hammers would have any use for disconnected handles; thus without the whole there can be no exchange value. Likewise, it is at the level of the sentence that the use value and the exchange value of any statement unfold into view.

As such, the sentence is the hinge unit of any literary product.

Larger literary products, such as poems, are like completed machines. Any individual sentence might be a piston. It will not get you down the road by itself, but you cannot move the automobile without it.

I have said that the sentence is a unit of prose writing. Certainly sentences exist in literature before the arrival of prose literature. Grammar, and thus the idea of the sentence, not only extended from models of high discourse, but was and has always been taught and predicated on the idea of such models. As Shklovsky noted, prose enters literature with the rise of printing a little more than five hundred years ago. As such, its social role as an index of education became progressively more important as education spread to the bourgeois classes. The more educated the individual, the more likely her utterances would have the characteristics of well-formed sentences. The sentence, well-formed and complete, was and still is an index of class in society.

Now prose fiction to a significant extent derives from the narrative epics of poetry, but moves toward a very different sense of form and organization. Exterior formal devices, such as rhyme and linebreak, diminish and the units of prose become the sentence and the paragraph. In the place of external devices, which function to keep the reader's or listener's experience at least partly in the present, consuming the text, fiction foregrounds the syllogistic leap or integration above the level of the sentence to create a fully referential tale.

This does not mean that the prose fiction paragraph is without significant form, even in the most compelling narrative. Consider this paragraph from Conrad's *The Secret Agent:*

In front of the great doorway a dismal row of newspaper sellers standing clear of the pavement dealt out their wares from the gutter. It was a raw, gloomy day of the early spring; and the grimy sky, the mud of the streets, the rags of the dirty men harmonized excellently with the eruption of the damp, rubbishy sheets of paper soiled with printers' ink. The posters, maculated with filth, garnished like tapistry the sweep of the curbstone. The trade in afternoon papers was brisk, yet, in comparison with the swift, constant march of foot traffic, the effect was of indifference, of disregarded distribution. Ossipon looked hurriedly both ways before stepping out into the cross-currents, but the Professor was already out of sight.

Only the last of these five sentences actually furthers the narrative. The rest serve to set the scene, but do so in the most elegant manner imaginable. Every sentence here is constructed around some kind of opposition. The first takes us from the "great doorway" to a "dismal row" in the "gutter." The second contrasts "spring" with "raw and gloomy," and then has the "grimy sky," "the mud," "the rags of the dirty men" "harmonize excellently" with the "damp rubbishy sheets soiled with ink." And so forth, even to the presence of Ossipon and the absence of the Professor.

This kind of structure might well be foregrounded in a poem, by placing key terms in critical places along the line, by putting certain oppositions in literal rhyme, and by writing the whole perhaps in the present tense. Fiction has a much greater tendency toward the aorist or past tense in general. More importantly, the lack of these foregrounding devices permits the syllogistic or fetishistic capacity of the language to become dominant.

It is this condition of prose that we find also in the work of Russell Edson, the best known English language writer of the prose poem. This is from "The Sardine Can Dormitory":

A man opens a sardine can and finds a row of tiny cots full of tiny dead people; it is a dormitory flooded with oil.

He lifts out the tiny bodies with a fork and lays them on a slice of bread; puts a leaf of lettuce over them, and closes the sandwich with another slice of bread.

He wonders what he should do with the tiny cots; wondering if they are not eatable, too?

He looks into the can and sees a tiny cat floating in the oil.

The bottom of the can, under the oil, is full of little shoes and stockings. . .

Other than the hallucinated quality of the tale, derived from surrealism and the short stories of Kafka, there is really nothing here of great difference from the conditions of prose as one finds it in fiction. If anything, it has less of the formal qualities of poetry than the Conrad passage above.

In good part, what makes Edson a prose poet is where he publishes. The poems in *Edson's Mentality*, from which this was taken, were first published in *Poetry Now, Oink!*, and the *Iowa Review*. By publishing among poets, Edson has taken on the public role of a poet, but a poet whose work participates entirely in the tactics and units of fiction.

Edson is a good example of why the prose poem—even that name is awkward—has come to be thought of as a bastard form.

Even today in America the prose poem barely has any legitimacy. There are no prose poems at all in Hayden Carruth's anthology, *The Voice That Is Great Within Us.*

Nor in Donald Allen's *The New American Poetry.*

Nor in the Kelly/Leary anthology, *A Controversy of Poets.*

The prose poem came into existence in France. From 1699, the rules of versification set down by the French Academy proved so rigid that some writers simply chose to sidestep them, composing instead in a "poctic" prose style, writing epics and pastorals in this mode in the eighteenth century. At the same time, poetry from other languages was being translated into French prose. It was Aloysius Bertrand who, in 1827, first began to compose poems in prose. He published these works in a book called *Gaspard de la Nuit.* By the end of the nineteenth century, the prose poem had been incorporated fully into French literature by Baudelaire, Mallarmé, and Rimbaud.

The French found the prose poem to be an ideal device for the dematerialization of writing per se. Gone were the external devices of form that naggingly held the reader at least partially in the present. Sentences could be lengthened, stretched even further than the already long sentences which characterized Mallarmé's verse, without befuddling the reader or disengaging her from the poem. And longer sentences also suspended for greater periods of time the pulse of closure which enters into prose as the mark of rhythm. It was perfect for hallucinated, fantastic and dreamlike contents, for pieces with multiple locales and times squeezed into a few words. Here is a six sentence poem by Mallarmé, translated by Keith Bosley as "The Pipe":

> Yesterday I found my pipe as I was dreaming about a long evening's work, fine winter work. Throwing away cigarettes with all the childish joys of summer into the past lit by sun-blue leaves, the muslin dresses and taking up again my earnest pipe as a serious man who wants a long undisturbed smoke, in order to work better: but I was not expecting the surprise this abandoned creature was preparing, hardly had I taken the first puff when I forgot my great books to be done, amazed, affected, I breathed last winter coming back. I had not touched the faithful friend since my return to France, and all London, London as I lived the whole of it by myself, a year ago appeared; first the dear fogs which snugly wrap our brains and have there, a smell of their own, when they get in under the casement. My tobacco smelt of a dark room with leather furniture seasoned by coaldust on which the lean black cat luxuriated; the big fires! and the maid with red arms tipping out the coals, and the noise of these coals falling from the steel scuttle into the iron grate in the morning—the time of the postman's solemn double knock, which brought me to life! I saw again through the windows those sick trees in the deserted square—I saw the open sea, so often crossed that winter, shivering on the bridge of the steamer wet with drizzle and blackened by smoke—with my poor wandering loved one, in travelling clothes with a long dull dress the color of road dust, a cloak sticking damp to her cold shoulders, one of those straw hats without a feather and almost without ribbons, which rich ladies throw away on arrival, so tattered are they by the sea air and which poor loved ones retrim for a few good seasons more. Round her neck was wound the terrible handkerchief we wave when we say goodbye for ever.

Here we almost have a prefiguring of the new sentence: the absence of external poetic devices, but not their interiorization in the sentence. Mallarmé has extended their absence by reducing the text to the minimum number of sentences. The dematerialization of the text in this manner is an example of prose shaping poetic form and beginning to alter sentence structure. But note that there is no attempt whatsoever to prevent the integration of linguistic units into higher levels. These sentences take us not toward language, but away from it.

The prose poem did not take root in England or America. Oscar Wilde and Amy Lowell made stabs at it. The influence of poems in other languages being translated into English prose, such as Tagore's rendering of the Indian songs, *Gitanjali,* was quite visible.

Alfred Kreymbourg's 1930 anthology, *Lyric America,* has four prose poems. One is a long and tedious one by Arturo Giovanni, called "The Walker." The other three are by the black poet Fenton Johnson. I'm going to read the longest of these because Johnson uses a device here which points in the direction of the new sentence. Each sentence is a complete paragraph: run-on sentences are treated as one paragraph each, but two paragraphs begin with conjunctions. Structured thus, Johnson's is the first American prose poem with a clear, if simple, sentence:paragraph relation.

The Minister

I mastered pastoral theology, the Greek of the Apostles, and all the difficult subjects in a minister's curriculum.

I was learned as any in this country when the Bishop ordained me.

And I went to preside over Mount Moriah, largest flock in the Conference.

I preached the Word as I felt it, I visited the sick and dying and comforted the afflicted in spirit.

I loved my work because I loved God.

But I lost my charge to Sam Jenkins, who has not been to school four years in his life.

I lost my charge because I could not make my congregation shout.

And my dollar money was small, very small.

Sam Jenkins can tear a Bible to tatters and his congregation destroys the pews with their shouting and stamping.

Sam Jenkins leads in the gift of raising dollar money.

Such is religion.

Johnson is clearly influenced by Edgar Lee Masters, but his sentence:paragraph device brings the reader's attention back time and again to the voice of the narrator in this poem. It is the first instance in English of a prose poem which calls attention to a discursive or poetic effect. Even though the referential content is always evident, the use of the paragraph here limits the reader's ability to get away from the language itself.

But Fenton Johnson may not be the first American prose poet of consequence. Here, from *Kora In Hell: Improvisations,* is the third entry in the twentieth grouping, accompanied by its commentary:

One need not be hopelessly cast down because he cannot cut onyx into a ring to fit a lady's finger. You hang your head. There is neither onyx nor porphyry on these roads—only brown dirt. For all that, one may see his face in a flower along it—even in this light. Eyes only and for a flash only. Oh, keep the neck bent, plod with the back to the split dark! Walk in the curled mudcrusts to one side, hands hanging. Ah well... Thoughts are trees! Ha, ha, ha, ha! Leaves load the branches and upon them white night sits kicking her heels against the shore.

A poem can be made of anything. This is a portrait of a disreputable farm hand made out of the stuff of his environment.

Certainly we have strategies here which echo the French prose poem, such as the constantly shifting point of view. More important: the sentences allow only the most minimal syllogistic shift to the level of reference, and some, such as the laughter, permit no such shift whatsoever.

But note the word "portrait" in Williams's commentary. His model here is not the French prose poem so much as the so-called cubist prose of Gertrude Stein, who as early as 1911 wrote *Tender Buttons:*

Custard

Custard is this. It has aches, aches when. Not to be. Not to be narrowly. This makes a whole little hill.

It is better than a little thing that has mellow real mellow. It is better than lakes whole lakes, it is better than seeding.

Roast Potatoes

Roast potatoes for.

Stein says in "Poetry and Grammar" that she did not intend to make *Tender Buttons* poetry, but it just happened that way. It is sufficiently unlike much that she later called poetry to suggest that it is something other than that. The portraits in *Tender Buttons* **are** portraits. The syllogistic move above the sentence level to an exterior reference is possible, but the nature of the book reverses the direction of this movement. Rather than making the shift in an automatic and gestalt sort of way, the reader is forced to deduce it from the partial views and associations posited in each sentence. The portrait of custard is marvelously accurate.

The sentences also deserve some examination. They are fragmented here in a way that is without precedent in English. Who but Stein would have written a sentence in 1911 that ends in the middle of a prepositional phrase? Her use of elliptical sentences—"Not to be. Not to be narrowly."—deliberately leaves the subject out of sight. Custard does not want to be a hard fact. And the anaphoric pronoun of "this makes a whole little hill" refers not to custard, but the negated verb phrases of the two previous sentences. Likewise in "Roast Potatoes," Stein uses the preposition "for" to convert "roast" from an adjective into a verb.

Stein has written at great length about sentences and paragraphs. Her essays on them are works in themselves, and in them, she reveals herself to have thought more seriously about the differences here than any other poet in English.

Because of the nature of her arguments, I'm going to simply quote, in order, some passages which shed some light on the issue in the terms in which I have been talking about it. From "Sentences and Paragraphs," a section of *How To Write* (1931):

1. Within itself. A part of a sentence may be sentence without their meaning.
2. Every sentence has a beginning. Will he begin.
Every sentence which has a beginning makes it be left more to them.
3. A sentence should be arbitrary it should not please be better.
4. The difference between a short story and a paragraph. There is none.
5. There are three kinds of sentences are there. Do sentences follow the three. There are three kinds of sentences. Are there three kinds of sentences that follow the three.

This of course refers to the simple, compound, complex division of traditional grammars.

From the essay, "Sentences," in the same book:

6. A sentence is an interval in which there is a finally forward and back. A sentence is an interval during which if there is a difficulty they will do away with it. A sentence is a part of the way when they wish to be secure. A sentence is their politeness in asking for a cessation. And when it happens they look up.

7. There are two kinds of sentences. When they go. They are given to me. There are these two kinds of sentences. Whenever they go they are given to me. There are there these two kinds of sentences there. One kind is when they like and the other kind is as often as they please. The two kinds of sentences relate when they manage to be for less with once whenever they are retaken. Two kinds of sentences make it do neither of them dividing in a noun.

Stein is here equating clauses, which divide as indicated into dependent and independent, with sentences. Anything as high up the chain of language as a clause is already partially a kind of sentence. It can move syllogistically as a sentence in itself to a higher order of meaning. That's an important and original perception.

8. Remember a sentence should not have a name. A name is familiar. A sentence should not be familiar. All names are familiar there for there should not be a name in a sentence. If there is a name in a sentence a name which is familiar makes a data and therefor there is no equilibrium.

This explains Stein's distaste for nouns quite adequately. The concern for equilibrium is an example of grammar as meter, which points us clearly toward the new sentence.

In her 1934 American lecture, "Poetry and Grammar," Stein makes a few additional comments which shed light on the relation of sentences to prose, and hence prose poems. The first is, I believe, the best single statement on the problem as it is faced by a writer:

9. What had periods to do with it. Inevitably no matter how completely I had to have writing go on, physically one had to again and again stop sometime and if one had to again and

again stop some time then periods had to exist. Besides I had always liked the look of periods and I liked what they did. Stopping sometime did not really keep one from going on, it was nothing that interfered, it was only something that happened, and as it happened as a perfectly natural happening, I did believe in periods and I used them. I never really stopped using them.

10. Sentences and paragraphs. Sentences are not emotional but paragraphs are. I can say that as often as I like and it always remains as it is, something that is.

I said I found this out in listening to Basket my dog drinking. And anybody listening to any dog's drinking will see what I mean.

Stein later gives some examples of sentences she has written, also from *How To Write*, which exist as one sentence paragraphs and capture the balance between the unemotional sentence and the emotional paragraph. My favorite is "A dog which you have never had before has sighed."

11. We do know a little now what prose is. Prose is the balance the emotional balance that makes the reality of paragraphs and the unemotional balance that makes the reality of sentences and having realized completely realized that sentences are not emotional while paragraphs are, prose can be the essential balance that is made inside something that combines the sentence and the paragraph . . .

What Stein means about paragraphs being emotional and sentences not is precisely the point made by Emile Beneviste: that linguistic units integrate only up to the level of the sentence, but higher orders of meaning—such as emotion—integrate at higher levels than the sentence and occur only in the presence of either many sentences or, at least Stein's example suggests this, in the presence of certain complex sentences in which dependent clauses integrate with independent ones.

So what is the new sentence?

We are now ready to ask that question. It has to do with prose poems, but only some prose poems. It does not have to do with surrealist prose poems, whether of the European or American variety, or the nonsurrealist prose poems of the middle-American variety, which is poetry by function of social context. The Surrealists, on the other hand, manipulate meaning only at the higher or outer layers well beyond the horizon of the sentence.

Bob Grenier's *Sentences* directly anticipates the new sentence. By removal of context, Grenier prevents most leaps beyond the level of grammatic integration. This is the extreme case for the new sentence. However, most of Bob's "sentences" are more properly utterances and in that sense follow Olson and Pound and a significant portion of Creeley's work in that area.

Periodically, some sentences and paragraphs in Creeley's *A Day Book* and *Presences* carry the pressurized quality of the new sentence, in that the convolutions of syntax often suggest the internal presence of once exteriorized poetic forms, although here identified much with the forms of speech.

One glimpses it in the work of Charles Bernstein, Clark Coolidge and Bernadette Mayer, East Coast poets with much relevance to many of us in San Francisco. But one doesn't see it consistently there.

A paragraph from the eighteenth section of "Weathers," by Clark Coolidge:

> At most a book the porch. Flames that are at all rails of snow. Flower down winter to vanish. Mite hand stroking flint to a card. Names that it blue. Wheel locked to pyramid through stocking the metal realms. Hit leaves. Participle.

In other contexts, any one of these could become a new sentence, in the sense that any sentence properly posed and staged could. Each focuses attention at the level of the language in front of one. But seldom at the level of the sentence. Mostly at the level of the phrase or, at most, the clause. "Flower down winter to vanish" can be a grammatical sentence in the traditional sense if flower is taken as a verb and the sentence as a command. But "Names that it blue" resists even that much integrating energy. Coolidge refuses to carve connotative domains from words. They are still largely decontextualized—save for the physical-acoustic elements—ready-mades.

This is not an example of the new sentence because it works primarily below the level of the sentence. However, there is another important element here as a result of that: the length of sentences and the use of the period are now wholly rhythmic. Grammar has become, to recall Barthes' words, prosody. As we shall see, this is an element whenever the new sentence is present.

Here are two paragraphs of new sentences:

An inspected geography leans in with the landscape's repetitions. He lived here, under the assumptions. The hill suddenly vanished, proving him right. I was left holding the bag. I peered into it.

The ground was approaching fast. It was a side of himself he rarely showed. The car's tracks disappeared in the middle of the road. The dialog with objects is becoming more strained. Both sides gather their forces. Clouds enlarge. The wind picks up. He held onto the side of the barn by his fingertips.

These paragraphs are from *a.k.a.*, by Bob Perelman.

In them we note these qualities: (1) The paragraph organizes the sentences in fundamentally the same way a stanza does lines of verse. There are roughly the same number of sentences in each paragraph and the number is low enough to establish a clear sentence:paragraph ratio. Why is this not simply a matter of the way sentences are normally organized into paragraphs? Because there is no specific referential focus. The paragraph here is a unit of measure—as it was also in "Weathers." (2) The sentences are all sentences. By which I mean that the syntax of each resolves up to the level of the sentence. Not that these sentences make sense in the ordinary way. For example, "He lived here, under the assumptions." This sentence could be rewritten, or have been derived, from a sentence such as "He lived here, under the elm trees," or, "He lived here, under the assumption *that* etc." (3) This continual torquing of sentences is a traditional quality of poetry, but in poetry it is most often accomplished by linebreaks, and earlier on by rhyme as well. Here poetic form has moved into the interiors of prose.

Consider, by way of contrast, this first stanza of Alan Bernheimer's "Carapace":

> The face of a stranger
> is a privilege to see
> each breath a signature
> and the same sunset fifty years later
> though familiarity is an education

There are shifts and torquings here also, but these occur hinged by external poetic form: linebreaks. In "Carapace," the individual line is so-called ordinary language and is without this torque or pressurization of syntax. Torquing occurs in "Carapace" through the addition of the lines, one to another.

a.k.a., by contrast, has redeployed the linebreak to two levels. As I noted, the length of the sentence is a matter now of quantity, of measure. But the torquing which is normally triggered by linebreaks, the function of which is to enhance ambiguity and polysemy, has now moved directly into the grammar of the sentence. At one level, the completed sentence (i.e., not the completed thought, but the maximum level of grammatic/linguistic integration) has become equivalent to a line, a condition not previously imposed on sentences.

Imagine what the major poems of literary history would look like if each sentence was identical to a line.

That is why an ordinary sentence, such as "I peered into it," can become a new sentence, that is, a sentence with an interior poetic structure in addition to interior ordinary grammatical structure. That is also why and how quoted lines from a Sonoma newspaper in David Bromige's "One Spring" can also become new sentences.

In fact, the increased sensitivity to syllogistic movement enables works of the new sentence a much greater capacity to incorporate ordinary sentences of the material world, because here form moves from the totality downward and the disjunction of a quoted sentence from a newspaper puts its referential content (*a*) into play with its own diction, as in the sentence "Danny always loved Ireland," (from *Tjanting*, referring to Dan White); (*b*) into play with the preceding and succeeding sentences, as quantity, syntax, and measure; and (*c*) into play with the paragraph as a whole, now understood as a unit not of logic or argument, but as quantity, a stanza.

Let's look at this play of syllogistic movement:

> I was left holding the bag. I peered into it.
>   The ground was approaching fast. It was a side of himself
> he rarely showed.

This is not the systematic distortion of the maximum or highest order of meaning, as in surrealism. Rather, each sentence plays with the preceding and following sentence. The first sounds figurative, because of the deliberate use of the cliche. The second, by using both a repetition of the word "I" and the anaphor "it," twists that, making it sound (*a*) literal and (*b*) narrative, in that the two sentences appear to refer to an identical content.

But the third sentence, which begins the next paragraph, works instead from the direction one might take in looking into a bag and associating from there the sense of gravity one feels looking down, as though falling.

The fourth sentence moves outside the voice of the narrative "I" and presents the sequence of previous sentences as leading to this humorous conclusion.

This double-relation of syllogistic movement, which nonetheless does not build up so far as to move the reader away from the level of language itself, is highly typical of the new sentence.

Further, the interior structure of sentences here reflects also how such issues as balance, normally issues of line organization, recast themselves inside sentences. A sentence like "Clouds enlarge" is no less concerned with such balance than those of Grenier's *Sentences:* the word "enlarged" is an ordinary word *en*larged.

Let's list these qualities of the new sentence, then read a poem, listening for their presence:

1. The paragraph organizes the sentences;
2. The paragraph is a unit of quantity, not logic or argument;
3. Sentence length is a unit of measure;
4. Sentence structure is altered for torque, or increased polysemy/ambiguity;
5. Syllogistic movement is (*a*) limited (*b*) controlled;
6. Primary syllogistic movement is between the preceding and following sentences;
7. Secondary syllogistic movement is toward the paragraph as a whole, or the total work;
8. The limiting of syllogistic movement keeps the reader's attention at or very close to the level of language, that is, most often at the sentence level or below.

My example is the poem "For She," by Carla Harryman. It is one paragraph:

The back of the hand resting on the pillow was not wasted. We couldn't hear each other speak. The puddle in the bathroom, the sassy one. There were many years between us. I stared the stranger into facing up to Maxine, who had come out of the forest wet from bad nights. I came from an odd bed, a vermillion riot attracted to loud dogs. Nonetheless I could pay my rent and provide for him. On this occasion she apologized. An arrangement that did not provoke inspection. Outside on the stagnant water was a motto. He was more than I perhaps though younger. I sweat at amphibians, managed to get home. The sunlight from the window played up his golden curls and a fist screwed over one eye. Right to left and left to right until the sides of her body were circuits. While dazed and hidden in the room, he sang to himself, severe songs, from a history he knew nothing of. Or should I say malicious? Some rustic gravure, soppy but delicate at pause. I wavered, held her up. I tremble, jack him up. Matted wallowings, I couldn't organize the memory. Where does he find his friends? Maxine said to me "but it was just you again." In spite of the cars and the smoke and the many languages, the radio and the appliances, the flat broad buzz of the tracks, the anxiety with which the eyes move to meet the phone and all the arbitrary colors, I am just the same. Unplug the glass, face the docks. I might have been in a more simple schoolyard.

I have just a few more things to say. One is that I first noticed the new sentence in the poem "Chamber Music" in Barrett Watten's *Decay*. I think that since then it has come forward in the work of not just one or two of us, but through the collective work and interinfluence of the entire local poetic community.

If "language writing" means anything, it means writing which does focus the reader onto the level of the sentence and below, as well as those units above. Heretofore, this has been accomplished by the deliberate exclusion of certain elements of signification, such as reference and syntax. The new sentence is the first mode of "language writing" which has been able to incorporate all the elements of language, from below the sentence level *and* above.

Everywhere there are spontaneous literary discussions. Something structurally new is always being referred to. These topics may be my very own dreams, which everyone takes a friendly interest in. The library extends for miles, under the ground.

"Plasma"

PERIOD

Charles Simic

Negative Capability and Its Children
1978

> *. . . that is, when a man is capable of being in*
> *uncertainties, mysteries, doubts, without any*
> *irritable reaching after fact and reason.*
> John Keats

Today what Keats said could be made even more specific. In place of "uncertainties," "mysteries" and "doubts," we could substitute a long list of intellectual and aesthetic events which question, revise and contradict one another on all fundamental issues. We could also bring in recent political history: all the wars, all the concentration camps and other assorted modern sufferings, and then return to Keats and ask how, in this context, are we capable of being in anything *but* uncertainties? Or, since we are thinking about poetry, ask how do we render this now overwhelming consciousness of uncertainty, mystery and doubt in our poems?

To be "capable of being in uncertainties" is to be literally in the midst. The poet is in the midst. The poem, too, is in the midst, a kind of magnet for complex historical, literary and psychological forces, as well as a way of maintaining oneself in the face of that multiplicity.

There are serious consequences to being in the midst. For instance, one is subject to influences. One experiences crises of identity. One suffers from self-consciousness. One longs for self-knowledge while realizing at the same time that under the circumstances self-knowledge can never be complete. When it comes to poetry, one has to confront the difficult question: Who or what vouches for the authenticity of the act? After more than a century of increasing and finally all-embracing suspicions regarding traditional descriptions of reality and self, the question of authenticity ceases to be merely an intellectual problem and becomes a practical one which confronts the poet daily as he or she sits down to write a poem. What words can I trust? How can *I know* that I trust them?

There are a number of replies, as we'll see, but in an age of uncertainties there has to be a particular kind of answer. It includes, for example, the notion of experiment, that concept borrowed from science and which already appears in Wordsworth's *Advertisement to Lyrical Ballads* (1798) and implies a test, a trial, any action or process undertaken to demonstrate something not yet known, or (and this is important) to demonstrate something known and forgotten. I was simply quoting Webster's definition and he reminded me that "experimental" means based on experience rather than on theory or authority. Empiricism, yes, but with a difference. In experimental poetry it will have to be an empiricism of imagination and consciousness.

Back to the notion of being in the midst. "Given the imperfect correspondence between mind and objective reality" (Hegel), given the fact that this "imperfect correspondence" is the product of a critique of language which since the Romantics has undermined the old unity of word and object, of concept and image, then modern poetics is nothing more than the dramatization of the epistemological consequences of that disruption. Certainly, to call it "dramatic" is to suggest contending voices. My purpose here is to identify some of them and establish, as it were, their order of appearance.

We can proceed with our "translation" of Keats. We can speak of Chance in place of his "uncertainty." Is it with Keats that Chance, that major preoccupation of modern experimental poetics, enters aesthetics?

One aspect of that history is clear. Dada and then surrealism made Chance famous, made it ontological. They turned it into a weapon. Cause and effect as the archenemies. Nietzsche had already claimed that "the alleged instinct for causality is nothing more than the fear of the unusual." Fear, of course, and its offspring, habit, which is there, presumably, to minimize that fear. But isn't poetry too a habit, a convention with specific expectations of content and form which have their own causal relationship? Certainly—and this I believe was understood by these poets. So the project became one of using Chance to break the spell of our habitual literary expectations and to approach the condition of what has been called "free imagination."

There's more to it, however. There's a story, almost a parable, of how Marcel Duchamp suspended a book of Euclidian geometry by a string outside his window for several months and in all kinds of weather, and then presented the result to his sister as a birthday present, and of course as an art object. A lovely idea. Almost a philosophical gesture, a kind of ironic critique of Euclid by the elements. Even more, this example and others like it offer a fundamental revision of what we mean by creativity. In that view, the poet is not a *maker,* but someone able to detect the presence of poetry in the accidental.

This is a curious discovery, that there should be poetry at all in the accidental, that there should even be lyricism. The implications are troubling. If we say "lyricism," we imply an assertion of a human presence and will, but how do we locate even a hint of human presence in operations that have no conscious intent and are left to Chance? Is it because there's a kind of significance (meaning) which is not the function of causality? In any case, you don't achieve anonymity when you submit yourself to the law of accident. "Chance," as Antonin Artaud said, "is myself." This is a magnificent insight. It humanizes the abstraction (Chance) and shifts the problem into an entirely different area.

Pound, Olson, and that whole other tradition we are heirs to, with its theory of "Energy," perhaps provides the next step. That theory, it seems to me, accounts for this astonishing discovery that the text is always here, that the content precedes us, that the labor of the poet is to become an instrument of discovery of what has always been with us, inconspicuous in its familiarity.

Olson says "a poem is energy transferred from where the poet got it . . . by the way of the poem itself to, all the way over to, the reader." Pound called it "Vortex." Both of them were pointing to the experience of one's own existence and its dynamics as the original condition which the poet aims to repossess. And for Olson, "there's only one thing you can do about kinetic, re-enact it."

That's the key term: re-enactment. Their definitions are concerned with locating the agent that fuels the poetic act. Their hope, above all, is to give us a taste of that original preconscious complexity and unselected-ness. The problem next is how to accomplish it? And the question remains. What does Chance re-enact?

Suppose what we call Chance is simply a submission to a message from the unconscious. The random then becomes a matter of obedience to inwardness and calls for an appropriate technique. The surrealists, as we know, took it over from professional mediums and renamed it "automatic writing." In any case, it's still an interior dictation they are after, a trance, an altered state of consciousness. Breton gives the prescription: "A monologue that flows as rapidly as possible, on which critical spirit of the subject brings no judgement to bear, which is therefore unmarred by any reticence, and which will reproduce as exactly as possible spoken thought."

Now anyone can cut up words from a newspaper and arrange them at random, while only a few have a gift of speaking in tongues, so the technique of automatic writing is problematic and in practice obviously less "automatic" than one would like. The hope that runs through Breton's writings is visionary. He was after the angelic orders. In his pronouncements there's an element of faith which in turn simplifies the actual experience.

On the surface of it, what the other modern tradition proposes has some similarity. Creeley, for example, quotes William Burroughs to describe his own technique: "There is only one thing a writer can write about: *What is in front of his senses in the moment of writing.*" Olson is even more categorical: "The objects which occur at every given moment of composition (of recognition, we can call it) are, can be, must be treated exactly as they occur therein, and not by any ideas or preconceptions from outside the poem." There's a difference, of course. The faculty implied and cultivated here, and conspicuously missing from automatic writing, is attention. Consequently, the emphasis in this kind of poetry is on clarity, precision, conciseness, although still without any attempt at interpretation. The object of attention is set down without a further comment. The aim is that "precise instant when a thing outward and objective transforms itself, or darts into the inward, the subjective." The cutting edge.

In both cases, however, the emphasis is on immediacy, and the purpose is an exchange of a particular kind of energy. In both instances, the ambition is identical: To discover an authentic ground where poetry has its being and on that spot build a new ontology.

Unfortunately, there's always the problem of language, the problem of conveying experience. It's in their respective views of language and what it does, that surrealism and imagism part company.

Surrealism suspects language and its representational powers. In its view, there's no intimacy between language and the world; the old equation, word equals object, is simply a function of habit. In addition, there's the problem of simultaneity of experience versus the linear requirements of grammar. Grammar moves in time. Only figurative language can hope to grasp the simultaneity of experience. Therefore, it's the connotative and not the denotative aspect of language that is of interest, the spark that sets off the figurative chain reaction and transcends the tyranny of the particular.

But Pound, Williams, Olson and Creeley are in turn suspicious of figures of speech. The figurative drains attention. It tends to take us elsewhere, to absent us from what is at hand. Furthermore, there's a strong commitment in their poetry to living speech. "Nothing," as Ford Madox Ford advised Pound, "that you couldn't in some circumstances, in the stress of some emotion *actually* say." As for grammar, we have their related ideas of prosody, form, and poetic line, which are nothing more than attempts to create a grammar of poetic utterance which would pay heed to the simultaneity of experience.

I think what emerges out of these apposite views is a new definition of content. The content of the poem is determined by the attitude we have toward language. Both the attentive act and the figurative act are profoundly prejudiced by the poet's subjectivity. (Heisenberg's discovery that observation alters the phenomena observed applies here.) The content is that *prejudice,* at the expense of the full range of language. This is a constant in modern poetics regardless of whether we conceive of language as the expression of a moment of attention or, as in the case of surrealism, as the imaginative flight out of that privileged moment.

Nevertheless, we find both traditions speaking of *the image,* and insisting on its importance. And yet, the contexts are very different and carry incompatible views of the nature of our common reality.

For surrealism, the characteristic of a strong image is that it derives from the spontaneous association of two very distinct realities whose relationship is grasped solely by the mind. Breton says, "the most effective image is the one that has the highest degree of arbitrariness." For the imagists, an image is "an intellectual and emotional complex in an instant of time," but a complex (we might add) derived from a perception of an existing thing. Imagism names what is there. Surrealism, on the other hand, endlessly renames what is there, as if by renaming it it could get closer to the thing itself. The goal in surrealism as in symbolism is a texture of greatest possible suggestiveness, a profusion of images whose meaning is unknown and unparaphrasable through a prior system of signification. The surrealist poet offers the imaginary as the new definition of reality, or more accurately, he equates the imaginary with a truth of a psychological order. Here, the separation between intuition and what is real is abolished. Everything is arbitrary except metaphor, which detects the essential kinship of all things.

For imagism, that "necessary angel" of Stevens's, that reality out there with its pressures and complexities is unavoidable. Imagism accepts our usual description of that reality. The image for Pound is a moment of lucidity when the world and its presence is re-enacted by consciousness in language. He calls for sincerity, care for detail, wonder, faith to the actual. Zukofsky compared what was attempted to a photo lens "free or independent of personal feelings, opinions . . . detached, unbiased." In this context, attention and imagination mean almost the same thing, a power which brings the world into focus.

The surprising outcome of many surrealist operations is that they uncover the archetypal—those great images that have mythical resonance. Perhaps we can say that the imagination (surrealist) could be best described as "mythical," providing we understand what that implies. The characteristic of that mode is that it doesn't admit dualism. It is decidedly anthropomorphic. It intuits a link between the freedom of the imagination and the world. Owen Barfield has observed that already "the Romantic image was an idol-smashing weapon meant to return men to their original participation in the phenomena." Rimbaud, too, as we know, wanted to bridge that gap. However, the vision of the romantics and symbolists was essentially tragic, while that of the surrealists is comic. The surrealist myth-maker is a comic persona in a world which is the product of a language-act, and an age in which these language-acts have proliferated.

When Arp writes of a "bladeless knife from which a handle is missing," when Norge speaks of a "time when the onion used to make people laugh," we have images, configurations, which employ archetypal elements but are not properly speaking archetypes. Instead, we have the emergence of entities which only by the force of utterance and the upheaval they cause in the imagination and thought acquire existence and even reality. These "useless objects" have a strange authority. Even as visionary acts, they consist of particulars and thus curiously provide us with a semblance of an actual experience.

For as the imagists would say, "knowledge is in particulars." Nothing is in the intellect that was not before in the senses, or Williams's well-known "no ideas but in things." At issue here is an attempt to recreate experience which preceded thought and to uncover its phenomenological ground. To allow phenomena to speak for itself. "To let that which shows itself be seen from itself in the very way in which it shows itself from itself" (Heidegger). There's a kind of responsibility here, care toward the actual, the sheer wonder of dailiness, the manner of our *being* in the world. Authenticity in imagism is primarily this confrontation with the sensuous for the sake of recreating its intensities.

The great ambition in each case is *thought*. How to think without recourse to abstractions, logic and categorical postulates? How to sensitize thought and involve it with the ambiguity of existence? Poems, in the words of the Russian formalistic critic Potebnia are a "method of simplifying the thinking process." The surrealist Benjamin Peret goes further. He says simply that "thought is one and indivisible." Eluard says somewhere that "images think for him." Breton, as we have seen, defines psychic automatism as "the actual functioning of thought." Not far is Pound with his poetry as "inspired mathematics," or Duncan's saying that a poem is "the drama of truth." These are outrageous claims, but only so if we equate thought with "reason" and its prerogatives. To say that Chance thinks wouldn't make much sense, but to admit that

Chance causes thought would be closer to what these statements intend. Again Olson raises an interesting question: "The degree to which projective (that is, the kind of poem I've been calling here imagist) involves a stance toward reality outside a poem as well as a new stance towards the reality of the poem itself." This is the whole point. Obviously, the rigorous phenomenological analysis of imagination and perception that surrealists and imagists have done has opened a whole new range of unknowns which address themselves to thought, and in the process alter the premises of the poems being written and the way in which they conceive of meaning.

Current criticism has unfortunately tended to simplify that historical predicament. It has seen the developments in recent poetry only within one or another literary movement, even when the strategies of these poetries have partaken of multiple sources. One can say with some confidence that the poet writing today can no longer be bound to any one standpoint, that he no longer has the option of being a surrealist or an imagist fifty years after and to the exclusion of everything else that has been understood since. Their questioning has involved us with large and fundamental issues. Their poetics have to do with the nature of perception, with being, with psyche, with time and consciousness. Not to subject oneself to their dialectics and uncertainties is truly not to experience the age we have inherited.

The aim of every new poetics is to evolve its own concept of meaning, its own idea of what is authentic. In our case, it is the principle of uncertainty. Uncertainty is the description of that gap which consciousness proclaims: Actuality versus contingency. A new and unofficial view of our human condition. The best poetry being written today is the utterance and record of that condition and its contradictions.

Louis Simpson

Reflections on Narrative Poetry
1980

Why tell stories in lines of verse? Isn't prose a more suitable medium?

It would be, if poets only had ideas and wished to convey them. But feeling is more urgent, and their feelings are expressed by the movement of lines. In poetry the form, more than the idea, creates the emotion we feel when we read the poem.

In everything else poets share the concerns of the writer of prose, and may indeed learn more about writing narrative poems from the novelist than from other poets, for in the past two hundred years it has been the novelist whose labor it was to imitate life, while the poet prided himself on his originality, his remoteness from the everyday. "Life" was the business of the middle class and the novelists who entertained it.

As a result, poetry has been impoverished. In the theory of poetry held by Poe and his French translators, poetry is lyrical and intense, the reflection of an unearthly beauty. Many people believe that poetry is a language we do not speak, and that the best poetry is that which we are least able to understand.

I wish to discuss another kind of poetry, that which undertakes to be an imitation of life. The aim of the narrative poet is the same as for the writer of prose fiction—to interpret experience, with the difference I have mentioned: his writing will move in measure. And this measure evokes a harmony that seems apart from life. I say "seems" because it would be impossible to prove that it exists. Readers of poetry, however, feel it. This harmony is what poetry is, as distinct from prose.

Let us learn from the novelist, however, how to deal with the world, for it is his specialty. We may learn from Chekhov, and Conrad, and Joyce, and a hundred other writers of fiction. I see no reason that a poet should not take notes, as prose writers do, or write out his story first in prose. I believe that Yeats sometimes worked in this way.

I once read an interview with a poet in which she spoke contemptuously of "subject-seeking" poets. It was Charles Olson's teaching, I believe, that the poet should not have a subject but should put himself into a dynamic relationship with the environment, and poetry would rise out of this. But when I read the books of the poet who was so down on subject-seekers, I found that her own poems always had a subject. In fact, she could be all too explicit, writing about her family or writing poems with a political message. Either she was deceived about the nature of her writing or felt that she could dispense with the rule she had made for others.*

There are kinds of poetry that seem visionary, having little resemblance to life. But even these rely on images, and the images, however farfetched, have points of contact with our experience. The room envisioned by Rimbaud at the bottom of a lake is still a room.

But I shall not insist on the point. Let us admit that there are kinds of poetry that are not representations of life. This does not concern us: we are speaking of narrative poetry. This has to do with actions and scenes. The action may be subtle, the scene barely sketched, but the aim is to move the reader, and to increase understanding, by touching the springs of nature.

But it is not enough to hold a mirror up to nature. As Henry James says in the preface to *The Spoils of Poynton*, "Life has no direct sense whatever for the subject and is capable, luckily for us, of nothing but splendid waste. Hence the opportunity for the sublime economy of art."

So you take what you need and rearrange it, and you invent. Invention is supposed to be the *sine qua non* of the so-called creative arts. It is what people usually mean when they use the word "imagination." The poet, says Longinus, thinks that he sees what he describes, and so is able to place it before the eyes of the reader.

Yes, of course. But I wonder how useful this description is

---

*This poet has informed me that it was the *seeking* for a subject that she objected to, not poetry with a subject. This gives an entirely different meaning to her words, one with which I concur wholeheartedly. —Author.

to the man who does the job? It may actually do more harm than good, by urging the writer to strain his powers of invention. Rather than try to work himself up to a pitch of imagination, the poet would do well to discover what is there, in the subject. Let him immerse himself in the scene and wait for something to happen . . . the right, true thing.

There is a form of meditation that consists of keeping distractions away . . . sounds from the street, itchings, and ideas. Emptying the mind in this way is hard work indeed. And for some writers the art of writing may consist of getting rid of distracting ideas. It may consist of saying repeatedly, "No, that is not it."

"There can be," says James, "evidently, only one logic for these things: there can be for [the writer] only one truth and one direction—the quarter in which his subject most completely expresses itself."

So you choose the direction that has most to offer. Some writers, however, are unwilling to go so far. It is instructive to take up a book of poems and see, with every poem, which direction the poet has chosen to take. Some poets take the easiest direction, an ending that will please most people. The sad thing about these poets is that they don't please anyone very much: for all their attempts to be good-natured the public will desert them for some poet whose writing is obscure and who seems to despise them. The mob does not admire those who flatter it—at any rate, not for long. They know they are only a mob and reserve their admiration for those who tell them so.

* * *

One day you were stopped on a street corner by an old panhandler. While the lights were changing and people hurrying by, he told you his story.

He served in Mexico with "Black Jack" Pershing, over forty years ago. He had a wife who was unfaithful. One day he followed her and confronted her with it. "Baby," he said, "I'm wise to you and the lieutenant."

A few days later you wrote a poem about it, trying to describe a Mexican landscape and evoke the atmosphere. But something was missing.

It was not until you asked yourself why you were interested

that the story began to move. The account of his following the woman touched upon some unease in your soul. The rest was merely scaffolding: you were not interested in the landscape or the history of the time. But the tale of jealousy affected you . . . you could imagine yourself in his shoes.

But though poetry rises out of feeling, the poem is not just personal. You could put yourself in the old man's shoes . . . you saw yourself following the woman through a lane in the dust and heat. But, and this is my point, you *saw* . . . you were a character in the story. Your feelings had been separated from yourself. You were therefore able to make them move in one direction or another. You were writing a poem to be read by others, not just getting a feeling out of your system.

Story-telling is an impersonal kind of art, even when the story appears to be about oneself. The "I" who appears in the poem is a dramatic character. "JE est un *autre*."

In recent years there was talk of "confessional poetry." Robert Lowell and Sylvia Plath, among others, were said to be confessional poets—that is, to be writing directly about their lives. But when we read the poems in *Life Studies* and *Ariel* we find that the incidents they relate have been shaped so as to make a point. The protagonist is seen as on a stage. In confessional poetry, on the other hand, there is no drama. The drama is not in the poem but outside it, in a life we cannot share.

I would advise the poet to be as objective about himself as possible. In this way you will not be locked into the treadmill of your own personal history, treading the same stairs again and again.

For twenty years there has been an outpouring of subjective art. There was a generation that believed that poetry should be nothing more than an expression of the poet's feelings. "Why talk about art? Be sincere and tell it like it is."

That was an unhappy generation. They could never advance beyond themselves. It is ironic that, at the same time that they were abolishing art, they complained of a lack of understanding. For art is a key to understanding.

Everyone has feelings—indeed it is impossible not to feel. But we need to understand one another.

* * *

Scripture tells us that all the ways of a man are right in his own eyes but the Lord pondereth the hearts. The ways of the poet James Merrill must surely be right in his own eyes, and I cannot explain my aversion to his style except as an aversion to the personality it presents. The style is the man.

> Tap on the door and in strolls Robert Morse,
> Closest of summer friends in Stonington.
> (The others are his Isabel, of course,
>
> And Grace and Eleanor—to think what fun
> We've had throughout the years on Water Street . . .)
> He, if no more the youthful fifty-one
>
> Of that first season, is no less the complete
> Amateur. Fugue by fugue Bach's honeycomb
> Drips from his wrist—then, whoops! the Dolly Suite.

What else can one possibly say on this subject? There is one thing: one can say, as an absolute rule, that poets must not use words loosely.

When I was a young man I wrote a poem in which I said that poetry had made me "nearly poor." I showed this to a friend, himself a writer, and he advised me to change "nearly poor" to "poor"—it would be more striking. I kept the line as it was, and never again did I pay attention to anything this critic had to say. A man who does not know the difference between being nearly poor and being poor, or who is willing to disregard it in order to make a better-sounding line, is not to be trusted. A man like that would say anything.

Since we have moved away from standard forms, the movement of the line, also, depends on the movement of the poet's soul, how he feels, and thinks, and breathes. As late as the nineteen-fifties American poets were expected to write in meter and rhyme. And a few years ago there was talk of songwriters' bringing about a renaissance of rhyme. But there has been no talk of this lately. Most American poets write free verse. This may fall into groups of lines that make a repeating pattern, but the pattern is still irregular. I do not know of any poet who writes in regular forms—meter, stanza, and rhyme—with the assurance of Robert Lowell and Richard Wilbur thirty years ago.

I believe that we shall continue to write free verse of one

kind and another, and that it is possible to write a sustained narrative in free verse just as effectively as though it were written in hexameters or the meters used by Walter Scott. The long narrative poem by Patrick Kavanagh titled "The Great Hunger" is a case in point. It moves just as well as writing in rhyme and meter, and, moreover, echoes the speech of a modern world, which meter and rhyme cannot.

I can see no reason for writing in the old forms of verse. Finding the form for the poem as one writes is half the joy of poetry.

* * *

Poets try to think of new images. But it does not matter whether the image be new or old—what matters is that it be true. Poets who think that by producing farfetched images they are changing our consciousness are doing nothing of the kind. One comes to expect the unexpected.

As the painter Magritte points out, everyone is familiar with the bird in a cage. Anyone can visualize a fish in a cage, or a shoe. But these images, though they are curious, are, unfortunately, arbitrary and accidental. If you wish to surprise, alarm, and alert the reader on the deeper levels of consciousness, visualize a large egg in the cage.

"There exists a secret affinity between certain images; it holds equally for the objects represented by these images."

* * *

One writes, refusing temptations, sailing past the siren voices. Are the lines about morphology really necessary? What worked for another may not work for you. All sorts of ideas come into a writer's head, but only some are in keeping with his nature, his way of saying a thing.

Imagine that you are reading your poem aloud, and that two or three people whose intelligence you respect are sitting in the audience. If you say something banal, or try to conceal a poverty of thought in a cloud of verbiage, you will see them yawn, their eyes beginning to close.

If you visualize an audience you won't go in for merely descriptive writing. It was description that killed the narrative poem in the nineteenth century. Think of the long poems of

Tennyson or Edwin Arlington Robinson. What was it the Victorians found in all that scenery? Perhaps it had something to do with sex. The shopkeepers who ruled Western Europe and, later, the United States, couldn't tolerate talk of sex in their houses. But the woods were loaded with naked bums and flying feet.

Since movies were invented we have had no time for descriptions of scenery and for long drawn-out transitions. Nor for the working out of an obvious plot. And still this kind of poetry continues to be written. The history of the conquistadors, and wagon trains, are favorite subjects. Sometimes these volumes are handsomely bound—American publishers are incurable optimists, they hope for another *John Brown's Body,* but what they are more likely to get is the equivalent of the Thanksgiving play, with scenes of the Pilgrim Fathers— the parts being taken by members of the town council—Red Indians, the minister and the minister's wife, and the farm-hand and his girl. It ends with bringing on a cow and baskets heaped with corn and pumpkins. Perhaps this is what people have in mind when they warn us of the danger of having a subject.

* * *

I have been reading an article on prose fiction in which the writer says that, without anyone's noticing, we have entered upon a new period of realism. I believe this to be true, and true of poetry as well.

"Most artists and critics," said Susan Sontag, writing in the sixties, "have discarded the theory of art as representation of an outer reality in favor of art as subjective expression."

Critics define movements in art just as they come to an end. For twenty years we have been reading poetry that expressed the personal feelings and opinions of the poet. The movement is exhausted—this is apparent in the visual arts as well as poetry and fiction. People long for understanding and a community of some kind.

The word "realism" can be misleading. I do not mean reporting, but writing that penetrates beneath the surface to currents of feeling and thought. Not Champfleury but Flaubert.

I do not know a better way to explain my ideas than by

showing how I have applied them. I shall therefore end with a poem.

The images have the affinities Magritte speaks of, though I do not think I should point them out—to do so would take away the pleasure of reading, for myself as well as the reader. I may point out, however, that realism allows for fantastic images and ideas . . . but they have a reason for being. The landscape that suddenly appears in the poem . . . the old man sitting with his back to the wall, the woman who appears in a doorway . . . are in the mind of one of the characters.

The Man She Loved

In the dusk
men with sidelocks, wearing hats
and long black coats walked side by side,
hands clasped behind their backs,
talking Yiddish. It was like being in a foreign country.

The members of the family
arrived one by one . . .
his aunts, his uncle, and his mother
talking about her business
in Venezuela. She had moved to a new building
with enough space and an excellent location.

To their simple, affectionate questions
he returned simple answers.
For how could he explain what it meant to be a writer . . .
a world that was entirely different,
and yet it would include the sofa
and the smell of chicken cooking.

Little did they know as they spoke
that one day they would be immortal
in a novel that commanded the sweep
of Tolstoy, a magnificent creation
that would bring within its compass
offices in Manhattan and jungles
of the Amazon. A grasp of psychology
and sense of the passing of time
that one can only compare to,
without exaggerating, Proust.

The path wound through undergrowth.
Palms rose at an angle from the humid plain.

He passed a hut with chickens and goats . . .
an old man who sat with his back to a wall,
not seeing. A woman came out of a door
and stared after him.
                              In the distance
the purple mountains shone, fading
as the heat increased.

"Let me take a look at it,"
said Joey. He took the watch
from Beth, pried open the back,
and laid it on the table before him.
Then from the pocket of his vest
he produced a jeweler's loupe.
He screwed this into his eye
and examined the works.
"I can fix it. It only needs an adjustment."

"Are you sure?" said his sister.
"I wouldn't want anything to happen to it.
Jack gave it to me."

The used-car tycoon. But they never married.
"I've got," he said, "a tiger by the tail,"
meaning the used-car business.

Joey stared at her.
"Don't you think I know my business?"

Siblings. Members of the one family,
tied by affection, and doubt . . .
right down to the funeral
when, looking at the face in the box,
you can be sure. "That's real enough."

Spreading her wings at the piano . . .
"The Man I Love." A pleasant voice
but thin.

She travelled to Central America
on the Grace Line, singing with a band.
White boats on a deep blue sea . . .
at night a trail of fireflies.
"Sitting at the Captain's table,"
"Teeing off at the Liguanea Club."

This picture was taken much earlier . . .
three flappers with knee-high skirts.
1921.
They were still living in Delancey Street.

The songs that year were "Say It With Music"
and "If You Would Care For Me."

W. D. Snodgrass

Tact and the Poet's Force
1958

I want to begin by reading, for my text, a poem from a children's record called "The Carrot Seed":

> Carrots grow from carrot seeds;
> I planted one to grow it.
> I'll water it; I'll pull the weeds.
> Carrots grow from carrot seeds.

On the record, this is the song of the hero, a little boy who plants one single carrot seed, believing it will come up. Every day he cultivates around the seed, waters it, pulls up weeds; every day he watches for his carrot. Meantime, his older brother stands around singing:

> Nyaa, nyaa, it won't come up;
> Nyaa, nyaa, it won't come up;
> Won't come up; won't come up;
> Nothing's coming up!

Even worse than that, this little boy has parents. They say, "Well, your carrot *might* come up, but you mustn't feel too badly, *if* . . ." and they have a little song:

> Grownups know a lot of things
> That little boys can't know,
> So don't be disappointed, if
> Your carrot doesn't grow.

Faced by this multitude of skeptics, our hero can only reply by singing, once again, his credo:

> Carrots grow from carrot seeds;
> I planted one to grow it.
> I'll water it; I'll pull the weeds.
> Carrots grow from carrot seeds.

This is a story, then, about faith. This little boy has a theory about life and growth in the universe, about his relation to natural processes; it is his answer to all questions, all doubts. One must admit that he has better luck with *his* theories than most of us have with ours: one day, in a mighty fanfare, a regular sunburst of trumpets and kettledrums, the biggest carrot in the whole world springs up. When his astonished family asks him what in the world's going on out there, he replies in the most matter-of-fact tone:

> The carrot. Came up.

He shows neither surprise nor triumph: this is exactly what *had* to happen; he had always *known* this.

After I had heard this record several times, I sat down to read the record jacket. I got a severe shock. I could recall that little boy's voice saying, with plangent certainty, "I know it." But those words weren't on the jacket. They weren't on the record either—he had never said them. I heard them, yet he had not said them. What happened, apparently, was this: when he sang

> Carrots grow from carrot seeds;
> I planted one to grow it.

I must have thought ahead, half-consciously, and tried to guess the rest of that old familiar stanza-form:

> I'll water it; I'll pull the weeds
> And it will grow, I know it.

Instead, when he got to that last line, he fooled me—he simply repeated the first line, his cherished principle:

> Carrots grow from carrot seeds.

Now the problem I want to raise is this: Why, when the story is already about a little boy's feeling that "he knows it," and when the poem so openly prepared a place for him to say that, why didn't he say it?

Let me leave that question hanging for a moment, to establish a second text—a slightly more conventional one. Early in the "Elegy Written in a Country Churchyard" is a passage where Gray describes the "solemn stillness" of the twilit landscape around the church. He can hear a few beetles droning, a few sheepbells tinkling; everything else is silent

> Save that from yonder ivy-mantled tow'r
> The moping owl does to the moon complain
> Of such as, wand'ring near her secret bow'r
> Molest her ancient solitary reign.

That passage admittedly does not share many qualities with "The Carrot Seed." Yet these two poems are alike, I think, in showing a very high degree of tact—a tact so highly refined that both passages are colored (perhaps even controlled) by crucial words or phrases which are never even spoken.

If you go back through the many different versions of this poem which Gray published during his lifetime, you discover something surprising. The earliest version and the deathbed version give that stanza exactly as I read it. All the many intervening versions, however, have instead of a "secret bower" a "sacred bower." And I submit that the purpose of the word "secret" is not to convey that the owl's bower is hidden—that's of no importance one way or the other—but rather to suggest that some "sacred" power, to which this owl is related, looks down over the scene.

Several factors contribute to this sense of sacredness. First, the physical presence of the church and graveyard; second, the similarity in sound between "secret" and "sacred"; third, both "secret" and "bower" already have holy connotations because of their use in the Bible and other earlier literature; finally, the interplay between "secret" and the phrase "ancient solitary reign." It's a mighty unusual owl that has an "ancient solitary reign"—you won't find him in Roger Tory Peterson. Thus, all resources have been used to suggest that crucial word "sacred." All resources, that is, *except* assertion.

The most interesting thing here, though, is that Gray had had that word "sacred" consciously in his mind, even published it. But he finally repressed it. For his final version, he must have decided that his first impulse—"secret"—was right; that the passage was better and the bower perhaps more sacred, if that sacredness was created by suggestion and atmosphere, not by assertion.

I must ask you to believe that poetic examples of this sort might be multiplied almost endlessly. The problem I want to address, then, is that old question asked so often by exasperated businessmen—my father among them—"Why don't you guys, you poets, say what you mean?"

I believe—and I hope this sounds either dangerously revolutionary, or else hopelessly old-fashioned—that it is a poet's business to say something interesting. Something so interesting and so valuable that people should stop whatever it is they are doing and listen . . . should stop thumbing through their order books, turning the dials on the TV, chasing the secretary around the desk. Truly, none of those things is trivial. The pursuit of a living, of some opinion to shape your life, of love—you must offer people something more valuable so they can dare to stop.

Of course, I am not saying that people *will* listen if you do say something interesting; quite the reverse is true. Unfortunately, people prefer writing that is dull, so most writing is intentionally dulled for its reader. Its real aim is the domination of that reader's spirit by the writer, or by those who pay him. That is best accomplished by being dull and so stultifying the reader's intelligence, his ability to discriminate, to make his own choice. This is true, of course, not only of such written material as newspapers, novels, and magazines, but of all forms of communication—radio, television, movies, nine-tenths of the talking done by merchants, teachers, parents. Their aim is to control—to get us to choose this whisky or that political group, this tobacco or that god, this brand of coffin or that system of values. In order to control our choice, they limit our area of vision, our awareness of the choices; the best way to do that is simply to say over and over again the things we have already heard and given at least nominal acceptance.

To such purposes, the artist—the man who wants to be interesting—stands constantly opposed. He always says something we have not heard before; he always suggests possibilities. This, however, makes him suspect if not actually hated, for we resist anything new with terrible ferocity.

That is understandable. We have done much magnificent theorizing about the world; the world remains a mystery. Man may become extinct, tyranny may prevail, your business fail, your wife leave you, tomorrow. There is a strong possibility that no idea works *all* the time. All the ideas carry guarantees, of course; the only trouble is that nobody knows where you go to get your money, or your life, back. This terrifying possibility that no idea always works is suggested every time someone offers us a new fact or a new idea. The more ignorant we are, the more sluggishly we think, then the more desperately we cling to the hope that our ideas are adequate. They clearly are not. The only way we can reassure ourselves is simply to deny the existence of anything which does not fit our preconceptions. So, all tyrants pander to our prejudices. We, in relief and gratitude, will give over control of our lives to anyone or anything that will just repeat to us those dangerously comforting half-truths we have invented about our world.

If, however, we fear any new fact or idea because it implies freedom of vision, we fear far more any new person, because he implies freedom of choice. We hate the man we can't disarm by slipping him into a stereotype, the man who won't fit our preconceptions about Man. Feeling as inadequate as we do, we automatically assume that anyone different must be better. And *that* we do not permit. So, we enforce our weaknesses upon each other. We hate the man who reminds us of the value of our differences.

We hate him even more because he reminds us that we are ourselves, not by force of circumstance, but largely by our own choice. If we do not approve of ourselves, we could have chosen differently; we can still choose differently tomorrow.

Unfortunately for the writer, he will always have to frighten people, and in just these ways. He can say nothing worth hearing, nothing worth stopping for, unless he says something new and different. He can only do that in one of three obvious ways:

First, he might have a new idea.
Second, he may have a new set of details and facts structured within old ideas.
Third, he may have a new style; that is, he may have a way of talking which symbolizes a new and different person.

If there are other ways to be interesting in a poem I have not seen them.

I want to devote the rest of my paper, then, to an analysis of the problems presented by this classification. First, and though many modern critics would disagree, I do believe a poem may have value simply for the idea it expresses. This is true, however, only if the idea is a new one—and there is nothing about which people more willingly fool themselves. It rather seldom happens; still it is possible: a writer *could* have a new idea. Let me give an example by the British poet Philip Larkin: a poem addressed to Sally Amis, the newborn daughter of his friend Kingsley Amis.

Born Yesterday

for Sally Amis

Tightly-folded bud,
I have wished you something
None of the others would:
Not the usual stuff
About being beautiful,
Or running off a spring
Of innocence and love—
They will all wish you that,
And should it prove possible,
Well, you're a lucky girl.

But if it shouldn't, then
May you be ordinary;
Have, like other women,
An average of talents:
Not ugly, not good-looking,
Nothing uncustomary
To pull you off your balance,
That, unworkable itself,
Stops all the rest from working.
In fact, may you be dull—
If that is what a skilled,
Vigilant, flexible,
Unemphasised, enthralled
Catching of happiness is called.

This idea—that Sally may be luckier to grow up neither specially gifted nor good-looking—is only new in some relative sense. We have all suspected it at some time—perhaps about our own children—but it so quietly overthrows our ordinary values about success and happiness that we usually repress it. So, in some vital sense, a new idea. And it is worth our time to listen to a man who believes this so earnestly that he can look at the newborn daughter of his friend and can honestly wish her to be ordinary so that she can be happy.

In this poem the idea has interest *as* an idea. Larkin gives almost no concrete details—he doesn't need them. Again, there is almost nothing of interest in the style, the voice; the man who could honestly speak this new idea was, automatically, a new and interesting man. Unfortunately for any of us who write, though, the bloom is already rubbed off that subject—in that poem, by that poet. From now on, a writer cannot merely by its use say anything new or valuable; that's been done.

So, one of the things I am doing here is to rebel against an old commandment of my schooldays: Thou shalt not use abstract words or ideas in thy poem. Although the abstract words—truth, justice, happiness, democracy, love, kindness, etc.—are usually dull, that is because they are normally used to narrow the field of vision, to keep people from seeing. There is no reason they cannot be used to widen vision, if the writer is either more honest or more capable of abstract thought than most of his culture is. It is not impossible to be interesting when talking about ideas or when using ideational language; it is merely improbable. The poet's chosen vocation is to try something improbable.

There are, however, two hints. First, most people who are very anxious to tell you their ideas have none. That's why they're anxious to tell them. Second, if you *are* looking for a new idea, you are more likely to find it close to home. Any truth worth mentioning is probably something we all know far too well already but which we are laboring to obscure. Freud once remarked that he was considered one of the geniuses of his age because he had made three discoveries— no one of which was unknown to any nursemaid on the whole continent! When Larkin says, "May you be dull" or, in another poem, "We all hate home / And having to be there" he has widened our vision to include something we always knew. This releases the energy we have wasted trying to hold it out of sight; at the same time, it suggests whole new areas of possible choice. It does not control which of the choices we shall make; it only makes us freer to choose, more responsible to the thing we *do* choose, and stronger to support it.

Now I certainly am not suggesting that a poem can never state any idea unless that is a new idea. In any poem, there

may very well be a statement of idea, which poem we, how-
ever, will value for other qualities. This can come about in a
great number of ways. It happens perhaps most commonly,
certainly most significantly, when an idea is discovered by the
poem itself to be already underlying one of its own patterns of
words and facts. The *discovery* of any such idea (or emotion—I
am using the terms quite interchangeably) is one of the most
exciting events in our world; it has a value quite distinct from
any value inhering to the idea *as* an idea. Consequently, just
such a discovery is very often the climactic action of a poem.
Let me give a single example, a poem by Rilke, which I give in
a rough prose translation:

An Archaic Torso of Apollo

We will not ever know his legendary head
Wherein the eyes, like apples, ripened. Yet,
His torso glows like a candelabra
In which his vision, merely turned down low,

Still holds and gleams. If this were not so, the curve
Of the breast could not so blind you, nor this smile
Pass lightly through the soft turn of the loins
Into that center where procreation flared.

If this were not so, this stone would stand defaced, maimed,
Under the transparent cascade of the shoulder,
Not glimmering that way, like a wild beast's pelt,

Nor breaking out of all its contours
Like a star; for there is no place here
That does not see you. You must change your life.

You must change your life. You wouldn't walk across the
street to hear *that.* How many people tell you that each week?
And with what a multitude of ulterior motives! Enjoy life; eat
at Fred's! Give wings to your heart; Northwest Orient Air-
lines! The poet's motive is only that you become someone
discovering that; someone looking at the statue and having
the impression that its lost eyes have somehow spread
through the whole trunk. Now the whole body seems to watch
you; you came to the museum to look at the statue; it is look-
ing at you. Suddenly, the discovery of this idea—You must

change your life—transforms the whole poem. You see that this body, maimed as it is, does not show you *its* inadequacy, but *yours.* This experience, and the emergence of the idea from it, is worth crawling miles for. What you do with that experience is your business.

So much for the handling of ideas. Let me turn now to the problems of tact in handling details. I want to take an extreme example: "Protocols" by Randall Jarrell. In this poem, several German children tell of their trip to the concentration camp at Birkenau in Odessa, and of how they were put to death in gas chambers which were disguised as shower rooms. You may not know that the poison gas, phosgene, smells like clover or hay—hence, the smell of hay mentioned at the end of the poem. Again, as the children are entering the camp, they see a smokestack; they think it's a factory.

Protocols

We went there on the train. *They had big barges*
   that they towed,
We stood up, there were so many I was squashed.
There was a smoke-stack, then they made me wash.
It was a factory, I think. *My mother held me up*
And I could see the ship that made the smoke.

When I was tired my mother carried me.
She said, "Don't be afraid." But I was only tired.
Where we went there is no more Odessa.
They had water in a pipe—like rain, but hot;
The water there is deeper than the world

And I was tired and fell in in my sleep
And the water drank me. That is what I think.
And I said to my mother, "Now I'm washed and dried,"
My mother hugged me, and it smelled like hay
And that is how you die. And that is how you die.

How many poets tried to write this poem and failed! How many could not resist saying that this is evil—that it is wrong to kill children. That is not worth saying. If the reader doesn't know that by now, there is no use *your* telling him. Everyone agrees that other people should not kill children; we only disagree as to when it may be necessary, what might be more important, and whether or not children *are* being killed. Jarrell's business, here, is to show that this reality exists, children *are* being killed. He has had the tact to see that any statement of idea would have weakened his poem.

But beyond this, he has seen the need for an extreme tact in choice of details. How many poets could have resisted the brutal guard who would beat the children and curse them for Jewish swine?—the weeping and hysterical sobbing?—the final horror when the Jews discovered the phosgene in the shower, the rush for the door, the strangling and trampling? They are all true—all happened at some time. Why are they kept out of the poem?

First, the strategy of argument suggests that when the facts are so strong you make a better case by showing your opponent's argument at its best. If at its best it is horrifying, you needn't argue the rest. This is Jarrell's strategy. The children rather enjoy the trip; everything is exciting, like a trip to a big city department store. The guards appear only as "they" who give orders to wash. Thus, we are not distracted into questions of manner; the real problem here is not *how* people should kill children, it is the reality that people *do* kill children.

But there is another reason why restraint is so crucial here. This subject lies in an area where we give habitual consent without real belief. For years, all the communication media told us about the German extermination camps; as a result, many of us were surprised to find that they really *did* exist. Not that we had ever said, even to ourselves, that the news reports were false. Rather we accepted them in their own spirit: as self-comforting rationalizations proving our own moral superiority and justifying our policies. Yet, we knew that the existence of such camps did not really account for our foreign policy; knew that we would have been told roughly the same things even if they had not been true; knew that even if the facts were true, they could be selected in accordance with any desired effect. We accepted the stories about concentration camps much as we accepted the advertisements that appeared beside them: we don't believe the tobacco really *is* better, we just buy it. Most of us already desired or accepted our government's policies, so we accepted the stories about concentration camps without really *believing* them.

We had so often used these truths *as if* they were lies, we could no longer believe in them. Such subjects become almost impossible to write about—during the war, in fact, Auden said they *were* impossible. Yet, if you cannot write about these, almost the key subjects to our civilization, why would anyone go to the terribly hard work that writing is? Jarrell shows what is required—a complete removal from any ulterior motive, an absolute dedication to the object and the experience.

Oddly enough, we find that Jarrell's understated version is nearer the literal fact than is the propagandist's version. In such camps there was little public brutality; that would cause hysteria or resistance and hinder the efficient operation of extermination procedures. Besides, the guards, however much trained in brutality, remained pretty much ordinary people. They reacted much as you or I might have. Unloading bodies from gas chambers drove most of them mad in about three months. That job had to be given over to trustees (*sonderkommando*) who could themselves be gassed when *they* went mad. Of course, some of the guards were brutal—many of us, when we think we're doing something wrong, do it with greater emphasis, hoping this proves it right. But most of us react differently. Most of us who operate gas chambers, hang nooses, or electric chairs prefer to do so with every demonstration of kindly concern, since we too want to believe ourselves kindly and gentle people.

Yet this question of nearness to literal truth can be very misleading. What the writer seeks is imaginative truth; and *that* Jarrell's poem has. You know at once that this is no news editor trying to arouse your feelings (or his own) to the support of some particular line of action; these are merely several children who died there, who tell you exactly, simply and directly, what it was like, how it felt. They would not *dream* of enlisting you. Hence they are more real than propaganda's children ever become; too real for anyone's comfort. They might be of any nationality; so might their guards. And this makes the poem terribly threatening, indeed. It does not say "He did it," or even "You did it"—it merely says "This is." It leaves open the horrifying possibility: "I did it. We *all* did it. We all *could* do it."

To write this poem, you must first be willing to imagine yourself as a child in the situation—a *real* child, who might even enjoy parts of the trip. Then, you must be willing to imagine yourself a guard—this is the real test—and see how you would act. You must admit that moral weakness *could* lead you into such a position, could at least strongly tempt you. Until you are willing to admit that you share some part of humanity's baseness and degradation, you cannot write about humanity's dignity and gentleness. Of all the ulterior motives, none is more common, none more debilitating, none more damning, than the pretense to moral superiority.

To show what happens in the absence of this kind of tact, let me take a passage from a man who, in his earlier works, had been a very fine poet indeed, Kenneth Rexroth. *The Dragon and the Unicorn* tells about a journey through Europe shortly after World War II. After describing the miseries of the poor in Capri, Naples, and Sorrento, Rexroth turns to address an imaginary reader:

> Sitting there, reading this in your
> Psychoanalyst's waiting room,
> Thirty-five years old, faintly
> Perfumed, expensively dressed,
> Sheer nylons strapped to freezing thighs,
> Brain removed at Bennington
> Or Sarah Lawrence, . . .
> . . . you
> Think this is all just Art—contrast—
> Naples—New York. It is not. Every time
> You open your frigidaire
> A dead Neapolitan baby
> Drops out.

This is probably one of the most significant of ideas for us—that our prosperity is based on the poverty, even the starvation, of others. Yet no man in his right mind could think that a new idea; any man capable of hearing that has heard it. What does Rexroth offer in voice and detail, what of himself does he contribute, to bring his idea to life again? Only the most blatant hyperbole, whose purpose clearly is not to introduce people to a reality they want to ignore, but rather to impress upon them his moral superiority. This amounts to an act of spiritual violence intended to dominate the reader and force his acceptance.

Such spiritual colonialism is as inimical to art as its techniques are inimical to peace when employed by nations. Such a failure of tact could come about, I think, only because of a deep insecurity in the writer. If he really thought his idea were adequate, would he quite so desperately need my agreement? Yet this kind of insecurity tends to dog the heels of any older idea, since the longer an idea is around, the more we will be aware of that idea's failures to cover the complexities of the world and of our minds. As John Jay Chapman remarked, anything you've believed more than three weeks is a lie. Yet it's true, too—as true as the first day you found it. But if your mind is at all active, so many qualifications will soon arise in your consciousness (not to mention the subconscious) that even that idea's complementary opposite must also be represented if we are to do justice to our minds.

Carrots *do* grow from carrot seeds. However, after planting a garden several years ago, I can report to you that carrots also do *not* grow from carrot seeds. This may have something to do with the fact that farmers plant them broadcast.

Our prosperity is based on the poverty of others. I would furnish you no excuse for ignoring that. Yet we must also see that it is based on the prosperity of others; many other people's prosperity is based on *ours*. Many valuable things and many revolting things exist because of that prosperity; you will not sum up your knowledge of it or your feelings about it in any simple statement.

The problem is that most people, once committed to any line of thought, cannot endure the unavoidable weaknesses and complexities of their position. They shout their idea louder and louder, hoping to quiet everyone else's doubts and especially their own. Soon, every claim to certainty is a proof of doubt. The man who really *does* know something will show it in his actions and his tone of voice—like the little boy in "The Carrot Seed." And it does seem that somewhere we must mention that however much we admire his confidence, his faith, he *was* wrong.

Too many people, however, outgrow Rexroth's kind of naïveté only to adopt its complementary opposite—a spurious superiority. They mature enough to see that no idea will permit them to be right all the time, so they reject *all* ideas. They become intellectuals. They live only to demonstrate their detachment from all positions, their utter superiority to any belief or any feeling. To them, the greatest sin is passion or energy. *Our* problem, I think, is to discriminate, yet not lose the ability to believe and act; to belong energetically to the world without being an idiot. We can do this only if we have the strength to live inside human limitations, to know that it *is* better to have lived, even though this means being wrong a good part of the time.

In contrast to Rexroth's poem, I want to quote another poem on the same subject, "The Golf Links" by Sarah Cleghorn. I think that these four lines demonstrate, as little else can, the strength that comes into the poet's voice when he has the inner security to let the facts speak in their own ungarnished strength.

The Golf Links

The golf links lie so near the mill
That almost every day
The laboring children can look out
And see the men at play.

This brings me to the problems of tact in style—and in a certain sense I have been talking about this problem all along, since the way we use ideas or facts is a part of our style. The particular point of my argument has been to prevent some misuse of facts or ideas from destroying the poet's voice in his poem.

If that is not to happen, a very great deal must be left to the tone of voice, the choice of language, the suggestiveness of words. As an example, let me take one of the most familiar poems in the language:

Stopping by Woods on a Snowy Evening
Robert Frost

Whose woods these are I think I know.
His house is in the village though;
He will not see me stopping here
To watch his woods fill up with snow.

My little horse must think it queer
To stop without a farmhouse near
Between the woods and frozen lake
The darkest evening of the year.

He gives his harness bells a shake
To ask if there is some mistake.

The only other sound's the sweep
Of easy wind and downy flake.

The woods are lovely, dark and deep,
But I have promises to keep,
And miles to go before I sleep,
And miles to go before I sleep.

Why *does* so much have to depend on the furtive tone of "He
will not see me"? On the despair implied by "The darkest
evening of the year"? (Some readers apparently thought they
could find that on their light meter!) On the sleep and death
associations of "easy" and "downy"?

Simply because Frost must remain faithful to the truth of
the experience; must resist the temptation to a spurious
superiority. When the woods speak to you, they don't say,
"Commit suicide"—or if they do, you'd better have someone
look to your woods; they're getting thinned out. If you hate
yourself, they say (as they say in a poem of Robert Lowell's),
"Cut your own throat. Cut your own throat. Now. Now." If
you hate your world, they say—in the softest, gentlest voice,
"You are *so* tired; surely you deserve a *little* sleep. We are
lovely, dark and deep." To weaken the seduction of that voice
would be to destroy the poem.

Just as the writer must give up all pretense to intellectual
superiority, he must give up also all pretense to moral
superiority. No man detached enough to use the word
"suicide" would be standing there to "watch [those] woods fill
up with snow." "Suicide" is committee language. It is always
easy to say "I am a terrible sinner" or "I have suicidal urges"
or "I have an Oedipus complex." You *say* you have troubles;
you sound so superior to them that you belie your own state-
ment in making it. The hard thing, the strong thing, is to say
in simple, personal language, how that problem affects the
pattern of your life.

Frost unquestionably knew he was writing about a suicidal
urge; he may have known that this was probably related to a
desire for the womb. To have said so would have been a gross
failure in humility. Again, however, this humility is terribly
threatening to those who do not happen to share it. We all
would like to think ourselves far above such feelings. But just
as Larkin's poem cannot choose in favor of home (as it does)
until it has faced the fact that "we all hate home," so Frost's

poem cannot honestly choose life (as it does) until it has humbly admitted how good death sometimes looks.

Studying the worksheets of this poem, it appears that "downy" was one of the last words added to the poem—it appears that Frost felt once he had found this word he had guaranteed the poem's experience, the seductive call of the woods to just step in and fall asleep, to have it downier and easier than this life ever gives it to you. No doubt, Frost could easily have picked a more "deathy" word and so have made his meaning unmistakable—even to those with a vested interest in misunderstanding. At the same time, this would demonstrate his command of the situation, his detachment from it. Not only would this distract his attention from the experience; it would strongly suggest that his real aim was our admiration for him, not our participation with him.

Why, finally, is all this tact required? Why must ideas and emotions be repressed from conscious statement into details and facts; repressed again from facts into the texture of language, the choice of words, connotations; repressed finally into technical factors like rhyme and echoes of other words? Why must we even depend on words like "sacred" or "I know it" which aren't in the printed poem at all? For two reasons which are really one: we aim at truth to experience and we aim at powerful expression. We are concerned here with problems of inmost belief and of strong emotion—and these again are areas of habitual disbelief. We simply do not credit people's conscious statements in these areas. And for very good reasons—most people simply do not use their conscious minds for the discernment or the revelation of the truth. They use their conscious minds to disguise themselves from others and from themselves, to make themselves look better than they are.

We simply do not believe anyone who talks very easily about matters of great feeling or ultimate belief. We are more impressed by the man who implies, almost by accident, that a bower is sacred to him or that "He knows it." We are not impressed with this kind of talk unless we see that the feeling is strong enough to force its way out past some sort of reticence.

Auden once wrote:

> The mouse we banished yesterday
> Is an enraged rhinoceros today

432 / W. D. SNODGRASS

He was referring to the way we often repress some idea or feeling, which then collects great strength and spreads through the whole pattern of our lives. Often enough this process is terribly destructive; sometimes it is very useful. The poet's chief business is the revelation of the pattern of our lives, regardless of whether he approves of that or not. Thus, he has more use for an enraged rhinoceros in his poem than for a mouse. Too much consciousness, misapplied, leads directly to mousy poems.

So the poet imitates life, often, by carrying on in his poem a process similar to that of our life. He takes some idea, ordinary enough in itself, and represses it from conscious assertion, so that it can spread into the details, the style, the formal technique. Like the lost eyes of Rilke's statue, this lost consciousness spreads throughout the whole trunk; it soon stares out from every pore. Since it is out of the reach of conscious assertion, we know it is less liable to manipulation toward any false motive; its genuineness is more nearly guaranteed.

Thus, in his work, the poet faces that same problem faced daily by the individual conscience. We know that we must restrain some part of our energies or we destroy ourselves. Yet, as we turn our energies back against ourselves, they too may destroy us. In the case of mental and emotional energies, they can make us shortsighted, cramped in mind, dull, dispirited. We must learn to restrain and refocus our powers in such a way that we will not be right at the expense of being dead and worthless; must learn to be, though necessarily both right and wrong, yet stronger, livelier, fitter to survive, and more worth the effort of preserving.

Gary Snyder

Poetry and the Primitive
Notes on Poetry as an Ecological Survival Technique
1967

Bilateral Symmetry

"Poetry" as the skilled and inspired use of the voice and language to embody rare and powerful states of mind that are in immediate origin personal to the singer, but at deep levels common to all who listen. "Primitive" as those societies which have remained nonliterate and nonpolitical while necessarily exploring and developing in directions that civilized societies have tended to ignore. Having fewer tools, no concern with history, a living oral tradition rather than an accumulated library, no overriding social goals, and considerable freedom of sexual and inner life, such people live vastly in the present. Their daily reality is a fabric of friends and family, the field of feeling and energy that one's own body is, the earth they stand on and the wind that wraps around it; and various areas of consciousness.

At this point some might be tempted to say that the primitive's real life is no different from anybody else's. I think this is not so. To live in the "mythological present" in close relation to nature and in basic but disciplined body/mind states suggests a wider-ranging imagination and a closer subjective knowledge of one's own physical properties than is usually available to men living (as they themselves describe it) impotently and inadequately in "history"—their mind-content programmed, and their caressing of nature complicated by the extensions and abstractions which elaborate tools are. A hand pushing a button may wield great power, but that hand will never learn what a hand can do. Unused capacities go sour.

Poetry must sing or speak from authentic experience. Of all the streams of civilized tradition with roots in the paleolithic, poetry is one of the few that can realistically claim

434

an unchanged function and a relevance which will outlast most of the activities that surround us today. Poets, as few others, must live close to the world that primitive men are in: the world, in its nakedness, which is fundamental for all of us—birth, love, death; the sheer fact of being alive.

Music, dance, religion, and philosophy of course have archaic roots—a shared origin with poetry. Religion has tended to become the social justifier, a lackey to power, instead of the vehicle of hair-raising liberating and healing realizations. Dance has mostly lost its connection with ritual drama, the miming of animals, or tracing the maze of the spiritual journey. Most music takes too many tools. The poet can make it on his own voice and mother tongue, while steering a course between crystal clouds of utterly incommunicable nonverbal states—and the gleaming daggers and glittering nets of language.

In one school of Mahayana Buddhism, they talk about the "Three Mysteries." These are Body, Voice, and Mind. The things that are what living *is* for us, in life. Poetry is the vehicle of the mystery of voice. The universe, as they sometimes say, is a vast breathing body.

With artists, certain kinds of scientists, yogins, and poets, a kind of mind-sense is not only surviving but modestly flourishing in the twentieth century. Claude Lévi-Strauss (*The Savage Mind*) sees no problem in the continuity:

> . . . it is neither the mind of savages nor that of primitive or archaic humanity, but rather mind in its untamed state as distinct from mind cultivated or domesticated for yielding a return. . . . We are better able to understand today that it is possible for the two to coexist and interpenetrate in the same way that (in theory at least) it is possible for natural species, of which some are in their savage state and others transformed by agriculture and domestication, to coexist and cross . . whether one deplores or rejoices in the fact, there are still zones in which savage thought, like savage species, is relatively protected. This is the case of art, to which our civilization accords the status of a national park.

Making Love with Animals

By civilized times, hunting was a sport of kings. The early Chinese emperors had vast fenced hunting reserves; peasants were not allowed to shoot deer. Millennia of experience, the proud knowledges of hunting magic—animal habits—and the skills of wild plant and herb gathering were all but scrubbed away. Much has been said about the frontier in American history, but overlooking perhaps some key points: the American confrontation with a vast wild ecology, an earthly paradise of grass, water, and game, was mind-shaking. Americans lived next to vigorous primitives whom they could not help but respect and even envy, for three hundred years. Finally, as ordinary men supporting their families, they often hunted for food. Although marginal peasants in Europe and Asia did remain part-time hunters at the bottom of the social scale, these Americans were the vanguard of an expanding culture. For Americans, "nature" means wilderness, the untamed realm of total freedom—not brutish and nasty, but beautiful and terrible. Something is always eating at the American heart like acid: it is the knowledge of what we have done to our continent, and to the American Indian.

Other civilizations have done the same, but at a pace too slow to be remembered. One finds evidence in T'ang and Sung poetry that the barren hills of central and northern China were once richly forested. The Far Eastern love of nature has become fear of nature: gardens and pine trees are tormented and controlled. Chinese nature poets were too often retired bureaucrats living on two or three acres of trees trimmed by hired gardeners. The professional nature-aesthetes of modern Japan, tea-teachers and flower-arrangers, are amazed to hear that only a century ago dozens of species of birds passed through Kyoto where today only swallows and sparrows can be seen; and the aesthetes can scarcely distinguish those. "Wild" in the Far East means uncontrollable, objectionable, crude, sexually unrestrained, violent; actually ritually polluting. China cast off mythology, which means its own dreams, with hairy cocks and gaping pudenda, millennia ago; and modern Japanese families participating in an "economic miracle" can have daughters in college who are not sure which hole babies come out of. One of the most remarkable intuitions in Western thought was Rousseau's Noble Savage: the idea that perhaps civilization has something to learn from the primitive.

Man is a beautiful animal. We know this because other animals admire us and love us. Almost all animals are beautiful, and paleolithic hunters were deeply moved by it. To hunt means to use your body and senses to the fullest: to strain your consciousness to feel what the deer are thinking today, this moment; to sit still and let your self go into the birds and wind while waiting by a game trail. Hunting magic is designed to bring the game to you—the creature who has heard your song, witnessed your sincerity, and out of compassion comes within your range. Hunting magic is not only aimed at bringing beasts to their death, but to assist in their birth—to promote their fertility. Thus the great Iberian cave paintings are not of hunting alone—but of animals mating and giving birth. A Spanish farmer who saw some reproductions from Altamira is reported to have said, "How beautifully this cow gives birth to a calf!" Breuil has said, "The religion of those days did *not* elevate the animal to the position of a god ... but it was *humbly entreated* to be fertile." A Haida incantation goes:

> "The Great One coming up against the current
>   begins thinking of it.
> The Great One coming putting gravel in his mouth
>   thinks of it
> You look at it with white stone eyes—
>   Great Eater begins thinking of it."

People of primitive cultures appreciate animals as other people off on various trips. Snakes move without limbs, and are like free penises. Birds fly, sing, and dance; they gather food for their babies; they disappear for months and then come back. Fish can breathe water and are brilliant colors. Mammals are like us, they fuck and give birth to babies while panting and purring; their young suck their mothers' breasts; they know terror and delight, they play.

Lévi-Strauss quotes Swanton's report on the Chickasaw, the tribe's own amusing game of seeing the different clans as acting out the lives of their totemic emblems:

The Raccoon people were said to live on fish and wild fruit, those of the Puma lived in the mountains, avoided water of which they were very frightened and lived principally on game. The Wild Cat clan slept in the daytime and hunted at night, for they had keen eyes; they were indifferent to women. Members of the Bird clan were up before daybreak: "They were like real birds in that they would not bother anybody . . . the people of this clan have different sorts of minds, just as there are different species of birds." They were said to live well, to be polygamous, disinclined to work, and prolific . . . the inhabitants of the "bending-post-oak" house group lived in the woods . . . the High Corncrib house people were respected in spite of their arrogance: they were good gardeners, very industrious but poor hunters; they bartered their maize for game. They were said to be truthful and stubborn, and skilled at forecasting the weather. As for the Redskunk house group: they lived in dugouts underground.

We all know what primitive cultures don't have. What they *do* have is this knowledge of connection and responsibility which amounts to a spiritual ascesis for the whole community. Monks of Christianity or Buddhism, "leaving the world" (which means the games of society) are trying, in a decadent way, to achieve what whole primitive communities—men, women, and children—live by daily; and with more wholeness. The shaman-poet is simply the man whose mind reaches easily out into all manners of shapes and other lives, and gives song to dreams. Poets have carried this function forward all through civilized times: poets don't sing about society, they sing about nature—even if the closest they ever get to nature is their lady's queynt. Class-structured civilized society is a kind of mass ego. To transcend the ego is to go beyond society as well. "Beyond" there lies, inwardly, the unconscious. Outwardly, the equivalent of the unconscious is the wilderness: both of these terms meet, one step even farther on, as *one*.

One religious tradition of this communion with nature which has survived into historic Western times is what has been called witchcraft. The antlered and pelted figure painted on the cave wall of Trois Frères, a shaman-dancer-poet, is a prototype of both Shiva and the Devil.

Animal marriages (and supernatural marriages) are a common motif of folklore the world around. A recent article by Lynn White puts the blame for the present ecological crisis on the Judaeo-Christian tradition—animals don't have souls and can't be saved; nature is merely a ground for us to exploit while working out our drama of free will and salvation under the watch of Jehovah. The Devil? "The Deivill apeired vnto her in the liknes of ane prettie boy in grein clothes . . . and at that tyme the Deivil gaive hir his markis; and went away from her in the liknes of ane blak dowg." "He wold haw carnall dealling with ws in the shap of a deir, or in any vther shap, now and then, somtyme he vold be lyk a stirk, a bull, a deir, a rae, or a dowg, etc, and haw dealling with us."

The archaic and primitive ritual dramas, which acknowledged all the sides of human nature, including the destructive, demonic, and ambivalent, were liberating and harmonizing. Freud said *he* didn't discover the unconscious, poets had centuries before. The purpose of California Shamanism was "to heal disease and resist death, with a power acquired from dreams." An Arapaho dancer of the Ghost Dance came back from his trance to sing:

"I circle around, I circle around

The boundaries of the earth,
The boundaries of the earth

Wearing the long wing feathers as I fly
Wearing the long wing feathers as I fly."

The Voice as a Girl

"Everything was alive—the trees, grasses, and winds were dancing with me, talking with me; I could understand the songs of the birds." This ancient experience is not so much—in spite of later commentators—"religious" as it is a pure perception of beauty. The phenomenal world experienced at certain pitches is totally living, exciting, mysterious, filling one with a trembling awe, leaving one grateful and humble. The wonder of the mystery returns direct to one's own senses and consciousness: inside and outside; the voice breathes, "Ah!"

Breath is the outer world coming into one's body. With pulse—the two always harmonizing—the source of our inward sense of rhythm. Breath is spirit, "inspiration." Expiration, "voiced," makes the signals by which the species connects. Certain emotions and states occasionally seize the body, one becomes a whole tube of air vibrating; all voice. In mantra chanting, the magic utterances, built of seed-syllables such as "OM" and "AYING" and "AH," repeated over and over, fold and curl on the breath until—when most weary and bored—a new voice enters, a voice speaks through you clearer and stronger than what you know of yourself; with a sureness and melody of its own, singing out the inner song of the self, and of the planet.

Poetry, it should not have to be said, is not writing or books. Non-literature cultures with their traditional training methods of hearing and reciting, carry thousands of poems— death, war, love, dream, work, and spirit-power songs—through time. The voice of inspiration as an "other" has long been known in the West as The Muse. Widely speaking, the muse is anything other that touches you and moves you. Be it a mountain range, a band of people, the morning star, or a diesel generator. Breaks through the ego-barrier. But this touching-deep is as a mirror, and man in his sexual nature has found the clearest mirror to be his human lover. As the West moved into increasing complexities and hierarchies with civilization, Woman as nature, beauty, and The Other came to be an all-dominating symbol; secretly striving through the last three millennia with the Jehovah or Imperator God-figure, a projection of the gathered power of anti-nature social forces. Thus in the Western tradition the Muse and Romantic Love became part of the same energy, and woman as nature the field for experiencing the universe as sacramental. The lovers' bed was the sole place to enact the dances and ritual dramas that link primitive people to their geology and the Milky Way. The contemporary decline of the cult of romance is linked to the rise of the sense of the primitive, and the knowledge of the variety of spiritual practices and paths to beauty that cultural anthropology has brought us. We begin to move away now, in this interesting historical spiral, from monogamy and monotheism.

Yet the muse remains a woman. Poetry is voice, and according to Indian tradition, voice, vāk (*vox*)—is a goddess. Vāk is also called Sarasvati, she is the lover of Brahma and his actual creative energy; she rides a peacock, wears white, carries a book-scroll and a vina. The name Sarasvati means "the flowing one." "She is again the Divine in the aspect of wisdom and learning, for she is the Mother of Veda; that is of all knowledge touching Brahman and the universe. She is the Word of which it was born and She is that which is the issue of her great womb, Mahāyoni. Not therefore idly have men worshipped Vāk, or Sarasvati, as the Supreme Power."

As Vāk is wife to Brahma ("wife" means "wave" means "vibrator" in Indo-European etymology) so the voice, in everyone, is a mirror of his own deepest self. The voice rises to answer an inner need; or as BusTon says, "The voice of the Buddha arises, being called forth by the thought of the living beings." In esoteric Buddhism this becomes the basis of a mandala meditation practice: "In their midst is Nayika, the essence of *Ali*, the vowel series—she possesses the true nature of Vajrasattva, and is Queen of the Vajra-realm. She is known as the Lady, as Suchness, as Void, as Perfection of Wisdom, as limit of Reality, as Absence of Self."

The conch shell is an ancient symbol of the sense of hearing, and of the female; the vulva and the fruitful womb. At Koptos there is a bas-relief of a four-point buck, on the statue of the god Min, licking his tongue out toward two conches. There are many Magdalenian bone and horn engravings of bear, bison, and deer licking abstract penises and vulvas. At this point (and from our most archaic past transmitted) the mystery of voice becomes one with the mystery of body.

How does this work among primitive peoples in practice? James Mooney, discussing the Ghost Dance religion, says "There is no limit to the number of these [Ghost Dance] songs, as every trance at every dance produces a new one, the trance subject after regaining consciousness embodying his experience in the spirit world in the form of a song, which is sung at the next dance and succeeding performances until superseded by other songs originating in the same way. Thus a single dance may easily result in twenty or thirty new songs. While songs are thus born and die, certain ones which appeal especially to the Indian heart, on account of their mythology, pathos, or peculiar sweetness, live and are perpetuated."

Modern poets in America, Europe, and Japan, are discovering the breath, the voice, and trance. It is also for some a discovery to realize that the universe is not a dead thing but a continual creation, the song of Sarasvati springing from the trance of Brahma. "Reverence to Her who is eternal, Raudrī, Gaurī, Dhātri, reverence and again reverence, to Her who is the Consciousness in all beings, reverence and again reverence.... Candī says."

Hopscotch and Cats Cradles

The clouds are "Shining Heaven" with his
different bird-blankets on

Haida

The human race, as it immediately concerns us, has a vertical axis of about 40,000 years and as of 1900 A.D. a horizontal spread of roughly 3000 different languages and 1000 different cultures. Every living culture and language is the result of countless cross-fertilizations—not a "rise and fall" of civilizations, but more like a flowerlike periodic absorbing—blooming—bursting and scattering of seed. Today we are aware as never before of the plurality of human life-styles and possibilities, while at the same time being tied, like in an old silent movie, to a runaway locomotive rushing headlong toward a very singular catastrophe. Science, as far as it is capable of looking "on beauty bare" is on our side. Part of our being modern is the very fact of our awareness that we are one with our beginnings—contemporary with all periods—members of all cultures. The seeds of every social structure or custom are in the mind.

The anthropologist Stanley Diamond has said "The sickness of civilization consists in its failure to incorporate (and only then) to move beyond the limits of the primitive." Civilization is so to speak a lack of faith, a human laziness, a willingness to accept the perceptions and decisions of others in place of your own—to be less than a full man. Plus, perhaps, a primate inheritance of excessive socializing; and surviving submission/dominance traits (as can be observed in monkey or baboon bands) closely related to exploitative sexuality. If evolution has any meaning at all we must hope to slowly move away from such biological limitations, just as it is within our power to move away from the self-imposed limitations of small-minded social systems. We all live within skin, ego, society, and species boundaries. Consciousness has boundaries of a different order, "the mind is free." College students trying something different because "they do it in New Guinea" is part of the real work of modern man: to uncover the inner structure and actual boundaries of the mind. The third Mystery. The charts and maps of this realm are called mandalas in Sanskrit. (A poem by the Sixth Dalai

Lama runs "Drawing diagrams I measured / Movement of the stars / Though her tender flesh is near / Her mind I cannot measure.") Buddhist and Hindu philosophers have gone deeper into this than almost anyone else but the work is just beginning. We are now gathering all the threads of history together and linking modern science to the primitive and archaic sources.

The stability of certain folklore motifs and themes—evidences of linguistic borrowing—the deeper meaning of linguistic drift—the laws by which styles and structures, art forms and grammars, songs and ways of courting, relate and reflect each other are all mirrors of the self. Even the uses of the word "nature," as in the seventeenth-century witch Isobel Gowdie's testimony about what it was like to make love to the Devil—"I found his nature cold within me as spring-well-water"—throw light on human nature.

Thus nature leads into nature—the wilderness—and the reciprocities and balances by which man lives on earth. Ecology: "eco" (*oikos*) meaning "house" (cf. "ecumenical"): Housekeeping on Earth. Economics, which is merely the housekeeping of various social orders—taking out more than it puts back—must learn the rules of the greater realm. Ancient and primitive cultures had this knowledge more surely and with almost as much empirical precision (see H. C. Conklin's work on Hanunoo plant-knowledge, for example) as the most concerned biologist today. Inner and outer: the Brihadāranyaka Upanishad says,

> Now this Self is the state of being of all contingent beings. In so far as a man pours libations and offers sacrifice, he is in the sphere of the gods; in so far as he recites the Veda he is in the sphere of the seers; in so far as he offers cakes and water to the ancestors, in so far as he gives food and lodging to men, he is of the sphere of men. In so far as he finds grass and water for domestic animals, he is in the sphere of domestic animals; in so far as wild beasts and birds, even down to ants, find something to live on in his house, he is of their sphere.

The primitive world view, far-out scientific knowledge, and the poetic imagination are related forces which may help if not to save the world or humanity, at least to save the redwoods. The goal of revolution is transformation. Mystical traditions within the great religions of civilized times have taught a doctrine of Great Effort for the achievement of Transcendence. This must have been their necessary compromise with civilization, which needed for its period to turn man's vision away from nature, to nourish the growth of the social energy. The archaic, the esoteric, and the primitive traditions alike all teach that beyond transcendence is Great Play, and Transformation. After the mind-breaking Void, the emptiness of a million universes appearing and disappearing, all created things rushing into Krishna's devouring mouth; beyond the enlightenment that can say "these beings are dead already; go ahead and kill them, Arjuna" is a loving, simple awareness of the absolute beauty and preciousness of mice and weeds.

Tsong-kha-pa tells us of a transformed universe:

1. This is a Buddha-realm of infinite beauty
2. All men are divine, are subjects
3. Whatever we use or own are vehicles of worship
4. All acts are authentic, not escapes.

Such authenticity is at the heart of many a primitive world view. For the Anaguta of the Jos plateau, Northern Nigeria, North is called "up"; South is called "down." East is called "morning" and West is called "evening." Hence (according to Dr. Stanley Diamond in his *Anaguta Cosmography*), "Time flows past the permanent central position . . . they live at a place called noon, at the center of the world, the only place where space and time intersect." The Australian aborigines live in a world of ongoing recurrence—comradeship with the landscape and continual exchanges of being and form and position; every person, animals, forces, all are related via a web of reincarnation—or rather, they are "interborn." It may well be that rebirth (or interbirth, for we are actually mutually creating each other and all things while living) is the objective fact of existence which we have not yet brought into conscious knowledge and practice.

It is clear that the empirically observable interconnectedness of nature is but a corner of the vast "jewelled net" which moves from without to within. The spiral (think of nebulae) and spiral conch (vulva/womb) is a symbol of the Great Goddess. It is charming to note that physical properties of spiral conches approximate the Indian notion of the world-creating dance, "expanding form"—

> We see that the successive chambers of a spiral Nautilus or of a straight Orthoceras, each whorl or part of a whorl of a periwinkle or other gastropod, each additional increment of an elephant's tusk, or each new chamber of a spiral foraminifer, has its leading characteristic at once described and its form so far described by the simple statement that it constitutes a *gnomon* to the whole previously existing structure.
>
> D'Arcy Thompson

The maze dances, spiral processions, cats cradles, Micronesian string star-charts, mandalas and symbolic journeys of the old wild world are with us still in the universally distributed childrens' game. Let poetry and Bushmen lead the way in a great hop forward:

> In the following game of long hopscotch, the part marked
> H is for Heaven: it is played in the usual way except that
> when you are finishing the first part, on the way up, you throw
> your tor into Heaven. Then you hop to 11, pick up your tor,
> jump to the very spot where your tor landed in Heaven,
> and say, as fast as you can,
> the alphabet forwards and backwards,
> your name, address and telephone number (if you have one),
> your age,
> and the name of your boyfriend or girl-friend (if you have
> one of those).
>
> Patricia Evans, *Hopscotch*

The Yogin and the Philosopher
1974

We live in a universe, "one turn" in which, it is widely felt, all is one and at the same time all is many. The extra rooster and I were subject and object until one evening we became one. As the discriminating, self-centered awareness of civilized man has increasingly improved his material survival potential, it has correspondingly moved him farther and farther from a spontaneous feeling of being part of the natural world. It often takes, ironically, an analytical and rational presentation of man's interdependence with other life forms from the biological sciences to move modern people toward questioning their own role as major planetary exploiter. This brings us to the use of terms like "Rights of Non-human Nature" or questions such as, "do trees have standing?" From the standpoint of "all is one" the question need never arise. The Chinese Buddhist philosopher-monk Chan-jan argued that even inanimate things possess the Buddha-nature as follows: "The man who is of all-round perfection knows from beginning to end that no objects exist apart from Mind. Who then is 'animate' and who 'inanimate?' Within the Assembly of the Lotus, all are present without division."

From the standpoint of the seventies and eighties it serves us well to examine the way we relate to these objects we take to be outside ourselves—non-human, non-intelligent, or whatever. If we are to treat the world (and ourselves) better, we must first ask, how can we know what the non-human realm is truly like? And second, if one gets a glimmer of an answer from there—how can it be translated, communicated, to the realm of mankind with its courts, congresses, and zoning laws? How do we listen? How do we speak?

The Cahuilla Indians who lived in the Palm Springs desert and the mountains above gathered plants from valley floor to mountain peak with precise knowledge. They said not everybody will do it, but almost anybody can, if he pays enough attention and is patient, hear a little voice from plants. The Papago of southern Arizona said that a man who was humble and brave and persistent, would some night hear a song in his dream, brought by the birds that fly in from the Gulf of California; or a hawk, a cloud, the wind, or the red rain spider; and that song would be his—would add to his knowledge and power.

What of this attention and patience; or the hearing of songs in dreams? The philosopher speaks the language of reason, which is the language of public discourse, with the intention of being intelligible to anyone, without putting special demands on them apart from basic intelligence and education. Then there is religious discourse, involving acceptance of certain beliefs. There is also a third key style: the yogin. The yogin is an experimenter. He experiments on himself. Yoga, from the root *Yuj* (related to the English "yoke") means to be at work, engaged. In India the distinction between philosopher and yogin was clearly and usefully made—even though sometimes the same individual might be both. The yogin has specific exercises, disciplines, by which he hopes to penetrate deeper in understanding than the purely rational function will allow. Practices, such as breathing, meditation, chanting, and so forth, are open to anyone to follow if he so wishes; and the yogic traditions have long asserted that various people who followed through a given course of practice usually came up with similar results. The yogins hold, then, that certain concepts of an apparently philosophical nature cannot actually be grasped except by proceeding through a set of disciplines. Thus the literature of the yogic tradition diverges from true philosophical writing in that it makes special requirements of its readers. Note the difference between Plato, and the school of Pythagoras. The latter was much closer to the schools of India—ashrams, with special rules and dietary prohibitions. The alchemical, occult, neoplatonic, and various sorts of Gnostic traditions of what might be called occidental counter-philosophy are strongly yogic in this way. Gnosticism took as its patroness Sophia, Wisdom, a goddess known in India under various names and in Buddhism under the name of Tara, "She who Saves" or leads across to the opposite shore. Witchcraft, a folk tradition going back to the paleolithic, has its own associations of magic, feminine powers, and plant-knowledge. As Robert Graves points out in *The*

White Goddess, the convergence of many ancient religions and shamanistic lines produces the western lore of the Muse. Some sorts of poetry are the mode of expression of certain yogic-type schools of practice. In fact, song, singing, comes very close to being a sort of meditation in its own right—some recent research holds that song is a "right hemisphere of the brain" function—drawing on the intuitive, creative, non-verbal side of man's consciousness. Since speech is a left-hemisphere function, poetry (word and song together) is surely a marriage of the two halves.

The philosopher, poet, and yogin all three have standing not too far behind them the shaman; with his or her pelt and antlers, or various other guises; songs going back to the Pleistocene and before. The shaman speaks for wild animals, the spirits of plants, the spirits of mountains, of watersheds. He or she sings for them. They sing through him. This capacity has often been achieved via special disciplines. In the shaman's world, wilderness and the unconscious become analogous: he who knows and is at ease in one, will be at home in the other.

The elaborate, yearly, cyclical production of grand ritual dramas in the societies of Pueblo Indians of North America (for one example) can be seen as a process by which the whole society consults the nonhuman (in-human, inner-human?) powers and allows some individuals to step totally out of their human roles to put on the mask, costume, and *mind* of Bison, Bear, Squash, Corn, or Pleiades; to re-enter the human circle in that form and by song, mime, and dance, convey a greeting from the other realm. Thus, a speech on the floor of congress from a whale.

The long "pagan" battle of western poetry against state and church, the survival of the Muse down to modern times, shows that in a sense poetry has been a long and not particularly successful defending action. Defending "the groves"— sacred to the Goddess—and logged, so to speak, under orders from Exodus 34:13 "you shall destroy their images and cut down their groves."

The evidence of anthropology is that countless men and women, through history and pre-history, have experienced a deep sense of communion and communication with nature and with specific non-human beings. Moreover, they often experienced this communication with a being they customarily ate. Men of goodwill who cannot see a *reasonable* mode of either listening to, or speaking for, nature, except by analytical and scientific means, must surely learn to take this complex, profound, moving, and in many ways highly appropriate, world view of the yogins, shamans, and ultimately all our ancestors, into account. One of the few modes of speech that gives us access to that other yogic or shamanistic view (in which all is one and all is many, and the many are all precious) is poetry or song.

William Stafford

A Way of Writing
1970

A writer is not so much someone who has something to say as he is someone who has found a process that will bring about new things he would not have thought of if he had not started to say them. That is, he does not draw on a reservoir; instead, he engages in an activity that brings to him a whole succession of unforeseen stories, poems, essays, plays, laws, philosophies, religions, or—but wait!

Back in school, from the first when I began to try to write things, I felt this richness. One thing would lead to another; the world would give and give. Now, after twenty years or so of trying, I live by that certain richness, an idea hard to pin, difficult to say, and perhaps offensive to some. For there are strange implications in it.

One implication is the importance of just plain receptivity. When I write, I like to have an interval before me when I am not likely to be interrupted. For me, this means usually the early morning, before others are awake. I get pen and paper, take a glance out of the window (often it is dark out there), and wait. It is like fishing. But I do not wait very long, for there is always a nibble—and this is where receptivity comes in. To get started I will accept anything that occurs to me. Something always occurs, of course, to any of us. We can't keep from thinking. Maybe I have to settle for an immediate impression: it's cold, or hot, or dark, or bright, or in between! Or—well, the possibilities are endless. If I put down something, that thing will help the next thing come, and I'm off. If I let the process go on, things will occur to me that were not at all in my mind when I started. These things, odd or trivial as they may be, are somehow connected. And if I let them string out, surprising things will happen.

If I let them string out.... Along with initial receptivity, then, there is another readiness: I must be willing to fail. If I am to keep on writing, I cannot bother to insist on high standards. I must get into action and not let anything stop me, or even slow me much. By "standards" I do not mean "correctness"—spelling, punctuation, and so on. These details become mechanical for anyone who writes for a while. I am thinking about such matters as social significance, positive values, consistency, etc. I resolutely disregard these. Something better, greater, is happening! I am following a process that leads so wildly and originally into new territory that no judgment can at the moment be made about values, significance, and so on. I am making something new, something that has not been judged before. Later others—and maybe I myself—will make judgments. Now, I am headlong to discover. Any distraction may harm the creating.

So, receptive, careless of failure, I spin out things on the page. And a wonderful freedom comes. If something occurs to me, it is all right to accept it. It has one justification: it occurs to me. No one else can guide me. I must follow my own weak, wandering, diffident impulses.

A strange bonus happens. At times, without my insisting on it, my writings become coherent; the successive elements that occur to me are clearly related. They lead by themselves to new connections. Sometimes the language, even the syllables that happen along, may start a trend. Sometimes the materials alert me to something waiting in my mind, ready for sustained attention. At such times, I allow myself to be eloquent, or intentional, or for great swoops (Treacherous! Not to be trusted!) reasonable. But I do not insist on any of that; for I know that back of my activity there will be the coherence of my self, and that indulgence of my impulses will bring recurrent patterns and meanings again.

This attitude toward the process of writing creatively suggests a problem for me, in terms of what others say. They talk about "skills" in writing. Without denying that I do have experience, wide reading, automatic orthodoxies and maneuvers of various kinds, I still must insist that I am often baffled about what "skill" has to do with the precious little area of confusion when I do not know what I am going to say and then I find out what I am going to say. That precious interval I am unable to bridge by skill. What can I witness about it? It remains mysterious, just as all of us must feel puzzled about how we are so inventive as to be able to talk along through complexities with our friends, not needing to plan what we are going to say, but never stalled for long in our confident forward progress. Skill? If so, it is the skill we all have, something we must have learned before the age of three or four.

A writer is one who has become accustomed to trusting that grace, or luck, or—skill.

Yet another attitude I find necessary: most of what I write, like most of what I say in casual conversation, will not amount to much. Even I will realize, and even at the time, that it is not negotiable. It will be like practice. In conversation I allow myself random remarks—in fact, as I recall, that is the way I learned to talk—so in writing I launch many expendable efforts. A result of this free way of writing is that I am not writing for others, mostly; they will not see the product at all unless the activity eventuates in something that later appears to be worthy. My guide is the self, and its adventuring in the language brings about communication.

This process-rather-than-substance view of writing invites a final, dual reflection:

1. Writers may not be special—sensitive or talented in any usual sense. They are simply engaged in sustained use of a language skill we all have. Their "creations" come about through confident reliance on stray impulses that will, with trust, find occasional patterns that are satisfying.

2. But writing itself is one of the great, free human activities. There is scope for individuality, and elation, and discovery, in writing. For the person who follows with trust and forgiveness what occurs to him, the world remains always ready and deep, an inexhaustible environment, with the combined vividness of an actuality and flexibility of a dream. Working back and forth between experience and thought, writers have more than space and time can offer. They have the whole unexplored realm of human vision.

Mark Strand

Notes on the Craft of Poetry
1978

For some of us, the less said about the way we do things the better. And I for one am not even sure that I have a recognizable way of doing things, or if I did that I could talk about it. That is, I do not have a secret method of writing, nor do I have a set of dos and don'ts. Each poem demands that I treat it differently from the rest, come to terms with it, seek out its own best beginning and ending. And yet, I would be kidding myself if I believed that nothing continuous existed in the transactions between myself and my poems. I suppose this is what we mean by craft, those transactions that become so continuous we not only associate ourselves with them, but allow them to represent the means by which we make art. But since they rarely declare themselves in procedural terms, how do we talk about them? It is true, I believe, that these transactions I have chosen to call craft are the sole property of the individual poet and cannot be transferred to or adopted by others. One of the reasons for this is that they are largely unknown at the time of writing and are discovered afterwards, if at all.

One of the essays that had great importance for me when I began to write was George Orwell's "Politics and the English Language." Reading it, I encountered for the first time a moral statement about good writing. True, Orwell was not considering the literary use of language, but language as an instrument for expressing and not for concealing or preventing thought. His point was that just as our English can become ugly and inaccurate because our thoughts are foolish, so the slovenliness of our language makes it easier for us to have foolish thoughts. He lists the following rules that can be relied on when the writer is in doubt about the effect of a word or phrase and his instinct fails him:

1. Never use a metaphor, simile or other figure of speech which you are used to seeing in print.

2. Never use a long word where a short one will do.

3. If it is possible to cut a word out, always cut it out.

4. Never use the passive where you can use the active.

5. Never use a foreign phrase, a scientific word or jargon word if you can think of an everyday English equivalent.

6. Break any of these rules sooner than say anything outright barbarous.

These are of course very elementary rules and you could, as Orwell admits, keep all of them and still write bad English, though not as bad as you might have. But how far will they take us in the writing of a poem? And how much of that transaction I mentioned earlier is described by them? The answers, I believe, are obvious. If following a simple set of rules guaranteed the success of a poem, poems would not be held in very high esteem, as, of course, they are. And far too many people would find it easy to write them, which, naturally, is not the case. For the poems that are of greatest value are those that break rules so that they may exist, whose urgency makes rules about how to write or not write poems irrelevant.

I believe that all poetry is formal in that it exists within limits, limits that are either inherited by tradition or limits that language itself imposes. These limits exist in turn within the limits of the individual poet's conception of what is or is not a poem. For if the would-be poet has no idea of what a poem is, then he has no standard for determining or qualifying his actions as a poet, i.e., his poems. Form, it should be remembered, is a word that has several meanings, some of which are near opposites. For instance, form has to do with the structure or outward appearance of something but it also has to do with its essence. In discussions of poetry it is a powerful word for just that reason; structure and essence seem to come together, as do the disposition of words and their meanings.

It hardly seems worthwhile to point out the shortsightedness of those practitioners who would have us believe that the form of the poem is merely its shape. They argue that there is formal poetry and poetry without form, free verse in other words, and that formal poetry has dimensions that are rhythmic or stanzaic, etc., and consequently measurable, while free verse exists as a sprawl whose disposition is arbitrary and as such is nonmeasurable. But if we have learned anything from the poetry of the last twenty or thirty years, it is that free verse is as formal as any other verse. There is ample evidence that it uses a full range of mnemonic devices, the most common being anaphoral and parallelistic structures, both as syntactically restrictive as they are rhythmically binding. I do not want to suggest that measured verse and free verse represent opposing mnemonics; I would rather we considered them together, both being structured or shaped and thus formal, or at least formal in outward, easily described ways.

The *essential* character of form is manifested most clearly in the apparatus of argument and image or, put another way, plot and figures of speech. This aspect of form is more difficult to discuss because it is less clear-cut; it happens also to be the area in which poems achieve their greatest individuality and where, as a result, they are more personal. This being the case, how is it possible to apply ideas of craft? Well, we might say that mixed metaphors are bad, that contradictions, unless they constitute intentional paradox, must be avoided, that this or that image is inappropriate, etc. All of which is either too vague, too narrow, or beside the point. That is, for me they are, although there are many creative-writing teachers who have no difficulty discussing these more variable and hidden characteristics of form. And I use the word "hidden" because somehow when we approach the question of what a poem means we are moving very close to its source or what brought it into being. To be sure, there is no easy prescription, like George Orwell's, of what to say and what not to say in a poem.

In discussing his poem "The Old Woman and the Statue," Wallace Stevens said:

> While there is nothing automatic about the poem, nevertheless it has an automatic aspect in the sense that it is what I wanted it to be without knowing before it was written what I wanted it to be, even though I knew before it was written what I wanted to do.

This is as precise a statement of what is referred to as "the creative process" as I have ever read. And I think it makes clear why discussions of craft are at best precarious. We know only afterwards what it is we have done. Most poets, I think, are drawn to the unknown, and writing, for them, is a way of making the unknown, if not known, then at least visible. And if the object of one's quest is hidden or unknown, how is it to be approached by predictable means? I confess to a desire to forget knowing, especially when I sit down to work on a poem. Those continuous transactions I mentioned earlier take place in the dark. Jung understood this when he said: "As long as we ourselves are caught up in the process of creation, we neither see nor understand; indeed we ought not to understand, for nothing is more injurious to immediate experience than cognition." And Stevens, when he said: "You have somehow to know the sound that is the exact sound; and you do in fact know, without knowing how. Your knowledge is irrational." This is not to say that rationality is wrong or bad, but merely that it has little to do with the making of poems (as opposed, say, to the understanding of poems). Even so rational a figure as Paul Valery becomes oddly evasive when discussing the making of a poem. In his brilliant but peculiar essay "Poetry and Abstract Thought," he says the following:

> I have . . . noticed in myself certain states which I may well call *poetic,* since some of them were finally realized in poems. They came about from no apparent cause, arising from some accident or other; they developed according to their own nature, and consequently I found myself for a time jolted out of my habitual state of mind.

And he goes on to say that "*the state of poetry* is completely irregular, inconstant, and fragile, and that we lose it, as we find it, by accident," and that "a poet is a man who, as a result of a certain incident, undergoes a hidden transformation." At its most comic this is a Dr. Jekyll/Mr. Hyde situation. And I suppose at its most tragic it still is. But it is astonishing that craft, even in such a figure, is beside the point. One feels that Valery, if given more time, might have become Bachelard who said among other things that "intellectual criticism of poetry will never lead to the center where poetic images are formed."

And what does craft have to do with the formation of poetic images? What does it have to do with the unknown sources of a poem? I would say, "Nothing." For craft, as it is taught and discussed, functions clearly only if the poem is considered primarily as a form of communication. And yet, it is generally acknowledged that poetry invokes aspects of language other than that of communication, most significantly, for our purposes, as a variation, albeit diminished, of a sacred text. Given such status, a status it has for the poet while he is writing, it is not validated by an appeal to experience, but exists autonomously, or as autonomously as history will let it. In his essay "On the Relation of Analytical Psychology to Poetry," Jung comes closest to addressing this issue when he says:

> The work presents us with a finished picture, and this picture is amenable to analysis only to the extent that we can recognize it as a symbol. But if we are unable to discover any symbolic value in it, we have merely established that, so far as we are concerned, it means no more than what it says, or to put it another way, that it *is* no more than what it *seems* to be.

This strikes me as a generous statement for it allows poems an existence ultimately tautological. Freud, on the other hand, who suggests a connection between daydreams and poems— but does not elaborate—and who addresses himself to the fantasies of the "less pretentious writers of romances, novels and stories," making their works into protracted forms of wish fulfillment, seems most intent on establishing the priority of mental states. But the purpose of the poem is not disclosure or storytelling or the telling of a daydream, nor is a poem a symptom. A poem is itself and is the act by which it is born; it is self-referential and is not necessarily preceded by any known order.

If poems often do not refer to any known experience, to nothing that will characterize their being, and thus cannot be understood so much as absorbed, how can considerations of craft be applied when they are justified on the grounds that they enhance communication? This is perhaps one of the reasons why discussions of craft are not only boring, but fall short of dealing with the essentials of poetry. And yet, these days with the proliferation of workshops, craft is what is being taught.

Perhaps the poem is ultimately a metaphor for something unknown, its working-out a means of recovery. It may be that the retention of the absent origin is what is necessary for the continued life of the poem as *inexhaustible artifact*. (Though words may represent things or actions, in combination they may represent something else—the unspoken, hitherto unknown unity of which the poem is the example.) Furthermore, we might say that the degree to which a poem is explained is precisely the degree to which it ceases being a poem. If nothing is left of the poem, it has become the explanation of itself, and readers of the explanation will experience only the explanation and not the poem. It is for this reason that poems must exist not only in language, but beyond it.

Alice Walker

In Search of Our Mothers' Gardens
1974

I described her own nature and temperament. Told how they needed a larger life for their expression. . . . I pointed out that in lieu of proper channels, her emotions had overflowed into paths that dissipated them. I talked beautifully I thought, about an art that would be born, an art that would open the way for women the likes of her. I asked her to hope, and build up an inner life against the coming of that day. . . . I sang, with a strange quiver in my voice, a promise song.

"Avey," Jean Toomer, *Cane*

The poet speaking to a prostitute who falls asleep while he's talking—

When the poet Jean Toomer walked through the South in the early twenties, he discovered a curious thing: Black women whose spirituality was so intense, so deep, so *unconscious,* that they were themselves unaware of the richness they held. They stumbled blindly through their lives: creatures so abused and mutilated in body, so dimmed and confused by pain, that they considered themselves unworthy even of hope. In the selfless abstractions their bodies became to the men who used them, they became more than "sexual objects," more even than mere women: they became Saints. Instead of being perceived as whole persons, their bodies became shrines: what was thought to be their minds became temples suitable for worship. These crazy "Saints" stared out at the world, wildly, like lunatics—or quietly, like suicides; and the "God" that was in their gaze was as mute as a great stone.

Who were these "Saints"? These crazy, loony, pitiful women?

Some of them, without a doubt, were our mothers and grandmothers.

In the still heat of the post-Reconstruction South, this is how they seemed to Jean Toomer: exquisite butterflies trapped in an evil honey, toiling away their lives in an era, a century, that did not acknowledge them, except as "the *mule*

459

of the world." They dreamed dreams that no one knew—not even themselves, in any coherent fashion—and saw visions no one could understand. They wandered or sat about the countryside crooning lullabies to ghosts, and drawing the mother of Christ in charcoal on courthouse walls.

They forced their minds to desert their bodies and their striving spirits sought to rise, like frail whirlwinds from the hard red clay. And when those frail whirlwinds fell, in scattered particles, upon the ground, no one mourned. Instead, men lit candles to celebrate the emptiness that remained, as people do who enter a beautiful but vacant space to resurrect a God.

Our mothers and grandmothers, some of them: moving to music not yet written. And they waited.

They waited for a day when the unknown thing that was in them would be made known; but guessed, somehow in their darkness, that on the day of their revelation they would be long dead. Therefore to Toomer they walked, and even ran, in slow motion. For they were going nowhere immediate, and the future was not yet within their grasp. And men took our mothers and grandmothers, "but got no pleasure from it." So complex was their passion and their calm.

To Toomer, they lay vacant and fallow as autumn fields, with harvest time never in sight: and he saw them enter loveless marriages without joy; and become prostitutes, without resistance; and become mothers of children, without fulfillment.

For these grandmothers and mothers of ours were not "Saints," but Artists; driven to a numb and bleeding madness by the springs of creativity in them for which there was no release. They were Creators, who lived lives of spiritual waste, because they were so rich in spirituality—which is the basis of Art—that the strain of enduring their unused and unwanted talent drove them insane. Throwing away this spirituality was their pathetic attempt to lighten the soul to a weight their work-worn, sexually abused bodies could bear.

What did it mean for a Black woman to be an artist in our grandmothers' time? In our great-grandmothers' day? It is a question with an answer cruel enough to stop the blood.

Did you have a genius of a great-great-grandmother who died under some ignorant and depraved white overseer's lash? Or was she required to bake biscuits for a lazy backwater tramp, when she cried out in her soul to paint watercolors of sunsets, or the rain falling on the green and peaceful pasture-lands? Or was her body broken and forced to bear children (who were more often than not sold away from her)—eight, ten, fifteen, twenty children—when her one joy was the thought of modeling heroic figures of Rebellion, in stone or clay?

How was the creativity of the Black woman kept alive, year after year and century after century, when for most of the years Black people have been in America, it was a punishable crime for a Black person to read or write? And the freedom to paint, to sculpt, to expand the mind with action, did not exist. Consider, if you can bear to imagine it, what might have been the result if singing, too, had been forbidden by law. Listen to the voices of Bessie Smith, Billie Holiday, Nina Simone, Roberta Flack, and Aretha Franklin, among others, and imagine those voices muzzled for life. Then you may begin to comprehend the lives of our "crazy," "Sainted" mothers and grandmothers. The agony of the lives of women who might have been Poets, Novelists, Essayists, and Short Story Writers (over a period of centuries), who died with their real gifts stifled within them.

And, if this were the end of the story, we would have cause to cry out in my paraphrase of Okot p'Bitek's great poem:

> O, my clanswomen
> Let us all cry together!
> Come,
> Let us mourn the death of our mother,
> The death of a Queen
> The ash that was produced
> By a great fire!
> O this homestead is utterly dead
> Close the gates
> With *lacari* thorns,
> For our mother
> The creator of the Stool is lost!
> And all the young women
> Have perished in the wilderness!

But this is not the end of the story, for all the young women—our mothers and grandmothers, *ourselves*—have not perished in the wilderness. And if we ask ourselves why, and

search for and find the answer, we will know beyond all ef-
forts to erase it from our minds, just exactly who, and of what,
we Black American women are.

One example, perhaps the most pathetic, most misun-
derstood one, can provide a backdrop for our mothers' work:
Phillis Wheatley, a slave in the 1700s.

Virginia Woolf, in her book, *A Room of One's Own*, wrote
that in order for a woman to write fiction she must have two
things, certainly: a room of her own (with key and lock) and
enough money to support herself.

What then are we to make of Phillis Wheatley, a slave, who
owned not even herself? This sickly, frail, Black girl who re-
quired a servant of her own at times—her health was so
precarious—and who, had she been white, would have been
easily considered the intellectual superior of all the women
and most of the men in the society of her day.

Virginia Woolf wrote further, speaking of course not of
our Phillis, that "any woman born with a great gift in the
sixteenth century [insert *eighteenth century*, insert *Black woman*,
insert *born or made a slave*] would certainly have gone crazed,
shot herself, or ended her days in some lonely cottage outside
the village, half witch, half wizard [insert *Saint*], feared and
mocked at. For it needs little skill and psychology to be sure
that a highly gifted girl who had tried to use her gift for
poetry would have been so thwarted and hindered by con-
trary instincts [add *chains, guns, the lash, the ownership of one's
body by someone else, submission to an alien religion*], that she must
have lost her health and sanity to a certainty."

The key words, as they relate to Phillis, are "contrary in-
stincts." For when we read the poetry of Phillis Wheatley—as
when we read the novels of Nella Larsen or the oddly false-
sounding autobiography of that freest of all Black women
writers, Zora Hurston—evidence of "contrary instincts" is
everywhere. Her loyalties were completely divided, as was,
without question, her mind.

But how could this be otherwise? Captured at seven, a slave
of wealthy, doting whites who instilled in her the "savagery"
of the Africa they "rescued" her from . . . one wonders if she
was even able to remember her homeland as she had known
it, or as it really was.

Yet, because she did try to use her gift for poetry in a world
that made her a slave, she was "so thwarted and hindered

by . . . contrary instincts that she . . . lost her health. . . ." In the last years of her brief life, burdened not only with the need to express her gift but also with a penniless, friendless "freedom" and several small children for whom she was forced to do strenuous work to feed, she lost her health, certainly. Suffering from malnutrition and neglect and who knows what mental agonies, Phillis Wheatley died.

So torn by "contrary instincts" was Black, kidnapped, enslaved Phillis that her description of "the Goddess"—as she poetically called the Liberty she did not have—is ironically, cruelly humorous. And, in fact, has held Phillis up to ridicule for more than a century. It is usually read prior to hanging Phillis's memory as that of a fool. She wrote

> The Goddess comes, she moves divinely fair,
> Olive and laurel binds her *golden* hair:
> Wherever shines this native of the skies
> Unnumber'd charms and recent graces rise.
>
> [Emphasis added]

It is obvious that Phillis, the slave, combed the "Goddess's" hair every morning; prior, perhaps, to bringing in the milk, or fixing her mistress's lunch. She took her imagery from the one thing she saw elevated above all others.

With the benefit of hindsight we ask, "How could she?"

But at last, Phillis, we understand. No more snickering when your stiff, struggling, ambivalent lines are forced on us. We know now that you were not an idiot nor a traitor; only a sickly little Black girl, snatched from your home and country and made a slave; a woman who still struggled to sing the song that was your gift, although in a land of barbarians who praised you for your bewildered tongue. It is not so much what you sang, as that you kept alive, in so many of our ancestors, *the notion of song.*

II

Black women are called, in the folklore that so aptly identifies one's status in society, "the *mule* of the world," because we have been handed the burdens that everyone else—*everyone else*—refused to carry. We have also been called "Matriarchs," "Superwomen," and "Mean and Evil Bitches." Not to mention

"Castraters" and "Sapphire's Mama." When we have pleaded for understanding, our character has been distorted; when we have asked for simple caring, we have been handed empty inspirational appellations, then stuck in the farthest corner. When we have asked for love, we have been given children. In short, even our plainer gifts, our labors of fidelity and love, have been knocked down our throats. To be an Artist and a Black woman, even today, lowers our status in many respects, rather than raises it: and yet, Artists we will be.

Therefore we must fearlessly pull out of ourselves and look at and identify with our lives the living creativity some of our great-grandmothers were not allowed to know. I stress *some* of them because it is well known that the majority of our great-grandmothers knew, even without "knowing" it, the reality of their spirituality, even if they didn't recognize it beyond what happened in the singing at church—and they never had any intention of giving it up.

How they did it—those millions of Black women who were not Phillis Wheatley or Lucy Terry or Frances Harper or Zora Hurston or Nella Larsen or Bessie Smith, nor Elizabeth Catlett, nor Katherine Dunham, either—brings me to the title of this essay, "In Search of Our Mothers' Gardens," which is a personal account that is yet shared, in its theme and its meaning, by all of us. I found, while thinking about the far-reaching world of the creative Black woman, that often the truest answer to a question that really matters can be found very close. So I was not surprised when my own mother popped into my mind.

In the late 1920s my mother ran away from home to marry my father. Marriage, if not running away, was expected of seventeen-year-old girls. By the time she was twenty, she had two children and was pregnant with a third. Five children later, I was born. And this is how I came to know my mother: she seemed a large, soft, loving-eyed woman who was rarely impatient in our home. Her quick, violent temper was on view only a few times a year, when she battled with the white landlord who had the misfortune to suggest to her that her children did not need to go to school.

She made all the clothes we wore, even my brothers' overalls. She made all the towels and sheets we used. She spent the summers canning vegetables and fruits. She spent the winter evenings making quilts enough to cover all our beds.

During the "working" day, she labored beside—not behind—my father in the fields. Her day began before sunup, and did not end until late at night. There was never a moment for her to sit down, undisturbed, to unravel her own private thoughts; never a time free from interruption—by work or the noisy inquiries of her many children. And yet, it is to my mother—and all our mothers who were not famous—that I went in search of the secret of what has fed that muzzled and often mutilated, but vibrant, creative spirit that the Black woman has inherited, and that pops out in wild and unlikely places to this day.

But when, you will ask, did my overworked mother have time to know or care about feeding the creative spirit?

The answer is so simple that many of us have spent years discovering it. We have constantly looked high, when we should have looked high—and low.

For example: in the Smithsonian Institution in Washington, D.C., there hangs a quilt unlike any other in the world. In fanciful, inspired, and yet simple and identifiable figures, it portrays the story of the Crucifixion. It is considered rare, beyond price. Though it follows no known pattern of quiltmaking, and though it is made of bits and pieces of worthless rags, it is obviously the work of a person of powerful imagination and deep spiritual feeling. Below this quilt I saw a note that says it was made by "an anonymous Black woman in Alabama a hundred years ago."

If we could locate this "anonymous" Black woman from Alabama, she would turn out to be one of our grandmothers—an artist who left her mark in the only materials she could afford, and in the only medium her position in society allowed her to use.

As Virginia Woolf wrote further, in *A Room of One's Own:*

Yet genius of a sort must have existed among women as it must have existed among the working class. [Change this to *slaves* and *the wives and daughters of sharecroppers.*] Now and again an Emily Brontë or a Robert Burns [change this to *a Zora Hurston or a Richard Wright*] blazes out and proves its presence. But certainly it never got itself on to paper. When, however, one reads of a witch being ducked, of a woman possessed by devils [or *Sainthood*], of a wise woman selling herbs [our rootworkers], or even a very remarkable man who had a mother, then I think we are on the track of a lost novelist, a suppressed poet, of some mute and inglorious Jane Austen. . . . Indeed, I would venture to guess that Anon, who wrote so many poems without signing them, was often a woman. . . .

And so our mothers and grandmothers have, more often than not anonymously, handed on the creative spark, the seed of the flower they themselves never hoped to see: or like a sealed letter they could not plainly read.

And so it is, certainly, with my own mother. Unlike Ma Rainey's songs, which retained their creator's name even while blasting forth from Bessie Smith's mouth, no song or poem will bear my mother's name. Yet so many of the stories that I write, that we all write, are my mother's stories. Only recently did I fully realize this: that through years of listening to my mother's stories of her life, I have absorbed not only the stories themselves, but something of the manner in which she spoke, something of the urgency that involves the knowledge that her stories—like her life—must be recorded. It is probably for this reason that so much of what I have written is about characters whose counterparts in real life are so much older than I am.

But the telling of these stories, which came from my mother's lips as naturally as breathing, was not the only way my mother showed herself as an artist. For stories, too, were subject to being distracted, to dying without conclusion. Dinners must be started, and cotton must be gathered before the big rains. The artist that was and is my mother showed itself to me only after many years. This is what I finally noticed.

Like Mem, a character in *The Third Life of Grange Copeland*, my mother adorned with flowers whatever shabby house we were forced to live in. And not just your typical straggly country stand of zinnias, either. She planted ambitious gardens— and still does—with over fifty different varieties of plants that bloom profusely from early March until late November. Before she left home for the fields, she watered her flowers, chopped up the grass, and laid out new beds. When she returned from the fields she might divide clumps of bulbs, dig a cold pit, uproot and replant roses, or prune branches from her taller bushes or trees—until night came and it was too dark to see.

Whatever she planted grew as if by magic, and her fame as

a grower of flowers spread over three counties. Because of her creativity with her flowers, even my memories of poverty are seen through a screen of blooms—sunflowers, petunias, roses, dahlias, forsythia, spirea, delphiniums, verbena ... and on and on.

And I remember people coming to my mother's yard to be given cuttings from her flowers; I hear again the praise showered on her because whatever rocky soil she landed on, she turned into a garden. A garden so brilliant with colors, so original in its design, so magnificent with life and creativity, that to this day people drive by our house in Georgia—perfect strangers and imperfect strangers—and ask to stand or walk among my mother's art.

I notice that it is only when my mother is working in her flowers that she is radiant, almost to the point of being invisible—except as Creator: hand and eye. She is involved in work her soul must have. Ordering the universe in the image of her personal conception of Beauty.

Her face, as she prepares the Art that is her gift, is a legacy of respect she leaves to me, for all that illuminates and cherishes life. She had handed down respect for the possibilities—and the will to grasp them.

For her, so hindered and intruded upon in so many ways, being an artist has still been a daily part of her life. This ability to hold on, even in very simple ways, is work Black women have done for a very long time.

This poem is not enough, but it is something, for the woman who literally covered the holes in our walls with sunflowers:

> They were women then
> My mama's generation
> Husky of voice—Stout of
> Step
> With fists as well as
> Hands
> How they battered down
> Doors
> And ironed
> Starched white
> Shirts
> How they led
> Armies

Headragged Generals
Across mined
Fields
Booby-trapped
Kitchens
To discover books
Desks
A place for us
How they knew what we
Must know
Without knowing a page
Of it
Themselves.

Guided by my heritage of a love of beauty and a respect for strength—in search of my mother's garden, I found my own.

And perhaps in Africa over two hundred years ago, there was just such a mother; perhaps she painted vivid and daring decorations in oranges and yellows and greens on the walls of her hut; perhaps she sang—in a voice like Roberta Flack's—*sweetly* over the compounds of her village; perhaps she wove the most stunning mats or told the most ingenious stories of all the village story-tellers. Perhaps she was herself a poet—though only her daughter's name is signed to the poems that we know.

Perhaps Phillis Wheatley's mother was also an artist.

Perhaps in more than Phillis Wheatley's biological life is her mother's signature made clear.

Richard Wilbur

Poetry and Happiness
1966

Frankly, the word "significance" gives me a chill, and so the title of these remarks is not "Poetry and Significance," but "Poetry and Happiness." I do fervently hope, however, that happiness will turn out to be significant.

I am not perfectly certain what our forefathers understood by "the pursuit of happiness." Of the friends whom I have asked for an opinion, the majority have taken that phrase to mean the pursuit of self-realization, or of a full humane life. Some darker-minded people have translated "happiness" as material well-being, or as the freedom to do as you damn please. I cannot adjudicate the matter, but even if the darker-minded people are right, we are entitled to ennoble the phrase and adapt it to the present purpose. I am going to say a few things about the ways in which poetry might be seen as pursuing happiness.

There are, as I. A. Richards has said, two main ways of understanding the word "poetry." We may think of poetry as a self-shaping activity of the whole society, a collective activity by means of which a society creates a vision of itself, arranges its values, and adopts or adapts a culture. it is this sense of "poetry" that we have in Wallace Stevens's poem "Men Made Out of Words," where he says

> The whole race is a poet that writes down
> The eccentric propositions of its fate.

But "poetry" may also mean what we more usually mean by it; it may mean verses written by poets, imaginative compositions

In spring of 1966 there was a symposium on the arts at the College of Wooster, in Wooster, Ohio. My assigned topic was something like "Poetry and the Pursuit of Significance," but I misheard it as given on the telephone, and so wrote as follows, scribbling in the first paragraph at the last minute.

that employ a condensed, rhythmic, resonant, and persuasive language. This second kind of poetry is not unconnected with the first; a poem written by a poet is a specific, expert, and tributary form of the general imaginative activity. Nevertheless, I should like to begin by considering poetry in the second and restricted sense only, as referring to verse productions written by individuals whose pleasure it is to write them.

Back in the days of white saddle shoes and the gentleman's grade of C, college undergraduates often found that they had an afternoon to kill. I can remember killing part of one afternoon, with a literary roommate, in composing what we called "A Complete List of Everything." We thought of ourselves, I suppose, as continuators of Dada, and our list, as we set it down on the typewriter, amounted to an intentionally crazy and disrelated sequence of nouns. A section of our list might have read like this: beauty, carburetor, sheepshank, pagoda, absence, chalk, vector, Amarillo, garters, dromedary, Tartarus, tupelo, omelet, caboose, ferrocyanide, and so on. As you can imagine, we did not complete our list; we got tired of it. As in random compositions of all kinds—musical, pictorial, or verbal—it was possible to sustain interest for only so long, in the absence of deliberate human meaning. Nevertheless, there had been a genuine impulse underlying our afternoon's diversion, and I think that it stemmed from a primitive desire that is radical to poetry—the desire to lay claim to as much of the world as possible through uttering the names of things.

This fundamental urge turns up in all reaches of literature, heavy or light. We have it, for example, in the eighteenth chapter of Hugh Lofting's *Story of Doctor Dolittle,* a chapter in which all children take particular joy. As you will remember, Doctor Dolittle and his animal friends, on their way back from Africa, come by chance into possession of a pirate ship, and find aboard her a little boy who has become separated from his red-haired, snuff-taking uncle. The Doctor promises to find the little boy's lost uncle, wherever he may be, and Jip the dog goes to the bow of the ship to see if he can smell any snuff on the North wind. Jip, it should be said, is a talking dog, and here is what he mutters to himself as he savors the air:

> Tar; spanish onions; kerosene oil; wet raincoats; crushed laurel-leaves; rubber burning; lace-curtains being washed— No, my mistake, lace-curtains hanging out to dry; and foxes—hundreds of 'em. . . .

These are the easy smells, Jip says; the strong ones. When he closes his eyes and concentrates on the more delicate odors which the wind is bringing, he has this to report:

> Bricks,—old yellow bricks, crumbling with age in a garden-wall; the sweet breath of young cows standing in a mountain-stream; the lead roof of a dove-cote—or perhaps a granary—with the mid-day sun on it; black kid gloves lying in a bureau-drawer of walnut-wood; a dusty road with a horses' drinking-trough beneath the sycamores; little mushrooms bursting through the rotting leaves. . . .

A catalogue of that sort pleases us in a number of ways. In the first place, it stimulates that dim and nostalgic thing the olfactory memory, and provokes us to recall the ghosts of various stinks and fragrances. In the second place, such a catalogue makes us feel vicariously alert; we participate in the extraordinary responsiveness of Doctor Dolittle's dog, and so feel the more alive to things. In the third place, we exult in Jip's power of instant designation, his ability to pin things down with names as fast as they come. The effect of the passage, in short, is to let us share in an articulate relishing and mastery of phenomena in general.

That is what the cataloguing impulse almost always expresses—a longing to possess the whole world, and to praise it, or at least to feel it. We see this most plainly and perfectly in the Latin canticle *Benedicite, omnia opera domini.* The first verses of that familiar canticle are:

> O all ye Works of the Lord, bless ye the Lord: praise him,
> and magnify him for ever.
> O ye Angels of the Lord, bless ye the Lord: praise him,
> and magnify him for ever.
> O ye Heavens, bless ye the Lord: praise him and magnify
> him for ever.
> O ye Waters that be above the firmament, bless ye the Lord:
> praise him and magnify him forever.

I need not go on to the close, because I am sure that you all know the logic of what follows. All the works of the Lord are called upon in turn—the sun, moon, and stars, the winds and several weathers of the sky, the creatures of earth and sea, and lastly mankind. There is nothing left out. The canticle may not speak of crushed laurel leaves and sycamores, but it does say more comprehensively, "O all ye Green Things upon the Earth, bless ye the Lord"; it may not speak of foxes and of young cows in a mountain stream, but it does say, "O all ye Beasts and Cattle, bless ye the Lord." What we have in the *Benedicite* is an exhaustive poetic progress from heaven, down through the spheres of the old cosmology, to earth and man at the center of things—a progress during which the whole hierarchy of creatures is cited in terms that, though general, do not seem abstract. It is a poem or song in which heaven and earth are surrounded and captured by words, and embraced by joyous feeling.

It is interesting to compare the strategy of the *Benedicite* to that of another and more personal poem of catalogue and praise, Gerard Manley Hopkins's "curtal sonnet" "Pied Beauty."

Glory be to God for dappled things—
　　For skies of couple-colour as a brinded cow;
　　　　For rose-moles all in stipple upon trout that swim;
Fresh-firecoal chestnut-falls; finches' wings;
　　Landscape plotted and pieced—fold, fallow, and plough;
　　　　And áll trádes, their gear and tackle and trim.

All things counter, original, spare, strange;
　　Whatever is fickle, freckled (who knows how?)
　　　　With swift, slow; sweet, sour; adazzle, dim;
He fathers-forth whose beauty is past change:
　　　　　　　　Praise him.

As in the old canticle, God is praised first and last; but what lies between is very different. Hopkins does not give us an inventory of the creation; rather, he sets out to celebrate one kind of beauty—pied beauty, the beauty of things that are patchy, particolored, variegated. And in his tally of variegated things there is no hierarchy or other logic: his mind jumps, seemingly at random, from sky to trout to chestnuts to finches, and finally, by way of landscape, to the gear and tackle of the various trades. The poem *sets out*, then, to give scattered examples of a single class of things; and yet in its final effect this is a poem of universal praise. Why does it work out that way?

It works that way, for one thing, because of the randomness which I have just pointed out; when a catalogue has a random air, when it seems to have been assembled by chance, it implies a vast reservoir of other things that might just as well have been mentioned. In the second place, Hopkins's poem may begin with dappled things, but when we come to "gear and tackle and trim," the idea of variegation is far less clear, and seems to be yielding to that of *character*. When, in the next line, Hopkins thanks God for "All things counter, original, spare, strange," we feel the poem opening out toward the celebration of the rich and quirky particularity of all things whatever.

The great tug-of-war in Hopkins's poetry is between his joy in the intense selfhood and *whatness* of earthly things, and his feeling that all delights must be referred and sacrificed to God. For Whitman, with whom Hopkins felt an uncomfortable affinity, there was no such tension. It is true that Whitman said, "I hear and behold God in every object," yet the locus of divinity in his poetry is not heaven but the mystic soul of the poet, which names all things, draws all things to unity in itself, and hallows all things without distinction. The divinely indiscriminate cataloguing consciousness of Whitman's poems can consume phenomena in any order and with any emphasis; it acknowledges no protocol; it operates, as Richard Lewis has said, "in a world . . . devoid of rank or hierarchy." In Section V of the "Song of Myself," Whitman describes an experience of mystic illumination, and then gives us these eight remarkable lines:

Swiftly arose and spread around me the peace and knowledge that
    pass all the argument of the earth,
And I know that the hand of God is the promise of my own,
And I know that the spirit of God is the brother of my own,
And that all the men ever born are also my brothers, and the women
    my sisters and lovers,
And that a kelson of the creation is love,
And limitless are leaves stiff or drooping in the fields,
And brown ants in the little wells beneath them,
And mossy scabs of the worm fence, heap'd stones, elder, mullein
    and pokeweed.

That passage happens to proceed from God to man to nature, but there is nothing hierarchical in its spirit. Quite the contrary. This is the Whitman who said, "I do not call one greater and one smaller. . . . The Insignificant is as big to me as any." He speaks in the same rapt voice of men and women and moss and pokeweed, and it is clear that he might have spoken to the same purpose of ducks or pebbles or angels. For Whitman, as for the Zen Buddhist, one thing is as good as another, a mouse is sufficient "to stagger sextillions of infidels," and any part, however small, includes by synecdoche the wonder of the whole.

I could go on to speak of still more list-making poets. I could quote the Rilke of the *Duino Elegies,* who asks

Are we perhaps here merely to say, House, Bridge, Fountain, Gate,
    Jug, Fruit-tree, Window,
Or Column, or Tower...

In our own immediate day there would be David Jones, Theodore Roethke, and Ruthven Todd in their later work; and indeed, there have been poets in all lands and ages who have sought to resume the universe in ordered categories, or to suggest its totality by the casual piling up of particulars.

But I have given enough examples already, and my aim here is not to make a catalogue of poetic catalogues, but to suggest by a few illustrations that the itch to call the roll of things is a major motive in the writing of poetry. Whether or not he composes actual catalogues like Whitman or Hopkins, every poet is driven by a compulsion to designate, and in respect of that drive the poet is not unlike people in general. We all want to be told, for no immediate practical reason, whether a certain column is Ionic or Corinthian, whether that cloud is stratus or cumulus, and what the Spanish word for "grocer" is. If we forget the name of a supporting actor in some film, or the roster of our Supreme Court bench, we are vexed and distracted until we remember, or look it up in some book of reference. If we travel to the tropics for the first time, and find ourselves surrounded not with oaks and maples but with a bristling wall of nameless flora, we hasten to arm ourselves with nature books and regain our control over the landscape.

The poet is like that, only more so. He is born, it appears, with a stronger-than-usual need for verbal adequacy, and so he is always mustering and reviewing his vocabulary, and forearming himself with terms he may need in the future. I recall the excitement of a poet friend when he discovered in a mushroom guide the word "duff," which signifies "decaying vegetable matter on the forest floor."

He was right to be excited, I think. Duff is a short, precise word which somehow sounds like what it means, and it is a word that poets must often have groped after in vain. My own recent discovery of that kind is the term for the depression in the center of one's upper lip. It had annoyed me, on and off, for many years that I had no word for something that was literally under my nose; and then at long last I had the sense to enquire of a dentist. He told me that the word is "philtrum," deriving from the Greek word for "love-potion," and implying, I should think, that the upper lip is an erogenous zone.

That sort of word-hunting and word-cherishing may sound frivolous to some, and it must be admitted that the poet's fascination with words can degenerate into fetishism and the pursuit of the exotic. More often, however, such researches are the necessary, playful groundwork for that serious business of naming which I have been discussing. Not all poets, especially in the present age, can articulate the universe with a *Benedicite,* or possess it by haphazard mysticism, but every poet is impelled to utter the whole of that world which is real to him, to respond to that world in some spirit, and to draw all its parts toward some coherence. The job is an endless one, because there are always aspects of life that we acknowledge to be real, but have not yet truly accepted.

For an obvious example, one has only to think of those machines which science has bestowed on us, and which Hart Crane said it was the great task of modern poetry to absorb. The iron horse has been with us for a century and a half, and the horseless carriage for eighty-odd years, but it is only in recent decades that "train" and "car" have consorted easily, in our verse, with "hill" and "ship" and "hawk" and "wagon" and "flower." And indeed there are still readers who think it unpoetic to bring a pickup truck into the landscape of a poem. The airplane has the aesthetic and moral advantage of resembling a bird and of seeming to aspire, but it took some hard writing in the thirties to install such words as "pylon" and "airfield" in the lexicon of modern verse. And for all our hard writing since, we have still not arrived at the point where, in Hart Crane's words, machinery can form "as spontaneous a terminology of poetic reference as the bucolic world of pasture, plow, and barn."

The urge of poetry is not, of course, to whoop it up for the automobile, the plane, the computer, and the spaceship, but only to bring them and their like into the felt world, where they may be variously taken, and to establish their names in the vocabulary of imagination. One perpetual task of the poet is to produce models of inclusive reaction and to let no word or thing be blackballed by sensibility. That is why I took a large pleasure, some years ago, in bringing off a line that convincingly employed the words "reinforced concrete." And that is why William Carlos Williams, with his insistence on noting and naming the bitterest details of the American urban scene, was such a hero of the modern spirit; he would not wear blinders in Rutherford and Paterson, but instead wrote beautifully of peeling billboards, wind-blown paper bags, and broken bottles in the gravel, claiming for poetry a territory that is part of our reality, and needs to be seen and said. For poetry, there is no such thing as no man's land.

The drive to get everything said is not merely a matter of acknowledging and absorbing the physical environment. The poet is also moved to designate human life in all its fullness, and it may be argued, for an extreme example, that the best of Henry Miller arises from a pure poetic compulsion to refer to certain realities by their real names. Mr. Miller's best is not very good, actually, and Aretino did it far better some centuries back; but there are passages in the *Tropics* that are clearly attempting, by means of an exuberant lyricism, to prove that the basic four-letter words are capable of augmenting our literary language without blowing it to pieces. I expressed this view not long ago, when testifying for Mr. Miller at an obscenity trial, and the judge replied only with a slow, sad shaking of the head. But I remain unshaken. I do not think that Mr. Miller succeeds very often in his aim, partly because the words he champions are what the theater calls bad ensemble players. But as for his aim, I recognize it as genuine and would call it essentially poetic.

Thus far I have been speaking of poetry as an inventory of external reality; now let me speak of poetry as discovery and projection of the self. The notion that art is self-expression, the expression of one's uniqueness, has provoked and excused a great deal of bad, solipsistic work in this century; nevertheless, the work of every good poet may be seen in one way or another as an exploration and declaration of the self.

In Emily Dickinson, for instance, we have a poet whose most electrifying work is the result of keen and dogged self-scrutiny. Having spied for a long time on her own psyche, she can report that "Wonder is not precisely knowing, / And not precisely knowing not." Or she can produce a little poem like this, about how anguish engrosses the sense of time:

> Pain has an element of blank;
> It cannot recollect
> When it began, or if there were
> A day when it was not.
> It has no future but itself,
> Its infinite realms contain
> Its past, enlightened to perceive
> New periods of pain.

Those lines are a pure trophy of introspection; they are not the rephrasing of something known, but the articulation of one person's intense inward observation. Yet because they are so articulate and so true, they light up both the poet's psychology and everyone else's.

Another version of self-discovery is implied in Edwin Muir's statement that "the task of a poet is to make his imaginative world clear to himself." What Muir meant was that every poet, owing to his character and early life, has a predisposition to project his sense of things by telling this or that story, by using this or that image or symbol. It may take a poet years to stumble on his destined story or symbol and set it forth, but for Muir they are always vaguely and archetypally there, at the back of the poet's mind.

When we say of a poet that he has found his subject, or found his voice, we are likely to be thinking about poetry in Muir's way, as a long struggle to objectify the soul. Marianne Moore sketching her first emblematic animal, Vachel Lindsay first attempting to catch the camp-meeting cadence, Frost first perceiving the symbolic possibilities of a stone wall—at such moments the poet is suddenly in possession of the formula of his feelings, the means of knowing himself and of making that self known. It was at such a moment that Rilke wrote in a letter, "I am a stamp which is about to make its impression."

As I have said, these moments of self-possession can be a long time in coming. Looking back at his early poems, and finding them cloudy and abortive, Yeats sadly wrote in his *Autobiography,* "It is so many years before one can believe enough in what one feels even to know what the feeling is." It was late in his life that a Scots poet whom I knew, while buckling his belt one morning, heard himself saying the Lord's Prayer, and concluded that he must be a Christian after all. Or to speak of a deconversion, there were eight years of silence between the clangorous, prophetic early books of Robert Lowell and the publication of *Life Studies,* in which a flexible, worldly voice suddenly speaks, with a whole personality behind it. What had happened to Lowell was, in Yeats's phrase, a "withering into the truth," and some such process must occur, I think, in the life of every poet.

It is Yeats above all, in the present age, who has preached and embodied the notion that poetry is self-projection; that the poet creates his world "lock, stock and barrel out of his bitter soul." "Revelation is from the self," he said; and though his way of putting it altered, he never ceased to think as he had done in 1893, when he wrote in his book *The Celtic Twilight,*

> What is literature but the expression of moods by the vehicle of symbol and incident? And are there not moods which need heaven, hell, purgatory and faeryland for their expression, no less than this dilapidated earth?

What's fundamental in poetry, according to that definition, is moods—that is, the poet's repertory of emotions, his spectrum of attitudes. All else is instrumental; persons, things, actions, and ideas are only means to externalizing the states of the poet's heart. Before Yeats was through, he had constructed a visionary system full of cycles and interpenetrating gyres which embraced all possible experience, all human types, all ages of man, all ages of history, this world and the next. It was a vision as inclusive as that of the *Benedicite,* but whereas the latter was for its poet an objective poem, Yeats's vision is all a deliberate ramification of his subjective life. The phases of the moon, the gong-tormented sea, the peacock's cry, hunchback and saint, Cuchulain—the ground of their reality is the various and conflicting spirit of the poet. When the young Yeats says

Before us lies eternity; our souls
Are love, and a continual farewell,

and when he later proclaims that "men dance on deathless feet," he is not expounding the doctrine of reincarnation, but exploiting that idea as a means of expressing his own heart's insatiable desire for life. The spirits who brought Yeats the substance of his system did not bring him an epitome of external truth; rather, they said, "We have come to give you metaphors for poetry." And when Yeats felt that certain of his expressive fictions were exhausted, he turned for a new start not to the world but to what he called, in a famous line, "the foul rag and bone shop of the heart."

I have said something now about two impulses of poetry—the impulse to name the world, and the impulse to clarify and embody the self. All poets are moved by both, but every poet inclines more to one than to the other, and a way of measuring any poet's inclination is to search his lines for moments of descriptive power. Description is, of course, an elaborate and enchanted form of naming, and among the great describers of the modern period are Hopkins, and Williams, and Lawrence in his animal poems, and Marianne Moore, who once described a butterfly as "bobbing away like wreckage on the sea." And then there is that thunderstorm in a poem of Elizabeth Bishop's, which moves away, as she tells it,

in a series
Of small, badly-lit battle scenes,
Each in "Another part of the field."

Or there is the beautifully realized little sandpiper, in her latest book, who runs "in a state of controlled panic" along a beach which "hisses like fat."

Now, Yeats had his sea birds, too, and in his youthful novel *John Sherman* there were some puffins very accurately observed; but soon he became concerned, as he said, with "passions that had nothing to do with observation," and the many birds of his subsequent work are a symbolic aviary of no descriptive interest. Yeats rarely gives us any pictorial pleasure, in birds or in anything else, being little concerned in his naming of things to possess them in their otherness and actuality. Nevertheless, he, like all poets, is a namer; and Miss Bishop, for all her descriptive genius, is like all poets a scholar of the heart. It is a matter of proportion only, a matter of one's imaginative balance.

And having said the word "balance," I want to offer a last quotation from Yeats, which speaks directly to the question of art and happiness. In a letter to Dorothy Wellesley, written sometime in the thirties, Yeats said,

> We are happy when for everything inside us there is a corresponding something outside us.

That is an observation about life in general, but above all it applies to poetry. We are happy as poets, Yeats says, when our thoughts and feelings have originals or counterparts in the world around us—when there is a perfect conversancy or congruence between self and world. In Yeats's poetry, the chief symbol for such happiness is the marriage bed, and his artful lovers Solomon and Sheba, each striving to incarnate the other's dream, represent the mutual attunement of imagination and reality. Keats's lovers Madeline and Porphyro, in "The Eve of St. Agnes," accomplish the same miracle and symbolize the same thing; each, without loss of reality, becomes the other's vision, and the poem is one solution to Keats's continuing enquiry into the right balance between vision and everyday experience. Elsewhere he employs or espouses other formulae, as in the poem "To Autumn," where imagination does not transmute and salvage the world, but, rather, accepts it in all its transient richness, and celebrates it as it is.

There is a similar quality of acceptance in Robert Frost's poems about imaginative happiness. Here is one called "Hyla Brook."

> By June our brook's run out of song and speed.
> Sought for much after that, it will be found
> Either to have gone groping underground
> (And taken with it all the Hyla breed
> That shouted in the mist a month ago,
> Like ghost of sleigh-bells in a ghost of snow)—
> Or flourished and come up in jewelweed,
> Weak foliage that is blown upon and bent
> Even against the way its waters went.
> Its bed is left a faded paper sheet
> Of dead leaves stuck together by the heat—

A brook to none but who remember long.
This as it will be seen is other far
Than with brooks taken otherwhere in song.
We love the things we love for what they are.

It does not trouble him, Frost says, that the brook on his farm runs dry by June, and becomes a gulley full of dead leaves and jewelweed; it may not be Arethusa or smooth-sliding Mincius; it may not, like Tennyson's brook, go on forever; but it has real and memorable beauties that meet his desire. Loving it for what it is, the poet does not try to elevate his subject, or metamorphose it, or turn it into pure symbol; it is sufficient that his words be lovingly adequate to the plain truth. In another and comparable poem, called "Mowing," Frost builds toward a similar moral: "The fact is the sweetest dream that labor knows." One does not think of Wallace Stevens, who so stressed the transforming power of imagination, as having much in common with Frost, and yet Stevens would agree that the best and happiest dreams of the poet are those that involve no denial of the fact. In his poem "Crude Foyer," Stevens acknowledges that poets are tempted to turn inward and conceive an interior paradise; but that is a false happiness; we can only, he says, be "content, / At last, there, when it turns out to be here." We cannot be content, we cannot enjoy poetic happiness, until the inner paradise is brought to terms with the world before us, and our vision fuses with the view from the window.

Regardless, then, of subjective bias or of a reverence for fact, poets of all kinds agree that it is the pleasure of the healthy imagination to achieve what Stevens called "ecstatic identities with the weather." When the sensibility is sufficient to the expression of the world, and when the world, in turn, is answerable to the poet's mind and heart, then the poet is happy, and can make his reader so.

Now, if I were satisfied with my use of the word "world," which I have been saying over and over in an almost liturgical fashion, I might feel that I had come near to the end of my argument. But world, in contemporary usage, is a particularly sneaky and ambiguous term. I see that I must try to use it more precisely, and that once I have done so there will be more to say. What might I mean by world? I might mean what Milton meant when he spoke of "this pendant world"; that is,

I might mean the universe. Or I might mean the planet Earth; or I might mean the human societies of Earth, taken together. Or if I defined world by reference to the soul or self, I might mean what a German philosopher called the "Non-Ego," or what Andrew Wyeth meant when he called one of his paintings "Christina's World." I am sure that you have all seen that touching painting of Wyeth's: it shows us a crippled girl sitting in a field of long grass, and looking off toward a house and barn; her "world" consists of what she can see, and the desolate mood in which she sees it.

Literary critics, nowadays, make continual use of the word "world" in this last sense. They write of Dylan Thomas's world of natural process, Conrad Aiken's world of psychic flux, John Ransom's gallant and ironic world of the South, or the boyish, amorous, and springtime world of E. E. Cummings. Any of us could assign a "world," in this sense, to any poet whose work we know; and in doing so, we would not necessarily be blaming him for any narrowness of scope. Robinson Jeffers on his mountaintop by the Pacific, writing forever of hawks and rocks and of the violent beauty of nature, was not prevented from speaking, through his own symbols and from his own vantage, of God and history and cities and the passions of men and women. Like any good poet of this American century, he found images and symbols that could manifest the moods of his heart, and elected a world of his own through which the greater world could someway be seen and accounted for.

And yet if one thinks back to the Italian fourteenth century, if one thinks of the "world" of Dante's imagination, how peripheral and cranky Jeffers seems! Dante's poetry is the work of one man, who even at this distance remains intensely individual in temper and in style; and yet the world of his great poem was, for his first readers, quite simply the world. This was possible because he was a poet of genius writing from the heart of a full and living culture. He lived and wrote, in Stevens's phrase, "at the center of a diamond."

I bring up Dante not merely to belabor the present with him, but because there is something that needs to be explained. We are talking of poetry as a mode of pursuing happiness; we live in a century during which America has possessed many poets of great ability; nevertheless, it is no secret that the personal histories of our poets, particularly in the last thirty years, are full of alcoholism, aberration, emotional breakdowns, the drying up of talent, and suicide. There is no need to learn this from gossip or biography; it is plainly enough set down in the poetry of our day. And it seems to me that the key to all this unhappiness may lie in the obligatory eccentricity, nowadays, of each poet's world, in the fact that our society has no sufficient cultural heart from which to write.

Alberto Moravia, in a recent article on a great American writer and suicide, Ernest Hemingway, describes our country as "a minor, degraded and anti-humanistic culture," and observes that our typical beginning novelist, lacking any faith in the resources of culture, "confines himself to recounting the story of his youth." Having done so once successfully, the novelist proceeds, for lack of any other subject, to do it again and again, and, as Moravia puts it, "mirrors increasingly, in the mechanization of his own work, the mechanization of the society for which he is writing." I am sorry to say that I cannot brush aside Signor Moravia's general judgment upon us. I wish that I could.

One can protest that not all of our novelists are the prisoners of their own early lives, and that most of our poets are cultured in the sense of being well schooled in the literary and artistic tradition. But one cannot deny that in the full sense of the word "culture"—the sense that has to do with the humane unity of a whole people—our nation is impoverished. We are not an articulate organism, and what most characterizes our life is a disjunction and incoherence aggravated by an intolerable rate of change. It is easy to prophesy against us. Our center of political power, Washington, is a literary and intellectual vacuum, or nearly so; the church, in our country, is broken into hundreds of sorry and provincial sects; colleges of Christian foundation hold classes as usual on Good Friday; our cities bristle like quartz clusters with faceless new buildings of aluminum and glass, bare of symbolic ornament because they have nothing to say; our painters and sculptors despair of achieving any human significance, and descend into the world of fashion to market their Coke bottles and optical toys; in the name of the public interest, highways are rammed through old townships and wildlife sanctuaries; all other public expenditure is begrudged, while the bulk of the people withdraw from community into an affluent privacy.

I could go on with such sweeping assertions, and soon, no doubt, I would go too far, and would have to admit that anarchy is not confined to America, and that here or there we have the promise of cultural coherence. But I would reluct at making too much of the present boom in education, or the growth of regional theaters and symphony orchestras. Such things may be good in themselves, but they are not the kind of culture I am talking about. Houston has an admirable symphony orchestra, but the nexus of human relations in that city is the credit card, and where art does not arise from and nourish a vital sense of community, it is little more than an incitement to schizophrenia.

The main fact about the American artist, as a good poet said to me the other day, is his feeling of isolation. To Dante, at the other extreme, the world appeared as one vast society, or as a number of intelligibly related societies, actual and spiritual; his *Commedia* was the embodiment and criticism of a comprehensive notion of things that he shared with his age. Or think, if you will, of the sure sense of social relevance with which Milton embarked on the writing of an epic poem which was to be "exemplary to a nation." Or think of that certainty of the moral consensus that lies behind the satires of Alexander Pope, and makes possible a wealth of assured nuance. How often, I wonder, has any American poet spoken so confidently from within the culture?

I began by distinguishing two ways of understanding the word "poetry": first, as verse compositions written by individuals, and second, as that ensemble of articulate values by means of which a society shapes and affirms itself. It is the natural business of the first kind of poetry to contribute to the second, clarifying, enriching, and refreshing it; and where the poet is unable to realize himself as the spokesman and loyal critic of an adequate culture, I think that his art and life are in some measure deprived of satisfaction and meaning.

To be sure, every poet is a citizen of the Republic of Letters, that imaginary society whose members come from every age and literature, and it is part of his happiness to converse, as it were, with the whole of tradition; but it is also his desire to put his gift at the service of the people of his own time and place. And that, as I have been saying, is a happiness not easily come by in contemporary America. It is possible, however isolated one may feel, to write out of one's private experiences of nature or God or love; but one's poetry will reflect, in one way or another, the frustration of one's desire to participate in a corporate myth. In some of our poets, the atomism of American life has led to a poetry without people, or an art of nostalgia for childhood. Elsewhere, we find a confessional poetry in which the disorder and distress of the poet's life mirrors that cultural disunity to which he, because of his calling, is peculiarly sensitive. When the poet addresses himself directly to our society, these days, it is commonly in a spirit of reproach or even secession, and seldom indeed in a spirit of celebration. I do not hold the poet responsible for that fact.

At the close of one of his eloquent poems, Archibald Mac-Leish exhorts the modern poet to "Invent the age! Invent the metaphor!" But it is simply not the business of poets to invent ages, and to fashion cultures singlehanded. It may be that Yeats's Ireland was in good part Yeats's own invention, and he may have made some of it stick; but America is too huge a muddle to be arbitrarily envisioned. The two modern poets who tried to put a high-sounding interpretation on our country—Lindsay, whose Michigan Avenue was a street in heaven, and Crane, whose Brooklyn Bridge leapt toward our spiritual destiny—ended by taking their own lives.

Now, all I wanted to say was that the poet hankers to write in and for a culture, countering its centrifugal development by continually fabricating a common and inclusive language in which all things are connected. But I got carried away by the present difficulty of attaining that happy utility.

Of course I have overstated the matter, and of course there are fortunate exceptions to be pointed out. Robert Frost was strongly aware of the danger that accelerating change might sweep our country bare of all custom and traditional continuity; some of his best poems, like "The Mountain," are about that threat, and it is significant that he defined the poem as "a momentary stay against confusion." Frost staved off confusion by taking his stand inside a New England rural culture which, during the height of his career, still possessed a certain vitality, and remains intelligible (if less vital) today. In general I should say that Frost *assumed*, rather than expounded, the governing ideas and ideals of that culture; but that, after all, is the way of poetry with ideas. It does not think them up; it does not argue them abstractly; what it does is to

realize them within that model of felt experience which is a
poem, and so reveal their emotional resonance and their
capacity for convincing embodiments.

I was looking the other day at what is doubtless the
best-loved American poem of this century, Robert Frost's
"Birches," and it occurred to me that it might be both perti-
nent and a little unexpected if I finished by quoting it and
saying one or two things about it.

> When I see birches bend to left and right
> Across the lines of straighter darker trees,
> I like to think some boy's been swinging them.
> But swinging doesn't bend them down to stay
> As ice storms do. Often you must have seen them
> Loaded with ice a sunny winter morning
> After a rain. They click upon themselves
> As the breeze rises, and turn many-colored
> As the stir cracks and crazes their enamel.
> Soon the sun's warmth makes them shed crystal shells
> Shattering and avalanching on the snow crust—
> Such heaps of broken glass to sweep away
> You'd think the inner dome of heaven had fallen.
> They are dragged to the withered bracken by the load,
> And they seem not to break; though once they are bowed
> So low for long, they never right themselves:
> You may see their trunks arching in the woods
> Years afterwards, trailing their leaves on the ground
> Like girls on hands and knees that throw their hair
> Before them over their heads to dry in the sun.
> But I was going to say when Truth broke in
> With all her matter of fact about the ice storm,
> I should prefer to have some boy bend them
> As he went out and in to fetch the cows—
> Some boy too far from town to learn baseball,
> Whose only play was what he found himself,
> Summer or winter, and could play alone.
> One by one he subdued his father's trees
> By riding them down over and over again
> Until he took the stiffness out of them,
> And not one but hung limp, not one was left
> For him to conquer. He learned all there was
> To learn about not launching out too soon
> And so not carrying the tree away
> Clear to the ground. He always kept his poise
> To the top branches, climbing carefully

With the same pains you use to fill a cup
Up to the brim, and even above the brim.
Then he flung outward, feet first, with a swish,
Kicking his way down through the air to the ground.
So was I once myself a swinger of birches.
And so I dream of going back to be.
It's when I'm weary of considerations,
And life is too much like a pathless wood
Where your face burns and tickles with the cobwebs
Broken across it, and one eye is weeping
From a twig's having lashed across it open.
I'd like to get away from earth awhile
And then come back to it and begin over.
May no fate willfully misunderstand me
And half grant what I wish and snatch me away
Not to return. Earth's the right place for love:
I don't know where it's likely to go better.
I'd like to go by climbing a birch tree,
And climb black branches up a snow-white trunk
Toward heaven, till the tree could bear no more,
But dipped its top and set me down again.
That would be good both going and coming back.
One could do worse than be a swinger of birches.

To begin with, this poem comes out of the farm and wood-
land country of northern New England, and everything in it
is named in the right language. Moreover, there are moments
of brilliant physical realization, as when the breeze "cracks
and crazes" the "enamel" of ice-laden birches, or the birch-
swinging boy flings out and falls in a perfect kinetic line,
"Kicking his way down through the air to the ground." The
poem presents a vivid regional milieu, and then subtly ex-
pands its range; naturally, and almost insensibly, the ground
and sky of New England are magnified into Heaven and
Earth.

Considered as self-projection, "Birches" is an example of
how the pentameter can be so counterpointed as to force the
reader to hear a sectional and personal accent. Frost's talking
voice is in the poem, and so, too, is his manner: the drift of the
argument is ostensibly casual or even whimsical, but behind
the apparent rambling is a strict intelligence; the language
lifts into rhetoric or a diffident lyricism, but promptly returns
to the colloquial, sometimes by way of humor. The humor of
Frost's poem is part of its meaning, because humor arises

from a sense of human limitations, and that is what Frost is talking about. His poem is a recommendation of limited aspiration, or high-minded earthliness, and the birch incarnates that idea perfectly, being a tree that lets you climb a while toward heaven but then "dips its top and sets you down again." This is a case in which thought and thing, inside and outside, self and world, admirably correspond.

Because of his colloquialism and his rustic settings, Frost has often been thought of as a nonliterary poet. That is a serious error. Frost was lovingly acquainted with poetic literature all the way back to Theocritus, and he was a conscious continuator and modifier of the tradition. Formally, he adapted the traditional meters and conventions to the natural cadence and tenor of New England speech. Then as for content, while he did not echo the poetry of the past so promiscuously as T. S. Eliot, he was always aware of what else had been written on any subject, and often implied as much. In "Hyla Brook," Frost makes a parenthetical acknowledgment that other poets—Tennyson, Milton, Theocritus perhaps—have dealt more flatteringly with brooks or streams than he feels the need to do.

In "Birches," Frost's reference is more specific, and I am going to reread a few lines now, in which I ask you to listen for the voice of Shelley:

> Often you must have seen them
> Loaded with ice a sunny winter morning
> After a rain. They click upon themselves
> As the breeze rises, and turn many-colored
> As the stir cracks and crazes their enamel.
> Soon the sun's warmth makes them shed crystal shells
> Shattering and avalanching on the snow crust—
> Such heaps of broken glass to sweep away
> You'd think the inner dome of heaven had fallen.

"Many-colored." "Glass." "The inner dome of heaven." It would not have been possible for Frost to pack so many echoes of Shelley into six lines and not be aware of it. He is slyly recalling the two most celebrated lines of Shelley's *Adonais:*

> Life, like a dome of many-colored glass,
> Stains the white radiance of eternity.

Such a reminiscence is at the very least a courtesy, a tribute to the beauty of Shelley's lines. But there is more to it than that. Anyone who lets himself be guided by Frost's reference, and reads over the latter stanzas of Shelley's lament for Keats, will find that "Birches," taken as a whole, is in fact an answer to Shelley's kind of boundless neo-Platonic aspiration. It would be laborious, here and now, to point out all the pertinent lines in *Adonais;* suffice it to say that by the close of the poem Keats's soul has been translated to Eternity, to the eternal fountain of beauty, light, and love, and that Shelley, spurning the Earth, is embarking on a one-way upward voyage to the Absolute. The closing stanza goes like this:

> The breath whose might I have invoked in song
> Descends on me; my spirit's bark is driven
> Far from the shore, far from the trembling throng
> Whose sails were never to the tempest given;
> The massy earth and spherèd skies are riven!
> I am borne darkly, fearfully, afar;
> Whilst, burning through the inmost veil of Heaven,
> The soul of Adonais, like a star,
> Beacons from the abode where the Eternal are.

Frost's answer to that is "Earth's the right place for love." In his dealings with Shelley's poem, Frost is doing a number of things. He is for one thing conversing timelessly with a great poem out of the English tradition; he is, for another thing, contending with that poem in favor of another version of spirituality. And in his quarrel with Shelley, Frost is speaking not only for his own temper but for the practical idealism of the New England spirit. Frost's poem does justice to world, to self, to literary tradition, and to a culture; it is happy in all the ways in which a poem can be happy; and I leave it with you as the best possible kind of answer to the question I have been addressing.

Notes on Contributors

A. R. AMMONS (b. 1926) grew up in North Carolina, where he took a degree at Wake Forest College. He served in the Navy, was principal of an elementary school, and spent ten years as a businessman in New Jersey. From 1969 until 1981 he taught at Cornell University; in 1981 he became a MacArthur Fellow. His *Collected Poems 1951–1971* won the National Book Award in 1973, and in 1975 he received the Bollingen Prize. His first book of poems was *Ommateum,* 1955; *Corson's Inlet,* 1965, first gained him attention. Subsequent volumes include the long poems, *Tape for the Turn of the Year,* 1965, and *Sphere: The Form of a Motion,* 1974. In 1977 he published *Selected Poems 1951–1977.*

MARVIN BELL (b. 1937) grew up on Long Island and earned an MFA at the University of Iowa where he now teaches. He published three volumes with small presses before *A Probable Volume of Dreams,* 1969, the Lamont Poetry Selection. Further books of poems include *The Escape Into You: A Sequence,* 1971; *Residue of Song,* 1974; *Stars Which See, Stars Which Do Not See,* 1977; and *These Green-Going-to-Yellow,* 1981. His essays on poetry are collected in *Old Snow Just Melting,* 1982.

WENDELL BERRY (b. 1934) was educated at the University of Kentucky, migrated to New York and California for a few years, and settled down in Kentucky. He taught for some years but quit in 1977 to write and edit and farm. He is author of three novels and seven collections of essays, including *The Unsettling of America,* published by the Sierra Club in 1977. His books of poems begin with *The Broken Ground,* 1964; and include *Openings,* 1969; *Farming: A Handbook,* 1971; *The Country of Marriage,* 1973; *Clearing,* 1977; and *In Part,* 1980.

ROBERT BLY (b. 1926) went to St. Olaf's College in his home state of Minnesota for a year before transferring to Harvard University, from which he graduated in 1950. He lives in his home state—writing, translating, and editing—and travels to give readings at hundreds of American colleges. He has edited a magazine variously called *The Fifties, The Sixties,* and *The Seventies,* and a press named after the magazine. His first book was *Silence in the Snowy Fields,* 1962.

Since then he has published *The Light Around the Body*, 1967, which won the National Book Award; *Sleepers Joining Hands*, 1973; *The Morning Glory*, 1975; *This Body Is Made of Camphor and Gopherwood*, 1977; *This Tree Will Be Here for a Thousand Years*, 1979; and *The Man in the Black Coat Turns*, 1981. Interviews and essays are collected in *Talking All Morning*, 1980.

HAYDEN CARRUTH (b. 1921) attended the University of North Carolina at Chapel Hill, did graduate work at the University of Chicago, and edited *Poetry* from 1949 to 1950. In recent decades he has lived largely in Vermont. In 1978 he became Professor of English at Syracuse University in New York. *The Crow and the Heart* was his first book, published by Macmillan in 1959. *Brothers, I Loved You All* appeared in 1978, and *The Sleeping Beauty*, a long poem, in 1982.

ROBERT CREELEY (b. 1926) grew up in New England, lived in Majorca and Guatemala, and taught at Black Mountain College where he edited the *Black Mountain Review*. In recent years he has taught at the University of Buffalo and the University of New Mexico. His first major collection of poems was *For Love: Poems 1950–1962*, followed by *Words*, 1967; and most recently *Selected Poems*, 1976; and *Later*, 1979. He has written short stories, a novel, and much criticism; his essays are collected in *A Quick Graph: Collected Notes and Essays*, 1970; and *Was That a Real Poem and Other Essays*, 1979.

ROBERT DUNCAN (b. 1919) has lived most of his life in northern California where he was born. Like Creeley he taught at Black Mountain College. Some of his books are *The Opening of the Field*, 1960; *Roots and Branches*, 1964; *Bending the Bow*, 1968; *Writing Writing*, 1964; and *The Years as Catches*, 1966.

RUSSELL EDSON (b. 1935) lives in Stamford, Connecticut, where he writes prose poems at night. Some of his books are *The Very Thing That Happens: Fables and Drawings*, 1964; *What a Man Can See*, 1969; *The Clam Theatre*, 1973; *The Intuitive Journey and Other Works*, 1976; and *The Reason Why the Closet-Man Is Never Sad*, 1977. He has also written a book of plays called *The Falling Sickness*, 1975.

TESS GALLAGHER (b. 1943) grew up in the Pacific Northwest and attended the University of Iowa. Two of her books are *Instructions to the Double*, 1975; and *Under Stars*, 1978. She teaches at Syracuse University, and writes essays and short stories as well as poems.

SANDRA GILBERT (b. 1936) who teaches at the University of

California at Davis, has written a book on D. H. Lawrence's poems, *Acts of Attention*, 1973, and has collaborated with Susan Gubar on *The Madwoman in the Attic*, 1979. In 1979 she published a book of poems, *In the Fourth World*.

JOHN HAINES (b. 1924) was born in Norfolk, Virginia, and homesteaded for twelve years in Alaska. He published *Winter News* in 1966, followed by *The Stone Harp*, 1971, and *Cicada*, 1977. His book of essays, *Living Off the Country*, appeared in 1981.

DONALD HALL (b. 1928) grew up in Connecticut, took degrees at Harvard and Oxford, and taught at the University of Michigan. In 1975 he moved to New Hampshire to write full-time. His books of poems began with *Exiles and Marriages,* 1955, and include *The Alligator Bride,* 1969, and *Kicking the Leaves,* 1978. He has written biography (*Henry Moore,* 1966, and *Dock Ellis in the Country of Baseball,* 1976) and memoir (*String Too Short to be Saved,* 1961, and *Remembering Poets,* 1978).

ROBERT HASS (b. 1941) grew up in California where he now lives and teaches, after spending several years in the East. *Field Guide* was published in 1973, followed by *Praise,* 1980.

DICK HIGGINS (b. 1938) cofounded Happenings and Fluxus (1958, 1961) before starting the *Something Else Press* (1964–74) and naming the concept of Intermedia (1965). At present he runs *Printed Editions* (P.O. Box 27, Barrytown, N.Y. 12507) and works in Berlin, Germany, on a D.A.A.D. Fellowship (1981–82).

JOHN HOLLANDER (b. 1929) is a Manhattan native who teaches at Yale University. His *A Crackling of Thorns* appeared in the Yale Series of Younger Poets in 1958. Further collections include *Movie-Going and Other Poems,* 1962; *Types of Shape,* 1969; *Tales Told of the Fathers,* 1975; *Reflections on Espionage,* 1976; *Spectral Emanations: New and Selected Poems,* 1978; and *Blue Wine and Other Poems,* 1979. *Vision and Resonance,* a critical and scholarly work, appeared in 1975. In 1981 he published another critical book, *The Figure of Echo,* and "a didactic collection of examples of verse form, structure, system" called *Rhyme's Reason.*

RICHARD HUGO (b. 1923) was born and educated in the Pacific Northwest, and teaches at the University of Montana. His books of poems include *A Run of Jacks,* 1961; *Death of the Kapowsin Tavern,* 1965; *Selected Poems,* 1979; and *The Right Madness of Skye,* 1980. He collected lectures and essays in *The Triggering Town,* 1979.

DAVID IGNATOW (b.1914) was born in Brooklyn and spent many years in business before he became a teacher. *Say Pardon* appeared in 1961, followed by *Figures of the Human*, 1964; *Rescue the Dead*, 1968; *Poems 1934–69*, 1970; *Facing the Tree*, 1975; *Tread the Dark*, 1978; and *Whisper to the Earth*, 1981. Ralph Mills edited *The Notebooks of David Ignatow* in 1973, and a collection of essays and interviews, *Open Between Us*, in 1980.

DONALD JUSTICE (b. 1925) was born in Miami, and has taught at many American colleges, most particularly the University of Iowa. His first book of poems was *The Summer Anniversaries*, 1960, followed by *Night Light*, 1967; *Departures*, 1974; and *Selected Poems*, 1979, which won a Pulitzer Prize.

X. J. KENNEDY (b. 1929) is the pseudonym of Joseph Charles Kennedy. He grew up in New Jersey, received his undergraduate degree from Seton Hall, and did graduate work at the University of Michigan. He taught at Tufts University until his resignation in 1979. An editor of *Counter/Measures* magazine, he has also compiled influential textbooks and written poetry for children. His adult poetry appears in *Nude Descending a Staircase*, 1961; *Growing into Love*, 1969; and *Emily Dickinson in Southern California*, 1973.

BLIEM KERN (b. 1943) is "an exponent and master of Yoga as outlined by Lord Krishna in The Bhagavadgita and in Patanjali's Yoga Sutras." His selected poems 1964–73 are contained in *Meditationsmeditationsmeditations*, followed by *Nuclear Prayer*, 1978; *Text of Amen*, 1980; and *Word Farm*, 1981. He has worked as a graphic designer for magazines, films, book publishers. He has performed his sound poetry in the United States, France, and Italy; he has exhibited in England, Japan, Australia, Brazil, and Egypt.

GALWAY KINNELL (b. 1927) divides his time between a Manhattan apartment and a farm in Vermont. He has taught at many colleges, including Sarah Lawrence, the University of Hawaii, and New York University. His first book of poems was *What a Kingdom It Was*, 1960, followed by *Flower Herding on Mount Monadnock*, 1964; *Body Rags*, 1968; *The Book of Nightmares*, 1971; and *Mortal Acts, Mortal Words*, 1980. His collected interviews appear in *Walking Down the Stairs*, 1978.

RICHARD KOSTELANETZ (b. 1940) is a New Yorker who edits magazines called *Precisely* and *Assembling*, and publishes short stories, novels, and poems. His criticism and literary journalism include *The End of Intelligent Writing*, 1974; *Grants and the Future of Literature*, 1978; *Twenties in the Sixties*, 1978; and *The Old Poetries and the New*,

1981. His poetry includes *Visual Language*, 1970; *Portraits from Memory*, 1975; and *Rain Rains Rain*, 1976.

DENISE LEVERTOV (b. 1923) was born in England and came to the United States in 1948. She published her first book of poems in London in 1946, *The Double Image*. In America she has published *Here and Now*, 1956; *Overland to the Islands*, 1958; *To Stay Alive*, 1971; *Footprints*, 1972; *The Freeing of the Dust*, 1975; *Life in the Forest*, 1978; and *Collected Earlier Poems 1940–1960*, 1979. Some of her prose is collected in *The Poet in the World*, 1974.

JOHN LOGAN (b. 1923) was born and studied in Iowa. He has taught at the University of Notre Dame, the University of Buffalo, and the University of Hawaii. His books of poems include *A Cycle for Mother Cabrini*, 1955; *Ghosts of the Heart*, 1960; *Spring of the Thief*, 1963; and *The Anonymous Lover*, 1973. In 1981 he published *Only the Dreamer Can Change the Dream* (selected poems). *A Ballet for the Ear*, essays and interviews, appeared in 1982.

AUDRE LORDE (b. 1934) was born and lives in New York City. Some of her books are *Cables to Rage*, 1970; *New York Head Shop and Museum*, 1974; *Coal*, 1976; and *The Black Unicorn*, 1978.

THOMAS MCGRATH (b. 1916) grew up in North Dakota, and has lived in South Dakota, Hollywood, Mexico, and western Minnesota. Some of his books are *Figures from a Double World*, 1955; *Letter to An Imaginary Friend, Parts I and II*, 1970; *The Movie at the End of the World: Collected Poems*, 1973; and *Open Songs: Sixty Short Poems*, 1977.

JACKSON MAC LOW (b. 1922) was born in Chicago and lives in New York City. Some of his collections include *The Pronouns*, 1964; *Stanzas for Iris Lezak*, 1970; and *Asymmetries 1-262*, 1978. *Representative Works* appeared from Ross-Erikson in 1981.

W. S. MERWIN (b. 1927) attended Princeton University along with Galway Kinnell, and, after graduation, tutored Robert Graves's son in Mallorca. His publication began when he was Yale Younger Poet in 1952 with *A Mask for Janus*. The early work has been collected in *The First Four Books of Poems*, 1975. Some other titles are *The Moving Target*, 1963; *The Lice*, 1967; *The Carrier of Ladders*, 1970; *Writings to an Unfinished Accompaniment*, 1974; and *The Compass Flower*, 1977. He has published more than fifteen volumes of translations.

FRANK O'HARA (1926–66) grew up in Massachusetts, served in the Navy, and attended Harvard. He was associate curator at the Museum of Modern Art in New York City at the time of his death;

much of his work has been published posthumously. During his lifetime, he published *Oranges,* 1953; *Meditations in an Emergency,* 1957; *Second Avenue,* 1960; and *Lunch Poems,* 1965. Friends collected *In Memory of My Feelings,* 1967, and in 1971 Donald Allen edited *The Collected Poems of Frank O'Hara.*

ALICIA OSTRIKER (b. 1937) is author of *Vision and Verse in William Blake,* 1965; her book of essays, *Writing Like a Woman,* will soon be published by the University of Michigan Press. She teaches at Rutgers University. Her poems have appeared in *A Dream of Springtime,* 1979; *The Mother/Child Papers,* 1980; and *A Woman under the Surface,* 1982.

RON PADGETT (b. 1942) was born in Tulsa and lives on the lower East Side of New York City. He published *Bean Spasms* with Ted Berrigan in 1967; *Bun* with Tom Clark in 1968; *Great Balls of Fire,* 1969; and *Toujours l'Amour* in 1976.

ROBERT PINSKY (b. 1940) grew up in New Jersey, attended Rutgers University, and earned a Ph.D. at Stanford University. For many years a teacher at Wellesley College in Massachusetts, he recently moved to the University of California at Berkeley. He has written one critical book—*The Situation of Poetry,* 1976—and two books of poems: *Sadness and Happiness,* 1975, and *An Explanation of America,* 1979.

ADRIENNE RICH (b. 1929) grew up in Baltimore, Maryland, attended Radcliffe College, and has taught at various American universities. She now lives in western Massachusetts. Her prose includes *Of Woman Born: Motherhood as Experience and Institution,* 1976, and *On Lies, Secrets, and Silence,* 1979. She began to publish her poetry as the Yale Younger Poet in 1951 with *A Change of World.* Subsequent volumes include *The Diamond Cutters,* 1955; *Snapshots of a Daughter-in-Law,* 1963; *Necessities of Life,* 1966; *Leaflets,* 1969; *The Will to Change,* 1971; *Diving into the Wreck,* 1973; *Poems Selected and New,* 1975; and *The Dream of a Common Language,* 1978; and *A Wild Patience Has Taken Me This Far,* 1981.

MICHAEL RYAN (b. 1946) won the Yale Younger Poet Award with his first book, *Threats Instead of Trees,* 1973. His second book, *In Winter,* 1981, was a selection of the National Poetry Series.

RON SILLIMAN (b. 1946) has been a community organizer and political activist as Community Outreach Director for Central City Hospitality House in San Francisco. He has published seven volumes of poetry, including *Ketjak,* 1980, and *Tjanting,* 1981.

CHARLES SIMIC (b. 1938) moved to the United States from Yugoslavia in 1949. He has taught in California and New Hampshire, and his books include *Dismantling the Silence*, 1971; *White*, 1972; *Return to a Place Lit by a Glass of Milk*, 1974; *Charon's Cosmology*, 1977; and *Classic Ballroom Dances*, 1980.

LOUIS SIMPSON (b. 1923) was born in Jamaica and came to the United States when he was seventeen. His criticism is collected in *Three on the Tower*, 1975; *A Revolution in Taste*, 1978; and *A Company of Poets*, 1981. His first book of poems was *The Arrivistes*, 1949. More recently he has published *Selected Poems*, 1965; *Adventures of the Letter I*, 1971; *Searching for the Ox*, 1976; and *Caviare at the Funeral*, 1980.

W. D. SNODGRASS (b. 1926) grew up in Beaver Falls, Pennsylvania, and did graduate work at the University of Iowa. He taught for many years at Syracuse University, and at present teaches at the University of Delaware. His critical essays were collected in *In Radical Pursuit*, 1975. His books of poems are *Hearts's Needle*, 1959; *After Experience*, 1968; and *The Fuhrer Bunker*, 1977.

GARY SNYDER (b. 1930) grew up on the West Coast and attended Reed College. He spent many years studying Zen Buddhism in Kyoto, Japan. Books of poems include *The Back Country*, 1967; *Regarding Wave*, 1970; and *Turtle Island*, 1974. His prose appears in *Earth House Hold*, 1969; *The Old Ways*, 1977; and *The Real Work*, 1980.

WILLIAM STAFFORD (b. 1914) grew up in Kansas and has lived for many years in Oregon. *Writing the Australian Crawl*, 1978, collects his essays and interviews. His books of poems began with *West of Your City*, 1960, and *Traveling Through the Dark*, 1962, which won the National Book Award. His poems are collected in *Stories That Could Be True*, 1977.

MARK STRAND (b. 1934) was born in Canada, studied at Iowa, and lives in Salt Lake City, Utah. He has been a translator and an anthologist. His books of poems include *Reasons for Moving*, 1968; *Darker*, 1970; *The Story of Our Lives*, 1973; *The Late Hour*, 1978; and *Selected Poems*, 1980.

ALICE WALKER (b. 1944) is author of *Langston Hughes, American Poet*, 1974, and books of poems which include *Revolutionary Petunias and Other Poems*, 1978; *Once: Poems*, 1976; and *Good Night, Willie Lee, I'll See You in the Morning*, 1979.

RICHARD WILBUR (b. 1921) attended Amherst College in Massachusetts, served in the Army during the Second World War, and was a Junior Fellow in the Society of Fellows at Harvard. For many years a professor at Wesleyan University in Connecticut, since 1977 he has been Writer-in-Residence at Smith College in Massachusetts. His prose is collected in *Responses,* 1976. He has translated five plays by Molière, and his books of poems are *The Beautiful Changes,* 1947; *Ceremony,* 1950; *Things of This World,* 1956 (Pulitzer Prize and the National Book Award); *Advice to a Prophet,* 1961; *Walking to Sleep,* 1969; and *The Mind-Reader,* 1976.

UNDER DISCUSSION
David Lehman, General Editor
Donald Hall, Founding Editor

Volumes in the Under Discussion series collect reviews and essays about
individual poets. The series is concerned with contemporary American and
English poets about whom the consensus has not yet been formed and the
final vote has not been taken. Titles in the series include: